─MILLER'S─
CollectableS
PRICE ◆ GUIDE

Don't Throw Away A Fortune!
Invest In
Miller's Price Guides

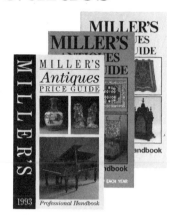

ORDER FORM
Please send me the following editions:

Miller's Antiques Price Guide 1985 £12.95

Miller's Antiques Price Guide 1987 £12.95

Miller's Antiques Price Guide 1988 £14.95

Miller's Antiques Price Guide 1989 £14.95

Miller's Antiques Price Guide 1990 £16.95

Miller's Antiques Price Guide 1991 £17.95

Miller's Antiques Price Guide 1992 £19.99

Miller's Antiques Price Guide 1993 £19.99

Miller's Picture Price Guide 1993 £19.99

Miller's Collectables Price Guide 1990-1991 £12.95 (reprint)

Miller's Collectables Price Guide 1991-1992 £14.95

Miller's Collectables Price Guide 1992-1993 £14.99

Miller's Collectables Price Guide 1993-1994 £15.99

I enclose my remittance for .... post free (UK only)
or please debit my Access/Barclaycard account number

NAME _____

ADDRESS _____

_____

SIGNATURE _____

If you do not wish to deface this volume, either write the above details on a separate sheet and send it to Millers Publications Ltd, Performance Books, P.O. Box 7, Heathfield, East Sussex TN21 0YS, or telephone (04353) 2588. This offer is subject to availability.

MILLER'S
CollectableS
PRICE ◆ GUIDE

(Volume V)

Compiled and Edited by
Judith and Martin Miller

General Editor: Robert Murfin

MILLER'S COLLECTABLES PRICE GUIDE

Compiled, edited and designed by
Millers Publications
The Cellars, High Street,
Tenterden, Kent. TN30 6BN
Telephone (05806) 6411

Compiled and edited by
Judith & Martin Miller

General Editor: Robert Murfin
Editorial Co-ordinator: Sue Boyd
Editorial Assistants: Marion Rickman, Jo Wood, Jill Charles
Artwork: Stephen Parry, Jody Taylor, Darren Manser
Photographic Co-ordinator and Advertising Executive: Elizabeth Smith
Display Advertisements: Elizabeth Warwick, Sally Marshall
Index compiled: DD Editorial Services, Beccles
Additional photography: Ian Booth, Robin Saker

Copyright © 1993 Millers Publications

First published as *Miller's Collectables Price Guide 1993/94*

Reissued 1995

A CIP catalogue record for this book is
available from the British Library

ISBN 1-85152-890-3

Bromide output: The Final Word, Tonbridge, Kent
Illustrations: G. H. Graphics, St. Leonards-on-Sea
Colour origination: Scantrans, Singapore
Printed and bound in England by William Clowes Ltd.,
Beccles and London

CONTENTS

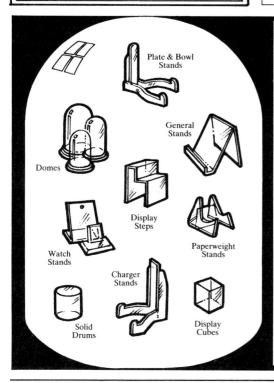

Acknowledgements

The publishers would like to acknowledge the great assistance given by our consultants.

ART DECO*:*	**Beverley,** 30 Church Street, London NW8
BOOKS:	**Peter Harrington,** Harrington Bros. The Chelsea Antique Market, 253 King's Road, London SW3
CONTINENTAL CRACKLE WARE:	**David & Sylvia Powell,** Decorative Arts 1860-1960, 28 The Mall, Camden Passage, N1
GOSS & CRESTED WARE:	**Nicholas Pine,** Goss & Crested China Ltd., 62 Murray Road, Horndean, Hants
SCOTTISH POTTERY:	**George Haggarty,** Bow Well Antiques, 103 West Bow, Edinburgh
EPHEMERA:	**Trevor Vennett-Smith, FRICS, FSVA, CAAV,** 11 Nottingham Road, Gotham, Nottingham
COMICS:	**Phil Clark,** Nostalgia & Comics, 14-16 Smallbrook Queensway, City Centre, Birmingham
SIXTIES & SEVENTIES:	**Liam Woolnough,** 130 Queens Road, Nuneaton, Warwickshire
STANHOPES:	**Douglas Jull,** Cissbury, Worthing, Sussex
ROCKING HORSES:	**Stevenson Brothers,** The Workshop, Ashford Road, Bethersden, Ashford, Kent

A teddy-dog, a prototype from Chad Valley, stuffed with straw, with glass eyes and mohair coat, c1930, 12in (31cm) long.
£100-150 *STK*

This toy was not popular so, therefore, rare.

INDEX TO ADVERTISERS

A Lyons' Milk Chocolate 1d Bar
box, c1920, 11in (28cm) wide.
£20-25 *ACh*

A Rowntree's insert, c1928, 8in
(20cm) high. **£10-15** *ACh*

A Cadbury's Milk Tray box,
in purple and gold, c1950
4in (10cm) high.
£2-3 *ACh*

A Fry's Chocolate Crunchies
advertisement, c1930,
9.5in (24cm) wide.
£18-25 *ACh*

An advertising die-cut show
card, 10in (25cm) high.
£20-25 *ACh*

Key to Illustrations

Each illustration and descriptive caption is accompanied by a letter code. By reference to the following list of Auctioneers (denoted by *) and Dealers (•), the source of any item may be immediately determined. In no way does this constitute or imply a contract or binding offer on the part of any of our contributors to supply or sell the goods illustrated, or similar articles, at the prices stated. Advertisers in this year's directory are denoted by †.

AA • Ambeline Antiques, By George Antique Centre, St. Albans, Herts Tel: 0727 53032 & 081 445 8025

AAM • Anything American (Chris Pearce), 33-35 Duddenhill Lane, London NW10. Tel: 081 451 0320

AAR * Amersham Auction Rooms, 125 Station Road, Amersham, Bucks. Tel: 0494 729292

ABS • Abstract, 58-60 Kensington Church Street, London W8. Tel: 071 376 2652

ACC •† Albert's, 113 London Road, Twickenham, Middx. Tel: 081 891 3067

ACh • Alan Chappell Tel: 0938 84543

ACL • Academy Costumes Ltd., 25 Murphy Street, London SE1. Tel: 071 620 0771

ADC • Art Deco Ceramics, Sheep Street Antique Centre and Ely Street Antique Market, Stratford-upon-Avon, Warwicks. Tel: 0789 297496/297244

AGM • The Button Museum, Kyrle Street, Ross-on-Wye, Hereford & Worcs. Tel: 0989 66089

AH * Andrew Hartley, Victoria Hall, Little Lane, Ilkley, W. Yorks. Tel: 0943 816363

AI • Antiques & Interiors, 22 Ashford Road, Tenterden, Kent. Tel: 05806 5462

AL •† Ann Lingard, Ropewalk Antiques, Ropewalk, Rye, East Sussex. Tel: 0797 223486

ALL * Allen & Harris, Bristol Auction Rooms, St. John's Place, Apsley Road, Clifton, Bristol, Avon. Tel: 0272 737201

AMH • Amhurst Antiques, 23 London Road, Riverhead, Kent. Tel: 0732 455047

AOS •† Antiques on the Square, Church Stretton, Shropshire. Tel: 0694 724111

APO • Apollo Antiques Ltd., The Saltisford, Birmingham Road, Warwick. Tel: 0926 494746

ASA • AS Antiques & Decorative Arts, 26 Broad Street, Pendleton, Salford 6, Manchester. Tel: 061 737 5938

ASB •† Andrew Spencer Bottomley, The Coach House, 173A Huddersfield Road, Thongsbridge, Holmfirth, Huddersfield, Yorks. Tel: 0484 685234

ASc • Ascott Antiques, Narborough, Leics. Tel: 0533 863190

ASH • Ashburton Marbles, Grate Hall, North Street, Ashburton, Devon. Tel: 0364 53189

B * Boardman, Station Road Corner, Haverhill, Suffolk. Tel: 0440 703784

BBA * Bloomsbury Book Auctions, 3/4 Hardwick Street, Off Rosebery Avenue, London EC1. Tel: 071 833 2636/6361945

BBR *† BBR Auctions, c/o Elsecar Project, Wath Road, Elsecar, Barnsley, S. Yorks. Tel: 0226 745156.

Bea * Bearnes, Rainbow, Avenue Road, Torquay, Devon. Tel: 0803 296277

BEE •† Beehive House, Janice Paull, 125 Warwick Road, Kenilworth, Warwickshire CV8 1HY Tel: 0926 55253

BGA • By George Antique Centre, 23 George Street, St. Albans, Herts. Tel: 0727 53032

BHE •† British Heritage Telephones, 11 Rhodes Drive, Unsworth, Bury, Lancs. Tel: 061-767 9259

Bon *† Bonhams, Montpelier Galleries, Montpelier Street, Knightsbridge, London SW7. Tel: 071 584 9161

BOW •† Simon Bowler, Smith Street Antique Centre, Warwick. Tel: 0926 400554 & 021 783 8930

BWA • Bow-Well Antiques, 103 West Bow, Edinburgh. Tel: 031 225 3335.

BWe * Biddle & Webb of Birmingham, Ladywood Middleway, Birmingham. Tel: 021 455 8042

C * Christie, Manson & Woods Ltd., 8 King Street, St James's, London SW1. Tel: 071 839 9060

CAA • Central Antique Arms & Militaria, Smith Street Antique Centre, 7 Smith Street, Warwick, CV34 4JA Tel: 0926 400554

CAB •† Candlestick & Bakelite, PO Box 308, Orpington, Kent. Tel: 081 467 3743.

CAG * Canterbury Auction Galleries, 40 Station Road West, Canterbury, Kent. Tel: 0227 763337.

CB • Christine Bridge Antiques, 78 Castlenau, London SW1 Tel: 081 741 5501

CCC •† The Crested China Co., The Station House, Driffield, E. Yorks. Tel: 0377 47042

CD • The China Doll, 31 Walcot Street, Bath, Avon. Tel: 0225 465849

C(G) * Christie's (International) S.A., 8 Place de la Tocannerie, 1204 Geneva. Tel: 010 4122 311 1766

CHa • Carol Hammond, Unit 8, Kensington Church Street Antiques Centre, 58/60 Kensington Church Street, London W8. Tel: 071 938 4405

CHA • Chapel House Antiques, 32 Pentood Industrial Estate, Pendre, Cardigan, Dyfed. Tel: 0239 614868 & 613268

CJS • Collectable Jukeboxes (Terry Price), PO Box 1964, Selly Oak, Birmingham B29 4B2. Tel: 021 475 6540.

CLA • Classic Costumes, Northcote Road Antique Market, 155a Northcote Road, Battersea, London SW11. Tel: 081 764 8858

COB •† Cobwebs, 78 Northam Road, Southampton. Tel: 0703 227458

COL •† Collectables, P.O. Box 130, Chatham, Kent. Tel: 0634 828767

CNY * Christie, Manson & Woods International Inc., 502 Park Avenue, New York, NY 10022, USA. Tel: (212) 546 1000 (including Christie's East)

CP •† Cat Pottery, 1 Grammar School Road, North Walsham, Norfolk Tel: 0692 402962

CPT • Chris Partington, 41 Berwick Road, Shrewsbury, Shropshire SY1 2LS Tel: 0743 369373

CS •† Christopher Sykes Antiques, The Old Parsonage, Woburn, Bucks. Tel: 0525 290259/290467

C(S) * Christie's Scotland Ltd., 164-166 Bath Street, Glasgow. Tel: 041 332 8134

CSA • Church Street Antiques, 15 Church Street, Godalming, Surrey. Tel: 0483 860894

CSC • The Chicago Sound Company, Northmoor House, Colesbrook, Gillingham, Dorset. Tel: 0747 824338

CSK *† Christie's (South Kensington) Ltd., 85 Old Brompton Road, London SW7. Tel: 071 581 7611

DA * Dee & Atkinson, The Exchange Saleroom, Driffield, Yorks YO25 7LJ. Tel: 0377 43151

DaD • David Dockree, 224 Moss Lane, Bramhall, Stockport Cheshire. Tel: 061 485 1258

DHO • Derek Howard, The Original Chelsea Antiques Market, 245/253 King's Road, London SW3. Tel: 071-352 4113

DID • Didier Antiques, 58-60 Kensington Church Street, London W8. Tel: 071 938 2537 & 0836 232634

DN * Dreweatt Neate, Donnington Priory, Donnington, Newbury, Berks. Tel: 0635 31234

DRU • Drummonds of Bramley, Birtley Farm, Horsham Road, Bramley, Guildford, Surrey. Tel: 0483 898766.

EB • E. Brook, Smith Street Antique Centre, Warwick. Tel: 0926 497864

EP * Evans & Partridge, Agriculture House, High Street, Stockbridge, Hants. Tel: 0264 810702

FAB • FAB, 130 Queen's Road, Nuneaton, Warwicks. Tel: 0203 382399

FMN •† Forget Me Not Antiques (Heather Sharp), By George Antique Centre, 23 George Street, St. Albans, Herts. Tel: 0727 53032 & 0923 261172

G&CC •† Goss and Crested China Ltd. (Nicholas J. Pine), 62 Murray Road, Horndean, Hants. Tel: 0705 597440

GAK • G. A. Key, 8 Market Place, Aylsham, Norwich, Norfolk. Tel: 0263 733195

GAZ • Gazelles, 31 Northam Road, Southampton. Tel: 0703 235291/780798

GH * Giles Haywood, The Auction House, St. John's Road, Stourbridge, W. Midlands. Tel: 0384 370891

GHA • Garden House Antiques, 116-118 High Street, Tenterden, Kent. Tel: 05806 3664

GRF • Grange Farm Ltd., Grange Farm, Tongham, Surrey. Tel: 0258 2993/2804

HB •† Harrington Bros., The Chelsea Antique Market, 253 King's Road, London SW3 5EL. Tel: 071 352 5689 & 1720.

HCH * Hobbs & Chambers, Market Place, Cirencester, Glos. Tel: 0285 4736

HEG • Stuart Heggie, 58 Northgate, Canterbury, Kent CT1 1BB Tel: 0227 470422

HEW •† Muir Hewett, Halifax Antiques Centre, Queen's Road Mills, Queen's Road/Gibbet Street, Halifax, W. Yorks. Tel: 0422 366657

HEY • Heyford Antiques, 7 Church Street, Nether Heyford, Northampton. Tel: 0327 40749

HOW • Howards Antiques, 10 Alexandra Road, Aberystwyth, Dyfed. Tel: 0970 624973

HSS * Henry Spencer & Sons, 20 The Square, Retford, Notts. Tel: 0777 708633.

ING • Inglewood Antiques, Ely St. Antique Centre, Stratford-upon-Avon, Warwicks. Tel: 0789 297496

IS •† Ian Sharp Antiques, 23 Front Street, Tynemouth. Tel: 091-296 0656

IW	•†	Islwyn Watkins, 1 High Street, 29 Market Street, Knighton, Powys. Tel: 0547 520145 & 528940
JAC	•	John & Anne Clegg, 12 Old Street, Ludlow, Shropshire Tel: 0584 873176
JBB	•†	Jessie's Button Box, Great Western Antique Centre, Bartlett Street, Bath, Avon. Tel: 0225 310388
JH	*	Jacobs & Hunt, Lavant Street, Petersfield, Hants. Tel: 0730 62744
JHo	•	Jonathan Horne (Antiques) Ltd., 66B & C Kensington Church Street, London W8. Tel: 071 221 5658.
JMC	•	J & M Collectables, The Cranbrook Antique Centre, High Street, Cranbrook, Kent. Tel: 0580 891657
JMG	•†	Jamie Maxtone Graham, Lyne Haugh, Lyne Station, Peebles, Scotland. Tel: 07214 304.
K	•†	Keith Gretton, Unit 14 Northcote Road Antique Market, Battersea, London SW11. Tel: 071 228 0741 & 071 228 6850
KAC	•	Kensington Antique Centre, 58-60 Kensington Church Street, London W8. Tel: 071 376 0425
L	*	Lawrence Fine Art, South Street, Crewkerne, Somerset. Tel: 0460 73041
LB	•	The Lace Basket, la East Cross, Tenterden, Kent. Tel: 05806 3923/3664
LBL	•	Laurance Black Ltd. Antiques of Scotland, 45 Cumberland Street, Edinburgh. Tel: 031 557 4545
LF	*	Lambert & Foster, 102 High Street, Tenterden, Kent. TN30 6HU. Tel: 05806 3233.
LIO	•†	Lion's Den, 31 Henley Street, Stratford-upon-Avon, Warwicks. Tel: 0789 415802.
LR	•	Leonard Russell, 21 King's Avenue, Mount Pleasant, Newhaven, E. Sussex. Tel: 0273 515153
LRG	•	Lots Road Galleries, 71 Lots Road, London SW10 0RN. Tel: 071 351 7771
MA	•	Manor Antiques, 2a High Street, Westerham, Kent. Tel: 0959 64810
MAS	•	Maskerade (Lynn Waller), Unit 15, The Antique Centre, 58 Kensington Church Street, London W8. Tel: 071 937 8974
MCA	*	Mervyn Carey Auctions, Twysden Cottage, Benenden, Cranbrook, Kent. Tel: 0580 240283
MJB	*	Michael J. Bowman, 6 Haccombe House, Netherton, Newton Abbot, Devon. Tel: 0626 872890
ML	•	Magic Lantern (Josie Marsden), By George Antique Centre, 23 George Street, St. Albans, Herts. Tel: 0727 53032
MR	*	Martyn Rowe, The Truro Auction Centre, Calenick Street, Truro, Cornwall TR1 2SG. Tel: 0872 260020.
MRT	•	Mark Rees Tools, Barrow Mead Cottage, Rush Hill, Bath BA2 2QR Tel: 0225 837031

N	*	Neales, 192-194 Mansfield Road, Nottingham NG1 3HX Tel: 0602 624141
NA	•	Nostalgia Amusements, 22 Greenwood Close, Thames Ditton, Surrey. Tel: 081 398 2141
NB	•	Nicolaus Boston, Kensington Church Street Antique Centre, London W8. Tel: 071 376 0425 & 0722 326906
NCA	•†	New Century Art Pottery, 69 Kensington Church Street, London W8. Tel: 071 376 2810
ND	*†	Nock Deighton, Livestock & Auction Centre, Tasley, Bridgnorth, Shropshire WV16 40R. Tel: 0746 762666
NF	•	Nick Fletcher, PO Box 411, Longton, Stoke-on-Trent ST3 4SS.
NOS	•	Nostalgia Comics, 14-16 Smallbrook Queensway, City Centre, Birmingham. Tel: 021 643 0143
NOW	•	Now & Then, 7 & 9 West Crosscauseway, Edinburgh EH8 9JW. Tel: 031 668 2927/0860 278774
NP	•†	Neville Pundole, PO Box 6, Attleborough, Norfolk. Tel: 0953 454106
OD	•	Offa's Dyke Antique Centre, 4 High Street, Knighton, Powys, Wales. Tel: 0547 528635
ONS	*	Onslow's Metrostore, Townmead Road, London SW6. Tel: 071 793 0240
ORG	•	Oriental Rug Gallery, 42 Verulam Road, St. Albans, Herts AL3 4DQ Tel: 0727 41046
PAG	•	Prinny's Antiques Gallery (F. Whitney Antiques), 3 Meeting House Lane, Brighton. Tel: 0273 204554
PAR	•	Park House Antiques, Park Street, Stow-on-the-Wold, Nr Cheltenham, Glos.
PC		Private Collection
PCh	*	Peter Cheney, Western Road Auction Rooms, Western Road, Littlehampton, Sussex. Tel: 0903 722264 & 713418
P(L)	*	Phillips, Hepper House, 17a East Parade, Leeds LS1 2BU Tel: 0532 448011
PLO	•	Mrs I. Morton-Smith, The Plough, Maysleith, Milland, Nr. Liphook, Hants Tel: 0428 76323
POW	•†	Sylvia Powell Decorative Arts, 28 The Mall, Camden Passage, London N1. Tel: 071 354 2977/081 458 4543.
PR	•	Pamela Richards, Sheep Street Antique Centre, Stratford-upon-Avon, Warwicks.
P(S)	*	Phillips, 49 London Road, Sevenoaks, Kent. Tel: 0732 740310
PSA	•	Pantiles Spa Antiques, 6 Union House, Eridge Road, Tunbridge Wells, Kent. Tel: 0892 541377
RAG	*	Rye Auction Galleries, Rock Channel, Rye, Sussex. Tel: 0797 222124.
RBB	*	Russell, Baldwin & Bright, Fine Art Salerooms, Ryelands Road, Leominster, Hereford. Tel: 0568 611166

RdeR • Rogers de Rin, 76 Hospital Road, Paradise Walk, London SW3. Tel: 071 352 9007

RE • Ron's Emporium, 98 Church Lane, Sholden, Deal, Kent. Tel: 0304 374784

REL • Relic Antiques at Brillscote Farm, Lea, Malmesbury, Wilts. Tel: 0666 822332

RFA • Rochester Fine Arts, 86 High Street, Rochester, Kent. Tel: 0634 814129

RIC • Rich Designs, 11 Union Street, Stratford-upon-Avon, Warwicks. Tel: 0789 772111.

RID * Riddetts of Bournemouth, 26 Richmond Hill, Bournemouth, Dorset Tel: 0202 555686

ROS • Roses, 60 King's Street, Sandwich, Kent. Tel: 0304 615303

ROW • Rowena Blackford at Penny Lampard's Antique Centre, 31-33 High Street, Headcorn, Kent. Tel: 0622 890682 & 861360

RP • Robert Pugh, Pennard House Antiques, 3/4 Piccadilly, London Road, Bath. Tel: 0225 314713/313791

RR • Jonathan Hill, 2-4 Brook Street, Bampton, Devon. Tel: 0398 331532

RWB • Roy W. Bunn Antiques, 34-36 Church Street, Barnoldswick, Colne, Lancs. Tel: 0282 813703

S * Sotheby's, 34-35 New Bond Street, London W1. Tel: 071 493 8080

S(AM) * Sotheby's, 102 Rokin, 1012 KZ, Amsterdam, Holland. Tel: 31 (20) 627 56 56

S(Mon) * Sotheby's Monaco, BP 45-98001, Monaco. Tel: 93 30 88 80

S(NY) * Sotheby's New York, 1334 York Avenue, New York, NY 10021. Tel: 212 606 7000

S(S) * Sotheby's Sussex, Summers Place, Billingshurst, W. Sussex. Tel: 0403 783933

SAM • Samarkand Galleries, 2 Brewery Yard, Sheep Street, Stow-on-the-Wold, Glos. Tel: 0451 832322

SCO • Scot Hay House Antiques, 7 Nantwich Road, Woore, Shropshire. Tel: 063081 7118

SCR •† The Scripophily Shop, Britannia House, Grosvenor Square, London W1. Tel: 071 495 0580

SCW • The Sussex Commemorative Ware Centre, 88 Western Road, Hove, Sussex BN3 1JB. Tel: 0273 773911.

Sim * Simmons & Sons, 32 Bell Street, Henley-on-Thames, Oxon. Tel: 0491 591111

Som • Somervale Antiques, 6 Radstock Road, Midsomer Norton, Bath, Avon. Tel: 0761 412686

SRA *† Sheffield Railwayana Auctions, 43 Little Norton Lane, Sheffield, Yorks. Tel: 0742 745085 & 0860 921519

STE •† Stevenson Brothers, The Workshop, Ashford Road, Bethersden, Ashford, Kent. Tel: 0233 820580

STK •† Stockbridge Antiques, 8 Deanhaugh Street, Edinburgh EH4 1LY. Tel: 031 332 1366

SUF • Suffolk Sales, Half Moon House, High Street, Clare, Suffolk. Tel: 0787 277993

SWO * Sworders, G. E. Sworder & Sons, 15 Northgate End, Bishops Stortford, Herts. Tel: 0279 51388

TED •† Teddy Bears of Witney, 99 High Street, Witney, Oxon. Tel: 0993 702616

TEM • Teddy's Emporium, 50 Northgate, Canterbury, Kent CT1 1BE Tel: 0227 769987

TH • Tony Horsley. Tel: 0273 732163

TOR • Tortoiseshell (Pixie Taylor), Trebedw Guest House, Henllan, Llandysul, Dyfed, Wales. Tel: 0559 370943.

TRU • The Trumpet, West End, Minchinhampton, Glos. Tel: 0453 883027

TS • Tim's Spot, Ely St. Antique Centre, Stratford-upon-Avon, Warwicks. Tel: 0789 297496

TVA • Teme Valley Antiques, 1 The Bull Ring, Ludlow, Shropshire. Tel: 0584 874686.

VB • Variety Box, 16 Chapel Place, Tunbridge Wells, Kent. Tel: 0892 31868 & 21589

VBu •† Valerie Burman, Market Fayre, 69 High Street, Broadstairs, Kent. Tel: 0843 862563

VH • Valerie Howard, 131e Kensington Church Street, London W8. Tel: 071 792 9702

VS *† T. Vennett-Smith, 11 Nottingham Road, Gotham, Nottingham. Tel: 0602 830541

WA •† Windmill Antiques, 4 Montpelier Mews, Harrogate, Yorks. Tel: 0423 530502 & 0845 401330

WAC •† Walsall Antiques Centre, 7a Digbeth Arcade, Walsall, W. Midlands. Tel: 0922 725163/5

WAL *† Wallis & Wallis, West Street Auction Galleries, Lewes, E. Sussex. Tel: 0273 480208

WEL • Wells Reclamation & Co., The Old Cider Farm, Coxley, Nr Wells, Somerset Tel: 0749 77087/77484

Wil • Willcocks Antiques, G3 Chenil Galleries, 181-183 King's Road, London SW3. Tel: 071 351 6816.

WIL * Peter Wilson, Victoria Gallery, Market Street, Nantwich, Cheshire. Tel: 0270 623878

WW * Woolley & Wallis, The Castle Auction Mart, Castle Street, Salisbury, Wilts Tel: 0722 321711

YV • Yvonne Willcocks, K3 Chenil Galleries, 183 King's Road, Chelsea, London SW3. Tel: 071 352 7384

ZEI • Zeitgeist, 58 Kensington Church Street, London W8. Tel: 071 938 4817

Aeronautica

A presentation silver salver and other memorabilia relating to Lt. G.L. Brinton, RN, (Flying Officer RAF), a member of the Schneider Trophy Team, 1931.
£2,900-3,000 *S(S)*

A Gloster Meteor control column handgrip, with firing buttons, in as new condition with packing, in original box, 8in (20cm) wide.
£125-150 *CSK*

A portrait of a WRAF pilot, 26in (66cm) long.
£125-175 *RE*

An RAF World War II period sector clock, the case stamped MCA21B713, with RAF crest, 17.25in (43.8cm) diam., unrestored.
£1,800-2,000 *CSK*

A bomb aimer's computer, 1940s.
£15-18 *COB*

An RAF sector clock, with 5 minute red, blue and yellow sectors, mahogany case stamped on the back S.Davall & Sons, Goswell Road, dated 1939, lacking glass and winding key, case with traces of paint.
£850-900 *S(S)*

Air Chief Marshal Lord Dowding's handwritten draft 'farewell' message to Fighter Command, November 1940.
£9,000-10,000 *S(S)*

A Supermarine Spitfire blind flying panel, with connecting pipes, 14in (30.5cm) wide.
£460-480 *CSK*

An Air Ministry pattern astro-compass manufactured by Sperti Inc. Cincinnati, Ohio; an RAF sextant MkV; and an aircraft octant in case, 8.25in (21cm) wide.
£25-30 *CSK*
and a bubble sextant Mk VIII by H. Hughes & Son Limited, 10.5in (27cm) wide, in case and a U.S. pattern Army Air Force pattern bubble sextant, in case 12.75in (32.5cm) wide.
£60-70 *CSK*

A rare RNAS station bell, with original clapper and white painted rope handle, 16in (40.5cm) high.
£1,600-1,700 *S(S)*

A Brooklands Aero Club car badge, nickel plated with enamelling in 5 colours, the reverse numbered 130, some damage, early 1930s.
£575-600 *S(S)*

A Luftwaffe pilot's wristwatch, 1940s. **£450-500** *S(S)*

Cross Reference
Wristwatches

An 'Aviation' board game, The Aerial Tactics Game of Attack and Defence, with original printed cards on metal stands and board, in original box.
£80-100 *CSK*

Part of the propellor of a Mark I Spitfire, 1940s, 6.5in (16cm) square.
£15-20 *OD*

A silver and enamelled RFC cigarette case, the gilt interior engraved Capt. A. D. Pass. RFC 23 Queens Gate Terrace, S.W., some enamel missing, hallmarked London 1916, 5in (13.5cm) high.
£100-120 *S(S)*

An RAF Operations Room Sector clock, with painted dial divided into coloured triangles of red, yellow and blue for 2.5 minute periods, in mahogany case, stamped 16573 Made by W. Elliott Ltd. England 1941, 14in (35.5cm) diam, with key.
£1,500-1,600 *CSK*

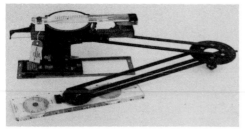

A complete Kelvin Hughes Craig computer, for course and speed calculation, with original instruction book in mint condition, in original transit case, 28in (71cm) long.
£275-300 *CSK*

A teddy bear, Edward St. John Biggin, complete with flying outfit decorated with numerous badges and a Flying Log Book, showing many types flown, with photographs and display case containing further badges.
£450-500 *S(S)*

Cross Reference
Teddy Bears

Part of a crashed spitfire.
£25-28 *COB*

A bronze medallion commemorating the Montgolfier brothers' ascent, with moulded signature N. Galteaux, 1.5in (4cm) diam. **£150-200** CSK

A silk Union Jack, inscribed in ink 'Flown on Apollo 15 26th July- 7th Aug 1971' and signed by the astronaut Al Worden, with silk crew badge for Scott, Worden and Irwin, framed and glazed, with hand written card by Al Worden certifying authenticity.
£1,800-1,900 *CSK*

A gilt bronze medallion, embossed 'Lindbergh Medal of the Congress of the United States of America', signed 'Lavra Gardia Fraser Sculptor', 'Act May 4 1928', 2.75in (7cm).
£120-140 *CSK*

A collection of World War II period wooden scale model construction kits.
£120-150 *CSK*

Dress

A USAAF issue silk lined leather flying jacket, the back decorated with an F86 Sabre surrounded by stars. **£200-220** *CSK*

A RAF flying helmet, complete with visor, microphones, etc, 1970s.
£60-65 *COB*

An Air Transport Auxiliary (Ferry Pilots) blue service tunic, skirt and side cap, with ATA wings and First Officer rank.
£475-525 *ONS*

A USAAF flying suit and helmet, the lightweight suit in orange cotton with Colonel insignia, type K-2B, label dated 13 November 1963, and transfers, including 155th Fighter Group.
£650-700 *S(S)*

Ephemera

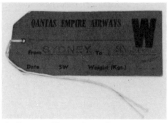

A Qantas flying boat luggage label, 1940.
£3-4 *COB*

A WRAF pilot's helmet and spats, c1930.
£90-110 RE

A USAAF officer's service tunic and trousers, WWII period.
£250-275 *S(S)*

A rare group of early RAF uniform and flying clothing, 1918.
£950-1,100 *S(S)*

A box of approximately 200 1940s aircraft recognition cards. **£40-45** *COB*

H.S. Williamson, Imperial Airways, London, Scylla, lithograph in colours, 1934, backed on linen, 20 by 25in (51 by 64cm).
£625-650 *CSK*

A selection of illustrated German aviation books, with original dust jackets.
£10-20 each *CSK*

Models

A flying scale model of Junkers D1 single seat fighter, wooden airframe covered with simulated corrugated aluminium, with working control surfaces, finished in green and purple camouflage, wingspan 76in (193cm).
£1,250-1,350 *CSK*

A Tippco clockwork lithographed tinplate high wing bomber, cat. ref. 29, with operating propeller, undercarriage and bomb dropping action, c1936, pilot, bombs and bombing mechanism missing.
£375-400 *CSK*

A 1:72 scale aluminium model of a Fokker DR1, 'The Red Baron Werner Voss' by D. Vann, wingspan 7.5in (19.5cm).
£225-250 *CSK*

A flying scale model of a Fokker DVII, the single seat fighter with fabric covered wooden airframe and working control surfaces, finished in camouflage red, blue and white, wingspan 57in (145cm). **£350-375** *CSK*

A flying scale model of a Hawker Fury, with fabric covered wooden airframe and working control surfaces, finished in the colours of No. 43 Sqn. RAF the famous 'Fighting Cocks', wingspan 60in (152.5cm).
£460-480 *CSK*

A flying scale model of a Sparmann P-1, with fabric covered wooden airframe and working control surfaces, finished in Swedish Air Force silver livery, wingspan 82in (208cm). **£575-600** CSK

A detailed flying scale model of a Bristol Bulldog, with fabric covered wooden airframe, and working control surfaces, finished in the colours of No. 3 Sqn. RAF, wingspan 64in (162.5cm). **£450-475** *CSK*

A model aircraft centrepiece, by Doug Vann, modern, 8in (20.5cm) high. **£900-1,000** *S(S)*

A flying scale model of a Curtis Owl, finished in USA AF camouflage, wingspan 82in (208cm). **£400-425** *CSK*

A 1:144 scale aluminium model of the Hawker Hurricane, mounted by D. Vann, wingspan, 6.75in (17.2cm). **£120-130** *CSK*

A flying scale model of a de Havilland Mosquito FB.VI, with wooden airframe, working rudder, elevators, ailerons and flaps, finished in RCAF camouflage of 418 (City of Edmonton), wingspan 72in (183cm). **£1,500-1,600** *CSK*

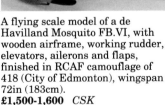

A flying scale model of a Bucker Bu131 Jungmann, with fabric covered wooden airframe and working control surfaces, finished in Luftwaffe markings and camouflage, wingspan 72in (183cm). **£650-680** *CSK*

A flying scale model of a Hawker Hurricane, with working control surfaces, finished in blue, wingspan 66in (177.5cm). **£475-500** *CSK*

l. A static display model of a Sopwith Pup, with cockpit with flying and engine controls, 9.5in (24cm) long. **£300-325**

r. A detailed scale static display model of the Sopwith 5F.1. Dolphin, Serial No. E5429, with fabric covered wings fuselage and empennage, cockpit with flying and engine controls, windscreen and 2 machine guns with telescopic sight, 9 cylinder rotary engine, propeller, undercarriage and other details, finished in RFC camouflage 9.5in (24cm) long. **£420-450** *CSK*

A flying scale model of the Gloster Gladiator, with wooden airframe and working control surfaces, finished in the colours of No. 43 Sqn. RAF, wingspan 56in (142cm). **£460-480** *CSK*

A flying scale model of a Fokker DVI, with fabric covered wooden airframe, working control surfaces, finished in green, purple and white with markings, wingspan 73in (185.5cm). **£1,250-1,400** *CSK*

Photographs

A set of 9 World War II Luftwaffe photo mechanical colour reproductions, slight tear, 10 by 11.5in (25 by 29cm). **£200-225** *CSK*

A collection of 13 photographs, some in colour, including Avro Lancaster ED 592, and a selection of aviation 'Profile' booklets. **£50-60** *CSK*

Postcards

A collection of 35 signed commemorative philatelic covers related to the NASA Space Programme, including Mercury, Apollo, Gemini and Space Shuttle flights. **£850-875** *CSK*

Signatures include: Major General Walter Dornberger, ex commandant, Peenemunde, Wernher von Braun, Willy Messerschmitt, John Glenn, Cdr. Scott Carpenter, Col. James McDivitt, Capt. James Lovell, Neil Armstrong, 'Buzz' Aldrin, Alexander Ivanchenkov, Vladimir Kovalenok and many others.

> **Cross Reference**
> Postcards

A collection of 10 coloured and photographic postcards. **£170-190** *CSK*

A collection of 20 early aviation postcards. **£110-125** *CSK*

A collection of 11 official photographic reproduction postcards depicting LZ 127, 'Graf Zeppelin'. **£210-230** *CSK*

Cross Reference
Zeppelins

Posters

DORNIER-WERKE

DMZ Deutsche Motor-Zeitshrift, various issues 1933-39, unbound, some complete years, containing advertisements for German aircraft manufacturers, and a quantity of technical books. **£75-85** *CSK*

An Imperial Airways lithograph in colours, backed on linen, c1936, 38 by 25in (98 by 63cm). **£725-750** *CSK*

An Imperial Airways flying boat map, 1930s. **£20-25** *COB*

Prints

James Goulding, Heinkel He 162 A 2, 19.5 by 15in (49.5 by 38cm). **£210-230** *CSK*

Original artwork for 'Profile' and other publications.

Frank Wootton, born 1911, Lockheed Super Constellation of Linea Aeropostal Venezuela, signed and inscribed, oil sketch on board, unframed, 21.25 by 25.25in (54 by 64cm). **£775-800** *CSK*

A collection of 6 aircraft pictures, including a Dewoitine 730, 9.5 by 12.5in (24 by 32cm). **£120-140** *CSK*

Frank Wootton, born 1911, BOAC Super Constellation at Nassau, pencil and black crayon, signed and inscribed Frank Wootton. **£285-300** *CSK*

A Short built Felixtowe F5s, in 'dazzle' camouflage on convoy patrol, watercolour, 17 by 22in (43 by 56cm).   **£60-80** *CSK*

Munro, 'Wapiti', signed, inscribed and dated, pencil and watercolour, 12.5 by 19.25in (32 by 49cm). **£60-70** *CSK*

C. Rupert Moore, a Dragon Rapide of North Sea Air Transport Ltd., airborne, signed and dated 1947, pencil and bodycolour heightened with white, 23.5 by 17.25in (60 by 44cm). **£80-100** *CSK*

A rare Vickers Supermarine Spitfire Sales Brochure, dated June 1939, spiral bound, sepia and blue, photos and text. **£620-640** *CSK*
Provenance: ex R.J. Mitchell and thence by descent.

A collection of 14 original artworks for 'Profile' publications. **£350-370** *CSK*

Ross Nicoll, The Vickers Valiant prototype, signed, gouache and watercolour, 16.25 by 22.75in (41 by 58cm).   **£125-145** *CSK*

W.J. Gaskin, Handley Page Heyford bombers in mock combat with flight of Hawker Furies, signed, pencil and watercolour, 10.75 by 15.5in (27.5 by 40cm).   **£100-120** *CSK*

Roffe, Fokker triplanes, and SE5s about to close for action, gouache, signed, 12.25 by 18.25in (31 by 46.5cm).
£80-100 *CSK*

A collection of original artworks including de Havilland Rapide, for 'Profile' publications.
£350-370 *CSK*

A limited edition print, Return of the Few, after Robert Taylor, 7/50, signed in pencil by 52 Battle of Britain pilots, including Brian Kingcome, Bob Stanford-Tuck, Frank Carey, Pete Brothers and Al Deere, 24 by 16in (61 by 41cm), mounted, framed and glazed.
£850-1,000 *S(S)*

A collection of 16 original artworks for 'Profile' publications.
£220-240 *CSK*

Propellers

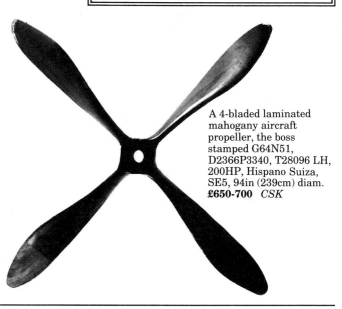

A laminated mahogany 2-blade propeller, with canvas covered tips and brass leading edges, the boss stamped 'DRG No.Z64 80 HP. CIRRUS MkII. D 6'4". P4'8" A G 51482 DEC/33', one blade with transfer The Airscrew Co. Weybridge Surrey, 76in (193cm) diam.
£160-180 *CSK*

A 4-bladed laminated mahogany aircraft propeller, the boss stamped G64N51, D2366P3340, T28096 LH, 200HP, Hispano Suiza, SE5, 94in (239cm) diam.
£650-700 *CSK*

A rare 4-blade laminated wood propeller, the 4 tips with brass sheaths stamped around the shaft hull '2869 Darracq Motor Engineering Co. Ltd., London, 100hp Monosoupape Gnome FE8, W.D. 17586 T 7928' bearing the original Darracq circular transfer to the reverse of the blade.
£800-900 *MR*

This propeller is one of a batch of 245 plus 50 more completed by Vickers of the Durracq-built FE8 Biplane Fighter with pusher propeller of late 1916. It was used by No. 40 or No. 41 Squadron Royal Flying Corps.
With full provenance from its retainment after World War I to its present owner.

A two-bladed laminated mahogany propeller, boss stamped D2500 P1800 886, 98in (249cm) span.
£475-525 *S(S)*

A laminated mahogany two-blade propeller, applied with transfers for F Tibbenham, Ipswich, 104in (264cm) diam.
£450-460 *CSK*

A laminated mahogany 4-blade propeller, built in 2 sections and with brass leading edges, the bosses stamped GF 0572 No.2 (the other 2A) DRG.No.5097.4.25 D 2660P2180 De H 50, 107in (271.8cm).
£950-1,000 *CSK*

Zeppelins

A menu card, The Graf Zeppelin over New York, from the first Europe Pan-American flight, issued by the Louis Sherry Hotel N.Y.
£250-275 *CSK*

A collection of photographs from the personal album of Heinrich Kubis, some taken on board LZ 127 'Graf Zeppelin', and a chromium plated shaped entrée dish carried aboard LZ 129 'Hindenburg' during the 1936 'Olympiafahrt', 11.5in (28.9cm) wide.
£3,400-3,500 *CSK*

A Veedol lithograph poster in colours, backed on linen, 50 by 29.5in (127 by 75cm).
£575-600 *CSK*

A clockwork lithographed tinplate Graf Zeppelin D LZ 127, equipped for electric light, bulb holder missing.
£350-375 *CSK*

A leatherette and silk lined correspondence folder, embossed in gilt 'Graf Zeppelin', with a pictorial representation of LZ 127, 17.5in (44.5cm) wide open, and a collection of original Deutsche Zeppelin-Reederei notepaper, envelopes and a broadsheet, carried aboard, c1929.
£550-575 *CSK*

A collection of 6 commemorative postcards, 3 colour including one dated 17-9-29 'Au Bord des Luftschiffes Graf Zeppelin,', and a photograph of LZ127 Graf Zeppelin alighting on the Bodensee.
£110-125 *CSK*

A gilt-bronze and enamel commemorative plaque, inscribed ZIELFAHRT ZUR ZEPPELIN-LANDUNG, 1931, 3.25in (8.2cm) wide.
£220-240 *CSK*

A wood and plated metal Art Deco period window static display model of Graf Zeppelin, 16.75 by 30in (42.5 by 76.2cm).
£950-1,000 *CSK*

FURTHER READING

History of British Aviation, Brett R. Dallas, 2 vols 1908-14 and 1913-14
British Flying Boats and Amphibians, G. R. Duval, 1909-52 London 1953
The Fighters: The Men and Machines of the First Air War, Thomas R. Funderburk, London 1966
The History of Aeronautics in Britain, J. E. Hodgson, 1924
Janes All The World's Aircraft - Published annually
Airmails 1870-1970, James A. Mackay, London 1971.
Combat Aircraft of the World, F. C. Swanborough, London 1962

A scarce commemorative painted metal money box, recording a zeppelin landing on 5th August, 1908, made by Märklin, 5in (13cm).
£525-575 *S(S)*

A LZ130 'Graf Zeppelin' folding broadsheet, with detailed cut-away and publicity information for this, the last Zeppelin built, dated 5/39.
£175-200 *CSK*

Automobilia

A Price's Motorine Motor Oil, double sided sign, 18in (46cm) diam.
£80-100 *ONS*

A BP Motor Spirit double sided union flag, 16 by 24in (41 by 62cm).
£150-170 *ONS*

A Jaguar car badge, 4in (10cm) long.
£4-6 *RE*

A Bedford Drivers Club badge, 3.25in (11cm) diam.
£2-5 *PC*

A Runeasy cycle oil can, 1920s. **£9-11** *COB*

A Henry Le Monnier Automobile Unic Poster, lithograph in colours, 1928, backed on linen, 45 by 61in (115 by 155cm).
£1,000-1,200 *CSK*

A Louis Vuitton fine tan leather small accessory trunk, with leather corners, leather strap and carrying handles, brass studded, on casters, inside lid and base lined with brown felt, labelled LV No 789794, lock No 073685, 24 by 19 by 15.5in (62 by 48 by 39cm).
£1,500-1,700 *ONS*

Three tinplate clockwork toy racing cars, English, 1930-1940s. **£110-120** *S*

Two wood scratch built models of Bluebird, c1936, the largest 20in (51cm) long. **£175-200** *S*

Cross Reference
Toys/Tinplate

A collection of 6 posters advertising Concours d'Elegance, Pebble Beach, California, from the 1960s.
£950-1,200 *CNY*

Cross Reference
Toys

Mascots

A Wolseley radiator cap,
4.75in (12cm) long.
£10-15 *RE*

A Mohican Indian Head
chromium plated bronze
mascot, mounded on
wood base, by Darel,
c1930, 4.75in (12cm)
high.
£200-220 *CSK*

A Lalique smoked grey glass
'Sanglier' mascot, etched and
moulded R. Lalique, 2 small chips,
1930s, 2.75in (7cm) high.
£450-490 *S*

A Farman Icarus mascot, chromium
plated bronze, stamped and marked
Colin George, 20 782, Made in
France, 10, base stamped Finnigans
London, 1922, 6in (15cm) high.
£600-650 *S*

A monkey mascot, with an
elongated mouth, brass mounted on
brass base, c1920, 4in (10.5cm)
high.
£150-160 *CSK*
*It is believed this is one of 5
manufactured by Napier Cars for
an Indian prince who commissioned
a gold one as a wedding gift.*

A Lalique car mascot, moulded in
the form of a dragonfly with wings
closed, moulded mark Lalique and
engraved R. Lalique, France,
c1920s, 6.25in (15.5cm) long.
£700-730 *WIL*

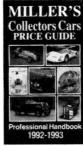

Art Deco

Art Deco, the style that epitomises the twenties and thirties, derived its name from the Paris Exhibition of 1925. The 'Exposition des Arts Decoratifs et Industriels Modernes', sponsored by the French Government, was a showcase of all that was modern. Designed to generate trade in post war Europe, it was a huge success. The Exhibition coupled with the launch of the liner SS Normandie in 1935 established Art Deco as one of the most innovative and exciting styles of the 20thC. Almost everything imaginable on the Normandie, from the glasses and tableware to the bathroom tiles, demonstrated the Art Deco style, establishing the designers as leaders in their respective fields.

Art Deco took a long time to become recognised by collectors. It was not until the sixties that attentions moved from the Art Nouveau period to Art Deco with the jewellery of Jean Fouquet and the glass of René Lalique leading the field.

Most modern collectors seem attracted to the practical wares; ceramics, glass and household accessories, particularly as furniture and those wonderful figures and sculptures became prohibitively expensive.

We have included a good selection of household goods in this year's edition and would remind you to cross reference to the glass and ceramic sections.

A chrome covered tea and coffee pot, c1930.
£25-35 each *CAB*

A Christofle 'Gallia' sugar shaker, in original box, c1920, 4.5in (12cm) high.
£300-350 *ABS*

An Art Deco chrome photograph frame, 6in (15cm) high.
£12-15 *ROW*

> **Cross Reference**
> Picture Frames

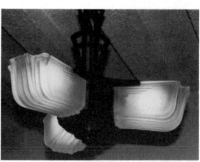

A French Art Deco gilt bronze and glass lamp, c1930.
£200-400 *ASA*

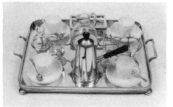

An Art Deco coffee and liqueur set, tray 17in (43.5cm) wide.
£400-600 *ASA*

> **Cross Reference**
> Radios

A radio by Walter Dorwin Teague, with mirrored glass and painted wood case, c1936, 17.5in (44.5cm) wide.
£850-900 *S*

An Art Deco figure lamp, with alabaster orb and shade.
£500-650 *ASA*

A lacquer cigarette case, c1920.
£300-350 *ABS*

A Ziggurat Art Deco oak photograph frame, 6in (15cm) high. **£12-15** *ROW*

Cross Reference
Smoking

An Art Deco chrome and black barometer, c1935 10in (25cm) wide. **£80-100** *CAB*

A cold painted bronze, ivory, and marble 'Bat Dancer' clock, by Ferdinand Preiss, marked F. Preiss, c1925, 15in (39cm) high.
£4,250-4,750 *S*

An Art Deco cold painted metal figure lamp, c1930.
£450-650 *ASA*

A set of 5 Art Deco ceiling and wall lights. **£600-1,000** *ASA*

Cross Reference
Continental Art Deco Ceramics

An Art Deco mirror, hand painted under the glass and signed P. A. Pilley, in a dark green lacquered frame, 25.5in (65cm) high.
£65-75 *ROW*

An Art Deco tea tray, with a coloured silver paper crinoline lady under black glass, in an oak frame, 16in (40.5cm) long.
£20-25 *ROW*

Clocks

A Modernist nickel plated metal and glass clock, attributed to Léon Hatot, c1930, 13in (33cm) high.
£675-700 *S*

A silver coloured metal clock with lightly hammered gilt metal finish, VII numeral missing, marked Imhof, 6in (16cm) high.
£700-750 *S*

A silver mounted clock with 30 hour movement, Birmingham 1923, 6in (15cm) high.
£100-125 *TRU*

Figures

A spelter figure of a girl fencer, 9.5in (24cm) high.
£300-350 *HEW*

'Scarf Dancer', a silvered bronze and onyx figure, by Demetre H. Chiparus, marked D H Chiparus, c1925, 26in (67cm) high.
£4,250-4,750 *S*

'Oriental Dancer', a cold painted bronze and onyx figure, by Demetre H. Chiparus, marked Chiparus, c1920, 16in (40cm) high.
£3,750-4,000 *S*

A cold painted bronze and ivory Devil and Girl, marked Roland Paris, on a marble stand, minor damage, c1920, 16in (40cm) high.
£1,600-1,700 *S*

An Art Deco carved wooden sculpture of frogs, 8in (20cm) high.
£80-150 *ASA*

Art Nouveau

The Art Nouveau style which had developed by about 1880 traced its origins to the earlier Arts and Crafts Movement. The same flowing floral designs were incorporated with the use of modern materials and craftsmanship. The styles were a great success at the Paris Exhibition of 1900 and artists and designers sold their wares at the gallery 'Maison de l'Art Nouveau' owned by the entrepreneur Siegfried Bing. Artists such as Tiffany, Gailliard and Emile Gallé soon became very popular. The term Art Nouveau is traditionally reputed to have derived from the title of Bing's gallery. The French referred to the movement as 'Le Style Anglais' and the Italians as 'Stile Liberty', much to the surprise of the founder of the store Arthur Liberty who constantly called it Art Nouveau!

Art Nouveau was a natural progression for collectors as the art and designs of the Victorian period became harder to find and consequently more expensive. By the 1960s Art Nouveau was firmly established as a collecting area in its own right.

We have concentrated our selection on more affordable practical household items, but would strongly recommend you to cross refer to the ceramic and glass sections, and particularly the work of Alphonse Mucha and Aubrey Beardsley in the Ephemera Section.

A pair of Keswick copper repoussé vases, by W.H. Mawson, 10in (25cm). **£150-175** *ZEI*

A Zsolnay ewer, in stoneware and gilt, c1900, 21.5in (55cm) high.
£600-800 *ABS*

A Keswick copper muffin dish, 9in (23cm).
£100-150 *ZEI*

A Newlyn copper punch bowl, with repoussé fruit and foliage, 11in (28cm).
£200-300 *ZEI*

A pair of WMF classical vases, in silvered pewter with cut crystal liners, 13in (33cm).
£600-800 *ZEI*

A neo-Gothic tea set in silvered Britannia metal for Spurrier and Cornforth, 1880s.
£600-800 *ZEI*

A pair of Liberty Tudric pewter vases, designed by Knox.
£500-600 *ZEI*

An iridescent glass three-handled dish, attributed to Marie Kirschner, for Loetz, c1905, 10in (25cm) diam.
£600-625 *S*

An Art Nouveau silver standing bowl, on shaped square base with 4 curved supports to the shaped square bowl top, London 1907, by Mappin & Webb, 18.5ozs.
£280-320 *GAK*

A lightly hammered silver inkwell, with cabochons, maker's mark London, inscribed Omar Ramsden et Alwyn Carr me fecerunt, c1912, 3.5in (9cm).
£875-925 *S*

A Keswick copper charger with repoussé design, 19in (48cm).
£200-300 *ZEI*

A Victorian terracotta planter, Arts & Crafts Movement, 26in (66cm) high.
£300-350 *GRF*

An Austrian pewter mounted vase, by Loetz, 9in (23cm).
£200-300 *ZEI*

A WMF Art Nouveau centrepiece, in silvered pewter with cut crystal liners, 20in (51cm) high.
£800-1,000 *ZEI*

A WMF oval flower dish, in silver plated pewter with green cut crystal liner, 15in (38cm).
£500-600 *ZEI*

A Della Robbia vase, by Anne David, 10in (25cm).
£250-300 *ZEI*

A Silberzinn wine cooler in the Art Nouveau Whiplash style.
£400-600 *ZEI*

A WMF Gothic revival silver on brass jewel casket.
£100-150 *ZEI*

Candlesticks

A pair of WMF Arts & Crafts style candlesticks, 10in (25cm).
£300-350 *ZEI*

A pair of carved wood mirrors, with easel supports, c1905, 16.5in (42cm).
£1,100-1,300 *S*

An Art Nouveau oil lamp stand, painted green with yellow flowers, 35in (89cm) high.
£250-300 *PC*

Picture Frames

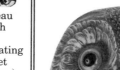

A pair of Goberg German Arts & Crafts candlesticks.
£100-150 *ZEI*

A WMF silver plated toilet mirror, 12in (32in).
£700-800 *ZEI*

An English Art Nouveau style silver photograph frame, with large flowerheads on undulating leafy stems, blue velvet easel back, 11in (27.9cm) high.
£135-150 *CNY*

Bells

A celluloid table or desk bell, moulded as an owl's head, with beak operating wind-up bell mechanism, c1930, 4in (10cm) diam. **£80-100** *PC*

For a further selection of bells please refer to Miller's Collectables Guide, Volume IV, pages 46-47

A pair of George V Art Nouveau style photograph frames, Chester 1913, 10in (25cm) high.
£650-675 *HSS*

Books

Twentieth Century book collecting is currently a very popular area attracting some very good prices. Currently sought after are early P. G. Wodehouse and Stephen King. Cookery books are always in demand.

As with all collectables, condition is paramount, the classic catalogue description is 'As new with similar dust jacket', however books showing signs of use should not be discarded, but condition must be reflected in the price.

What constitutes a valuable book? Is it the age, author, title, condition, first edition, the illustrator, the illustrations, the fact that it is signed by the author, the leather binding or the rarity? In truth it is generally a combination of all or some of these things.

Desirability together with availability have created a great interest in 20thC books. They are accessible, bargains can still be found and one can start with little capital. Popular authors are, by definition, printed in large quantities, although this may not be the case with their early works. If a film or T.V. series has been made of the work this will help it achieve a wider audience. If the author is American then the U.S. printing is generally preferred although it may not necessarily be the true first. Ernest Hemingway's 'Across the River and into the Trees' was first published in the U.K. and Winston Churchill's 'History of the Second World War' was first issued in America, for example.

In the end the best way to learn about books is to handle them, seek out reliable dealers and ask questions.

The Sleeping Beauty, retold by A.T. Quiller-Couch, illustrated by Edmund Dulac, 11 by 9in (28 by 23cm).
£160-180 *HB*

The Dryads and Other Tales, by Frank White, illustrated by A. M. Corah, published by Frederick Warne & Co., Copyright 1936. **£18-20** *TRU*

The Boy's Own Book of Indoor Games, c1920s.
£2.50-3.50 *TRU*

Round the World in Eighty Days, Jules Verne, published by Hutchinson & Co., poor condition, c1890s. **£2-3** *TRU*

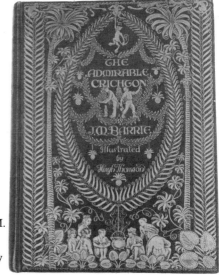

Cross Reference
Colour Review

The Admirable Crichton, by J.M. Barrie, published by Hodder & Stoughton, illustrated by Hugh Thomson, 10.75 by 8.25in (27 by 21cm). **£50-60** *HB*

Four Kate Greenaway
Almanacks, 1886/87/90/91, 4 by
3in (10 by 8cm) each.
£125-150 each   *HB*

Boy's Own Annuals, 1915-16 and
1919-20.
£2-3 each   *TRU*

Little Lord Fauntleroy, by Frances
Hodgson Burnett, published by
Frederick Warne & Co., 1890.
£2.50-3.50   *TRU*

Eagle Annual, No.7.
£3-4.50   *TRU*

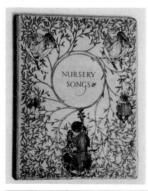

Ruthless Rhymes, published by Edward
Arnold, London, c1920.
£10-12.50   *TRU*

Nursery Songs,
published by T.C.
& E. C. Jac, London,
songs arranged by
Joseph Moorat and
pictures by Paul
Woodroffe.
£10-12.50   *TRU*

The Golden Age, by
Kenneth Grahame,
illustrated by Ernest
H. Shepard, 1st edition
and signed by Shepard,
7.5 by 5in (19 by 13cm).
£125-150 *HB*

Swinburne, selected
poems published by
The Bodley Head, 1st
edition 1928,
illustrated by Harry
Clarke, 9.75 by 6.5in
(24 by 16cm).
£65-75 *HB*

King Arthur and His Knights, by Harry G. Theaker,
published by Ward Lock & Co., c1930, some
tears to plates, 10 by 7.5in (25 by 19cm).
£30-40 *Wil*

Poems of Childhood, by Eugene
Field, published by Charles
Scribners & Sons, New York, 1st
edition, 1904, illustrated by
Maxfield Parrish, 9.5 by 7.25in
(24 by 18cm).
£55-60 *HB*

A Song of the English, by
Rudyard Kipling, published by
Hodder & Stoughton, illustrated
by W. Heath Robinson, 1st
edition, 11.25 by 9in (29 by 23cm).
£140-150 *HB*

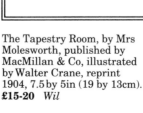

Through The Looking Glass,
by Lewis Carroll, published
by MacMillan & Co., 1893,
7.5 by 5in (19 by 13cm).
£40-45 *Wil*

The Tapestry Room, by Mrs
Molesworth, published by
MacMillan & Co, illustrated
by Walter Crane, reprint
1904, 7.5 by 5in (19 by 13cm).
£15-20 *Wil*

Le Village Aérien - Voyages
Extraordinaires, Collection
Hetzel, by Jules Verne, 1st
edition, 11 by 7.5in
(28 by 19cm).
£225-250 *HB*

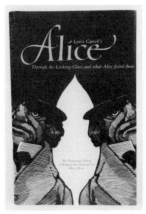

Alice Through the Looking Glass, and what Alice found there, The Pennyroyal Edition, published by University of California Press 1983, illustrated by Barry Moser, 13.5 by 8.75in (34 by 22cm).
£40-45 *Wil*

Peter Pan in Kensington Gardens, by J.M. Barrie, illustrated by Arthur Rackham, 1st edition, 1906, 10 by 7.75in (25 by 20cm).
£150-180 *HB*

Flower Legends for Children, told by Hilda Murray, published by Longmans Green & Co., pictured by J.S. Eland, 8.75 by 11.25in (22 by 29cm).
£65-70 *Wil*

The Water Babies, by Charles Kingsley, published by Hodder & Stoughton for Boots Pure Drug Co., illustrated by Jessie Willcox Smith.
£65-75 *Wil*

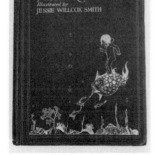

A Midsummer Night's Dream, published by Constable & Co. Ltd., London, 1st edition, 1914, illustrated by W. Heath Robinson, 11.5 by 9in (29 by 23cm).
£125-150 *HB*

The Complete Alice & The Hunting Of The Snark, by Lewis Carroll, published by Jonathan Cape, 1st edition 1975, illustrated by Ralph Steadman, 11.5 by 8.25in (29 by 21cm).
£40-45 *Wil*

The Tale of Two Bad Mice, by Beatrix Potter, published by F. Warne & Co., 1st edition 1904, 5.75 by 4.25in (15 by 11cm). **£125-145** *HB*

Alice's Adventures in Wonderland, by Lewis Carroll, published by William Heinemann, illustrated by Arthur Rackham, 1st edition 1907, with a poem by Austin Dobson, 8.25 by 6.25in (21 by 16cm). **£100-120** *HB*

The Princess And Curdie, published by Blackie, illustrated by Helen Stratton, 12 colour illustrations and 29 text illustrations in black and white, 8 by 6in (20 by 15cm). **£80-85** *Wil*

The Tale of Mr Tod, by Beatrix Potter, published F. Warne & Co., 1st edition 1912, 5.5 by 4.5in (14 by 12cm). **£125-150** *HB*

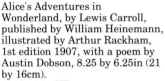

Bunter The Ventriloquist, by Frank Richards, 1st edition, 1961, 7.5 by 5in (19 by 13cm). **£20-25** *HB*

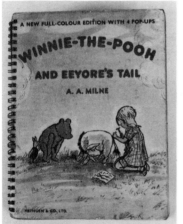

A complete set of 23 titles in presentation Peter Rabbit's Book Shelf, published by F. Warne & Co. Ltd., c1970. **£45-55** *ROW*

Winnie-The-Pooh And Eeyore's Tail, by A.A. Milne, published by Methuen & Co. Ltd., 9.5 by 7.5in (24 by 19cm). **£60-70** *HB*

The Tale of Tom Kitten, by Beatrix Potter, published by F. Warne & Co., 1st edition 1907, 5.5 by 4.5in (14 by 12cm). **£125-150** *HB*

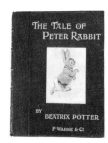

The Tale of Peter Rabbit, by Beatrix Potter, published by F. Warne & Co., early edition. **£70-75** *HB*

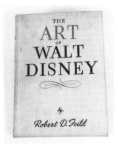

The Tale of Mrs Tiggy-Winkle, by Beatrix Potter, published by F. Warne & Co., 1st edition 1905, 5.5 by 4.5in (14 by 12cm). **£125-150** *HB*

The Art of Walt Disney, by Robert D. Field, 1st edition, 1944, 11 by 8.5in (29 by 21cm). **£65-75** *HB*

Billy Bunter's Bargain, by Frank Richards, 1st edition, 1958, 7.5 by 5in (19 by 13cm). **£25-30** *HB*

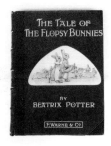

The Tale of The Flopsy Bunnies, by Beatrix Potter, published by F. Warne & Co., 1st edition 1909, 5.5 by 4.5in (14 by 12cm). **£125-150** *HB*

Maigret's Memoirs, by Simenon, published by Hamish Hamilton, 1st edition, 1963, 7.5 by 5.25in (19 by 13cm). **£30-35** *HB*

Set of 12 newspaper books of Financial Times 1967-74, 23.5 by 16in (60 by 41cm). **£200-300** *APO*

Maigret's Little Joke, by Simenon, published by Hamish Hamilton, 1957, 7.5 by 5in (19 by 13cm). **£30-35** *HB*

Maigret and the Burglar's Wife, by Simenon, published by Hamish Hamilton, 1st edition, 1955, 7.5 by 5.25in (19 by 13cm). **£30-35** *HB*

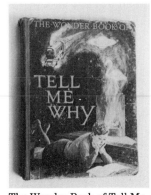

The Wonder Book of Tell Me Why, 1930s. **£3.50-4.50** *TRU*

Gnomeland, Teatime Tales for Tiny Tots, by Uncle Elgo. **£1-2** *TRU*

Language of Flowers, published by George Routledge & Sons, London, 1st edition, c1888, illustrated by Kate Greenaway, with 125 flower illustrations, 6 by 5in (15 by 13cm). **£100-120** *HB*

Hawthorne's Wonder Book, published by Hodder & Stoughton, 1st edition, illustrated by Arthur Rackham, 10 by 8in (25 by 20cm). **£120-180** *HB*

Rubáiyát of Omar Khayam, 1926, with decorative leather binding, 10.25 by 8in (26 by 20cm). **£100-120** *HB*

The Legend of Sleepy Hollow, published by George G. Harrap & Co. Ltd., London, 1928, illustrated by Arthur Rackham, 8 colour illustrations, black and white line drawings, pictorial end papers, 10 by 8in (25 by 20cm). **£140-150** *HB*

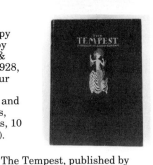

The Tempest, published by Heinemann, 1st edition, illustrated by Arthur Rackham, 10 by 7.5in (25 by 19cm). **£170-180** *HB*

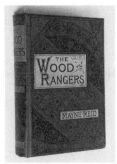

London, by A.R. Hope Moncrieff, published by A & C Black, 1916, 9 by 6.5in (23 by 16cm). **£50-60** *HB*

Undine, by De La Motte Fouqué, adapted from the German by W.L. Courtney, published by William Heinemann, London 1909, illustrated by Arthur Rackham, 15 colour plates, 10.5 by 7.5in (26 by 19cm). **£80-90** *HB*

The Wood Rangers, by Captain Mayne Reid, G. Roulledge & Sons, reasonable condition. **£3-4** *TRU*

The Arthur Rackham Fairy Book, re-print George Harrap & Co., reprint 1939, 9 by 6.25in (23 by 16cm).
£50-55 *Wil*

Bunter Out Of Bounds, by Frank Richards, 1st edition, 1959, 7.5 by 5in (19 by 13cm).
£25-30 *HB*

The Tale of Pigling Bland, by Beatrix Potter, published by Frederick Warne & Co., 1st edition 1913, 5.5 by 4.5in (14 by 12cm).
£120-140 *HB*

Rogues in Porcelain, compiled and decorated by John Austen, 1924, 10 by 6.5in (25 by 16cm). **£80-85** *Wil*

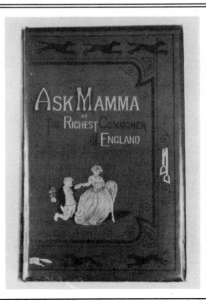

Ask Mamma or The Richest Commoner in England, published by Bradley Agnew & Co., March 31, 1858, illustrated by John Leech, 9 by 6in (23 by 15cm).
£45-50 *Wil*

Boot Scrapers

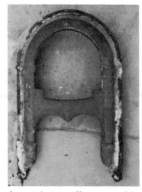

A cast iron wall mounted boot scraper from the Chinese Embassy, No. 41 Portland Place, c1880, 16in (41cm) high.
£30-40 *DRU*

A wrought iron boot scraper, from The Nurses' Home, Charing Cross Hospital, c1900, 15in (38cm) wide.
£45-50 *DRU*

A cast iron boot scraper, 11.5in (29cm) high.
£30-40 *DRU*

Cross Reference
Metalware Kitchenalia Tools

A wall mounted boot scraper, 12in (31cm) wide.
£20-30 *DRU*

A cast iron boot scraper, 10in (25cm) high.
£30-40 *DRU*

A cast iron boot scraper, 20in (51cm) high.
£40-50 *DRU*

A boot scraper, late 19thC, 12.5in (32cm) high.
£30-40 *DRU*

A Victorian wall mounted cast iron boot scraper, 16.5in (42cm) high.
£40-60 *DRU*

A foot scraper from the extension to Chelsea Police Station, 10in (25 cm) high.
£40-50 *DRU*

A boot scraper, late 18thC, 7.5in (19cm).
£30-40 *DRU*

Bottles

An English wine bottle,
c1765, 12in (31cm) high.
£75-95 *LIO*

A Persian green bottle, c1700,
11.5in (29cm) high.
£55-75 *LIO*

A Staffordshire pottery potato
flask, c1785, 7.5in (19cm) long.
£55-75 *LIO*

An Indian green bottle, c1700,
11in (28cm) high.
£50-70 *LIO*

An English onion bottle, c1705,
6in (15cm) high.
£140-160 *LIO*

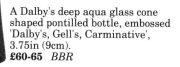

A Dalby's deep aqua glass cone
shaped pontilled bottle, embossed
'Dalby's, Gell's, Carminative',
3.75in (9cm).
£60-65 *BBR*

An early clear glass feeder, 8.75in (22cm) long.
£35-40 *BBR*

A Hamilton aqua glass embossed bottle,
'A S Watson & Co Ltd, Hong Kong, China
& Manila', cracked, 9.25in (24cm) long.
£15-20 *BBR*

A blue cylinder
glass with blob
lip, front embossed
'Jas Mackie &
Sons, Est 1835,
Newcastle', some
wear, 6.75in
(17cm) high.
£40-45 *BBR*

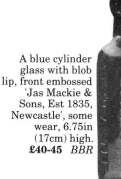

A round bottomed aqua glass
cylinder, embossed in ribbon
around shoulder. 'Carrara Water
Maughams Patent Registered 31
May 1845'
£40-45 *BBR*

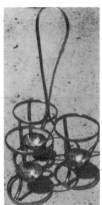

A plated Hamilton stand, for 3 bottles, stamped 'Mappin Brothers, 2062/A', slight tarnishing, 13in (33cm) high.
£60-65 *BBR*

A Barrett & Elers aqua glass bottle, embossed 'Barrett & Co Vauxhall, London', and around base edge 'Lumb & Co/Makers, Castleford', 9.25in (24cm) high.
£15-17 *BBR*

A Hamilton aqua glass bottle, embossed 'N Paul & Burrow, Real, Soda Water, 5 Bow Street, Covent Garden 1802', 8.5in (21cm) long.
£40-45 *BBR*

> **Cross Reference**
>
> Glass

Medicine Bottles

A round cobalt poison bottle, with 'Liq Arsenic' in white lettering to front panel and 'Poison' near base, chipped, 7.25in (18cm).
£60-65 *BBR*

An aqua glass medicine bottle, embossed 'Man Or Animals', and triangular 'T.M. RD296 969', embossed around base, 4.75in (12cm).
£16-18 *BBR*

A Tipper & Son cobalt blue glass bottle, embossed 'Tipper & Son M.R.C.V.S./By Examination Birmingham, Not To Be Taken', 6.75in (17cm) high.
£75-80 *BBR*

A ribbed circular cobalt poison bottle, with 'Liq. Ammon. Fort' in white lettering on front panel, and 'Poison' in orange lettering near base, with stopper, chipped, 9in (23cm) high.
£85-95 *BBR*

A cobalt 'Admiralty' poison bottle, ribbed on 3 sides, '16ozN' on front, complete with stopper, 6.5in (16cm) high.
£60-65 *BBR*

A Quines patent light blue aqua bottle, unusual circular wedge shape, rising upwards at an angle, embossed 'Poison' both sides and '2oz' beneath neck, 4.75in (12cm) long.
£225-250 *BBR*

One of the U.K.'s rarest glass poison bottles.

Stoneware

A stone bottle, inscribed 'J Robertson & Co Edinburgh Brewed Ginger Beer', 8.25in (21cm) high.
£40-45 *BBR*

A Jenner & Butterworth stone bottle, with Crown cork closure, picture of Blackpool Tower, 8.5in (21cm) high.
£90-100 *BBR*

A bottle inscribed 'R.A.C.S., Olde Fashioned, Stone Ginger Beer', green top, with small chips, 7in (18cm) high.
£60-65 *BBR*

A stone bottle inscribed 'The Cyclists Favourite Ginger Beer Dorchester', with transfer of cyclists, 6.75in (17cm) high.
£40-45 *BBR*

Cross Reference
Packaging & Advertising

A bottle inscribed 'Underwoods, Brewed Ginger Beer, Carlisle', a picture of the factory and 'Awarded Certificate of Merit 1896', 8in (20cm) high.
£75-80 *BBR*

A stone bottle, 10in (25cm) high.
£6-8 *SCO*

A stone bottle inscribed 'Probyn's Ginger Beer/Gold Medal Brewers Exhibition 1896' with picture of a Grecian lady, 6.75in (17cm) high. **£30-35** *BBR*

Boxes

Cross Reference

Tea Caddies

A brass mounted stationery box, with single long drawer, fall front and fitted interior, early 20thC, 12.5in (32in high).
£200-220 *GAK*

A Victorian figured walnut brass bound lap desk, with fitted interior, 11in (28cm) wide.
£165-185 *GAK*

A Continental silver gilt and enamelled box, the lid painted with a maiden, the sides with resting maidens and cherubs, base sepia painted with landscape, enamelled interior with centre panel of birds and flowers, 19thC, 2.5in (6cm) diam.
£1,100-1,200 *GAK*

A selection of ivory, bone and coquilla nut egg boxes.
£9-13 each *VB*

An Ottaviani crested crane box, in palisander wood, enamel, and silver coloured metal, engraved 'Ottaviani' and stamped '8 MC', 1960s, 9.5in (24cm) wide.
£700-775 *S*

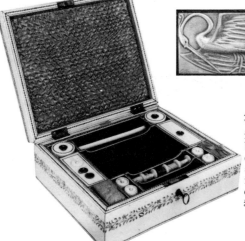

An Anglo Indian Vizigapatnam ivory sewing box, with incised design of flowers and fitted interior, early 19thC.
£450-500 *LRG*

A walnut and brass bound stationery box with dome top, late 19thC, 9.5in (24cm) wide.
£130-150 *PCh*

A pair of boxes in olive wood and walnut, 19thC.
£200-225 *Sim*

An enamelled steel deed box, 15.75in (40cm). **£60-70** *LBL*

Buckles

A Liberty Cymric buckle, Birmingham 1903, 3in (8cm).
£250-280 *JBB*

A silver buckle by Archibald Knox for Liberty & Co., stamped Cymric, maker's mark and number '5', Birmingham, c1902, 3.5in (9cm) wide.
£550-600 *S*

An Art Deco celluloid buckle, 1.25in (3cm) square.
£2-3 *COL*

A silver plated clasp, 3.5in (9cm).
£30-40 *JBB*

A paste clasp with centre pink stone, c1900, 3.5in (9cm).
£30-40 *JBB*

A Victorian cloak clasp, 4.5in (12cm).
£20-25 *JBB*

An Art Nouveau parcel gilt and silver coloured metal buckle, stamped '24', c1900, 3.5in (9cm).
£425-475 *S*

An enamel clasp, c1910, 3.5in (9cm).
£30-35 *JBB*

A brass buckle, with diamanté and black stones, 3in (8cm) wide.
£4-6 *COL*

An early Victorian cut steel clasp.
£50-55 *JBB*

Button Hooks

A silver button hook, set with Scottish agate, c1880, 7in (18cm) long.   **£40-60** *BWA*

For a further selection of Button Hooks, please refer to previous editions of Miller's Collectables Price Guides.

Buttons

A selection of gentlemens trouser buttons, from bespoke tailors.
5-10p each *AGM*

Local research can identify the location and dates of the shops.

A mogul painting on ivory button, c1840.
£70-75 *JBB*

Peanuts character buttons.
5-10p each *AGM*

A ceramic button.
£2-3 *JBB*

| Cross Reference |
| Art Deco |

An Artid button, 1940s.
£1-2 *JBB*

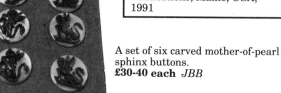

A set of six carved mother-of-pearl sphinx buttons.
£30-40 each *JBB*

Art Deco inlaid wood buttons. **£25-30** *JBB*

FURTHER READING
The Complete Button Book, Lilian Smith Albert and Cathryn Kent, London 1952
The Collector's Encyclopedia of Buttons, Sally C. Luscomb, New York 1967
Buttons: A Guide for Collectors, Gwen Squire, London 1972
Buttons, Diana Epstein and Millicent Safro, Newleaf Publications, Maine, USA, 1991

A set of 6 silver buttons, boxed.
£60-70 *TRU*

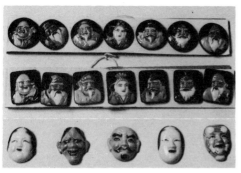

Two boxes of Imari seven Gods of Wisdom buttons.
£40-45 each and
One box of Imari five Gods of Wisdom buttons.
£30-40 *JBB*

Fossilized walrus tooth buttons, Scrimshaw from Alaska buttons.
£25-30 each *JBB*

Cross Reference
Paperweights

A paperweight button.
£10-12 each JBB

A lady's head button.
£8-10 *JBB*

An enamel on silver buckle and button set, Birmingham 1910.
£120-140 *JBB*

Victorian porcelain buttons.
£50-60 each *JBB*

An ivory netsuke button.
£30-35 *JBB*

An embroidered swan button.
£6-8 *JBB*

Fox head horn buttons.
£1-3 each
JBB

Beatrix Potter character buttons.
5-10p each *AGM*

A boxed set of 8 Victorian enamelled buttons.
£200-225
JBB

Cameras

This year we have concentrated on the more unusual cameras that collectors may come across. We have focused in particular on a fascinating selection of 'Spy' cameras.

We recommend you refer to previous editions of Collectables, especially Volume IV, 1992-93, pages 62-70, for the more usual plate and modern single lens reflex cameras.

The camera market is steady and the more unusual items, as featured here, are keenly sought by collectors and dealers alike. Please note the cross reference to the Scientific Instrument section.

A Rollei-Werke, West Germany, 16mm Rollei 16S camera, with chrome and snakeskin trim body covering, a Rollei Honeywell badge, and a Carl Zeiss Tessar f2.8 25mm lens, in maker's ever ready case, in maker's fitted presentation case.
£190-200   *CSK*

A Contessa-Nettel 6 x 9cm tropical Deck-Rullo camera, with polished teak body, nickel fittings, tan leather bellows and a Carl Zeiss Jena Tessar f4.5 12cm lens.
£1,400-1,600   *CSK*

An Expo Camera Co., 30 x 28mm focal-plane police camera with black metal body, nickel fittings, rotating viewfinder, focal-plane shutter, film holder, and instruction booklet, in maker's box.
£1,100-1,200   *CSK*

The focal-plane Expo police camera was advertised for a very brief period. This is the only known example. The original sold for $7.50 rather than the $5 for the ordinary model which may explain its apparent rarity. The camera features a rotating waist level and a slightly different body construction.

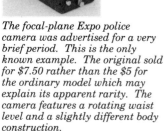

A Thornton-Pickard Mfg. Co. Ltd., London, 6 x 9cm tropical Duplex Ruby reflex camera, with polished teak body, brass binding, tan leather viewing hood and bellows and a T.T.H. Cooke Anastigmat 6.25 in f158mm lens.
£1,300-1,400   *CSK*

A Phönix 9 x 12cm tropical camera, with polished teak body, brass fittings, tan coloured bellows and a Schneider Xenar f/4.5 13.5cm lens, in a dial set Compur shutter.   **£375-400**   *CSK*

A Bernard Wolf, Switzerland, 4.5 x 6cm collapsible camera, with hinged clam section, chromed struts, inset sports finder engraved + 80703, unpleated soft leather bellows, lens section with sliding apertures, meniscus lens, single speed shutter and ground glass focusing screen.
£1,600-1,700   *CSK*

The number marked on the camera related to a Swiss patent dated 25 November 1918 granted to Bernard Wolf of Basle, Switzerland.

A Molteni, Paris, 9 x 12cm detective camera, with polished mahogany body, brass fittings, hinged front and back sections, internally contained dark slides and a brass bound lens, signed.
£375-400 *CSK*

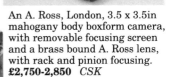

An A. Ross, London, 3.5 x 3.5in mahogany body boxform camera, with removable focusing screen and a brass bound A. Ross lens, with rack and pinion focusing.
£2,750-2,850 *CSK*

An F. Koristka, Milan, 1.5 x 1.5in mahogany body boxform camera, with brass fittings, internally contained single metal plate holders and a brass bound Zeiss Anastigmat f2.5 62mm lens.
£1,000-1,100 *CSK*

A Dr Adolf Hesekiel & Co., Berlin, 9 x 12cm reflex camera , with polished wood body, brass fittings, black cloth viewing hood, a Dopple-Anastigmat 120mm lens.
£3,000-3,250 *CSK*

A Houghton-Butcher Mfg. Co. Ltd., London 6 x 9cm tropical Ensign Cameo camera, with brass and brown metal fittings, tan leather bellows and a Dallmeyer, London Dalmac f3.5 4.75in lens, in a rimset Compur shutter.
£240-260 *CSK*

A George Hare, London, quarter plate brass and mahogany tailboard camera, with red leather square cut bellows, a brass bound Perken, Son and Rayment 5 x 4 Rapid Euryscope Optimus lens and maker's plate.
£475-525 *CSK*

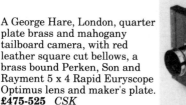

A Rowland Ward & Co., London, 1.25 x 1.25in Naturalist's camera, with wood body, brass fittings, rotary shutter, direct vision finder, side mounted rack and plate advancing mechanism, base mounted 12 plate plateholder, instruction sheet and maker's box with printed instruction label.
£5,250-5,500 *CSK*

The Naturalist's camera is virtually identical to Marion and Cos Academy camera and the instruction sheet carries the name Academy.

A J. Lancaster & Son, Birmingham, quarter plate The Rover camera, with polished mahogany body and brass bound lens, in a Lancaster See-Saw shutter.
£450-500 *CSK*

A 4 x 5in wood body American pattern boxform camera, with inlay decoration, focusing screen and a brass bound lens.
£175-200 *CSK*

A G.G.S., Italy, 35mm Luckyflex camera, with a Solar Anastigmat f3.2 50mm viewing lens and a Solar Anastigmat f3.2 50mm lens.
£1,275-1,350 *CSK*

A Nettel, Sontheim, 9 x 12cm tropical Sonnet camera, with polished teak and tan leather body, brass fittings, tan leather bellows and a Carl Zeiss Jena Tessar f4.5 15cm lens, in a Compound shutter.
£200-250 *CSK*

A Steinheil, München, 9 x 12cm wood body detective camera, with brass fittings, internally contained single metal slides, maker's plate and a brass bound lens. **£480-500** *CSK*

A Soho Ltd., London, 127-rollfilm collapsible camera, No. 2202 with bronzed metal body, red leather bellows and a Kershaw Annar f8 lens. **£110-120** *CSK*

A Bell Camera Co., Grinnell, 11.5 x 3.5in rollfilm Bell's Straight Working Panoram camera no. 72, with red leather bellows and a Wollensak lens. **£675-700** *CSK*

A 1.5 x 1.5in mahogany boxform camera, with waist level viewfinder, lens and dark slide, camera body stamped, Gesetzl Geschletzt. **£425-475** *CSK*

A Voigtländer, Germany, 4.5 x 6cm Bergheil deluxe camera, with tan leather body covering and bellows, gilt fittings and a Voigtländer Heliar 75mm f4.5 lens in a dial set Compur shutter.
£950-1,000 *CSK*

A Showa Optical Works Ltd., Japan, 14 x 14mm Gemflex twin lens reflex camera, with metal and black leather covered body, side panel with aperture adjustment and winding knob, opposite side panel with viewing hood release button, back plate engraved Made in Occupied Japan, a Gem viewing lens, Gem f3.5 25mm taking lens in a Swallow shutter.
£525-575 *CSK*

A 14 x 14mm triangular shaped Sun camera, with black body covering and chrome top and baseplates, waistlevel finder, I and B shutter and a Sanko 35mm lens.
£550-575 *CSK*

An H.J. Redding & Gyles, London, 120-rollfilm 6 x 6cm mahogany body Luzo camera, with round viewfinder, film punch, lens, shutter, maker's plate and in maker's leather case.
£875-925 *CSK*

A Graflex camera and case, 11in (28cm) wide.
£150-160 *BWA*

A W. Kunik, West Germany, 14 x 14mm Petietux camera, with built in light meter, flash syncronisation and a helical focusing Kratz Optic f2.8 25mm lens.
£350-380 *CSK*

A replica Doppel-Sport pigeon camera, with black metal body and alloy fittings, rotating shutter and fixing straps.
£680-700 *CSK*

A Sanwa Syokai Ltd., Tokyo, 14 x 14mm Myracle model II camera, with black body covering and chrome top and baseplates and a Hope Anastigmat f4.5 lens, in maker's leather ever ready case, in maker's box stamped Made in Occupied Japan.
£275-300 *CSK*

A S.C.A.T., Italy, 16mm camera, with black body covering, a f3.5 lens with helical focusing and a yellow filter, in a green case and instruction leaflet, in maker's box.
£180-220 *CSK*

A Minica O.L., Japan, 17 x 17mm Mini camera, with black body covering and chrome finished trim, top plate with swinging frame finder, lens panel and back plate engraved Minica O.L. Made in Occupied Japan.
£975-1,000 *CSK*

A Schatz & Son, Germany, 16mm Sola camera, with polished metal and black leather covered body, swinging waist level viewfinder, top plate mounted sportsfinder, baseplate mounted clockwork film advance and a Schneider Kinoplan f3 2.5cm lens.
£2,600-2,800 *CSK*

The Sola was patented on 29 October 1934 and started sales in c1938. It could take up to 6 photographs at around 1.5 frames per second, using 16mm film in special cassettes. The camera featured one of the first spring wound motors which could advance the whole film at one winding. The camera was used by the German Schutz-Staffel who used it to take rapid sequence photographs.

An Expo Camera Co., New York, 1.25 x 1in Expo Police camera, with black metal body, nickel fittings, waist level finder, shutter, interior transfer Expo Police Camera Pat. throughout the world, US Pat. Jan 31st 1911, and film holder, direction book for Expo Police camera and slip case, in maker's box.
£575-600 *CSK*

An E. B. Koopman 1.5in square hand camera, The Presto with metal body, top plate mounted film or plate advance, front mounted wheel stops and internal four plate holder.
£350-375 *CSK*

This was invented by Herman Casler.

The American Camera Co., London, 1.75in diam. metal body camera, The Demon, with spring shutter, metal plate cover and back plate.
£1,250-1,350 *CSK*

A Petal Optical Co., Japan., 22mm diameter octagonal Evarax A camera, with polished chrome body, front plate with red and blue decorative floral engraving, legend Evarax A Patents, 25 and B shutter, release engraved Made in Occupied Japan, a box of panchromatic Petal film.
£1,850-1,950 *CSK*

A Lancart, Paris, 12 x 15mm XYZ camera, with nickel plated body, side panel with film advance, top plate with collapsible sportsfinder, back panel and front panel decoratively engraved, Kynor f3.5 lens and one film spool.
£1,800-2,000 *CSK*

The XYZ camera dates from c1935.

An S.P.S. Co., Japan, 12 x 14mm Peace Baby Flex twin lens reflex camera, with black leather and metal body, a 20mm taking lens in a Time and Instantaneous shutter and two film spools.
£1,500-1,600 *CSK*

A Fotofex-Kameras, Berlin, 16mm Mini Fex camera, with black leather covered body, chrome trim, a direct vision optical viewfinder and a Ludwig Victar f3.5 25mm lens in a Vario shutter. **£730-780** *CSK*

The Mini Fex is considered the first serious sophisticated subminiature of the 20thC.

An O.I.P., Brussels, 35mm Cinescopie camera, with polished metal, leather covered and black enamel body, top-plate with film winding knob, removable lens section with removable parallax correcting viewfinder stamped 5, a f3.5 50mm. lens, in a self setting Ibsor shutter.
£875-925 *CSK*

This was an early 35mm camera for 24 x 24mm negatives.

A 14 x 14mm Baby Flex twin lens reflex camera with black leather and metal body, a Sanko f3.5 20mm taking lens in a Peace III R.K. Instantaneous and Time shutter and one film spool.
£1,200-1,300 *CSK*

A Carmen, France, 25mm square Pygmee camera, with black metal and nickel fitted body, viewfinder, *P* and *I* shutter, lens and interior with label, in maker's box.
£125-150 *CSK*

The Pygmee was also sold under the name Carmen.

A James A. Sinclair & Co. Ltd.,London quarter plate tropical Una camera, with polished mahogany body, brass binding, leather bellows and a Contessa-Nettel Sonnar anastigmat f4.5 13.5cm lens.
£1,600-1,800 *CSK*

A Concava S.A.,16mm Tessina camera, Switzerland, with red metal and chrome body, waist level finder, a Tessina 25mm f/2.8 lens, removable Tessina 17 jewel watch mounted on accessory shoe and a leather wrist strap with camera mounting plate.
£3,000-£3,250 *CSK*

A Riken Optical Co., Japan, 16mm Ricoh 16 camera, with black covered and chrome body and a Riken Ricoh f2.8 2.5cm lens, a 16mm Golden Ricoh 16 camera, with black covered and gold plated body, a gold plated barrel Riken Ricoh f3.5 2.5cm. lens and gold plated tripod adapter and instruction booklet.
£275-300 *CSK*

The Tessina watch is a very rare accessory, and probably only 100 were made for the American market.

An A. Dubroni, Paris, 5 x 5cm boxform camera, with a brass bound Dubroni lens, spirit burner and 6 glass chemical bottles, in maker's fitted wood box.
£2,500-2,700 *CSK*

A Waldes & Co., Dresden 4 x 4cm Foto-Fips cardboard body camera, comprising bellows and shutter and metal support structs, mounted in a box, with chemical bottle and plates.
£340-360 *CSK*

The camera is labelled in Czechoslovakian and dates to c1925. This example is in very good condition.

An E. & H.T. Anthony, New York, quarter plate wood body Schmidt patent detective, camera No. 36, with brass fittings, rotary shutter and lens.
£2,500-2,750 *CSK*

l. A Concava S.A., Switzerland, 35mm Tessina Automat 35 camera, with chrome body, waist level finder and a Tessinon 25mm f2.8 lens, and a removable accessory shoe-mounted Metraphot 2 photo-electric light meter.
£750-775 *CSK*

This camera was reputedly made for the Tessina designer Dr. Steineck. It has a different finished metal and fittings.

r. A Concava S.A., 35mm Tessina 35 camera, with polished chrome body, waist level finder, a 25mm f2.8 lens, nickel-prototype automatic clockwork winder, and a black leather Tessina wriststrap.
£1,300-1,400 *CSK*

The Canadian mounted police ordered Tessina cameras with motor winders and it is possible that this is a prototype for these.

A Compendica Vaduz, Liechtenstein, 16mm Compendica 88/16a camera, No. 504, with green crackle metal body, rear mounted combined shutter/aperture control, light meter, and a helically focusing Compendica f/2.9 25mm lens, camera blueprint, press print and press handout. **£2,250-2,500** *CSK*

The American Safety Razor Corp., USA, 22 x 24mm ASR Fotodisc camera, with black crackle and polished metal body, direct vision finder, a Rapodis 32mm lens and backplate, with user instructions, and a Fotodisc film magazine.
£740-780 *CSK*

A C. P. Goerz, Vienna, 16mm Minicord camera, with a black leather covered metal body, and a C. P. Goerz Helgor f2 2.5cm lens. **£185-200** *CSK*

Spy Cameras

A C. P. Stirn, Germany, 1.75in diam. Concealed Vest camera, with polished metal body, top mounted back opening catch, front panel with 6 position exposure counter lens, back plate engraved Pat'd July 27. 1886, and internally contained 5in diam. exposed plate, in maker's fitted mahogany box opening door, nickel handle and base mounted tripod bush.
£2,750-3,000 *CSK*

An A. Lehmann, Berlin, replica Ben Akiba walking stick camera, with polished chrome plated body with decorative engraving, film winding key, shutter, lens and 5 internally contained film spools.
£1,750-2,000 *CSK*

Binocular Cameras

A 1.5in square replica Krugener Photo-Carnet camera, with wooden body, sector shutter, lens, leather panel stamped Photo-Carnet de Dr Krugener inventeur A. Schaeffner, and single metal slides.
£1,000-1,100 *CSK*

A Toko Photo Co., 10 x 14mm Teleca combined binocular camera, with a pair of leather covered barrel binocular lenses, a Telesigmar f4.5 3.5in and a film cassette, in maker's leather case.
£980-1,250 *CSK*

A Binoca Co., Japan, 16mm Binoca combined opera glass camera, with white plastic casing and brassed metal fittings, an integral pair of individually focusing 2.5 by 25 binocular lenses, a Bicon f4.5 40mm taking lens and film cassette.
£575-600 *CSK*

A Möller Wedel, West Germany, 16mm CamBinox combined camera/binocular, with a pair of binocular lenses with individual rear sight adjustment, a central camera section with a top section, back section with combined exposure counter and shutter setting knob and an interchangeable J. D. Möller Jdemar f3.5 90mm taking lens and instruction booklet.
£1,100-1,200 *CSK*

A Toko Photo Co., Japan, 10 x 14mm Cyclops combined binocular camera, with a pair of leather covered binocular lenses and a Telesigmar f4.5 3.5in taking lens, in maker's fitted leather case.
£1,100-1,200 *CSK*

A Nichiryo International Co., Japan, 35mm Nicnon binocular camera, with a pair of 7 x 50 binocular lenses with dioptre adjustment, an integral Nicnon 165mm f3.5 taking lens and an attached camera section with clockwork wind.
£480-500 *CSK*

Cigarette Packet Cameras

Four 110-film disguised cigarette packet cameras, each with plastic casing and integral cameras, comprising Peer 100, Marlboro, Mild Seven and 555.
£300-400 each *CSK*

A 16mm disguised cigarette box camera with black paint body with gilt JPS logo, integral shutter and 23mm f3.5 lens.
£750-780 *CSK*

A W. Kunik, West Germany, brown Vanity lighter outfit, comprising a 16mm Petie camera, with black crackle and chrome metal body and a 25mm f11 lens, in a tan coloured leather covered body with integral petrol lighter. **£750-775** *CSK*

Cigarette Lighter Cameras

Advertisements for this camera began to appear in 1987. It had similar specifications to a camera made by Nikkoh and was designated the 2000 CL camera by one US distributor.

l. A Suzuki Optical Works, Japan, 6 x 6mm Echo 8 camera lighter, inside camera section with waist level finder, 2 film cassettes and lighter section, and original instruction sheet.
£1,800-2,000 *CSK*

r. A Suzuki Optical Co. 6 x 6mm Camera-Lite camera lighter with chrome body, 2 film cassettes and metal lighter section, in maker's grey plastic slip case, and original instruction sheet.
£2,000-2,250 *CSK*

A 8 x 13mm gold plated cigarette lighter camera, with film advance, single speed shutter, lighter, Minox film chamber and baseplate engraved 18K-20my SIPE-Germany.
£3,750-3,950 *CSK*

A Speccam combined camera/table top cigarette lighter with gold plated and black snakeskin covered body.
£350-400 *CSK*

Gun Cameras

A Doryu Camera Co. Ltd., Japan, 16mm Doryu 2-16 flash camera, with black plastic and polished metal body and a Dorymar wide angle 15mm f2.2 lens, mounted on an integral pistol stock and facility for magnesium flash pellets.
£13,000-15,000 *CSK*

The Doryu pistol camera was introduced in 1955.

An E. Krauss, Paris, 28 x 21mm Le Photo-Revolver camera, with black metal and nickel body section, top plate with folding sportsfinder and front panel with helical focusing lens and shutter controls, mounted on a leather covered and nickel magazine back.
£2,500-2,700 *CSK*

An ERAC Selling Company Ltd., London, 16mm Erac pistol camera, with a metal body camera mounted in a black plastic casing shaped as a pistol.
£375-400 *CSK*

Matchbox Cameras

A metal body Matchbox camera with collapsible sportsfinder, 2 sliding apertures, and a Carl Zeiss Jena Tessar f2.7 2.5cm lens, baseplate painted to resemble a matchbox.
£6,250-6,500 *CSK*

The camera was made in Germany c1938, and was extremely well made. Its underside had a Nazi eagle painted on a blue-grey background to resemble a matchbox.

An Eastman Kodak Co., Rochester, NY, 0.5 by 0.5in Matchbox camera model 2, with black Bakelite body, outer metal sleeve, winding knob with markings at 180° and simple Time and Instantaneous shutter, in maker's purse.
£2,500-2,800 *CSK*

The Kodak Matchbox camera was made between 1944 and 1945 and around 1,000 were made for the American Office of Secret Services in 2 batches of 500. The second model was made for reels of film.

A 16mm matchbox camera with nickel body, top plate with adjustable aperture control, side plate with shutter control.
£4,500-4,800 *CSK*

Two examples are known of which one had a fixed aperture (as in this case) and the other had an adjustable aperture. The action of pushing the camera forward inside the matchbox opened the front flap and released the shutter which was then reset on the reverse action.

Minox

A VEF, Riga, Latvia, 13 x 8mm Minox camera, with stainless steel body, top plate with focusing dial from 8"-∞, shutter release button, sliding yellow filter, baseplate engraved VEF Riga Minox. Made in Latvia. Pat. app. and a Minostigmat f3.5 15mm lens.
£580-600 *CSK*

A VEF, Riga, Minox enlarger, with brown Bakelite body, VEF light bulb, lens, electric cable and 2.25 x 3.25in paper holder, in maker's box; postcard paper holder in box, and a VEF Minox film processing tank, in maker's box.
£900-1,000 *CSK*

A VEF, Riga, 13 x8mm camera, with stainless steel body, top plate with focusing dial, exposure counter, shutter release button and shutter speed, casing locked, a Minostigmat 15mm f3.5 lens, baseplate engraved VEF Minox Riga., Made in Latvia and front plate engraved WA 506 with Nazi eagle insignia.
£2,750-3,000 *CSK*

This camera dates from the German occupation of the Baltic states before the advancing Red Army occupied Latvia.

A 8 x 11mm L'Appareil Espion Français camera, with ribbed brass/metal body, top plate, combined lens cover and shutter release, and direct vision viewfinder, lacking lens.
£800-850 *CSK*

The French espionage camera was made because of the shortage of Minox cameras and its design was based on Minox features. It took 45 frames 8 x 11mm on 9mm film. The camera was only made from 1939-41 and it is believed that fewer than 1,000 were made. They are usually found lacking their taking lens.

The Stylophot with right angle finder was made in very small numbers.

Pen Cameras

A Secam 16mm secret Stylophot colour camera, with black plastic body, right angle and direct vision finders, film advance with no coloured filter, aperture setting marked Noir Color, and 2 film cassettes, in maker's box marked Secreto.
£225-250 *CSK*

l. A Minox 8 x 11mm LX selection camera, with gold plated body, top plate with LED indicator lights, shutter release button and green, red and yellow LED's and a Minox f3.5 15mm lens, in maker's presentation box. **£680-700**

r. A 8 by 13mm dummy Minox B camera, with dummy lens and viewfinder and baseplate engraved Minox, Wetzlar F1589, Made in Germany.
£130-150 *CSK*

A Secam, France, 16mm Private Eye camera, with black plastic casing, film advance with inset orange filter, 2 position aperture Noir Color, blue lens shade and 2 film cassettes.
£275-300 *CSK*

A Harukawa, Japan, 16mm Septon pen camera, with plastic body, chrome and alloy fittings, direct vision finder, a Septon f2.8 20mm lens, integral propelling pencil, with instruction leaflet and maker's box.
£1,100-1,200 *CSK*

Radio Cameras

A Bell International Corp. 16mm Bell Kamra combined camera/radio, model KTC-62 No. 16728, in red plastic casing with metal trim, Prominar f3.5 23mm lens, in fitted presentation box; 3 Kowa Optical Co. 16mm Ramera combined camera/radio model KTC-62, in blue, black and white plastic casings, each with a Prominar f3.5 23mm lens, 2 in fitted presentation box. **£700-775** *CSK*

A Minolta Camera Co., Japan, 16mm Sonocon 16 combined camera/radio, with a black finish body, Rokkor f2.8 22mm lens, integral 7 transistor radio and charger. **£1,100-1,200** *CSK*

Ring Cameras

A Buttrio, Udine, Italy, 25mm diam. GF 81 ring camera No. 14, with polished gold plated body, helical focusing, depth of field indicator, rotary shutter, and removable waist level viewfinder, in turned wood case, 10 packets of unexposed disc films and 2 sets of instructions in Italian and English, in maker's box. **£3,750-4,000** *CSK*

The GF.81 camera appeared in 1981 and was made by Gian Paolo Ferro of Udine. Twenty of each of 2 models were made in polished or brushed gold.

A 3.5 x 5mm chrome metal body ring camera, with a Trioplan f2.8 10mm lens, iris diaphragm, single speed shutter, removable brass film insert section. **£5,750-6,000** *CSK*

Vanity Case Cameras

A W. Kunik, Petie vanity outfit, comprising a 16mm Petie camera with black crackle and chrome metal body and a 25mm f11 lens, in a vanity case covered in green, orange and black coloured leather with gilt tooling, powder compact, lipstick holder and film holder. **£1,300-1,500** *CSK*

A W. Kunik, West Germany, gilt Petie vanity outfit, comprising a 16mm Petie camera with grey-green and gilt metal body and a Röschlein Achromat 25mm f11 lens, in a mottled blue enamel finish and gilt metal trimmed vanity case with powder compact, lipstick holder and film holder. **£800-850** *CSK*

Watch Cameras

A Houghtons pattern Ticka camera, with lens cap, swinging viewfinder and interior label. **£1,100-1,200** *CSK*

An Expo Camera Co., USA, watch camera, with polished metal body, top plate, lens cap attached to body by chain, with instruction leaflet, in maker's box. **£1,100-1,300** *CSK*

A Houghtons Ltd., Ticka camera, with polished metal body with top plate, lens cap attached to body by chain, in maker's box, a Ticka film in maker's box, and an empty Ticka film box. **£800-900** *CSK*

An Expo Camera Co., USA, watch camera, with polished metal body with top plate, swinging viewfinder and spare film spool, in maker's fitted box with printed label.
£800-900 *CSK*

A Steineck Camera-Werk, West Germany, 25mm diam. Steineck ABC wristwatch camera, with alloy body, waist level mirror finder, a Steinheil VL f2.5 12.5mm lens, close-up lens, and a red leather strap, in maker's presentation case, body 42 by 32mm.
£3,250-3,500 *CSK*

FURTHER READING

An Age of Cameras,
Edward Holmes, 1974.
Subminiature Photography,
White, 1990.

Candle Extinguishers

A Royal Worcester candle extinguisher, 'Hush', shape no. 2844, with rare colour variation of cream dress edged with blue, blue ribbon and blonde hair, date code 1956, 3.5in (8cm) high.
£200-250 *TVA*

For a further selection of candle extinguishers refer to Miller's Collectables Price Guide Volume IV pages 71 to 73

Candlesticks

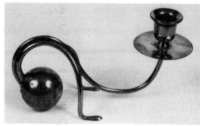

A copper and brass weighted candle holder, after a design by W.A.S. Benson.
£100-150 *ZEI*

A pair of early George III style silver candlesticks, with detachable nozzles, Sheffield 1903, 9in (23cm).
£375-400 *GAK*

Cross Reference
Art Nouveau

A pair of Lauder candlesticks, with bird, 12in (31cm) high.
£325-350 *NCA*

Card Cases

A mother-of-pearl card case, 4 by 3in (10 by 8cm).
£90-100 *COL*

For a further selection of Card Cases, please refer to Miller's Collectables Price Guide, Volume IV page 290.

A pair of Liberty Archibald Knox pewter and enamelled candlesticks.
£800-1,000 *ABS*

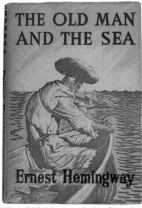

The Old Man and the Sea, by
Ernest Hemingway, published by
Jonathan Cape, lst Edition, 1953.
£30-35 *HB*

Billy Bunter The Hiker, by
Frank Richards, 1st
edition, 1958. **£25-30** *HB*

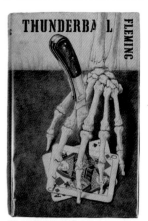

Thunderball, by Ian
Fleming, published by
Jonathan Cape, 1st edition,
1961. **£70-75** *HB*

The Lord of the Rings,
1st edition, by J.R.R.
Tolkien, signed.
£700-750 *HB*

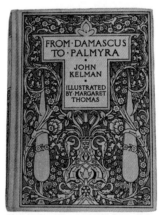

From Damascus to Palmyra, by
John Kelman, illustrated by
Margaret Thomas, 1908.
£65-75 *HB*

The Spy Who Loved Me,
by Ian Fleming, published
by Jonathan Cape, 1st
edition, 1962. **£70-75** *HB*

Maigret has Scruples, by
Simenon, published by
Hamish Hamilton, 1st
edition, 1959. **£30-35** *HB*

The Eyes of the Dragon, by
Stephen King, signed, 1st
edition, 1987. **£80-85** *HB*

Sunset at Blandings, by
P.G. Wodehouse, 1st
edition, 1977.
£25-30 *HB*

A set of 8 horse racing waistcoat buttons, 1890s-1920s. **£25-50 the set** *AGM*

A Glasgow University Athletic Club button. **50p-£2** *AGM*

A gentleman's sporting button, late 19thC. **50p-£2** *AGM*

A P S A Fencing Club button. **50p-£2** *AGM*

A York Rugby Football Union button. **50p-£2** *AGM*

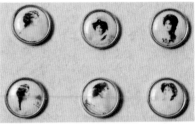

A set of gaiety girls buttons, worn on waistcoats, c1890s. **£25-50** *AGM*

A selection of silver Golf Club buttons, given as prizes, dated between 1920 and 1938. **£5-10 each** *AGM*

Four Golf Club blazer buttons. **£1-5 each** *AGM*

A gentleman's sporting button, late 19thC. **50p-£2** *AGM*

A set of footballers buttons. **£25-50** *AGM*

A gentleman's sporting button, late 19thC. **50p-£2** *AGM*

l. A selection of various yacht club buttons. **50p-£2 each** *AGM*

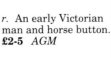

r. An early Victorian man and horse button. **£2-5** *AGM*

A Belleek caberet, 2nd period. **£280-300 the set.** Kettle. **£350-375** *PC*

A collection of Belleek Echinus, 1st period, bowls **£60-75 each**. Kettle and teapots **£300-395** *PC*

A collection of Belleek, 2nd period. **£150-200 each** *PC*

A Belleek mirror and boudoir candlestick, 1st period. **£750-800 each** *PC*

Two pairs of Belleek spill vases, 1st period. **£600-650 each pair** *PC*

A Belleek Echinus bread plate, 1st period. **£320-350** *PC*

A collection of Belleek crested pieces, 2nd period. **£60-150 each** *PC*

Two menu holders, with applied flowers, 2nd period. **£125-150 each** *PC*

Three Belleek amphora jars, 1st period. **£300-350 each** *PC*

A Masonic mantle plaque, by Obadiah Sherratt, c1825. **£1,500-1,800** *LR*

Thirty seven pieces of Spode dinner ware, early 19thC, each piece damaged or repaired. **£550-600** *PCh*

A barge ware teapot and lid, 'A present to Mrs. Pinkey from Florrie, 1914'. **£125-150** *PCh*

A printed lustre jug, c1830, 5in (12.5cm). **£200-250** *IW*

A Masonic creamware jug, Tyneside School, c1825, 6in (15cm). **£180-220** *IS*

A Sunderland pottery jug, with transfer commemorating 'Crimea', c1845. **£200-250** *HOW*

A Victorian hat pin holder, 5in (12.5cm). **£28-35** *AA*

A William Greatbatch teapot, Staffordshire, c1775, 5.5in (14cm). **£1,500-1,650** *JHo*

A Victorian toothbrush dish, with lid, 8in (20.5cm) long. **£40-50** *AI*

A pair of Ridgway's chamber pots, with moulded handles. **£100-150** *CB*

A Mason's Ironstone vase. **£220-245** *VH*

A Sunderland lustre jug, c1830. **£280-320** *RP*

A Mason's Ironstone punch bowl, impressed mark, c1820, 13in (33cm) diam. **£1,500-1,950** *BEE*

Ironstone china was introduced by Josiah Spode in Staffordshire in about 1805.

C. J. Mason patented his 'Ironstone China' in 1813 and it was made exclusively by his factory until 1827.

A Mason's Ironstone tureen and cover, printed and impressed mark, c1820. **£1,000-1,250** *BEE*

Two Mason's Ironstone jugs, c1815:
Footbath jug. **£1,000-1,200**
Toy jug. **£250-320** *BEE*

A Mason's Ironstone footbath, impressed mark, c1815, 15in (38cm) wide. **£1,750-2,000** *BEE*

l. A Mason's Ironstone letter rack, c1820. **£650-750**
r. A Mason's Ironstone spill vase, c1815. **£300-350** *BEE*

A Charlotte Rhead vase. **£80-140** *AOS*

A Royal Doulton vase, numbered 32, 1903, 10in (25cm) high. **£80-95** *POW*

A pair of Brannam vases, 1894, 9in (23cm) high. **£280-300** *NCA*

A Doulton Lambeth vase, signed, impressed mark H.B. 911. **£575-600** *PCh*

A Moorcroft pomegranate vase, 1914, 4in (10cm) high. **£250-350** *LIO*

A Charlotte Rhead vase with Lotus Leaves pattern, c1932, 8.5in (21cm) high. **£100-150** *AOS*

A Devonware Hawk vase, 12in (31cm). **£40-65** *AOS*

A Gouda pottery vase, 7in (18cm) high. **£50-60** *NCA*

A Minton 'Tube Line' jug, 14in (36cm) high. **£200-300** *ASA*

A Royal Doulton vase, Margaret Thompson, c1920, 6in (15cm) high. **£200-235** *POW*

Two Royal Doulton vases, Christine Abbot, 1923, 4.5in (11cm) high **£55-65**, 9in (23cm) **£90-105** *POW*

A Crown Devon posy bowl, 10in (25cm) diam. **£50-85** *AOS*

A Clarice Cliff vase, 6in (15cm) high.
£800-900 *RIC*

A Clarice Cliff lotus jug, 1929, 12in (31cm).
£1,500-2,000 *GAZ*

A Clarice Cliff vase, 1929, 8in (20cm).
£1,200-1,400 *GAZ*

A pair of Carlton Ware vases.
£300-400 *AOS*

A Forrester's Phoenix ware jug, Fuchsia pattern.
£70-80 *HEW*

A Burleigh jug, 8.5in (21cm) high.
£75-125 *AOS*

A Decoro vase, 1930s, 8in (20cm) high. **£50-75** *AOS*

A Clarice Cliff vase, for Newport Pottery, 1930s, 11.75in (30cm) high. **£575-600** *S*

r. A Clarice Cliff vase, shape No. 342.
£750-800 *ADC*

A Clarice Cliff Bizarre bowl, for Wilkinson Ltd., 1920s, 7.5in (19cm) diam. **£1,350-1,500** *S*

A Bough lady's powder bowl, marked, 1915.
£150-200 *BWA*

A Clarice Cliff ashtray, Gibraltar pattern.
£220-250 *RIC*

l. A Forrester's Phoenix ware bowl, c1930, 11in (28cm) diam. **£150-175** *HEW*

A Royal Doulton embossed jug, one of a limited edition of 600, 8in (20cm) high. **£200-260** *PCh*

A Longwy dish, c1900, marked, 7in (18cm) high. **£220-250** *CHa*

A pottery stove, complete with oil lamp, c1880. **£300-350** *LBL*

A Kingsware jug, Doulton base mark, 9in (23cm) high. **£175-200** *BBR*

Price's Cottage Ware, teapot, milk jug and sugar basin. **£10-30 each** *COL*

An earthenware grotesque dog, probably North Devon, c1900, 8in (20cm). **£50-60** *OD*

A Crown Ducal Charlotte Rhead decorated dish. **£55-65** *PCh*

A Moorcroft Liberty mug, c1919. **£450-500** *WAC*

A Brannam jug, c1883, 5.5in (14cm) high. **£100-120** *NCA*

Two Moorcroft commemorative mugs. **£300-350 each** *NA*

A Burleigh parrot jug, c1935, 7in (18cm) high. **£50-60** *PAG*

A Moorcroft commemorative flambé beaker. **£455-500** *WAC*

A blue crackleglaze bowl and pot, Boch Frères La Louvière, c1920, bowl **£200-225**, pot **£145-165** *POW*

A pair of Keramis 'La Maîtrise' vases, c1920. **£575-600** *POW*

A Bourne Denby owl jug **£30-45** and matching vase. **£40-55** *AOS*

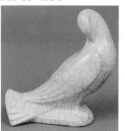

A Longwy crackleglaze dove, c1920. **£295-325** *POW*

A Longwy 'Prima Vera' , c1920. **£545-585** *POW*

A Keramis vase, c1920. **£275-300** *POW*

A Chameleon ware vase, George Clews. **£80-100** *NCA*

A Bough jug, in crocus design, marked, 6in (15cm) high. **£200-250** *BWA*

A Dunmore pottery jardinière, 8in (20cm) high. **£250-300** *BWA*

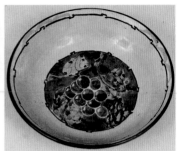

A Bough bowl, marked J.E.A. 1923, 8.5in (21cm) diam. **£200-250** *BWA*

A selection of Dunmore pottery pigs, including a money box. **£250-300 each** *BWA*

r. A Dunmore pottery toad, 6in (15cm). **£300-400** *BWA*

A Bough vase and cover, 15in (38cm) high. **£300-350** *BWA*

A Bough Toby jug, marked E.A., 1922. **£400-500** *BWA*

A Dunmore bust of General Gordon, 12in (31cm) high. **£500-700** *BWA*

A Bough vase, damaged, marked E.A. **£100-125** *BWA*

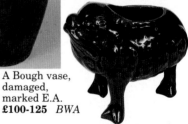

A Dunmore pottery toad, 6in (15cm) high. **£300-400** *BWA*

A Bough pottery biscuit barrel. **£200-250** *BWA*

A Dunmore pottery bear dish, 10in (25cm) long. **£700-1,000** *BWA*

r. A Bough teapot, marked C.C.A., 4.5in (12cm) high. **£200-250** *BWA*

A Dunmore pottery fish wall plaque, 9in (23cm) long. **£200-250** *BWA*

A Dunmore pottery jardinière, with dragon design. **£500-600** *BWA*

A Dunmore pottery owl jar, with removable head. **£1,000-1,200** *BWA*

A Dunmore pottery teapot, milk jug and sugar basin, teapot 4.5in (11cm) high. **£250-300 the set** *BWA*

A pair of Dunmore pottery chargers, 15.5in (39cm) diam. **£1,000-1,500** *BWA*

Two Dunmore pottery Burns character figures, 7.5 and 8in (19 and 20cm) high. **£300-400** *BWA*

A Dunmore pottery copy of a medieval cooking pot, 8in (20cm) high. **£200-250** *BWA*

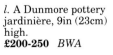

A Dunmore tobacco jar, 11.5in (29cm) high. **£1,000-1,200** *BWA*

l. A Dunmore pottery jardinière, 9in (23cm) high. **£200-250** *BWA*

A Dunmore pottery toad, 10in (25cm) high. **£800-1,200** *BWA*

A painted bowl, by Morven MaCleod, 7.5in (19m) diam. **£200-220** *BWA*

A Strathyre jug, painted by Jessie Wilson. **£100-120** *BWA*

A Bough three-handled loving cup, 7.5in (19cm) high. **£400-500** *BWA*

A Dunmore dragon jug, 13in (33cm). **£250-300** *BWA*

A Dunmore wall pocket. **£200-300** *BWA*

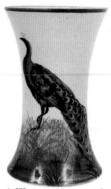

A Wemyss vase, with painted peacock. **£200-350** *RdeR*

A Strathyre jug, painted by Jessica Wilson, 6in (15cm) high. **£100-150** *BWA*

A Dunmore pottery crab wall pocket, 6in (15cm) long. **£300-350** *BWA*

A Macmerry cup and saucer. **£100-120** *BWA*

A Macmerry painted teapot, 8in (20cm) wide. **£400-450** *BWA*

A Wemyss chamber pot, with peaches, 8.25in (21cm) diam. **£250-350** *BWA*

A Prestonpans tea caddy, 5.5in (14cm) high. **£500-600** *BWA*

A zoo plate, 7.75in (19cm) diam. **£200-250** *BWA*

A bowl, by Peggy Foy, c1945.
£20-30 *IW*

A hand painted bowl, signed Florrie
Cliff, c1930. **£100-120** *ACh*

A wall mask, 7.5in
(19cm). **£100-120** *HEW*

Two Sylvac dogs, large
£85-130, small **£15-25** *AOS*

A Sadler teapot, c1950, 7.5in
(19cm). **£20-25** *OD*

A Cartlon Ware hand painted
plate. **£220-240** *GAZ*

A Wade trio, 'Hedgerow'.
£10-12 *COL*

r. Aunt Jemima, a hollow
doorstop, 1920s.
£70-100 *PC*

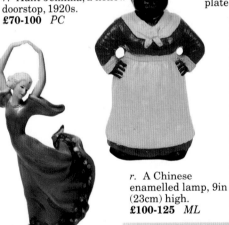

r. A Chinese
enamelled lamp, 9in
(23cm) high.
£100-125 *ML*

A Goebels hand painted
figure, 1930, 12in (31.5cm).
£320-350 *GAZ*

l. A Crown Devon lamp
base, 4.75in (12cm) high.
£250-275 *HEW*

A Myott fruit basket, 14in (36cm) wide.
£50-85 *AOS*

A pottery plate, probably Yorkshire, c1800.
£280-300 *RP*

A set of 4 Sèvres hand painted plates with gilt edges, 9.5in (24cm) diam.
£120-130 *PCh*

A Continental cabinet plate, with masks in gilding, c1840. **£180-220** *LIO*

A Quimper dish, marked H3 Quimper, c1900, 14.5in (37cm) wide. **£250-275** *VH*

A Victorian cabinet plate, unmarked, 9.5in (24cm) diam.
£100-140 *LIO*

A Crescent cabinet plate, decorated by Birbeck, c1910. **£110-140** *LIO*

A Doulton Series Ware fruit bowl.
£25-40 *AOS*

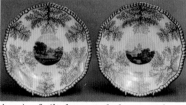

A pair of gilt decorated plates, with Okehampton Castle and Monks Rock Tenby, late 19thC. **£35-40** *PCh*

A Poole pottery commemorative plate, 11in (28cm) diam.
£50-60 *PCh*

A Wedgwood dessert dish, coloured in enamels, c1810, 10in (25cm) wide.
£180-200 *VH*

A Davenport cabinet plate, c1850, 9.5in (24cm) diam.
£120-150 *LIO*

A Fourmaintrau Frères pottery charger, marked, late 19thC.
£200-220 *VH*

A musical mug, 'I love Cyprus', plays 'Sing a Song of Sixpence', c1992. **£8-10** *PC*

A musical commemorative mug, plays 'Congratulations', 1986, 3.5in (9cm) high. **£50-100** *PC*

A George VI commemorative jug which plays 'For He's a Jolly Good Fellow', 1937. **£150-200** *PC*

A selection of Goss crested pottery, and Willow Art parian bust of Burns. **£65-75** *PCh*

A Crown Devon Fieldings musical Coronation jug, plays 'God Save The King', 1937. **£200-300** *PC*

A Worcester candle snuffer, 'The Witch', c1890. **£180-220** *TH*

A collection of Worcester candle snuffers, a monk, French cook, Japanese owl, old lady and Granny Snow. **£180-260 each** *TH*

A George V and Queen Mary Coronation plate, 1911, 8in (20cm) diam. **£30-40** *LIO*

A George V and Queen Mary Coronation mug, 1911, 4in (10cm) high. **£15-20** *LIO*

A Crown Devon one pint musical Coronation mug, plays 'Here's Health Unto His Majesty', May 12, 1937, 6.25in (16cm) high. **£200-250** *PC*

The Eaton Boating Song musical jug. **£400-500** *PC*

Twinkle Twinkle Little Star musical figure. **£150-200** *PC*

A Crown Devon musical Toby jug, There's a Tavern in the Town, 9in (23cm). **£150-200** *PC*

A musical Toby jug, The Night That We Danced. **£150-200** *PC*

Sally In Our Alley musical 1pt jug. **£400-500** *PC*

A John Peel whisky musical flagon. **£180-250** *PC*

A Crown Devon Fieldings Widdicombe Fair musical 1 pint jug. **£170-220** *PC*

A John Peel 1 pint musical tankard. **£100-150** *PC*

l. A musical tankard, Roll Out The Barrel. **£50-100** *PC*

On Ilka Moor Baht'at 1 pint tankard. **£150-200** *PC*

A Crown Devon musical 1 pint tankard, Daisy Daisy, 6in (15cm). **£130-180** *PC*

A Cherry Brandy musical bottle, The Hunting Song. **£50-100** *PC*

CERAMICS

This year we have arranged our Ceramics section slightly differently, to complement our Art Nouveau section. We have still maintained our basic principles to aid identification; that is we have grouped the featured items by factory, when the factory is clearly marked, and we have illustrated the main factory marks where necessary. We have also included the salient points of manufacturers' history, dates, locations and major artists and designers. In addition, this year we have featured particular geographical areas of production, notably the Low Countries and Scotland. These ceramics are becoming very collectable at the moment and offer new and varied fields for collectors who perhaps cannot manage the financial resources required for the more fashionable Art Deco pieces. It is worth reiterating that every year the ceramic section is wholly different and reflects market trends in popularity as well as prices. It is essential that previous editions are consulted to see, for example, Susie Cooper or Clarice Cliff, as featured last year, and refer to the cross references.

We have then, as usual, covered areas that are collected as particular items, for example teapots, which obviously come from a variety of makers.

Ceramics are as popular as ever with collectors of all ages, regardless of budgets, and if we have not yet featured what you collect please let us know.

Finally, remember that perfect pieces command the best prices and will prove to be the best investment, and as we always say, research your subject and buy the best you can afford.

Ault

● Founded by William Ault at Swadlincote, Nr Burton-on-Trent, Staffordshire.

● Produced earthenwares between 1887 and 1923.

● Became Ault Potteries in 1937, still producing earthenwares.

● Printed or impressed marks from 1887 onwards.

● Christopher Dresser (1834-1904) designed products for Ault and marked his work with his name (1891-96). He later worked for both Minton and Wedgwood.

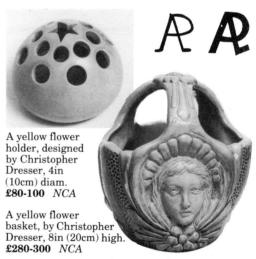

A yellow flower holder, designed by Christopher Dresser, 4in (10cm) diam.
£80-100 *NCA*

A yellow flower basket, by Christopher Dresser, 8in (20cm) high.
£280-300 *NCA*

Beswick

BESWICK ENGLAND

● Founded by John Beswick at Gold Street, Longton, Staffordshire, and produced earthenwares from c1936.

● Early wares not marked; later wares' printed marks as shown.

A hand painted wall mask, 1930s, 8in (20cm).
£150-200 *GAZ*

A terrier, 3.5in (9cm) long.
£15-20 *WAC*

A panda 2.75in (7cm) long.
£8-12 *WAC*

A retriever, 8in (20cm) long.
£25-30 *WAC*

A pigeon, 8in (20cm) long.
£30-35 *WAC*

A matt blue/green vase, 8in
(20cm) high. **£15-25** *AOS*

A joker mask, 5in (13cm) high.
£85-95 *WAC*

Bourne Denby

A Glyn Colledge vase, 7.5in (19cm) high. **£50-60** *NCA*

A Glyn Colledge vase, 8.5in (21cm) high. **£55-65** *NCA*

A Glyn Colledge vase, 14in (36cm) high. **£80-100** *NCA*

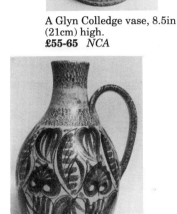

A Glyn Colledge bowl, 12.5in (32cm) diam. **£70-80** *NCA*

A Glyn Colledge ewer, 13in (33cm) high. **£80-100** *NCA*

A Glyn Colledge jug, 7.5in (19cm) high. **£40-50** *NCA*

Brannam

● C.H. Brannam Ltd produced earthenwares at the Litchdon Pottery, Barnstaple, Devon, from about 1879.

● Marks consisted of incised letters C.H. BRANNAM, sometimes dated and BARUM (the Roman name for Barnstaple).

For a further selection of Brannam earthenware refer to previous volumes of Miller's Collectables Price Guides, available from Millers Publications.

A vase, c1886, 7in (18cm) high. **£280-300** *NCA*

An oval green flower holder, 4in (10cm) high. **£250-280** *NCA*

A bowl, c1883, 3.25in (9cm) high. **£80-100** *NCA*

A jug with mythical bird decoration, 1881, 8in (20cm) high. **£250-275** *NCA*

A blue puffin jug, 6.25in (16cm) high. **£60-70** *NCA*

A frog vase, 1894, 3in (8cm) high. **£100-120** *NCA*

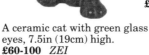

An 'Oriental' bowl, 7in (18cm) diam. **£60-70** *NCA*

Bretby

● Bretby Art Pottery was a partnership formed during the early 1880s by Willam Tooth (Linthorpe Art Pottery) and William Ault.

● Factory was at Woodville, near Burton-on-Trent, Derbyshire.

● Products marked as shown. The word 'ENGLAND' was added from c1891.

● William Ault left the partnership in 1886. The company became 'Tooth and Co' from the 1920s.

A vase, 4.5in (11cm) high. **£20-30** *NCA*

A ceramic cat with green glass eyes, 7.5in (19cm) high. **£60-100** *ZEI*

A two-handled loving cup, 4.5in (11cm). **£60-70** *NCA*

A pair of 'Oriental' bowls, 8in (20cm) diam. **£60-75** *NCA*

An 'Oriental' vase, 8in (20cm) high. **£90-100** *NCA*

Buckley

A rustic garden trio, comprising a seat and 2 urns, possibly different potteries, seat 17in (43cm) high, urns 26.5in (67cm) high.
£800-900 the set *IW*

A bird whistle, c1880, 9in (23cm) high.
£240-260 *IW*

Burgess & Leigh

A flower jug, 'The Kingfisher', 1930s, 7in (18cm) high.
£45-55 *GAZ*

A flower jug, 'Parrot' design, 1930s, 7in (18cm) high.
£45-55 *GAZ*

Cross Reference
Jugs

A flower jug, 'The Highwayman', c1930, 8in (20cm) high. **£200-250** *GAZ*

Burmantofts

● Burmantofts Art Pottery was produced by Messrs Wilcox & Co. (Ltd) of Leeds, Yorkshire, between 1882-1904.

● The Art Pottery was discontinued in 1904, some later terracotta ware was marked Leeds Fire-Clay Co. Ltd.

Two V. Kremer vases, 5in (13cm) high.
£120-130 each *NCA*

A two-handled vase,
10in (25cm)
high.
£140-160 *NCA*

A dragon chamberstick,
4.5in (11cm) high.
£180-200 *NCA*

An Isnik onion shaped vase, with
white and blue flower decoration
on deep blue ground, impressed
and printed mark, 19thC, 9.75in
(25cm) high. **£530-550** *AH*

> **Cross Reference**
> Art Nouveau

Carlton Ware

● Produced since 1890 at the Carlton
Works at Stoke-on-Trent.

● Art Pottery produced during the
1920s; household domestic wares very
heavily Art Deco influenced.

● Particularly famous for Guinness
advertising figures and animals.

● Later marks sometimes feature
previous name Wiltshaw & Robinson
Ltd.

A mug, c1925, 3.75in (9cm) high. **£20-25** *OD*

An Australian one-person set, 12in (31cm) long.
£230-260 *GAZ*

An Australian grape pattern
milk jug, 6.5in (16cm) high.
£120-140 *GAZ*

> **Cross Reference**
> Commemorative

A mushroom
cruet, 5.5in
(14cm) diam.
£20-25
WAC

A black cat teapot, c1960, 7.5in (19cm) high. **£30-40** *LIO*

A green vase with poppy and daisy design, 8in (20cm) high. **£250-300** *GAZ*

An Australian raspberry design jug, 5.5in (14cm) high. **£120-150** *GAZ*

George Clews & Co.

A pair of Chameleon Ware vases, 5.5in (14cm) high. **£80-100** *NCA*

A Chameleon Ware vase, in shades of yellow ochre, 10in (25cm) high. **£90-110** *NCA*

A Chameleon Ware Aladdin's Lamp, 8.5in (21cm) high. **£90-110** *NCA*

A Chameleon Ware vase, 9.5in (24cm) high. **£90-110** *NCA*

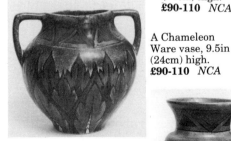

A two-handled Chameleon Ware vase, 6.5in (16cm) high. **£60-75** *NCA*

Charlotte Rhead

A bowl in pattern no. 5802, c1939.
£100-150 *AOS*

A tube line design plaque, by
Crown Ducal Co., 1930, 14.5in
(37cm).
£160-200 *GAZ*

A pottery wall plaque by Crown
Ducal, 16.5in (42cm).
£430-450 *GAK*

An octagonal bowl.
£75-125 *AOS*

Clarice Cliff

Cross Reference
Night Lights

● Originally Clarice Cliff worked for
Arthur J. Wilkinson (Ltd).

● Produced designs for Newport
Pottery marked as below from 1938.

A Goblin Ware child's night light,
3.5in (9cm) high.
£150-250 *RIC*

An Orange and Plums design
preserve pot.
£50-75 *AOS*

A Trees and House
pattern plate.
£100-150 *AOS*

A sandwich plate, 11.5in (29cm)
long. **£250-275** *RIC*

*Note the difference in price on
these sandwich plates, the pattern
used is vital to the value of a piece
- not the shape.*

A Floral Latona vase, hairline
crack, 6in (15cm) high.
£120-165 *RIC*

A Chloris pattern vase,
shape 358, 8in (20cm)
high. **£175-275** *AOS*

A Bizarre pattern sandwich plate, 11.5in (29cm) long.
£35-45 *RIC*

Part of a table centrepiece, in Bamboo pattern, 5in (13cm) wide.
£60-75 *RIC*

A biscuit barrel in Marguerite pattern, 7in (18cm) high.
£175-200 *RIC*

An ashtray, 5in (13cm) square.
£75-80 *RIC*

A Capri Orange squat candlestick, 3in (8cm) high.
£90-110 *RIC*

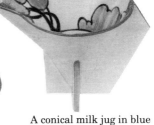

A conical milk jug in blue Autumn pattern, from a tea-for-6 set, 4in (10cm) high. **£175-200** *RIC*

A Biarritz shaped bowl, 6in (15cm) wide.
£18-22 *RIC*

A Marigold pattern sandwich plate, 11.5in (29cm) long. **£400-450** *RIC*

An early Geometric pattern sandwich plate, 11.5in (29cm) long.
£175-200 *RIC*

Part of a salad draining set, orange colourway, in Trees and House design, 8in (20cm).
£400-500 *GAZ*

A Bizarre shaped vase, in Secrets pattern, first produced 1939, 8in (20cm).
£500-600 *GAZ*

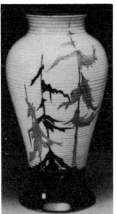

A Sunray pattern biscuit barrel, c1930, 6.5in (16cm).
£500-600 *GAZ*

A Bizarre glazed earthenware vase in Fir Tree pattern, marked Hand painted Bizarre by Clarice Cliff, Wilkinson Ltd, England, 1930s, 12.5in (32cm).
£575-600 *S*

A Celtic Harvest pattern preserve pot, with chrome lid, 4.5in (11cm) high.
£30-40 *RIC*

Decoro

● Decoro Pottery Co. (a part of R.H. & S.L. Plant Ltd) produced earthenwares at the Tuscan Works, Longton, Staffordshire, between 1933-49.

Decoro Pottery
MADE IN
ENGLAND

An octagonal fruit bowl, 8in (20cm) diam.
£75-125 *AOS*

A gourd shaped vase, Reg. No. 429479, 8in (20cm) high.
£75-125 *AOS*

TUSCAN
DECORO
POTTERY
MADE IN
ENGLAND

MAKE THE MOST OF MILLERS
Condition is absolutely vital when assessing the value of any item. Damaged pieces appreciate much less than perfect examples. However, a rare, desirable piece may command a high price even when damaged.

Devon Ware

A Honiton vase, 3in (8cm) high.
£8-10 *COL*

A Longpark cockerel teapot and cover, reverse with 'From Dawlish Dawntee be fraid 'aut now', 6in (15cm) diam.
£30-35 *PAR*

A Longpark cockerel coffee pot and cover, reverse with 'It's an ill wind that blows nobody good', 7in (18cm).
£30-35 *PAR*

A Longpark cockerel jam dish, impressed mark, 6in (15cm).
£18-20 *PAR*

A Longpark water jug, 7in (18cm) high.
£30-45 *AOS*

A Crown Devon cake plate, with stylised flowers pattern, 8in (20cm) diam.
£38-45 *ADC*

A Crown Devon coffee set, in geometric design, with lustre interior, c1930, coffee pot 7in (18cm) high.
£350-400 *GAZ*

A Crown Devon hand painted plate, 10.25in (26cm).
£85-95 *ADC*

A teapot, 6in (15cm) high.
£20-30 *AOS*

A Honiton 'Kenton' pattern jug, 7.75in (19cm) high.
£20-25 *COL*

Doulton

A baluster form stoneware jar, painted by Margaret E. Thompson, in blue and black enamels with the light brown body showing through, impressed and painted marks, 14.5in (37cm) high.
£330-350 *Bea*

'Gladiator' D 6550, designed by M. Henk, and produced between 1961-67, 7.5in (19cm) high.
£230-250 *WIL*

A character jug, in the form of Field Marshal Smuts, withdrawn 1948.
£560-580 *Bea*

A model of a bulldog, in a Union Jack cloak, printed mark, Rd.no. 645658, 6.25in (16cm) high.
£110-130 *P(S)*

'Gondolier' D 6589, designed by D. Biggs, produced from 1964-69, 8in (20cm) high.
£180-200 *WIL*

For a further selection of Doulton refer to Miller's Collectables Price Guide Volume I page 69, Volume III page 71 and Volume IV pages 82 and 83

Jackfield Ware

Two cups and saucers, cups 2.75in and 3in (8cm) diam. **£28-30 each** *AA*

A jug, 6.5in (16cm) high. **£25-30** *AA*

A jug, with pewter lid, 5.5in (14cm) high.
£25-30 *AA*

A cheese dish, 8in (20cm) diam.
£85-95 *AA*

Two teapot stands, 6 and 7.5in (15 and 19cm) diam.
£6-8 each *AA*

A Victorian teapot, 8in (20cm) high. **£65-75** *AA*

A teapot, 5.5in (14cm) high. **£50-60** *AA*

A teapot, 5.5in (14cm) high.
£65-75 *AA*

Cross Reference
Tea Pots

A jug, with pewter lid, 6in
(15cm) high.
£30-35 *AA*

A teapot.
£75-85
AA

George Jones & Sons

● These items were manufactured by one company George Jones & Son Ltd. who traded as the Trent Potteries and Crescent Potteries in South Wolfe Street, Stoke-on-Trent between 1861-1951

● Upon the death of George Jones, the founder, the business was carried on by several of his sons, one of whom, Horace Overton Jones, was an artist specialising in floral and topographical subjects.

● Some examples bear a monogram H.O.J. within the design.

A chocolate pot set, tray 12in(31cm) diam, pot 6in (15cm) high.
£180-200
WAC

A trio, marked George Jones Sons, Pyrethrum, plate 7in (18cm) diam. dated 1884,
£25-35 *WAC*

An afternoon tea cup and plate, 8.25in (21cm) wide. **£40-50 each** *WAC*

A violet design cream jug, sugar bowl and trio, plate 7in (18cm) cream and sugar **£30-36** Trio **£40-45** *WAC*

A Crescent china plate c1880, 8.75in (22cm) diam. **£20-25** *WAC*

A sucrier, 6in (15cm) high. **£35-40** *WAC*

A plate, unmarked, 9.75in (24cm) diam. **£12-15** *WAC*

An oval dish, marked Stoke Crescent, signed H.O.J., 8.75in (22cm) wide. **£45-50** *WAC*

A Crescent trio, marked George Jones & Sons, plate 7.25in (18cm) diam. **£18-25** *WAC*

A trio signed H.O.J. **£45-55 each** *WAC*

A plate, 8.25in (21cm) diam. **£25-30** *WAC*

A birds and bloom plate, marked George Jones & Sons, c1884, 9.75in (24cm) diam. **£12-18** *WAC*

A Crescent butter dish, George Jones & Sons, 6in (15cm) wide. **£15-20** *WAC*

A Stoke Crescent vase, George Jones & Sons, 5.75in (15cm) high. **£55-65** *WAC*

Lauder

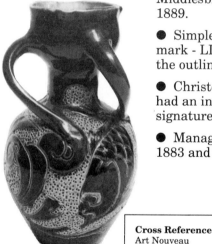

A chamberstick, 8in (20cm) high. **£75-85** *NCA*

A vase, 6in (15cm) high. **£80-90** *NCA*

Linthorpe

● Linthorpe pottery was produced at Middlesbrough, Yorks, between 1879-1889.

● Simple block lettered impressed mark - LINTHORPE (sometimes with the outline of a vase).

● Christopher Dresser designed works had an incised, impressed or painted signature.

● Managed by Henry Tooth before 1883 and monogrammed as below.

Cross Reference
Art Nouveau

A Christopher Dresser yellow floral jug, 6.5in (16cm) high. **£500-550** *NCA*

A Christopher Dresser plate, 8.5in (21cm) diam. **£90-110** *NCA*

A butterscotch glaze bowl, designed by Christopher Dresser with studding to sides, 9.5in (24cm) diam. **£200-300** *ZEI*

Moorcroft

● W. Moorcroft (Ltd) produced earthenwares at the Washington Works, Burslem, Staffordshire, from 1913.

● Simple impressed block lettered mark MOORCROFT BURSLEM.

● William Moorcroft's signature, was registered as a trademark in 1919. He died in 1945.

● Walter Moorcroft continued pottery in the traditional Moorcroft style with an initialled mark.

● Modern wares also have a printed mark MOORCROFT MADE IN ENGLAND.

A MacIntyre goblet, with red cornflowers, c1910, 9in (23cm). **£1,500-1,600** *NP*

A MacIntyre Flamminian vase, c1906, 8in (20cm). **£275-300** *NP*

A Moorcroft/MacIntyre ring holder, decorated with the poppy design, c1903, 4in (10cm) diam. **£300-350** *LIO*

A flambé glazed vase, in Clematis design, 12.5in (32cm). **£900-1,000** *NP*

A jardinière, Fairy Rings, design by Philip Richardson, introduced 1987, impressed Made in England and factory mark, John Moorcroft monogram, 9in (23cm) high. **£250-325** *VBu*

A buttercup vase, c1992, 16in (40.5cm) high. **£375-400** *NP*

A pansy design bowl, c1918, 6in
(15cm) high.
£1,100-1,200 *NP*

A MacIntyre Aurelian vase, in
cobalt blue and gold, c1898, 6in
(15cm).
£250-300 *NP*

A MacIntyre Florian bowl with
inverted rim, with blue
cornflowers, minor damage,
c1900, 8in (20cm) diam.
£300-350 *NP*

An arum lily pot, c1960, 6in
(15cm) high. **£200-250** *NP*

A William Moorcroft salt glaze
bowl, impressed marks and
facsimile signature, 1930s, 10in
(25.5cm).
£350-450 *VBu*

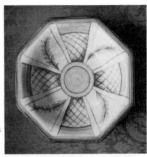

A carp plate, from a limited
edition of 250, 1989.
£175-200 *NP*

A Walter
Moorcroft bowl,
impressed Made
in England,
facsimile
signature and
royal warrant,
10in (25.5cm)
diam.
£200-300 *VBu*

A pottery pedestal jardinière, painted with mushrooms and toadstools on a mottled green ground, impressed No. 995, signed W. Moorcroft, with printed mark made for Liberty & Co., 8in (20cm) high.
£900-950 *Bea*

A pomegranate vase, c1924, 12in(30.5cm) high.**£300-325** *NP*

A pomegranate parasol top, made for the ladies at Ascot, c1917.
£80-100 *LIO*

A MacIntyre commemorative mug, inscribed from Mr & Mrs Lasenby, Liberty, 4in (10cm).
£350-400 *NP*

A dandelion vase, from a limited edition of 200, 1992.
£190-225 *NP*

Pilkington Lancastrian

- Pilkington's Tile & Pottery Co. Ltd, of Clifton Junction, Nr. Manchester, Lancs, produced earthenwares and lustre and glazed finishes.

- Art Pottery produced from about 1897-1938 and some later c1948-57.

- Early wares, if marked, had an incised 'P'.

- Several trade marks registered from 1904.

- Royal Lancastrian mark often accompanied by initial of designer.

A Pilkington Lancastrian pottery bowl, designed by Walter Crane, 6in (15cm). **£200-300** *ZEI*

> **Cross Reference**
> Art Nouveau

A Pilkington Lancastrian vase, designed by Gladys Rodgers, in grey matt glaze with multi-coloured chevrons, 17in (43cm) high. **£300-400** *ZEI*

later mark c1948-1957

Royal Winton

A moulded jug, 7in (18cm) high. **£25-45** *AOS*

A comport, c1935, 9.5in (24cm) diam. **£80-90** *COL*

> **DID YOU KNOW?**
> Miller's Collectables Price Guide is designed to build up, year by year, into the most comprehensive reference system available.

A sugar shaker in Paradise pattern. **£20-30** *AOS*

A jam pot in Springtime pattern. **£20-30** *AOS*

Royal Worcester

A plate painted with Roseck Abbey, probably by Robert Perling, impressed mark, c1870, 8.75in (22cm) diam.
£150-160 *TVA*

A honey pot and cover, pattern W5171, c1895, 4.5in (13cm).
£150-185 *TVA*

A vase, shape 1727, slight restoration, date code for 1897, 3.75in (9cm) high.
£100-150 *TVA*

A stork vase, shape no. 238, the ivory tusk section pierced and covered with flowering prunus, with a brown and gilt stork, bronze and green glaze rock formed base with tortoises, c1872, 11in (28cm) high.
£1,200-1,300 *GAK*

A tusk ice jug, shape 106, date 1886, 9in (23cm) high.
£400-500 *TVA*

A pair of bowls, with elephant supports, c1890, 5in (13cm) square.
£190-235 *TVA*

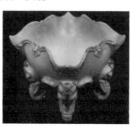

A Locke & Co. triple vase pattern no. 363, c1900, 7in (18cm) high.
£100-145 *TVA*

A Bamboo Rose jar and cover, shape 1326, 1898 date code, 4.5in (11cm) diam.
£100-150 *TVA*

A Locke & Co vase, decorated with a mirror image pattern, c1900, 3.25in (8cm) high.
£50-80 *TVA*

A shell dish, shape no 1413, date 1906, 4.5in (11cm) wide. **£100-140** *TVA*

A pair of leaf dishes, c1892, 5in (13cm) wide. **£100-120** *AMH*

A Locke & Co. vase, with finely painted pattern, shape no. 423, cracked, c1900, 5in (13cm) high. **£70-80** *TVA*

A globe vase, with violet pattern, shape 916, slight restoration, date code 1903, 4.5in (11cm) high. **£80-135** *TVA*

A dish, small chips, date code for 1900, 4.5in (11cm) diam. **£50-55** *AMH*

A model of H.R.H. The Duke of Edinburgh on his polo pony, modelled by Doris Lindner, No. 18 of a limited edition of 750, complete with certificate and wood stand. **£275-290** *Bea*

A porcelain model of Napoleon Bonaparte on a white charger, from the series of famous military commanders by Bernard Winskill, No. 18 of a limited edition of 750, complete with certificate and wood stand. **£2,000-2,250** *Bea*

A figure 'Grandmother's Dress', by Freda Doughty, shape no. 3081, c1945, 6.75in (17cm) high. **£100-150** *TVA*

A crinoline figure with cap, modelled as a tea cosy top, shape 2620, introduced 1916, 3in (8cm) high. **£400-450** *TVA*

A miniature patch box and cover, with hand painted birds, 1924, 1.5in (4cm) diam. **£100-150** *TVA*

A figure 'Marking Stones', 7.5in (19cm) high. **£400-500** *TH*

A figure of 'Ye Rat Catcher', 7.5in (19cm) high. **£400-500** *TH*

A figure of 'Ye Brush Man', 7.25in (18cm) high. **£400-500** *TH*

A figure 'Ye Prison Basket', 7.5in (19cm) high. **£400-500** *TH*

A figure of 'Ye Watchman' from the Cries of London series, 7.25in (18cm) high. **£400-500** *TH*

A pair of bird models, from the American game bird series, male and female Mallard, by Ronald Van Ruyckevelt, each No. 140 of a limited edition of 500, complete with certificates and wood stands. **£1,500-1,750** *Bea*

MAKE THE MOST OF MILLERS
Condition is absolutely vital when assessing the value of any item. Damaged pieces appreciate much less than perfect examples. However, a rare, desirable piece may command a high price even when damaged.

Ruskin

● Ruskin Pottery (W. Howson Taylor) of Smethwick, Birmingham, produced earthenwares between 1898 and 1935.

● Early wares were simply impressed TAYLOR.

● Painted or incised marks as below.

A crystaline glazed vase, 8in (20cm) high. **£100-150** *ZEI*

Cross Reference
Art Nouveau

A crystaline glazed vase, signed by W. Howson Taylor, 15in (38cm) high. **£600-800** *ZEI*

Rye

A bowl, with flecked body covered with applied green hops and leaves, the rim banded with sprigs, marked on base S.R.W. Rye, 9in (23cm).
£300-350 *RAG*

For a further selection of Rye Pottery, please refer to Miller's Collectables Price Guide, Volume III, page 62.

Sylvac

A rabbit, 5.5in (14cm) high.
£15-20 *WAC*

A vase, 6in (15cm) high.
£22-25 *COL*

A dog, 5.5in (14cm) high. **£15-22** *AOS*

Salopian

● The Salopian Art Pottery of Benthall, Nr Broseley, Shropshire, produced earthenwares between c1882 and 1912.

● Simple impressed mark on earthenwares SALOPIAN.

A blue vase, 5.5in (14cm) high. **£30-35** *NCA*

A vase, 4in (10cm) high. **£30-35** *NCA*

A child's mug, 3in
(8cm) high.
£10-12 *COL*

Cross Reference
Childrens & Nursery
Ceramics

A selection of Sylvac. **£18-25 each** *WAC*

A cat, 7in (18cm) high.
£15-20 *WAC*

A blue dog, 5.25in (13cm) high.
£10-15 *WAC*

A pixie, 4in (10cm) long.
£12-14 *WAC*

A spill holder/vase, 6.75in (17cm)
high.
£10-15 *WAC*

A poodle.
£15-25 *AOS*

A sunflower plate.
£10-15 *AOS*

A dog, 8in (20cm) long.
£15-20 *WAC*

A money box, 6in (15cm) high.
£10-12 *COL*

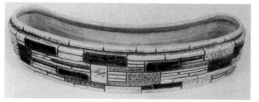

A posy planter, 13in (33cm) long. **£15-20** *COL*

A green and cream toast rack, 8in (20cm) long. **£15-20** *COL*

Upchurch

● The Upchurch Pottery (William and James Baker) produced earthenwares at Rainham in Kent between 1913 and 1961.

● Simple impressed marks UPCHURCH or UPCHURCH SEEBY.

● Seeby were their agents at Reading and Seeby sometimes appears as a painted mark.

Cross Reference
Art Nouveau

A matt glazed vase, 7in (18cm). **£50-70** *ZEI*

Wade Heath

● Formerly Wade & Colclough, Union Pottery, Burslem, Staffordshire, subsequently Wade Heath and Co., produced earthenwares between 1887 and 1927.

A matt glazed vase, 10in (25cm). **£70-100** *ZEI*

A twin handled vase with matt glaze, 6in (15cm). **£70-100** *ZEI*

● Wade Heath and Co. (Ltd), High Street Works, also Royal Victoria Pottery from 1938 marked their products in a variety of ways, all printed or impressed and including the word Wade.

FURTHER READING
The World of Wade Collectible Pottery & Porcelain, Ian Warner and Mike Posgay, 1991

A vase, c1935, 6.5in (16cm) high. **£25-35** *AOS*

A two-handled vase, c1935, 5in (13cm) high. **£20-30** *AOS*

A vase, c1935, 6in (15cm) high. **£25-35** *AOS*

Wedgwood

A plate, with transfer printed harbour scene, c1867, 9in (23cm) diam.
£120-150 *TVA*

A black basalt encaustic decorated two-handled oviform vase, painted in red, damaged and repaired, c1800, 10in (25cm) high.
£450-500 *C*

A black and white solid jasper copy of the Portland or Barberini vase type, by Thomas Lovatt, signed T.L. and impressed mark to base rim, c1880, 10in (25cm) **£1,100-1,200** *C*

A blue jasper dipped stoneware copy of the Portland or Barberini vase type, impressed mark and date code for 1887, 10in (25cm) high.
£575-600 *C*

A creamware oviform teapot and cover, painted in the manner of David Rhodes in yellow, iron red, pale green, dark brown and black, slight chips to rim of cover, c1768, 5.5in (14cm) high.
£1,900-2,000 *C*

Winstanley

A tabby cat licking its back, with closed eyes, marked J.Winstanley, England, 3, c1970, 8in (20cm) long.
£20-25 *CP*

A seated cat, marked J. Winstanley, 3, England, 8in (20cm) high.
£20-25 *CP*

A grey persian cat with white paws, marked J. Winstanley, England, 4, 8in (20cm) high.
£22-26 *CP*

A grey tabby cat, marked 5 J. Winstanley, England, 11.9.91, 12.5in (32cm) long. **£27-30** *CP*

A tabby cat with white crossed paws, marked J. Winstanley, England, 7, 9.9.91, 14.5in (37cm) long. **£35-40** *CP*

A tabby cat with white paws, marked J. Winstanley, 4, England, 9.5in (24cm) long. **£22-26** *CP*

Continental Art Deco Crackleware

A Boch Frères Keramis kingfisher, marked Ch. Catteau, c1920, 6.25in (16cm) high. **£80-95** *POW*

'Pierrot & Pierrette' by L. Fontinelle, in crackleglaze, c1925, 11.5in (29cm) long. **£450-475** *POW*

'Danse Moderne', pale pink banjo player and 2 dancers, Boch Frères Keramis, marked Ch. Catteau, c1920, 14.5in (37cm) long. **£475-525** *POW*

White crackleglaze cats, Odyv, c1915, 13in (33cm) long. **£140-165** *POW*

A dove, Adnet, c1930, 8in (20cm) high. **£150-185** *POW*

A pair of cockatoo book ends in white crackleglaze, Faiencerie Auguste Mouzin et Cie, c1925, 8in (20cm) high. **£150-175** *POW*

White crackleglaze Flamenco dancers, Auguste Maizin et Cie, c1920, 15in (38cm) high. **£170-195** *POW*

A white elephant, Zuid-Holland, 9in (23cm) high. **£180-200** *POW*

A pale pink crackleglaze double fish, c1920, 15in (38cm) high.
£150-195 *POW*

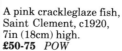

A pair of crackleglaze doves with gold tails, L. Guiraud Vallauris, 4in (10cm) long.
£150-195 *POW*

A pink crackleglaze fish, Saint Clement, c1920, 7in (18cm) high.
£50-75 *POW*

Three dancers, Etha Lempke, Zuid-Holland, c1930, 8in (20cm) high.
£220-260 *POW*

A crackleglaze figure, Marcel Guillard, Editions Etling, c1925, 9in (23cm) high.
£200-225 *POW*

A green crackleglaze fish, Le Jan, c1925, 16in (41cm) long.
£150-185 *POW*

A seal, Zuid-Holland c1930, 9in (23cm) high.
£120-145 *POW*

A white crackleglaze sailing boat, Le Jan, c1920, 19in (48cm) high.
£220-265 *POW*

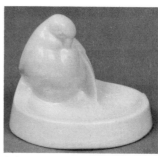

A dove ashtray, Boch Frères Keramis, Ch. Catteau, c1918, 5.25in (13cm) diam.
£100-135 *POW*

Cross Reference
Art Deco

A turquoise squirrel, Auguste Mouzin et Cie, c1925, 11in (28cm) high. **£100-125** *POW*

A pair of Pierrot white crackleglaze book ends, Odyv, c1925, 7in (18cm) high.
£225-265 *POW*

A white crackleglaze cubist knight on horseback, Odyv, c1925, 9in (23cm) high.
£140-165 *POW*

A turquoise crackleglaze dog, Le Jan, c1910, 13in (33cm) long.
£80-100 *POW*

Cubist crackleglaze birds, Angelo Hecq, c1930, limited edition 1/150, 13in (33cm) high. **£350-400** *POW*

A pair of crackleglaze fox book ends, Joset, c1930, 6.5in (16cm) high.
£75-95 *POW*

A pale green dove, Boch Frères Keramis, Ch. Catteau, c1920, 9in (23cm) high.
£150-185 *POW*

Dutch Art Deco/Art Nouveau Ceramics

A Zuid-Holland earthenware cache pot, in shades of blue, green, yellow and mauve, painted marks Gouda Juliana Ivora, c1915, 9in (22cm) diam. **£385-400** *S(AM)*

A pair of book ends D'Larrieu, c1910, 8.25in (21cm) high.
£400-425 *POW*

A crackleglaze peacock, Guillemin, c1920, 14in (36cm) long. **£120-145** *POW*

A pair of Zuid-Holland vases, amphora shape with loop handles, in shades of green, mauve and cream, chipped to base, painted marks, c1910, 14.5in (37cm) high.
£550-600 *S(AM)*

Two earthenware Gouda Ivora vases, with painted marks, c1915, 10.5in (26cm) high.
£200-225 *S(AM)*

SCOTTISH CERAMICS
Dunmore

- Situated on Dunmore Ness in Stirlingshire.

- Dunmore wares enjoyed royal patronage in the 1870s and were exhibited regularly in Edinburgh and Glasgow.

- Noted for grotesque animals, pedestals and commemorative busts; classic 19thC Scottish Art Pottery.

A pottery twig handled dish, 11in (28cm) wide.
£150-200
BWA

A pale green moon flask, 8.5in (21cm) high.
£150-200 *BWA*

A green, brown and ochre pottery planter, 8.5in (21cm) high.
£250-300 *BWA*

A bambo stick spill vase, 7.5in (19cm) high.
£100-130 *BWA*

A green and brown mottled pottery teapot, 7.5in (19cm) high.
£200-220 *BWA*

A green and ochre tazza, 8.5in (21cm) high.
£300-350 *BWA*

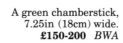

A two-handled brown treacle glazed frog mug, with 2 frogs, brown and cream, 6.5in (16cm) high.
£300-350 *BWA*

Four posy jars, 5in (13cm) high.
£100-130 *BWA*

A green chamberstick, 7.25in (18cm) wide.
£150-200 *BWA*

110

A blue owl,
6in (15cm)
high
£380-400
BWA

A red and ochre fern
leaf design vase,
10in (25cm) high.
£200-250 *BWA*

A green snake handled
vase, 9.5in (24cm) high.
£200-250 *BWA*

A pair of glazed blue
candlesticks, c1860,
13.5in (34cm) high.
£700-800 *BWA*

A black and green
two-handled
bowl, 11in
(28cm) wide.
£175-200 *BWA*

Cross Reference
Candlesticks

A pair of blue Grecian
vases, 13.5in (34cm) high.
£700-800 *BWA*

Holyrood

- Henry Taylor Wyse, 1870-1951, an accomplished artist, produced his first catalogue Simple Furniture in 1900.

- His pottery designs were produced during the first quarter of 20thC.

- Some blanks were purchased from David Methven & Sons of Kirkaldy and sold locally and exported to the Empire.

- Although Wyse's Holyrood Pottery became quite successful, his main interest was his full-time art teacher's job; he often encouraged both teachers and students to use his factory.

A blue, green and pink pottery
vase, 8in (20cm) high.
£150-175 *BWA*

A red and
green glazed
vase, 8in
(20cm) high.
£150-175
BWA

A blue and red vase,
6in (15cm) high.
£100-120 *BWA*

Prestonpans

- Industrial potteries date back to the mid-18thC. The original pottery was founded by William Cadell in 1750.

- The early wares were unmarked.

- Belfield & Co. established in mid-1830s by Charles Belfield at Seacliff.

A Gordon's green plate, with impressed mark, c1820, 8.5in (21cm) diam. **£30-50** *BWA*

Prestonpans Pottery mark

A Belfields teapot, early 20thC, 8.5in (21cm) high. **£75-85** *BWA*

A Gordon's Queen Caroline plate, in Pratt colours, 9in (23cm) diam. **£350-450** *BWA*

Strathyre

- Strathyre is a small town in Perthshire which, as well as producing its own pottery, also bought in 'blanks' for decoration by their 'Lady Artists' notably Mary Ramsey and Jessie Wilson.

- Most Strathyre pieces are clearly marked and generally signed or initialled by the artist.

- Industrial potteries date back to the mid-18thC. The original pottery was founded by William Cadell in 1750.

- The early wares were unmarked.

- Belfield & Co. established in mid-1830s by Charles Belfield at Seacliff.

A plate decorated by J.D. Wilson, 6.75in (17cm) diam. **£100-150** *BWA*

A dish, decorated by Mary A Ramsay, 11in (28cm) diam. **£150-200** *BWA*

Kilcoddy

A whisky flask, blue, red, green and yellow, dated 1832, 9in (23cm) high. **£200-300** *BWA*

A zoo jug, painted by Miles Johnson, 4.5in (11cm) high. **£150-175** *BWA*

A zoo jug, painted by Miles Johnson, 4.5in (11cm) high. **£150-175** *BWA*

A Morrison & Crawford blue and green named money box, 6.5in (16cm) high. **£100-120** *BWA*

A hand painted bowl, c1850, 11.75in (30cm) diam. **£100-150** *BWA*

Portobello

A Rathbone's blue and white bowl, variation of the Fallow Deer pattern, c1830, 7in (18cm) diam. **£100-150** *BWA*

A W & J A Bailey, Alloa, green and brown glazed plate, 9in (23cm) diam. **£30-40** *BWA*

A lustre jug, c1840, 3.5in (9cm) high. **£50-75** *BWA*

Wemyss

A jam pot, with plums design, 5.5in (14cm) high. **£150-200** *BWA*

A teapot, with sweet peas design, 5in (13cm) high. **£250-300** *BWA*

A vase, in wild roses pattern, 6.5in (16cm) high. **£200-250** *BWA*

A cockerel cream jug, 2.5in (6cm) high and a Bonjour bowl, 2in (5cm) high.
£200-250 the pair *BWA*

A chamber pot, with plums pattern, 8.5in (21cm) diam.
£200-250 *BWA*

A cat with black spots, green glass eyes and pink paws, with painted black mark, 12.25in (31cm) high.
£1,300-1,500 *AH*

A pair of 'Jazzy' vases, 7.5in (19cm) high.
£200-250 *BWA*

A goose vase, 8in (20cm) high.
£600-900 *BWA*

A teapot, with rose design, 5in (13cm) high.
£250-300 *BWA*

A tankard, with peacock, 5.75in (14cm) high.
£400-600 *BWA*

Welsh

A pitcher, probably Newport, with contemporary paint, c1880, 14.5in (37cm) high.
£60-70 *IW*

A set of four salt glaze lions, based on a pressed glass original, probably North Wales, c1860, 6.5in (17cm) high.
£380-420 the set *IW*

A Sweeney Mountain tobacco jar, 7.5in (19cm), early 19thC.
£40-45 *IW*

For a further selection of Welsh Pottery please refer to Miller's Collectables Price Guide Volume IV, p103.

Bowls & Dishes

A Phoenix Ware bowl, by Thomas Forester & Sons Ltd, peacock blue, exterior decorated with cream roses and gilt on black, c1920, 11.5in (29.5cm) diam.
£30-40 *ROW*

A bowl by John Pearson, 5in (13cm) wide.
£180-200 *NCA*

A shell shaped dessert dish, by Charles Bourne, pattern no. 60, c1820, 8.5in (21.5cm) wide.
£600-700 *TVA*

Barge Ware

A Measham Ware teapot, decorated in typical treacle glaze, applied with blue, white and print motifs, the cartouche reads 'A Present From A Friend', c1890, 12.5in (32cm) high.
£200-300 *HEY*

A teapot, c1900, 8in (20cm) high.
£115-165 *AA*

A jug, c1896, 8in (20cm) high.
£75-95 *AA*

A jug, c1885, 7.5in (19cm) high.
£75-95 *AA*

A Measham Ware teapot, with cream body, and green, blue and red applied design, c1880, 12in (30cm) high.
£350-450 *HEY*

A Measham Ware teapot, decorated in typical brown treacle glaze, with blue, pink and white applied decoration, c1890, 13.5in (34cm) high.
£300-400 *HEY*

Children's & Nursery Ware

A child's plate, with purple print, spurious Wedgwood type mark, c1840, 7in (17.5cm) diam. **£50-60** *IW*

A Doulton Bunnykins special edition two-handled mug, 1984, 3in (8cm) high. **£10-12** *COL*

A child's tea set, comprising: teapot, milk jug, sugar bowl, 2 cups, 2 saucers and 2 plates, each piece illustrated with a different nursery rhyme, teapot 4in (10cm) high. **£65-75** *ROW*

Two Victorian nursery plates, with black transfer printed picture, hand coloured in green and red, c1850, 6.5in (41cm) diam. **£50-60 each** *HEY*

A Doulton Bunnykins mug, 3in (7.5cm) high. **£5-8** *COL*

A Victorian nursery plate, in naturalistic underglaze colours and lustre under, with Joseph dressed in turquoise cloak, c1850, 7in (17.5cm) diam. **£35-45** *HEY*

A child's plate, possibly Davenport, 'Visit to the Zebra', c1840, 6.5in (16cm) diam. **£100-130** *IW*

A Doulton Bunnykins mug, 3.5in (8.5cm) high. **£5-6** *COL*

A Grimwades Peter Rabbit small tea set, comprising: 2 teapots, 2 jugs, bowl, 4 cups, saucers and plates, all decorated with scenes of Beatrix Potter's Peter Rabbit, on white ground with gilt edging, slight damage, cups 2in (5.5cm) high, in original box. **£500-550** *S(S)*

Coffee Pots

A Tams Ware hand painted green and white coffee set, c1930. **£40-50** *ROW*

A Wellington China coffee pot, sugar basin and cream jug, coffee pot 6in (15cm) high. **£10-15** *COL*

A pottery coffee pot, c1800, 11in (28cm) high.
£300-350 *JAC*

Commemorative

A commemorative cup and saucer, transfer painted enamel with gold decoration, saucer, c1880, saucer 6in (15cm) diam.
£55-65 *OD*

An earthenware jug with satirical print of Napoleon, overglaze print and enamel with lustre, some damage, c1814, 5.5in (14cm) high.
£130-150 *IW*

A Sunderland commemorative frog mug, with black transfer print, 4.5in (11.5cm) high.
£350-385 *JHo*

A Royal Doulton 'Peace' mug, 1919.
£30-35 *TRU*

A Denby Dale Pie plate, c1928, 9.5in (24cm) diam.
£60-70 *RP*

A commemorative frog mug, by Dixon Austin & Co., Sunderland, black transfer print with 'God Speed The Plough', 5in (13cm) high.
£345-365 *JHo*

Churchill

A Royal Doulton Winston Churchill Toby jug, 5.5in (14cm) high.
£20-25 *WAC*

Produced until 1991

A Winston Churchill head, modelled by Frank A. Potts, 1941, 6.5in (16.5cm) high.
£60-70 *WAC*

A Wedgwood bust of Churchill, modelled by Arnold Machin R.A., 1940, 7.5in (19cm) high.
£250-275 *WAC*

Political

A Wedgwood cream glazed pottery jug, commemorating Thomas Carlisle, dated for 30th April, 1881, 9in (23cm) high.
£120-140 *GAK*

A Roosevelt and Churchill cup, with 'Let's Drink To Peace', and 'Let's Drink To Victory', 5.5in (14cm) high.
£140-150 *WAC*

A Burleigh Ware cup, Champion of Democracy, with Roosevelt and Churchill, 6in (15cm) high.
£140-150 *WAC*

A Robert Peel jug, 5in (13cm).
£100-125 *WAC*

A blue printed commemorative jug of Sir R. Peel, M.P., c1840, slight damage, 4in (10cm) high. **£60-80** *LIO*

A mug from a limited edition of 250 items commemorating 3 election victories, Hayle, Cornwall, 3.5in (9cm). **£25-30** *WAC*

A Paragon mug, No 34 of a limited edition of 50 mugs, commemorating Neville Chamberlain, 'I am myself a man of Peace to the depths of my soul', 5in (13cm) high. **£600-650** *WAC*

A Reform jug, with re-used Napoleonic war print with added words 'Union Reform', c1832, 5.5in (14cm) high. **£180-220** *IW*

Royalty

A Paragon bone china jug, made for the 150th anniversary of Admiral Nelson's death, c1955, 4.5in (11.5cm) high. **£75-85** *WAC*

A Silver Jubilee 1910-1935 commemorative mug, 4in (10cm) high. **£18-22** *COL*

A Goodwin Bridgwood & Harris George IV commemorative silver-form jug, printed in black, damaged, black printed mark of lion over G.B.H. c1830, 5.5in (13.5cm) high. **£350-550** *S(S)*

Modern Royalty

A plate commemorating the wedding of Prince Andrew and Sarah Ferguson, by Sutherland China for Peter Jones Collection, Wakefield, 8.5in (21.5cm) diam. **£20-25** *WAC*

A Staffordshire pottery beaker, commemorating the wedding of Princess Anne and Captain Mark Phillips, 3.5in (8.5cm) high. **£8-12** *WAC*

A Sutherland plate, the Prince and Princess of Wales and bridesmaids, for Peter Jones Collection, Wakefield, 8.5in (21.5cm) diam. **£25-30** *WAC*

A Royal Wedding money box, 1981, 3.5in (9cm). **£8-12** *WAC*

A plate designed and produced by Panorama Studies, Ashburton Devon, depicting Earl Mountbatten, 10.5in (26.5cm) diam. **£45-50** *WAC*

A Duchy of Cornwall mug, Panorama Studies of Ashburton, Devon, John Bell design, 3.5in (9cm) high. **£15-20** *WAC*

A Wedgwood mug, commemorating the wedding of Princess Anne and Captain Mark Phillips, 4in (10cm) high. **£45-50** *WAC*

A child's part tea set. **£25-35** *WAC*

A mug commemorating H. M. Queen Elizabeth II's Silver Jubilee, black transfer ware. **£6-8** *COL*

A mug commemorating the Coronation, 2 June 1953, 2.5in (6.5cm) high. **£6-8** *COL*

A Coalport mug commemorating the birth of Prince William, 21 June 1982, 3.5in (9cm) high. **£30-35** *WAC*

A two-handled mug, 'Long Live Prince Henry Charles Albert David', 13 September 1984, 3.5in (9cm) high. **£20-25** *WAC*

Moorcroft Commemorative

A flambé square box, by Moorcroft, commemorating the Coronation of Edward VIII, damaged, 3. 5in (9cm). **£485-500** *WAC*

A Moorcroft tankard, commemorating King George VI, 4.5in (11.5cm) high. **£525-550** *WAC*

A Moorcroft salt glaze pot, commemorating King Edward VIII, 5in (13cm) diam. **£135-155** *WAC*

A mug commemorating the Coronation of King Edward VII and Queen Alexandra, given by Mr and Mrs Lasenby of Liberty's to all their staff, c1902, 3.5in (8.5cm) high. **£250-350** *WAC*

A Moorcroft jar commemorating King Edward VIII, 6in (15cm) high. **£285-300** *WAC*

A mug commemorating Edward VIII, 4.5in (11.5cm). **£575-600** *WAC*

Cruets

Faience

A French tureen and cover, modelled as a duck on a leaf-moulded circular base, glaze cracked, 15in (38cm) high. **£575-600** *CSK*

A monkey cruet, made in Japan, 4in (10cm) high. **£7-8** *WAC*

For a further selection of Cruets please refer to Miller's Collectables Price Guide Volume IV, pages 74-75.

A plate, c1900, 5in (12.5cm) diam. **£7-8** *OD*

A dish, marked S.B., c1900, 9in (22.5cm) wide. **£15-20** *OD*

A plate, c1900, 8in (20cm) diam. **£20-25** *OD*   Two plates, c1900, 5in (12.5cm) diam. **£7-8 each** *OD*

Ironstone

A Mason's Ironstone jug and basin set, 19thC. **£265-285** *JH*

A pair of Ashwoods Real Ironstone china tureens, white with blue, red and gilt underglaze c1880. **£250-300** *LRG*

Goss China

- Goss factory started producing Parian Ware in 1858.

- Historical models in porcelain were first produced in 1881 to be sold as souvenirs for trippers and holiday-makers.

- Only one agent was appointed in each town and by 1914 sixteen hundred agents had been appointed.

- 2,500 shapes were available with over 8,000 different coats-of-arms.

A selection of view ware. **£35-85 each** *CCC*

A group of 'Royal' interest ware.
£30-150 each *CCC*

John Knox's house.
£450-500 *CCC*

A bread platter, inscribed 'Give Us This Day Our Daily Bread', with the Brussels crest. **£100-125** *G&CC*

A Pompeian ewer.
£8-10 *G&CC*

A Carew cross.
£100-125 *G&CC*

A Dr Kenealy spill vase.
£150-200 *G&CC*

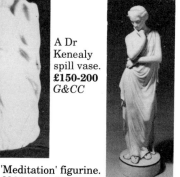

'Meditation' figurine.
£300-350 *G&CC*

Two figurines:
l. Classical.
r. Seasons.
£300-350
£400-450 *G&CC*

A Llewellyn Jewitt bust.
£2,250-2,500 *G&CC*

An Apollo bust.
£800-850 *G&CC*

FURTHER READING

The Concise Encyclopedia and Price Guide to Goss China and *The Price Guide to Arms and Decorations on Goss China,* Nicholas Pine (Milestone Publications), 62 Murray Road, Horndean, Hants.
William Henry Goss, The Story of the Staffordshire Family of Potters Who Invented Heraldic Porcelain, Lynda and Nicholas Pine.

Crested China

● Crested China was produced by many factories between about 1880 and 1940.

● Most famous main manufacturers were Arcadian, Carlton, Grafton, Shelley and Willow Art.

● More diverse model subjects than Goss, especially buildings, hats, animals, shoes etc.

● Many military subjects produced during the First World War to stimulate dwindling sales.

● Most companies were out of business by the start of the Second World War.

A selection of larger models. **£10-40 each** *CCC*

A selection of busts.
£45-95 *CCC*

A selection of birds. **£20-50 each** *CCC*

A selection of World War I figures and busts.
£50-80 each *CCC*

A selection of crested chairs.
£6-20 each *G&CC*

A selection of seaside souvenirs.
£3.50-25 each *G&CC*

An Arcadian jug,
£100-120 and a
figure,
£150-175 CCC

A selection of dogs.
£15-35 each *CCC*

Crested chess pieces.   **£7-30 each** *G&CC*

A selection of
figures, various
factories.
£35-120 each
CCC

FURTHER READING
Crested China, Sandy Andrews.
*The Price Guide to Crested
China,* Nicholas Pine
(Milestone Publications), 62
Murray Road, Horndean, Hants.

Jugs

A Spode New Oval shape cream jug, pattern No. 889, c1805, 5.5in (14cm) wide.
£100-150 *TVA*

An Arthur Wood moulded jug depicting Jack and The Beanstalk, c1935, 8.5in (21.5cm) high. **£50-80** *AOS*

A nature jug after Bernard Pallissy, 19thC.
£100-150 *AOS*

A jug depicting spinners, c1930, 5in (13cm) high.
£12-15 *OD*

An Empire Ware jug, c1938.
£15-20 *AOS*

A German Hunter jug, 19thC, 4.5in (11.5cm) high.
£8-10 *OD*

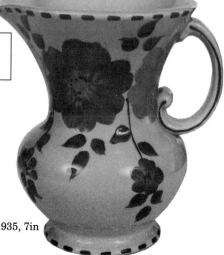

Cross Reference
Drinking
Pub Jugs

A set of 3 Arthur Wood jugs, 5.5 to 6.5in (14 to 16.5cm) high.
£65-85 *COL*

An Arthur Wood jug, c1935, 7in (17.5cm) high.
£20-30 *AOS*

Musical Jugs

- First launched in 1930 with the introduction of 'John Peel' series of half pint mug, pint mug and jug, shortly followed by a cigarette box, salad bowl and a whisky flagon.

- Further musical subjects included Widdicombe Fair, On Ilkla Moor Baht'at, Killarney and Auld Lang Syne.

- Rarer titles followed, including the Eton Boating Song and Gracie Fields.

- The production of musical novelties dwindled after World War II and had ceased by 1951.

A tankard playing The Floral Dance, 6in (15cm) high. **£150-200** *PC*

A Carlton Ware musical tankard, depicting Grandfather's Clock, 5in (13cm) high. **£150-200** *PC*

A Crown Devon Fielding painted one pint jug, playing 'Auld Lang Syne', 8.5in (21cm) high. **£125-200** *PC*

A half pint jug, depicting Windsor Castle, made at Burslem Pottery, playing 'Here's Health Unto His Majesty', 6in (15cm) high. **£200-250** *PC*

A Long John Silver musical Toby jug, unmarked, 10.5in (26.5cm) high. **£150-200** *PC*

Cross Reference
Toby Jugs

A half pint and a pint Sylvan Pottery tankard, playing John Peel, 6 and 7.5in (16.5 and 19cm) high.
£75-125 *PC*

A King George VI and Queen Elizabeth musical jug, playing 'God Save The King', 9in (23cm) high.
£250-350 *PC*

A half pint tankard, 'The Irish Jaunting Car', playing Killarney, 5in (13cm) high.
£150-200 *PC*

A half pint tankard, probably Winton, with Thorens movement playing Killarney, 6in (15cm) high.
£100-200 *PC*

A musical tankard, 'Widdicombe Fair', 5in (13cm) high. **£150-200** *PC*

A half pint Royal Winton Grimwades George VI Coronation tankard, playing the National Anthem, 6in (15cm) high.
£250-300 *PC*

A one pint jug, 'The Irish Jaunting Car', playing Killarney, 8in (20cm) high.
£200-250 *PC*

A Royal Doulton 'Old Charlie' jug, playing 'Here's Health Unto His Majesty', 5.5in (14cm) high.
£400-500 *PC*

Cross Reference
Doulton

A half pint musical tankard depicting John Peel, 4.5in (11.5cm) high.
£100-150 *PC*

Cross Reference
Colour Section

A half-pint tankard playing 'On Ilkla Moor Baht 'At', 4.5in (11.5cm) high.
£150-200 *PC*

Lustre Ware

A set of 3 graduated copper lustre jugs, slight damage.
£45-55 *LF*

A pink lustre tobacco jar, c1920, 4.5in (11.5cm) high.
£8-10 *OD*

A Gray's Gloria lustre jug, orange and black on white with gilding to rim and handle, c1925, 4.5in (11.5cm) high.
£45-50 *ROW*

Gloria lustre was developed by Susie Cooper in collaberation with Gordon Forsyth between 1925 and 1930.

Majolica

A modern Bavarian green lustre moustache cup and saucer, c1910, cup 6.5in (16.5cm) diam.
£20-25 *OD*

For further selection of Lustre Ware refer to Miller's Collectables, Price Guide, Volume IV, page 116.

An Egyptian revival jug, 8.5in (21.5cm) high.
£80-100 *NCA*

A Minton parrot, c1900, 11in (28cm) high.
£300-350 *NB*

Two Minton wall tiles, c1870, 8in (20cm).
£25-30 each *NB*

A Holdcroft sugar bowl, c1870, 4in (10cm) high.
£200-250 *NB*

A French majolica
vase, c1890,
10in (25.5cm).
£110-130 *NB*

A majolica fish flower holder,
c1890, 14in (35.5cm) long.
£130-150 *NB*

A Minton jug, c1860, 7in
(18cm).
£130-150 *NB*

A French majolica flower holder,
c1880, 6.5in (16cm) long.
£110-130 *NB*

A majolica strawberry dish,
c1870, 12in (30.5cm).
£150-180 *NB*

A kettle with fish design, c1875,
8in (20.5cm).
£200-250 *NB*

A French majolica plate,
c1890, 7in (18cm).
£20-25 *NB*

A pitcher, c1870, 9in
(23cm).
£50-75 *NB*

A Wedgwood shell plate,
c1870, 7.5in (19cm).
£40-50 *NB*

A French majolica figure,
c1900, 6in (15cm) high.
£30-40 *NB*

Mugs

A Pearlware blue painted
quart mug, inscribed
H. Rouse, c1800,
6in (15cm) high.
£100-120 *OD*

A French majolica jug,
c1890, 5in (13cm) high.
£20-25 *NB*

A majolica pitcher,
c1880, 8in (20cm) high.
£50-60 *NB*

An earthenware mug
with black and blue
banded decoration,
possibly Swansea,
c1840, 5in
(13cm) high.
£70-75 *OD*

Plates

A green Keith Murray dish and 5 plates.
£100-150 *ASA*

A green china wall plate, with yellow daffodils, c1920, 9in (23cm) diam.
£25-30 *ROW*

A British Anchor China cake plate, with chrome handle, c1932, 9in (23cm) diam.
£8-10 *COL*

A Hollinshead & Kirkham plate, 'Autumn' pattern, 9in (22cm) wide.
£35-45 *ADC*

A Bassano plate painted in the manner of Bartolomeo Terchi, c1740, 9in (22.5cm) diam.
£1,550-1,650 *C*

A blue and white delftware plate, painted in inky blue, inscribed Thos. Stevens, 1784, 9in (23cm) diam.
£350-450 *S(S)*

A Ridgway plate, pattern no. 941, c1815, 9in (23cm) diam.
£200-225 *TVA*

An underglaze blue painted plaque, c1795, 6in (15cm) diam.
£100-130 *IW*

Ribbon Plates

Two ribbon plates, typically to decorate a narrow boat, the left coloured black and red, the right blue and silver, c1900, 7.5in (19cm) diam. **£25-35 each** *HEY*

For a further selection of Ribbon Plates, refer to Miller's Collectables, Price Guide, Volume IV, pages 122 and 123.

A set of 6 Meir Ware dessert plates.
£25-35 *AOS*

Pot Lids

Russian Bear's Grease,
3.75in (9cm) diam.
£170-190 *BBR*

Stamp's Myrrhine Tooth
Paste, 3.75in (9cm) wide.
£35-40 *BBR*

Pratt Ware coloured pot lid of
Shakespeare's house, c1865,
4.25in (11cm) diam.
£55-75 *LIO*

Bear's Grease,
2.25in (6cm) diam.
£80-90 *BBR*

The Alexandra
Cherry Tooth Paste.
£185-200 *BBR*

Shakespeare, mauve transfer
print, 3.25in (8cm) diam.
£70-80 *BBR*

Bear's Grease, c1865, 3in (8cm) diam.
£45-65 *LIO*

Mrs Ellen Hales, 3in
(7.5cm) diam.
£45-50 *BBR*

Teapots

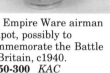

An Empire Ware airman
teapot, possibly to
commemorate the Battle
of Britain, c1940.
£250-300 *KAC*

A train teapot, by Ellgreaves, c1930.
£300-325 *KAC*

For a further selection of
Pot Lids, refer to
Miller's Collectables
Price Guide, Volume IV
pages 119 to 121.

A cat teapot, creamer
and sugar, by
Crown Ducal, c1930.
£100-125 *KAC*

A black cat teapot, with
a red bow, c1950.
£30-40 *KAC*

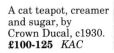

A Simple Simon teapot, with Georgie Porgie sugar, and Old Mother Hubbard creamer, by Devonmoor Pottery, c1930. **£130-150** *KAC*

A teapot in the form of Cinderella's pumpkin coach, with Mac and Jaq the mice helpers as creamer and sugar bowl, by Weetman, for Walt Disney Productions, 1960.   **£125-150** *KAC*

A Soho Pottery teapot in the form of corn on the cob, with stand, made to imitate earlier majolica pieces, c1930. **£130-150** *KAC*

A Price's Cottage Ware teapot, 5in (13cm) high. **£20-25** *COL*

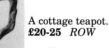

A Shelley bathing tent teapot, and a bucket for sugar and sea shell for creamer, designed by Hilda Cowham, 1928. **£950-1,100** *KAC*

A cottage teapot. **£20-25** *ROW*

A Price Brothers jester teapot, c1940. **£100-125** *KAC*

A German teddy bear teapot, c1940. **£60-75** *KAC*

A 'Scottie' golfer teapot, by Wade, and golf bag creamer and golf ball sugar, c1950.   **£150-175** *KAC*

Tea Sets

A Chamberlain trio, comprising coffee cup, tea cup, and saucer, pattern no. 886, c1820, saucer 5in (13cm) diam. **£150-225** *TVA*

A trio by Barker Brothers, hand painted design by John Guildford, c1930, plate 7in (18cm) diam. **£50-60** *GAZ*

A tea cup and saucer, hand painted in Paris, with silver lemon slice holder, Birmingham, c1905. **£35-45** *AMH*

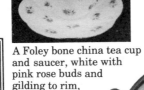

A tea bowl and saucer, by Penningtons, Liverpool, printed with floral sprays, tea bowl with hairline crack, c1750, saucer 5.5in (14cm) diam. **£100-120** *TVA*

A Foley bone china tea cup and saucer, white with gilded handle and rim, and pink interior to cup, c1896. **£15-18** *ROW*

A Derby tea cup and saucer, painted with Shropshire landscapes, by Robert Brewer, slight rubbing, c1810. **£650-700** *TVA*

A Foley bone china tea cup and saucer, white with pink rose buds and gilding to rim, c1896. **£15-18** *ROW*

A cup and saucer, by H. & R. Daniel, c1820, saucer 6in (15cm) diam. **£130-150** *TVA*

A tea set, design 2194, decorated with blue pansies, with WMF mounts, on a tray. **£100-130** *ASA*

A bowl, 6in (15cm) diam. **£100-125** *TVA*

A Wade trio, 'Mode', c1950. **£8-10** *COL*

A Pratt Ware cup and saucer with turquoise body, c1860. **£100-150** *HEY*

A trio, by Dunn Bennett & Co., 6in (15cm) diam.
£18-20 *OD*

A Charles Bourne, London, trio, pattern no. 208, c1820, saucer 5.5in (14cm) diam.
£300-400 *TVA*

Toby Jugs

The Snuff Taker, by Brampton, salt glazed, c1840, 9in (23cm) high.
£240-280 *IW*

Three modern limited edition Toby jugs: William Moorcroft, c1992, 8.5in (21.5cm) high, **£220- 240**, Clarice Cliff, 9in (22cm) high and Charlotte Rhead, 9.5in (23cm) high.
£350-450 each *ADC*

A character jug of John Peel, by Wilkinsons, signed by J. H. Thorpe, 14in (36cm) high.
£300-450 *AOS*

A Pratt type pearlware toby jug, sponged in blue, c1800, 10in (25cm) high.
£900-1,200 *S(S)*

A Yorkshire toby jug, decorated in Pratt colours, with impressed crown under base, c1810, 10in (25cm) high.
£800-900 *RWB*

A Ralph Wood style toby jug, some restoration, 9.5in (24cm) high.
£280-300 *Bea*

A Ralph Wood style Toby jug, with blue coat and ochre breeches, holding a jug of ale in one hand and beaker in the other, 9.5in (24cm) high.
£280-300 *Bea*

Toothbrush Trays

An Edwardian toothbrush dish and lid, 8in (20cm) long.
£18-20 *AI*

An Edwardian toothbrush dish and lid, 8.5in (21.5cm) long.
£20-25 *AI*

Vases

A pottery flower holder, by J. R. Malley & Co., 5in (13cm) wide.
£25-30 *NCA*

A green William Baron vase, 6in (15cm) high.
£80-100 *NCA*

A Mason's Ironstone Vase and Table pattern toothstick box and cover, c1815, 8in (20cm) long.
£270-300 *VH*

Cross Reference
Oriental

Two Noritake Japanese porcelain vases, with tube line design, c1930, largest 4in (10cm) high.
£60-80 each *GAZ*

A pair of Kutani porcelain vases, one with damaged rim, red three character seal mark, 14.5in (37cm) high. **£800-1,000** *P(S)*

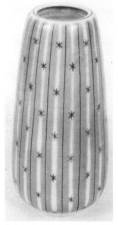

A pottery two-handled amphora vase, decorated with owls, 5.5in (14cm) high.
£40-50 *NCA*

Cross Reference
Devon Ware

A Copeland and Garrett spill vase, c1840, 4in (10cm) high.
£120-130 *TVA*

A Lauder Barum red pottery bottle vase, inscribed and painted, minor glaze damage, 17.5in (44cm) high.
£270-290 *Bea*

A Poole Pottery 'freeform' vase, c1950, 8.5in (21.5cm) high.
£140-180 *KAC*

A Chameleon Ware two-handled vase, designed by George Clews, 1930.
£85-135 *AOS*

Cross Reference
Art Nouveau

A Royal Cauldon vase, by Edith Gaiter, c1935, 8.5in (21.5cm) high.
£35-50 *AOS*

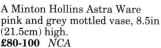

A Minton Hollins Astra Ware pink and grey mottled vase, 8.5in (21.5cm) high.
£80-100 *NCA*

A Rookwood Pottery matt glazed vase, 9in (23cm) high.
£200-300 *ZEI*

Victorian Staffordshire Pottery

A Staffordshire ochre, green and cream figure, c1800, 3.5in (9cm) long.
£1,600-1,700 *JHo*

A Staffordshire cow and calf spill holders, 19thC, 13in (33cm) high.
£350-375 *AA*

Two Staffordshire pottery figures of highlanders, 19thC: *l.* With horse and dead game, 10.5in (26cm).
£200-250 *r.* With spaniel, wearing blue frock coat and tartan sash, 11in (28cm). **£70-100** *AH*

A Staffordshire sheep, 19thC, 3in (8cm) long. **£60-70** *AA*

A pair of Staffordshire poodles and families, on blue bases, 5in (12.5cm). **£160-180** *GAK*

A Staffordshire figure of a
Highlander, 19thC, 12in (31cm)
high.
£100-120 *AA*

A Staffordshire earthenware jug, transfer printed in black and
hand coloured, inscribed John Matthews, Bricklayer's Arms,
1863, 9in (23cm). **£300-330** *S(S)*

A Staffordshire inkpot, 19thC.
£75-85 *AA*

A Staffordshire inkwell, 'The
Cobbler', 19thC, 4.5in (11cm)
high. **£170-180** *AA*

A grey transfer printed drainer,
19thC, 12in (31cm) wide.
£90-100 *TRU*

Two Staffordshire poodles, 19thC,
7 and 8in (18 and 20cm) high.
£120-130 *AA*

A pair of Staffordshire spaniels, with glass eyes,
19thC, 13in (33cm) high. **£180-190** *AA*

A pair of pearlware groups, the Sailors 'Departure' and 'Return', in enamel colours, both on red titled bases, c1810, 9in (23cm) high. **£500-600** *HEY*

A Staffordshire porcellaneous inkwell, modelled as a harpist and decorated in gilt, with shamrocks, c1840, 4.75in (12cm). **£160-180** *RWB*

A Walton pearlware group of 'Tenderness', on a titled green base moulded with blue scrolls, chipped, impressed mark, c1820, 7.5in (19cm) high. **£700-800** *S(S)*

A Staffordshire pottery figure of a woman standing by a birdcage, with a bird seated on her arm, c1855, 11.5in (29cm). **£145-160** *RWB*

A Staffordshire sheep spill holder, 19thC, 8in (20cm) high. **£140-150** *AA*

A Staffordshire pearlware figure entitled Show Woman, c1830. **£400-500** *S(S)*

A pair of Staffordshire vases, one damaged, 19thC. **£100-120** *SUF*

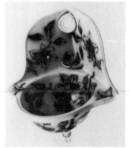

A late Victorian ceramic corner wash hand basin, white, decorated with blue floral transfers, hair line crack, back stamp for J. Dimmock & Co., Hanley. **£80-90** *WIL*

A Staffordshire spill vase, 19thC, 9in (23cm) high. **£125-135** *AA*

A Staffordshire figure of Giuseppe Garibaldi, c1864, 13.25in (34cm). **£250-280** *RWB*

A Staffordshire figure of Pope Pius IV, titled 'His Holiness the Pope', c1875, 18.25in (46cm). **£320-360** *RWB*

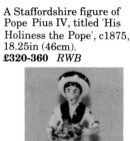

A Staffordshire pastille burner, modelled as a house, c1840, 4.5in (11cm). **£170-190** *RWB*

A Staffordshire porcellaneous figure of a girl with a flower basket, c1840, 6in (15cm). **£160-180** *RWB*

A Staffordshire spill vase, 19thC, 7in (18cm) high. **£90-100** *AA*

A Staffordshire Highland Couple, clock piece, 19thC, 15in (38cm) high. **£90-100** *AA*

A Walton pearlware figure of a youth, on a green mound base, some damage, impressed mark, c1820, 6in (15cm) high. **£350-450** *S(S)*

A jug, bowl, potty and matching dressing table set, decorated with pheasants and foliage, on a cream ground. **£150-160** *TRU*

A selection of brown and white Staffordshire spaniels, 19thC, 3.5 to 9in (9 to 23cm).
£85-130 each *AA*

A pair of Staffordshire figures of poodles with pups, c1850, 7in (18cm) high.
£380-420 *RWB*

A pair of Staffordshire Prussian generals, sparsely coloured in gilt, red and yellow, c1870, 12in (30cm) high.
£100-150 each *HEY*

A pair of Willow pattern tureens, late 19thC, 11in (28cm) wide. **£90-100** *TRU*

A Staffordshire spaniel and puppy, on cobalt blue base, 19thC, 6in (15cm) high. **£190-200** *AA*

Contemporary Ceramics

A Winchcombe pottery two- handled bowl, possibly by Michael Cardew, c1938, 8in (20cm) diam.
£200-240 *IW*

A Winchcombe cider jug, by Raymond Finch, 1938, 9.5in (24cm) high.
£85-95 *IW*

A mead bottle by John Leach, Michelney pottery, 1968, 7.5in (19cm) high. **£40-50** *IW*

A green salt kit, Weatheriggs pottery, Cumbria, c1930, 10.5in (26cm) high.
£30-40 *IW*

A buff coloured stoneware jug, Carter Stabler & Adams, Poole, c1920, 6in (15cm) high.
£60-70 *OD*

A Winchcombe Studio Pottery jug, with impressed pottery mark of Sydney Justin, c1930, 5.25in (13cm) high.
£40-50 *OD*

A Winchcombe pottery jug, by Raymond Finch, firing defects, 1954, 11.5in (29cm) high.
£75-85 *IW*

Wall Plaques

A Czechoslovakian hand painted wall masque, 1930s. **£200-250** *GAZ*

Cross Reference
Children's & Nursery Ware

A Czechoslovakian hand painted wall masque, c1930.
£200-250 *GAZ*

A celadon bowl by J.F. Walford, Redhill, Surrey, c1950, 3.25in (8cm) high. **£50-60** *IW*

Chimneypots

These Victorian chimney pots are mainly from the Lancashire area - predominantly Manchester - and are collected for use as flower pots.

A Victorian chimneypot, 16in (41cm) high.
£15-20 *AA*

A Victorian glazed chimneypot, 36in (91.5cm) high
£30-35 *AA*

A Victorian glazed chimneypot, 21in (53cm) high. **£30-35** *AA*

A Victorian unglazed chimneypot, 27in (68.5cm) high.
£25-30 *AA*

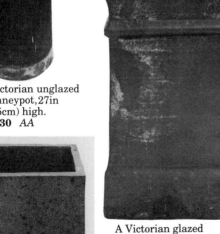

A Victorian glazed chimneypot, 23in (59cm) high. **£30-35** *AA*

A Victorian glazed chimneypot, 16in (41cm) high.
£20-25 *AA*

A Victorian unglazed chimneypot, 33.5in (85cm) high.
£55-65 *AA*

A Victorian chimneypot, 33.5in (85cm) high.
£55-65 *AA*

A Victorian chimneypot,
20in (50.5cm) high.
£15-20 *AA*

A Victorian glazed chimneypot,
25in (64cm) high.
£25-30 *AA*

A Victorian
unglazed
chimneypot,
15.5in
(39.5cm) high.
£10-15 *AA*

A Victorian glazed chimneypot,
23in (59cm) high.
£30-35 *AA*

A Victorian glazed
chimneypot, 38in
(96.5cm) high.
£30-35 *AA*

A Victorian
unglazed
chimneypot, 16.5in
(42cm) high.
£15-20 *AA*

A Victorian glazed
chimney pot,
26in (66.5cm)
high. **£25-30** *AA*

A Victorian glazed chimneypot,
27in (69cm) high. **£30-35** *AA*

A Victorian
chimneypot, 32in
(81cm) high.
£35-40 *AA*

A Victorian glazed
chimneypot, 22.5in
(56cm) high.
£30-35 *AA*

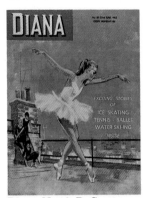

Rover, Nos 1148 and 1152, D. C.
Thompson, 1946.
£4-5 each *NOS*

Diana, No.18, D. C.
Thompson, 1963.
£3-4 *NOS*

Popular Comics, No. 45,
Dell Comics, 1939.
£30-32 *NOS*

Plastic Man, No.
64, last issue,
1956.
£35-37 *NOS*

T. V. Comic
Holiday Special,
T.V. Pubs. Ltd,
1966.
£10-12 *NOS*

Misty, No.1, Fleetway,
1978. **£2-3** *NOS*

Solo, No.8, City
Magazines/Century 21,
1967,
£4-5 *NOS*

Plug, No.1, D. C.
Thompson, 1977.
£3-4 *NOS*

All American, No. 68,
D. C. Comics, 1945.
£80-85 *NOS*

Magic,
No.1, D. C.
Thompson,
features
nephews of
Dandy and
Beano
characters.
£2.50-3
NOS

Goofy, No.1, I.P.C.,
with Disney strips,
1973.
£2-3 *NOS*

Tom and
Jerry, No.1,
Spotlight
Publications
Ltd, 1973.
£2-3 *NOS*

32 Captain Marvel Junior
comics, 1946-52.
£1,200-1,400 *S(NY)*

Captain Marvel Thrill Book,
1941, near mint condition.
£1,900-2,200 *S(NY)*

Marvel Comics, No.2 prototype
cover, Bill Everett, c1938.
£9,000-9,500 *S(NY)*

Pep Comics, No.1, M.J.L.
Magazines, January 1941.
£750-800 *S(NY)*

Captain Britain, No.1,
with cut out mask.
£2-3 *NOS*

Marvel Mystery Comics,
No.5, March 1940, Timely
Publications.
£2,500-3,000 *S(NY)*

Captain America, No.1, March
1941, Timely Publications.
£2,800-3,000 *S(NY)*

Whiz Comics, No.3, April
1940, Fawcett Publications.
£2,500-3,000 *S(NY)*

Popeye Feature Book, 1937,
David McKay Publications.
£1,750-2,000 *S(NY)*

12 Weird Fantasy comic books, by artists Frank Frazetta and Al Williamson, E. C. Publications, 1950s.
£520-560 *S(NY)*

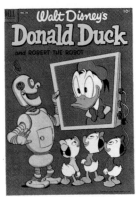

24 Donald Duck comic books, covers by artist Carl Barks, by Dell Publications, 1950s.
£500-520 *S(NY)*

A group of 94 Classic Comics, by Gilbertson Publications, 1940-1960.
£11,000-13,000 *S(NY)*

Two Daredevil comics by Lev Gleason Publications, 1941.
£7,000-7,500 *S(NY)*

Five Blue Beetle comics, Nos. 1-5, artist Will Eisner, by Fox Publications, c1939.
£3,200-3,500 *S(NY)*

Ten Shadow comics, by Street and Smith Publications, 1943-44.
£2,500-2,800 *S(NY)*

Twenty seven Walt Disney comics and stories, covers by Walt Kelly, Dell Publications.
£600-700 *S(NY)*

Four Flash Gordon comics, artist Alex Raymond, 1953.
£700-800 *S(NY)*

15 Bulletman comics, artist Mac Rayboy, Fawcett Pubs, 1941-46.
£6,300-6,600 *S(NY)*

A German bisque headed doll, with papier mâché toddler body. **£150-195** *PAR*

A bébé, by E. Denamur, wearing original underclothes and dress, c1885. **£2,000-3,000** *STK*

A Bru walking and kiss throwing bébé, original clothing, marked Bru Jne R9, 23in (59cm) high. **£3,500-4,500** *STK*

A pale bisque baby doll, by Swaine & Co., German, marked M 232, c1910, 22in (56cm). **£1,700-2,000** *STK*

An Ernst Heubach character baby, marked, c1915. **£450-550** *STK*

A Kammer & Reinhardt Kaiser Baby, with flock hair, wearing original crochet dress, 10in (25cm). **£400-600** *STK*

A Max Handwerck Bébé Elite, with jointed wood and papier mâché body, 24in (62cm). **£450-500** *PAR*

A Bru bébé, with original kid body, bisque arms, turned wooden legs, and mohair wig, marked Bru Jne 8, c1880. **£7,500-9,500** *STK*

A doll's dress, hand made using antique materials.
£45-50 *PAR*

A Mulatto bisque headed character doll, impressed Simon & Halbig.
£2,600-3,000 *CSK*

Two dolls using heads from the same mould, c1890: *l.* Roullet & Decamps. **£1,600-1,700** *r.* Simon & Halbig **£750-950** *STK*

A doll's dress, hand made using antique materials.
£50-55 *PAR*

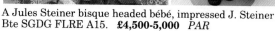

A Jules Steiner bisque headed bébé, impressed J. Steiner Bte SGDG FLRE A15. **£4,500-5,000** *PAR*

A pale bisque character boy doll, with toddler body, dressed in original suit, mohair wig, by Porzellanfabrik Mengers-gereuth, 15in (38.5cm).
£500-600 *STK*

A Jules Steiner bisque doll.
£1,800-2,500 *STK*

A doll's dress and bonnet, hand made from antique materials and lace.
£50-55 *PAR*

Mr Punch

'Boris', a red Steiff bear, c1920, 21in (53.5cm) high. **£3,000-5,000** *STK*

'Knickerbocker', an American bear, c1930, 18in (46cm). **£150-250** *STK*

Judy and the Baby

A set of Punch and Judy show characters, c1920, 9 to 19in (22.5 to 48.5cm) high. **£350-450 the set** *NOW*

The Devil and the Skeleton

The Crocodile

The Clown

A Decamps clockwork toy, 19thC. **£300-500** *NOW*

A Steiff bear, c1908. **£1,800-2,500** *NOW*

A Steiff teddy bear, with button in his ear, c1904. **£1,500-1,800** *TED*

A heart shaped mohair cushion with bear and musical box, German, c1930. **£200-300** *TED*

A mohair bear, by Twyfords, 1950s. **£70-100** *TED*

An English bear, stuffed with wood wool, 1920s. **£400-450** *TED*

A Schuco mohair lipstick and powder compact bear, 1930s. **£250-300** *TED*

r. A complete Steiff King Skittle set, with 8 other animals, c1895. **£3,000-5,000** *TED*

A traditional English bear, 1940s. **£60-80** *TED*

TEDDY BEARS

of Witney

In 1989 Ian Pout of 'Teddy Bears' gave £12,100 (a world record price) for Alfonzo, a red Steiff bear, owned by a Russian princess. This was an exceptional price for an exceptional bear.
We are always keen to offer a fair price for old bears, especially by **Steiff, Merrythought, Farnell, Deans, Chiltern and Chad Valley.**

Collectors catalogue of new bears (£2.00). Old bears for sale in shop but NOT by mail order.
OPEN: Monday-Saturday 9.30am-5.30pm, Sunday 11.30am-4.30pm.

Please contact Ian Pout at 'Teddy Bears'

99 High Street, Witney, Oxford OX8 6LY
Tel. (0993) 702616

A Petit et Dumontier pressed bisque bébé, impressed P 5 D, c1880. **£13,500-14,500** *S*

A Bru Jeune et Cie bisque swivel head bébé, unmarked, c1875. **£16,000-17,500** *S*

An A. Thuillier pressed bisque bébé, impressed A 14 T, c1875, 26in (66cm). **£35,000-38,000** *S*

l. A Kämmer & Reinhardt c1910 **£2,000-2,500** *c.* A Gebrüder Heubach, c1912 **£2,250-2,750** *r.* A François Gaultier, c1880. **£650-750** *S*

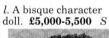

l. A bisque character doll. **£5,000-5,500** *S*

An Emile Jumeau pressed bisque doll, c1880. **£9,000-10,000** *S*

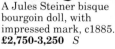

A Jules Steiner bisque bourgoin doll, with impressed mark, c1885. **£2,750-3,250** *S*

A Mothereau pressed bisque bébé doll, impressed B 6 M, c1885. **£10,500-11,500** *S*

A Jumeau pressed bisque portrait doll, impressed 1, together with trunk containing 6 outfits. **£7,500-8,000** *S*

Chocolate

This is another example of how a variety of goods and products with a single theme can be amassed to produce a magnificent and fascinating collection - in this case, chocolate.

A selection of chocolate wrappers, c1940.
£2-3 each *ACh*

A Cadbury's label from a wooden box, c1920, 11in (28cm) high.
£25-35 *ACh*

A Rowntree's insert for a free casket, c1920, 7in 17.5cm) wide.
Insert £5-6, Casket £8-12 *ACh*

Chocolate wrappers, c1930.
£2-3 each *ACh*

Two Bourneville Cocoa tins, with contents, poor condition, 5in (12.5cm) high.
l. unopened, c1930, **£4-5**
r. c1940, **£2-3** *ACh*

A Fry's original postcard, c1910. **£25-30** *ACh*

A Rowntree's insert, c1928, 8in (20cm) high. **£3-4** *ACh*

A Mars Snickers box, brought over by an American GI, c1941, 9in (22.5cm) wide. **£3-4** *ACh*

A Cadbury's chromolithograph label, c1900, 9.5in (24cm) wide.
£40-50 *ACh*

A Cadbury's Dairy Milk Chocolate box, with chromolithograph label, c1910, 12in (30.5cm) wide.
£40-50 *ACh*

Cross Reference
Packaging & Advertising

Two chocolate wrappers, c1950.
50p-£1 each *ACh*

A Fry's advertisement
show card, c1930, 15in
(38.5cm) high.
£40-60 *ACh*

Chocolate wrappers with
figures, **£5-6 each** *ACh*

Coca-Cola

A cardboard Coca-Cola bottle
carrier, 1960s.
£5-6 *COB*

A Coca-Cola wooden
guitar case, 1970s.
£30-35 *COB*

> **Cross Reference**
> Drinking

A Cadbury's Chocolate Coffee
Crèmes box, c1900.
£40-50 *ACh*

A glass Coca-Cola
advertisement, 1940s.
£20-25 *COB*

> **Cross Reference**
> Packaging &
> Advertising

A Fry's Chocolate Cream box
label, c1930, 8.5in (21cm) wide.
£15-18 *ACh*

A Coca-Cola metal flask in
a case, 1960s. **£9-10** *COB*

DOLLS

We have followed, as before, the generally accepted rules for the categorization of dolls; that is, by the medium from which the head is made. The French and German bisque headed dolls are further divided by manufacturer where clearly marked, but it is worth remembering that manufacturers often made heads for other doll makers and that the body may be made from some other material.

The market remains good, as always, for top quality examples. It is very important to check carefully for damage and restoration. Very early dolls before c1750 are commanding good prices despite the comparative crudeness of construction, detail and lack of original clothing.

A parian swivelhead shoulder doll, with closed mouth, fixed blue eyes, moulded hair and cloth body with bisque lower arms, legs missing, c1880, 9in (23cm) high . **£485-525** *S(S)*

A group of original googlie eye dolls, all bisque with jointed shoulders, c1912, 2.5 to 5in (6 to 13cm) high. **£350-400** *STK*

A papoose rubber doll, in buckskin outfit, made by Ojibwa, c1940, sold at Niagara Falls, 5in (13cm). **£25-35** *STK*

An Indonesian carved hardwood doll, with articulated arms, one-piece head and body, 19thC. **£150-200** *STK*

A Norah Wellings doll, wearing Victorian knickerbockers, c1925, 14in (36cm) high. **£60-70** *LB*

A R & B Drink'N Babe doll, completely original with trunk of accessories and original tag, marked Dream Baby, made for the American market, c1920. **£350-450** *STK*

A German papier mâché shoulder doll, with closed mouth, painted features, brush-stroke hair and straight kid body, in original costume, 10in (26cm) high. **£275-300** *S(S)*

A Russian composition doll, in original costume, c1930, 10in (25cm) high. **£25-35** *STK*

A Scandinavian costume doll, c1930, 8in (20cm) high. **£15-20** *STK*

A Pierotti-type poured wax shoulder doll, with closed mouth, fixed blue eyes, inserted blonde hair and cloth body, poured wax lower limbs and original costume, c1880, 16.5in (42cm) high. **£450-475** *S(S)*

Peruvian dolls, made from ancient ancestral cloth, approx. 1000 years old, but dolls made this century by Cuancay Indians, 5.5 and 9in (14 and 23cm) high. **£25-35 each group** *STK*

A Japanese doll, with 6 wigs, in original wooden box, c1935. **£75-100** *STK*

A French mechanical swimming bisque doll 'Ondine', with clockwork mechanism wound at navel, in original box, repaired and wear to box, with instruction sheets, 7in (18cm) high. **£1,200-1,300** *S*

A celluloid costume doll, c1915, 6in (15cm) high, **£15-20** *STK*

A Dean's rag doll, c1925, 25in (64cm) high. **£20-25** *OD*

A Farnell felt doll of Jean Harlow, with a blonde wig, and painted facial features, label on foot, Farnell's, Alpha Toys, Made in England, added Lenci label on clothes, 26in (66cm) high. **£400-450** *S(NY)*

A costume doll pen wiper, c1925, 3in (8cm) high. **£15-20** *STK*

'Margie' composition doll, Cameo Doll Company, with painted and moulded hair and painted facial features, and original paper label in its original box, 9in (23cm) high. **£60-70** *S(NY)*

A celluloid character lady doll, with inset brown eyes, blonde mohair wig and adult body, with turtle mark, 14.5in (37cm) high. **£675-700** *CSK*

A German child doll, with bisque head and limbs, c1890, 5.5in (14cm) high. **£100-150** *STK*

An Irish Rosebud doll, in original box, c1950, 6in (15cm). **£45-60** *STK*

A Chad Valley Mabel Lucie Attwell cloth doll, with pressed felt face, glass eyes and 5-piece velvet covered body, in original costume, c1936, 14in (36cm) high, in original cardboard box. **£240-250** *S(S)*

A half doll clothes brush, 4.5in (11cm) **£15-20** *LB*

A black dolls house man, c1880, 5in (13cm) high. **£60-80** *STK*

A Scottish costume doll, with original mohair wig, c1930, 8in (20cm) high. **£20-30** *STK*

Bisque Headed Dolls

The finest French and German dolls are bisque headed. Bisque is porcelain at the unglazed stage of manufacture and very easily damaged, therefore prospective purchases must be closely examined for damage and repair. Porcelain or china headed dolls are easily identified as they are glazed and appear shiny.

A bisque headed character baby doll, with blue sleeping eyes, wig, baby's body and embroidered dress, impressed J.D.K. 257 36, 14.5in (37cm) high.
£250-275 *CSK*

A C.M. Bergmann bisque socket head character baby doll, 16in (41cm) high.
£150-200 *HSS*

A DEP bisque doll, with weighted blue glass eyes, pierced ears and jointed wood and composition body, in original silk dress and bonnet, silk damaged, impressed DEP8, c1910.
£425-450 *S(S)*

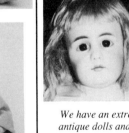

An Einco character boy doll, wearing original velvet and lace outfit, c1915, 10in (25cm).
£480-580 *STK*

A bisque head doll, with blue sleeping eyes, wood and composition ball jointed body, AM 390 A3M DRGM 246/1, 20in (51cm) high.
£270-300 *PAR*

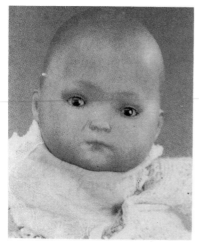

A Willi Weyh Mulatto bisque doll, with closed mouth, weighted brown eyes, domed head and cloth body, impressed W Weyh 2, c1926, 10.5in (27cm) high.
£300-350 *S(S)*

A French bisque head doll, with cork pate, brown wig, blue paperweight eyes, pierced ears and a closed mouth, on a 5-piece composition body, incised EDEN BEBE/Paris/M, 23in (59cm) high.
£500-550 *S(NY)*

A CET & Co. German character báby doll, with dimpled face and bright blue eyes, original mohair wig, underwear marked CET & Co. 66-7, c1910, 14in (36cm) high.
£250-350 *STK*

A bisque headed googlie-eyed doll, with water melon mouth, moulded curls and bent limbed composition body, broken thumb and foot, rub to cheek, impressed 172-1, 12in (31cm) high.
£850-900 *CSK*

FURTHER READING

Delightful Dolls, Thelma Bateman, Washington 1966.
The American Doll Artist, Helen Bullard, Boston 1965.
Dolls: Makers and Marks, Elizabeth A. Coleman, Washington 1963
The Collector's Encyclopedia of Dolls, Dorothy S., Elizabeth A. and Evelyn J. Coleman, New York 1968.
Dolls, Lady Antonia Fraser, London 1963.
Wonderful Dolls of Wax, Jo Elizabeth Gerken, Lincoln (Nebraska) 1964.
Directories of British, French and German Dolls, Luella Hart, Oaklands (Calif) 1964-65.
Dolls and Dollmakers, Mary Hillier, London 1968.
Dressing Dolls, A. Johnson, London 1969.
Dolls & Dolls Houses, Constance King, London 1977.
Dolls, J. Noble, London 1968.
Dolls of the World, G. White, London 1962.
European and American Dolls, G. White, London 1966.
Miller's Antiques Checklist, Dolls and Teddy Bears, Mitchell Beazley International Ltd., 1992

A French doll, with bisque head, real hair wig and jointed composition limbs, marked Fabrication Française A H & C Limoges, A6.
£250-275 *LF*

A Belgium bisque shoulderhead, with a blonde mohair wig, light blue painted eyes, eye shadow and a closed mouth, incised D.F./B./F.1., 6in (15cm) high.
£200-250 *S(NY)*

The head was made by the De Fuisseau around 1910 in Bandour, Belgium.

A German bisque headed black baby doll, with composition bent limb body, sleeping eyes, marked 241-3, 17in (43cm) high. **£225-250** *PAR*

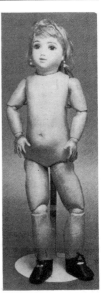

An A.T. bisque headed doll, with socket head, blue paperweight eyes, pierced ears, closed mouth, blonde wig, on a wood and composition body, damaged and repaired, incised A6T, 19in (48cm) high. **£5,000-5,500** *CNY*

A French bisque head doll, blue glass eyes, pierced ears and open mouth inset with upper teeth, on a jointed composition body, incised Limoges/France, 26in (66cm) high. **£300-350** *S(NY)*

A French swivel head bisque fashion doll, with closed mouth, fixed blue glass paperweight eyes, blonde wig and gussetted kid body, in original costume, cracks to face, impressed 4, c1880, 17in (44cm) high. **£850-900** *S(S)*

A Walthier & Son googlie eye doll, with bisque head, mohair wig and wearing original outfit, c1910, 8in (20cm) high. **£350-650** *STK*

A Limbach character boy, 'Walter', marked with the shamrock incised 8687, wearing original sailor suit, with flapper legs, c1920. **£350-450** *STK*

Dolls with flapper legs have joints half-way up the thigh so that it is covered when girl dolls wear flapper dresses.

A French bisque headed bébé, probably Petit & Dumontier, incised P 5 D, with a brown wig, pierced ears, brown paperweight eyes and an outlined closed mouth, on a wood and composition 8 ball-jointed body with metal hands, left small finger missing, hands repainted, 26in (66cm) high. **£10,500-11,500** *S(NY)*

A French bisque swivel head fashion doll, with brown wig, blue threaded glass eyes, pierced ears and closed mouth, on a kid body with individually stitched fingers, incised 3, 17in (43cm) high. **£1,300-1,500** *S(NY)*

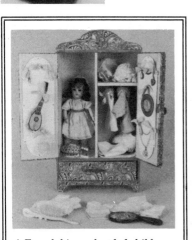

A 'Kaiser Baby' character doll, marked K * R 100, credited as being the first character baby doll made by Kammer & Reinhardt, c1910, 15in (38cm) high. **£450-650** *STK*

A French bisque headed child doll, with dark lashed sleeping eyes, fair mohair wig and jointed body, with original paper covered wardrobe, with complete trousseau, including iron, skipping rope, hot water bottle, buttons on card, mirror, brush and comb, wardrobe 15.5in (40cm) high. **£800-900** *CSK*

A Schoenau & Hoffmeister child doll, original wig, 1906, 24in (61cm) high. **£400-700** *STK*

A Bruno Schmidt bisque head doll, with ball jointed wood and composition body, brown glass eyes, c1910, 31in (79cm) high. **£1,400-1,500** *PAR*

Armand Marseille

Two child dolls produced from the same mould, marked 1894, AM 8/O dep 2/O., 16in (40.5cm):
l. with elaborate painting for the French market. with single stroke brows.
£350-500
r. with single stroke brows and slightly less elaborate painting for the German market,
£300-400 *STK*

An Armand Marseille doll.
£180-200 *MR*

A dream baby No. 351.with original wickerwork layette, original outfit and spare clothes, c1920.
£350-450 *STK*

A bisque head doll, with blue-grey sleeping eyes, straight arms and legs and composition body, AM390 A6M, 10in (25cm) high.
£180-200 *PAR*

Bru

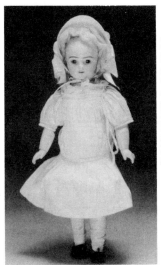

A French bisque headed bébé, with a blonde wig, cork pate, brown sleeping eyes, pierced ears and an outlined open mouth inset with upper teeth, on a wood and composition jointed body with straight legs, the doll throws kisses and has a voice box, one hand replaced, marked Bru, incised Bru Jne R/9, 21in (53cm) high.
£1,300-2,000 *S(NY)*

A Bébé Brevete, with carved wood body, paperweight eyes, wearing original costume, c1875, 14in (36cm) high.
£3,000-4,000 *STK*

A Bru swivel head fashion doll, with closed mouth, fixed blue eyes, sparse wig over cork pate, gussetted pink kid body, one arm detached, impressed A DEPOSE on left shoulder and B. Jne on right, c1866, 12in (31cm) high. **£1,000-1,100** *S(S)*

A bisque headed bébé, with cork pate, Bru metal neck joint, brown paperweight eyes, pierced ears and an outlined closed mouth, on a gussetted kid body with bisque lower arms, mark to face and one small finger broken, marked Bébé Brevete Bru, incised 5/0, 10.5in (26cm) high, **£3,500-4,500** *S(NY)*

Heubach

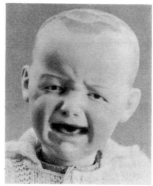

A character baby doll, in blue knitted suit, c1915, 10in (25cm) high. **£400-550** *STK*

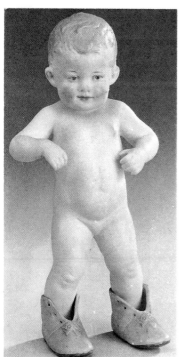

A laughing baby boy doll, with bisque head, intaglio eyes, original rompers, No. 7604, c1920. **£300-400** *STK*

An Ernst Heubach doll, with replacement clothes made from old material of the period. **£225-250** *PAR*

A bisque character 'Crying' doll, with open/closed crying mouth, intaglio eyes, domed head and curved limb composition body, impressed 8, c1912, 14.5in (37cm) high. **£1,200-1,300** *S(S)*

An all bisque 'Piano Baby' with painted features, moulded hair and oversized boots, c1914, 10in (25.5cm) high. **£450-480** *S(S)*

Jumeau

A bisque bébé doll, with brown hair, and azure eyes, silk dress, head marked Tête Jumeau, body marked Jumeau Médaille d'Or, c1885, 24.5in (62cm) high. **£1,500-2,500** *STK*

A bisque headed bébé doll, with cork pate, blonde wig, blue paperweight eyes, pierced ears, on 8-ball wood and composition body, 17in (43cm) high. **£5,000-6,000** *S(NY)*

A small bisque doll, with open mouth, fixed brown eyes, and jointed wood and composition body, slight damage, impressed 1 at neck socket, c1890. **£425-475** *S(S)*

A bisque headed bébé, with cork pate, spiral spring neck joint, blue threaded glass eyes, pierced ears, on a wood and composition ball-jointed body, arms replaced, head incised 1, stamped in blue Jumeau/Medaille D'Or/Paris, 11in (28cm) high. **£1,500-2,000** *S(NY)*

A bisque headed bébé, with cork pate, brown wig, blue paperweight eyes, pierced ears, closed mouth, on a jointed composition body with straight wrists, original dress and gloves, fingers scuffed, body stamped in blue Jumeau/ Medaille d'Or/Paris, head stamped in red Depose/Tête Jumeau/BTe. S.G.D.G./8, 18in (46cm) high. **£2,500-3,500** *S(NY)*

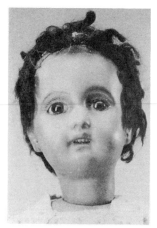

A Mulatto bisque doll, with open mouth, fixed brown eyes, pierced ears, black wig, cork pate, jointed wood and composition body, slight wig pull chips, impressed 4, c1907, 13in (34cm) high.
£750-800 *S(S)*

A bisque headed bébé, with cork pate, brown wig, brown threaded paperweight eyes, pierced ears, purple plush over eyes and closed mouth, on a jointed composition body with paper label Bébé Jumeau/Diplome d'Honneur, incised 4, 23in (59cm) high.
£7,500-8,500 *S(NY)*

A bisque headed bébé, with paperweight eyes, pierced ears, outlined mouth, on a wood and composition jointed body, stamped in blue Jumeau/Medaille d'Or /Paris, head stamped in red Depose/Tête Jumeau/BTe. S.G.D.G./9, with a voice box, 19.5in (50cm) high.
£2,000-3,000 *S(NY)*

A bisque headed bébé doll, with brown pate, original blonde wig, paperweight eyes, pierced ears, open mouth inset with upper teeth, on a jointed composition body, stamped in blue Bébé Jumeau/ BTe. S.G.D.G./Depose, original size 12 Bee marked shoes, 26in (66cm) high. **£1,500-2,000** *S(NY)*

A bisque headed bébé doll, with pierced ears, brown wig and jointed wood and composition body, dressed in spotted muslin and brown Jumeau shoes, crack to head, hands replaced, impressed 8, 20in (51cm) high.
£950-1,000 *CSK*

A bisque headed bébé, with cork pate, blonde wig, brown paperweight eyes, pierced ears, outlined closed mouth, on a jointed composition body with straight wrists, stamped in blue Jumeau/Diplome d'Honneur, head incised Depose/Tête Jumeau/12, 26in (66cm) high.
£2,000-3,000 *S(NY)*

A pressed bisque swivel headed fashion doll, with closed mouth, fixed blue paperweight eyes, pierced ears, blonde mohair wig over cork pate and gussetted kid body with separately stitched fingers, original dress and straw bonnet, head impressed 9, stamped on body Jumeau Medaille d'Or Paris, 23in (59cm) high. **£3,250-3,500** *S*

Kestner

A bisque headed doll, with closed mouth, original fleece wig and peg jointed body, wearing original outfit, marked 9, 9in (23cm) high. **£650-750** *STK*

A doll with closed mouth, painted face and eyes and wearing original outfit, marked 3917, probably by Kestner, c1880. **£350-450** *STK*

A bisque headed doll, with blonde wig, blue sleeping eyes, open mouth, on a wood and composition ball-jointed body, incised made in/K14/Germany/146, stamped in red Excelsior/D.R.P.No. 70685/Germany/4, 23in (59cm) high. **£300-350** *S(NY)*

Rabery & Delphieu

A bisque headed bébé, with cork pate, original blonde wig, blue paperweight eyes, pierced ears, closed mouth, on a jointed composition jointed body with straight wrists, incised R.2.D., 21.5in (54cm) high. **£2,200-3,000** *S(NY)*

A bisque bébé, with blue paperweight eyes, and closed mouth, wearing original outfit, c1880, 24in (62cm) high. **£2,500-3,500** *STK*

S.F.B.J.

A bisque headed character boy doll, with moulded hair, brown glass eyes, open/closed mouth with 2 moulded upper teeth, on a repainted jointed composition body, incised S.F.B.J./235/Paris/8, 19in (48cm) high. **£450-550** *S(NY)*

Simon & Halbig

A bisque headed doll, with blue glass eyes, pierced ears, open mouth, on a wood composition jointed body, wearing original dress, head incised Simon & Halbig/K*R/13, with Le Petit Parisien 1889 paper label on body, 17.5in (44cm) high.
£350-400 *S(NY)*

A bisque headed character doll, with blonde wig, blue sleeping eyes, an open/closed mouth, on a 5-piece composition baby body, incised 1428/4, 11in (28cm) high. **£500-550** *S(NY)*

A doll, with blue sleeping eyes and brown wig, 10.5in (27cm) high.
£200-250 *PAR*

Steiner

A bisque headed bébé doll, with blonde wig, cork pate, blue paperweight eyes, closed mouth, pierced ears, on a wood and composition jointed body, hairline crack to face, head incised A-13/Paris, stamped Le Parisien, 20.5in (52cm) high.
£900-1,000 *S(NY)*

A bisque headed bébé, with blonde wig, blue paperweight eyes, pierced ears, closed mouth, on a jointed composition body, wearing a white cotton c1890 chemise trimmed with lace, and leather shoes, head incised Sie C 6, body with J.St stamp, 21in (54cm) high.
£3,000-4,000 *S(NY)*

A bisque headed doll, with mohair wig and original silk underwear and cotton dress, marked HS3, 16in (41cm) high.
£450-550 *STK*

A bisque headed bébé, fixed blue eyes, pierced ears, and jointed papier mâché body with bisque hands, with new wig, impressed A-13 Paris, stamped on the hip Le Petit Parisien A. St Ste S.G.D.G. by Steiner.
£1,000-1,150 *CSK*

Felt Dolls

A pair of Maggie and Jiggs cloth dolls, Maggie holding a rolling pin, Jiggs smoking the usual cigar, c1925, 18 and 18.5in (46 and 47cm) high. **£2,000-3,000** *CNY*

Two Lenci felt dolls, from the 300 series, girl and boy doll with brown hair and painted facial features, 16 and 17in (41 and 43cm) high. **£850-950** *S(NY)*

A Lenci felt doll of a boy in a smoking jacket, from the 300 series, with a painted facial features, Lenci marked pipe in pocket and a tobacco pouch, c1925, 17in (43cm) high. **£2,000-2,500** *S(NY)*

Pedlar Dolls

A pair of Lenci Scottish felt dolls, the boy and girl with blonde hair and painted facial features, 17in (43cm) high each. **£2,000-3,000** *S(NY)*

These are from the 300 series with the hollow torsos. His hair is knotted as a hooked rug, her hair is in strips.

An early wooden pedlar doll in glass case. **£275-300** *PAR*

Wooden Dolls

An antique pedlar doll in glass dome. **£400-450** *PAR*

A Georgian oak doll, 12.5in (32cm) high. **£400-450** *JAC*

A Grödnertal wooden doll, with painted features, black painted skull, c1830, 8.5in (21cm) high. **£450-500** *S(S)*

A pedlar doll in glass dome. **£275-300** *PAR*

Dolls Houses

An Edwardian dolls house.
£330-360 *DaD*

A wooden dolls house, with papered brick facade, 2 bay windows, central front door, side opening to reveal the base with pull-out drawer forming a stylised garden, slight damage, English, c1860, 26in (66cm) high.
£1,700-2,500 *S(S)*

A further selection of dolls houses is featured in previous editions of Miller's Collectables Price Guides, available from Millers Publications.

Dolls Clothes

An antique dolls dress.
£45-50 *PAR*

A hand made couture dolls dress, made from old material.
£55-65 *PAR*

Two hand made dolls dresses, using antique materials and hand made lace.
£22-55 each *PAR*

A hand sewn dolls outfit, made from antique materials.
£50-60 *PAR*

A hand made dolls dress, made from antique materials and lace.
£45-50 *PAR*

A felt dolls coat and bonnet, 1930s.
£30-35 *PAR*

A dolls dress and jacket, 1930s.
£25-30 *PAR*

Dolls House Dolls

Seven German bisque headed dolls house dolls, 4 women and 3 men, c1880, 5.25 to 7.5in (13 to 19cm) high. **£1,300-1,500** *S*

A dolls house doll, c1880, 4.5in (11cm) high. **£40-60** *STK*

A French bisque headed dolls house doll, with set glass eyes, closed mouth, pin joined body, mohair wig, original costume, 3in (8cm) high. **£150-200** *STK*

Dolls House Furniture

A pair of matching fabric lined dolls trunks, with assorted contents, hinges replaced, c1890, 12in (31cm) wide. **£250-350** *STK*

A mid-Victorian mahogany miniature bureau, with false flap front and 3 long drawers and bracket feet, 8in (20cm) wide. **£150-250** *STK*

A brass fender and fire irons, fender 4in (10cm). **£100-150** *STK*

A late Victorian wooden dolls cradle, 14in (36cm) long. **£70-150** *STK*

| **Cross Reference** |
| Miniatures |

A tin fabric lined dolls trunk, with assorted contents, c1880, 14in (36cm) wide. **£150-250** *STK*

An early wickerwork dolls trunk, with assorted contents of dolls clothing, c1860, 11in (28cm) wide. **£150-250** *STK*

A child s toy tin scullery set, 'Alice in Kitchenland', with original box, 7in (18cm) high. **£15-18** *COL*

A miniature commode, base metal, 2in (5cm) high.
£15-20 *STK*

A tortoiseshell miniature toilet set.
£60-75 *PAR*

A pair of Victorian miniature chests, in rosewood and mahogany with boxwood stringing to the 2 long graduated drawers, with turned feet and shaped aprons, 7in (18cm) wide.
£200-250 *STK*

A group of painted metal, bone and wooden dolls house furniture and accessories, bisque and china miniature dolls, German and Anglo-Indian, some Rock and Graner, late 19thC.
£2,400-2,600 *S*

A Regency walnut and faux bamboo miniature dresser, with classical pediment above 2 shelves supported by 2 columns, base with one drawer and 2 doors, on turned feet, c1820, 15in (38cm) wide.
£300-400 *STK*

Dolls twin beds, 8in (20cm) long.
£65-75 *LB*

A selection of gilt metal dolls house chattels, including companion sets, a parrot cage and swing stand, a simulated bamboo framed picture, a clothes horse and magazine rack.
£850-900 *CSK*

A selection of tinplate dolls house furniture, c1950, dresser 4in (10cm) high, an Aga 2.25 by 3.25in (6 by 8cm) and a washing machine 3in (8cm) high.
£10-12 each *COL*

A group of dolls house miniatures and accessories, various dates.
£1,000-1,100 *S*

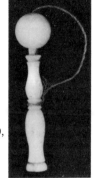

A dolls house bilboquet, c1880, 2in (5cm) high.
£30-45 *AMH*

A ceramic dolls house hip bath, 1920s, 3.5in (9cm) long.
£25-35 *STK*

A Victorian wickerwork cradle, 18in (46cm) long.
£50-60 *STK*

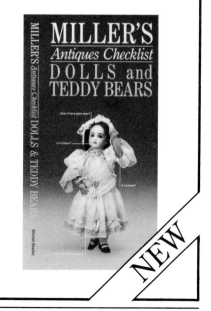

DRINKING

A Carlton Ware Flowers Brewery advertising ashtray, c1935, 9in (22.5cm) diam.
£35-55 *LIO*

A White Horse Whisky ceramic jug, with blue glaze and silver rim and handle, Shelley pottery mark, 5in (12.5cm) high.
£45-50 *BBR*

A Johnnie Walker character jug, by Ashtead Pottery, designed by Percy Metcalfe, 14in (35.5cm) high.
£250-350 *AOS*

A Truman's Ales & Stouts white glazed coaster, with Empire Works Stoke on Trent printed on base, 5.25in (13cm) diam.
£55-60 *BBR*

Meredith's Whiskey bottle, white with turquoise transfer, 7.5in (19cm) high.
£45-50 *BBR*

> **Cross Reference**
> Smoking
> Carlton Ware

A Cruiskeen Lawn Old Irish Whisky bottle, with Port Dundas Pottery mark, 7.25in (18cm) high.
£40-45 *BBR*

A carved and painted wood bottle stopper, with a lever in the back to raise the hat.
£10-15 *ROW*

A double-ended wine rack.
£40-45 *WEL*

Corkscrews

A silver-mounted boar tusk handle corkscrew with surface, Walker bell cap lifter and wire cutter, centre worm.
£250-275 *C*

A Thomason corkscrew, with decorated fruiting vines barrel, turned bone barrel, and cyphered helix worm, inner thread mechanism faulty.
£280-300 *C*

A French nickel plated single lever corkscrew, by Perille, c1880.
£120-150 *CS*

A souvenir key corkscrew, brass with antiqued verdigris finish.
£8-10 *CS*

A French Zig-Zag concertina corkscrew, c1920.
£25-35 *CS*

An all steel folding bow or harp corkscrew. **£10-15** *CS*

A Charles Hull's patent Royal Club corkscrew, 1864.
£750-800 *C*

An all steel four-pillar King's Screw, with turned bone handle, c1820.
£250-350 *CS*

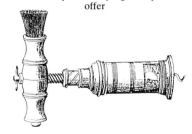

A mechanical corkscrew known as a London Rack, turned rosewood handle with steel body, c1860.
£55-65 *CS*

A Saml. Cotterrill Thomason corkscrew, with turned bone handle and brush, brass barrel and helix screw, 1802.
£230-250 *C*

A turned fruitwood handled T bar corkscrew, with dusting brush, c1830. **£15-25** *CS*

A turned walnut corkscrew, with T bar, brass stem and Henshall type button, c1840.
£35-45 *CS*

An English all steel seven tool pocket folding bow.
£90-100 *CS*

A King's Screw corkscrew, c1820.
£300-350 *CS*

A brass Farrow & Jackson type corkscrew, with wing-nut handle. **£65-75** *CS*

A corkscrew with patent ratchet mechanism, the barrel with applied gilt metal coat of arms, the turned bone handle fitted with a brush.
£230-250 *RBB*

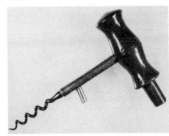

An English patent corkscrew combined Codd bottle marble ejector, marked Coney's Patent.
£35-45 *CS*

A hinged lever corkscrew, with wooden handle, helix screw stamped J. B. & Sons on shaft for J. Burgess and A. Fenton, tip short, 1874.
£1,500-1,750 *C*

A Thomason type brass barrel corkscrew, with Gothic window embossed decoration, bone handle with dusting brush, c1818. **£400-600** *CS*

A King's Screw with four-pillar open frame, turned bone handle and brush, steel raising handle and narrow side rack, helix screw. **£275-300** *C*

The Columbus, a German corkscrew with sprung stem, 19thC. **£35-45** *CS*

A German sprung stem corkscrew, with bladed worm, c1890. **£30-40** *CS*

A combination corkscrew, with turned ash wood handle and Codd bottle marble ejector. **£10-15** *CS*

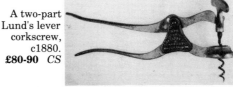

A two-part Lund's lever corkscrew, c1880. **£80-90** *CS*

A Rotary Eclipse brass mechanical cork drawer, c1880. **£400-500** *CS*

The circular base plate screws on to the top of a pub or coaching inn bar top.

A vintage barrel shaped brass corkscrew, with wooden handle. **£260-280** *GAK*

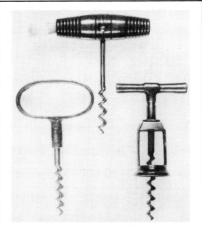

A turned barrel shaped handled corkscrew with dusting brush, an all steel Cellarmans type corkscrew, and an all steel Monopol corkscrew. **£10-30 each** *CS*

A combination corkscrew, with scissor type wire cutters, c1890. **£35-45** *CS*

A Holborn Signet corkscrew, with finger-ring set under the turned rosewood handle, and bladed worm, c1880. **£15-20** *CS*

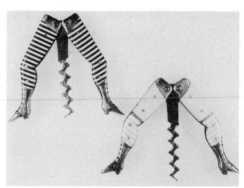

Two German Naughty Nineties corkscrews in celluloid and nickel silver, the ladies' legs flesh coloured with pink and white striped stockings. **£80-120** *CS*

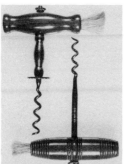

Two corkscrews with turned rosewood handles, both fitted with dusting brush and hanging ring, *top:* turned steel stem with Henshall Button, c1830. **£45-55,** *bottom:* turned barrel shaped handle, c1820. **£30-40** *CS*

A cast steel combination corkscrew, with crown cap opener and hooked blade, c1900. **£10-15** *CS*

Guinness

A Guinness barometer, c1960. **£20-25** *COB*

A Carlton Ware Guinness advertising lamp, in the form of a seal balancing a revolving metal sphere upon its nose. **£150-200** *PAR*

A Guinness clock, c1970. **£10-12** *COB*

A Carlton Ware penguin lamp for Arthur Guinness, with original revolving lampshade. **£150-175** *PAR*

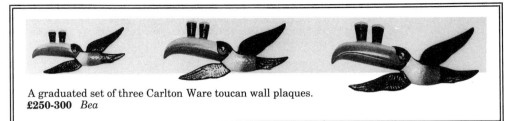

A graduated set of three Carlton Ware toucan wall plaques.
£250-300 *Bea*

A flower shaped 3 dimensional display with slots for bottles, inscribed 'Guinnessis Goodforia Andforallovus', c1950, 35.5in (90cm) high.
£120-130 *ONS*

A Carlton Ware Guinness advertising group, comprising: a man in an overall, a kangaroo in his pocket; a tortoise, a glass of Guinness on its back; a toucan; an ostrich; a sea- lion; and a kangaroo.
£400-500 the set *Bea*

Labels

Four Bacchanalian labels with mask, shell and vines border, die- stamped Claret, Sherry, Rum and Bucellas, c1825.
£280-300 *C*

Two escutcheon shaped labels, engraved Burgundy and Mountain, c1740, and 2 others.
£270-300 *C*

A Battersea enamel wine decanter label, inscribed Mountain, c1750.
£100-150 *CS*

A crescent shaped label, with pierced fretted edging, pierced Burgundy, Hester Bateman, c1770, and 3 others.
£350-375 *C*

Seven bisque pottery wine cellar bin labels, impressed on backs Wedgwood, Copeland Spode and Minton, c1850.
£20-70 each *CS*

A Sherry label by Peter and Anne Bateman, c1790, and 2 others.
£200-220 *C*

Egg Cups

A Victorian egg cup.
£15-20 *AA*

A sailor boy egg cup, 3.5in
(8.5cm) high.
£2-3 *ROS*

A porcelain egg cup, c1889.
£25-30 *AA*

A Worcester egg cup,
c1880. **£25-30** *AA*

A Mason's Ironstone egg
cup. **£18-22** *AA*

A set of 4 chrome Art Deco 'Style'
egg cups with covers, c1950.
£10-15 *COB*

A set of Shorter
Ware egg cups,
5in (12.5cm)
square.
£15-18 *COL*

A set of Doulton egg cups, c1920, 10in
(25cm) long. **£35-40** *AA*

A set of Crown Ducal egg cups.
£25-35 *AOS*

l. An egg cup, c1860, 2.5in
(6.5cm), **£25-30**
r. An egg cup, R. Hammersley &
Co., for T. Goode & Son, c1932,
2.5in (6.5cm) high, **£10-15** *AMH*

A set of porcelain egg cups, 19thC, 9in
(22.5cm) high. **£65-75** *AA*

EPHEMERA
Autographs

Henry Ford, signature on small card, VG. **£200-240** *VS*

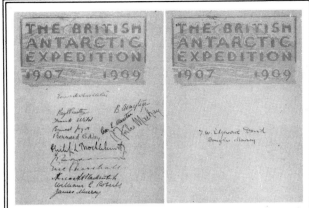

Ernest Shackleton, a set of 16 signatures of the members of the British Antarctic Expedition 1907-1909, on 2 sheets of headed notepaper. **£400-450** *VS*

George Bernard Shaw, signed piece, with one extra word in his hand, probably cut from the end of a letter, FR. **£55-60** *VS*

Cartoonists

Barry Appleby, an original Gambols 3-panel cartoon strip in pen and ink, 1984, G. **£40-60** *VS*

Thomas Edison, signature on large album page, G. **£80-125** *VS*

Reg Smythe, an original 3-panel Andy Capp cartoon strip in pen and ink, 1990, VG. **£60-80** *VS*

Charles M. Schulz, an original 3- panel Peanuts cartoon strip in pen and ink, 1991. **£325-350** *VS*

Charles M. Schulz, 2 individual album pages signed and inscribed and bearing original pen and ink sketch, G to VG. **£425-475** *VS*

Hank Ketcham, an original 12- panel Dennis the Menace cartoon strip in pen and ink, 1985, G. **£80-120** *VS*

Political

David Lloyd George, signed and mounted photograph by Lewis, silvering to top edge of image, G.
£65-75 *VS*

Mikhail Gorbachev, signed colour photograph, 11.75 by 9.25in (30 by 23cm), VG.
£375-400 *VS*

Sir Winston S Churchill, signed typed letter to Malcolm Dunbar, one page, 9th May 1958, FR-VG.
£500-550 *VS*

Lyndon B Johnson, signed colour heavystock magazine photograph, G.　　**£60-80** *VS*

Margaret Thatcher, signed photograph 8 by 6in (20 by 15cm), EX.
£80-100 *VS*

Sir Winston S Churchill, signed to mount, photograph by Walter Stoneman of London, extensive corner creasing, FR.
£725-775 *VS*

Ronald Reagan, signed photograph, inscribed 'To the Armed Service Directory Office in Hawaii', creased, 8 by 10in (20 by 25cm) VG.
£100-120 *VS*

Neville Chamberlain, signed hardback edition of The Struggle for Peace, dated June 1939, previously belonged to Sir Arthur N. Rucker, Chamberlain's private secretary as Minister of Health.
£120-150 *VS*

Theodore Roosevelt, signed postcard, G.
£150-165 *VS*

Royalty

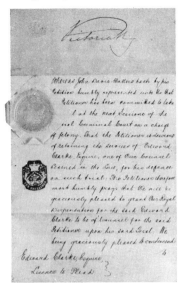

Queen Victoria, 2 pages, 8th November 1883, granting the lawyer Edward Clarke a Licence to plead in the trial of John Davis Walters, with embossed paper seal, VG.
£100-120 *VS*

Wallis, Duchess of Windsor, signed to mount, photograph by Dorothy Wilding also signed to mount, 7.5 by 5.25in (19 by 13cm), VG.
£280-320 *VS*

Queen Mary, Albert Duke of York (later King George VI) and Edward Prince of Wales (later King Edward VIII), one page given at the Court of Saint James's, 1st March 1929, granting the dignity of a Knight Grand Cross of the civil division of the Order of the British Empire to Sir Arthur Henry Crosfield, Baronet, G-VG.
£140-150 *VS*

Cross Reference
Royal Memorabilia

King George VI, 26th July 1941, a commission appointing Sir Wilfrid Edward Francis Jackson to be Governor and Commander-in-Chief of the Tanganyika Territory, VG.
£120-130 *VS*

Queen Alexandra, autograph telegram, to Captain Patterson, in pencil, G.   **£40-55** *VS*

EX	- Excellent
FR	- Fair
G	- Good
MT	- Mint
P	- Poor
VG	- Very Good

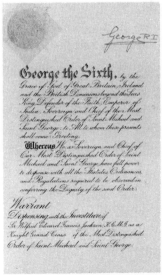

King George VI, 1st January 1943, signed document, granting the dignity of a Knight Grand Cross of the most Distinguished Order of Saint Michael and Saint George to Sir Wilfrid Edward Francis Jackson, VG.
£130-150 *VS*

Show Business

Enrico Caruso, signed
and inscribed postcard,
London 1907, FR-G.
£100-120 *VS*

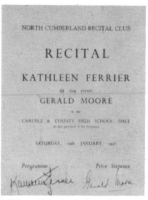

Kathleen Ferrier, signed concert
programme, also signed by Gerald
Moore, 19th January 1952, VG.
£100-120 *VS*

Charles Chaplin, signed sepia
photograph, 11 by 14.5in (28 by
37cm), P to FR.
£200-220 *VS*

Harpo Marx, signed
photograph, 8 by 10in
(20 by 25cm), G.
£110-130 *VS*

Kirk Douglas and Barbara
Stanwyck, signed and inscribed
photograph, 8.5 by 6.5in (21 by
16cm).
£30-40 *VS*

Edith Piaf, signed French
programme, VG.
£120-130 *VS*

Alfred Hitchcock, signed
photograph in white crayon, 11.5
by 7.5in (29 by 19cm), P-FR.
£150-175 *VS*

FRANK SINATRA

Frank Sinatra, signed
photograph, 1991, 8 by 10in (20
by 25cm), VG.
£60-75 *VS*

Jim Henson, signed and inscribed
7 by 7.5in (18 by 19cm) piece, also
signed Frank Oz, VG.
£40-60 *VS*

Errol Flynn, signed
photograph, 5.75 by
9in (14 by 23cm), FR.
£90-100 *VS*

Laurence Olivier,
signed postcard,
G.
£40-60 *VS*

Laurel and Hardy, signed and
inscribed sepia, 8 by 10in (20 by
25cm), FR to G.
£400-450 *VS*

Marilyn Monroe, black and white
photograph, signed and inscribed
To Bob Couture, small creases,
9.5 by 7.5in (24 by 19cm).
£900-1,000 *CNY*

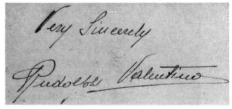

Rudolph Valentino, signed piece,
G to VG.
£200-220 *VS*

Lucille Ball, signed
photograph, 8.5 by
6.5in (21 by 16cm),
G-VG.
£40-60 *VS*

Richard Burton, in Roman
Costume, signed photograph , 6
by 9in (15 by 23cm), G.
£40-45 *VS*

Ghostbusters, signed by Dan
Ackroyd, Harold Ramis
and Rick Moranis, colour,
10.5 by 8.5in (26
by 21cm), VG.
£40-45 *VS*

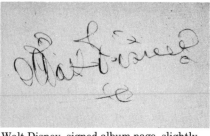

Walt Disney, signed album page, slightly scratchy ink, VG. **£300-350** *VS*

Mel Blanc, signed and inscribed colour photograph, half length sat at desk surrounded by various cartoon characters including Bugs Bunny, 21st September 1981, 8 by 10in (20 by 25cm), VG. **£30-40** *VS*

Charles Laughton, signed photograph, 7.5 by 9.5in (19 by 24cm), VG. **£40-60** *VS*

Mack Sennett, signed album page. **£70-85** *VS*

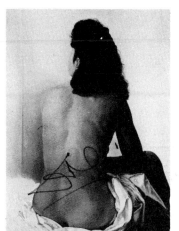

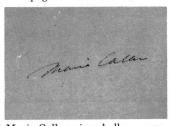

Maria Callas, signed album page, VG. **£80-120** *VS*

Elizabeth Taylor, signed photograph in costume from Beau Brummel inscribed to the photographer Fred Daniels, 10 by 7.5in (25 by 19cm), G. **£60-80** *VS*

Salvador Dali, signed colour magazine reproduction of one of his paintings featuring Gala, VG. **£65-70** *VS*

Ingrid Bergman, signed postcard, G. **£50-60** *VS*

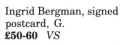

Brigitte Bardot, signed postcard, Picturegoer No. D682, VG. **£20-30** *VS*

John Wayne, signed postcard, Picturegoer No. W477, VG. **£100-120** *VS*

Jayne Mansfield, signed postcard, 2nd October, 1957, VG. **£100-120** *VS*

A collection of autographs and photographs from the cast of The Wizard Of Oz, MGM, 1939, including Judy Garland, pen and ink on paper matted and framed with a photograph of the movie star. **£2,200-2,500** *S(NY)*

Freddie Mercury, signed colour photograph 8.5 by 12in (21 by 31cm), EX.
£150-175 *VS*

Jimi Hendrix, signed photograph, also partially signed by Noel Redding, 6 by 4in (15 by 10cm).
£300-325 *VS*

The Rolling Stones, signed Decca EP to both sides of sleeve, FR-G.
£200-225 *VS*

Cross Reference
Rock & Pop

The Beatles, all 4 signatures on 4.25 by 4.75in (10.5 by 12cm) piece, VG-EX.
£600-650 *VS*

Cigarette Cards

John Player & Sons, Straight
Line Caricatures, set of 50, 1926.
Grade 2 £20-25
Grade 1 £40-50 *ACC*

W.D & H.O. Wills, Arms of Oxford
& Cambridge Colleges, set of 42, 1922.
Grade 2 £40-50
Grade 1 £85-95 *ACC*

W.D. & H.O. Wills, Household
Hints, set of 50, 1927.
Grade 2 £8-12
Grade 1 £18-22 *ACC*

W.D. & H.O. Wills,
Romance of the
Heavans, set of 50,
1928.
Grade 2 £15-18
Grade 1 £30-35
ACC

W.D. & H.O. Wills, Arms of
Universities, set of 25, 1923.
Grade 2 £25-35
Grade 1 £55-65 *ACC*

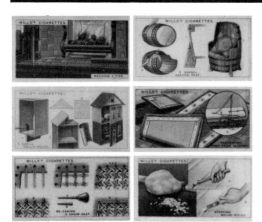

W.D. & H.O. Wills, Household
Hints, set of 50, 1930.
Grade 2 £16-20
Grade 1 £35-40 *ACC*

F. & J. Smith, Famous Explorers,
set of 50, slight foxing and
scuffing to reverse, otherwise VG.
£220-250 *VS*

W.D. & H.O. Wills, Old Furniture,
set of 25, 1923.
Grade 2 £70-80
Grade 1 £140-160 *ACC*

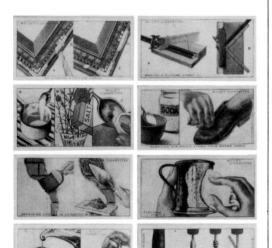

W.D. & H.O. Wills, Household
Hints, set of 50, 1936.
Grade 2 £6-8
Grade 1 £10-12 *ACC*

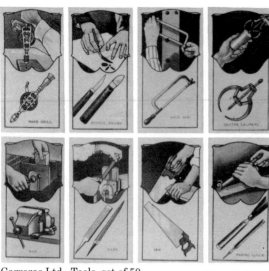

Carreras Ltd., Tools, set of 50,
1925.
Grade 2 £32-38
Grade 1 £65-75 *ACC*

W.D. & H.O. Wills, Old Silver, set
of 25, 1924.
Grade 2 £55-65
Grade 1 £110-130 *ACC*

Ardath Tobacco Co. Ltd., Empire
Personalities, set of 50, 1937.
Grade 2 £28-32
Grade 1 £48-52 *ACC*

Cavenders Ltd., Ancient Egypt,
set of 25, 1928.
Grade 2 £12-18
Grade 1 £28-32 *ACC*

W.A. & A.C. Churchman,
Holidays in Britain, set of 48,
1937.
Grade 2 £8-10
Grade 1 £12-15 *ACC*

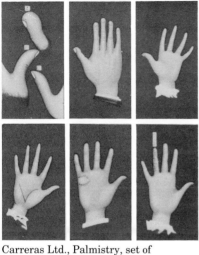

Carreras Ltd., Palmistry, set of
50, 1933.
Grade 2 £12-18
Grade 1 £22-28   *ACC*

W.D. & H.O. Wills, Gems of Russian Architecture, set
of 50, 1916.
Grade 2 £25-35
Grade 1 £55-65   *ACC*

Carreras Ltd., Notable M.Ps, set
of 50, 1929.
Grade 2 £32-38
Grade 1 £60-70

W.A. & A.C. Churchman,
Well Known Ties, Second
Series, set of 50, 1934.
Grade 2 £22-25
Grade 1 £38-42   *ACC*

Carreras Ltd., Happy Family,
set of 48, 1925.
Grade 2 £8-12
Grade 1 £20-22   *ACC*

Military

W.A. & A.C. Churchman, The
Navy at Work, set of 48, 1937.
Grade 2 £6-10
Grade 1 £12-16 *ACC*

Natural History

W.D. & H.O. Wills,
Animalloys,
set of 48, 1934.
Grade 2 £8-12
Grade 1 £18-22 *ACC*

Ogden's, Poultry, set of 25,
1916.
Grade 2 £55-65
Grade 1 £115-125 *ACC*

Gallaher Ltd., Army Badges, set
of 48, 1939.
Grade 2 £22-25
Grade 1 £35-38 *ACC*

W.A. & A.C. Churchman,
Warriors of all Nations, set of 25,
1929.
Grade 2 £55-65
Grade 1 £95-105 ACC

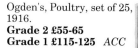

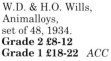

John Player & Sons, Animals of
the Countryside, set of 50, 1939.
Grade 2 £10-12
Grade 1 £18-20 *ACC*

W.D & H.O. Wills, Garden Flowers, set of 50, 1939.
Grade 2 £6-10   **Grade 1 £12-16** *ACC*

Show Business

Carreras Ltd., Glamour Girls, set
of 54, 1939.
Grade 2 £12-16
Grade 1 £18-24 *ACC*

W.D. & H.O. Wills, Flowering
Shrubs, set of 30, 1935.
Grade 2 £25-30
Grade 1 £55-60 ACC

Ardath Tobacco Co. Ltd., Famous
Film Stars, set of 50, 1934.
Grade 2 £32-38
Grade 1 £50-60 *ACC*

W.D. & H.O. Wills, Cinema Stars, set of 50, 1931.
Grade 2 £55-65
Grade 1 £110-130 *ACC*

Carreras Ltd., Film & Stage
Beauties, set of 54, 1939.
Grade 2 £10-14
Grade 1 £16-20 *ACC*

Grade 2 - Good Condition
Grade 1 - Excellent to Mint

Sport

W.A. & A.C. Churchman, Rugby
Internationals, set of 50, 1935.
Grade 2 £55-65
Grade 1 £110-130 *ACC*

John Player & Sons, Derby and
Grand National Winners, set of
50, 1933.
Grade 2 £75-80
Grade 1 £150-170 *ACC*

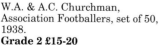

W.A. & A.C. Churchman,
Association Footballers, set of 50,
1938.
Grade 2 £15-20
Grade 1 £35-38 *ACC*

W.D. & H.O. Wills, British
Sporting Personalities, set of 48,
1927.
Grade 2 £22-28
Grade 1 £35-45 *ACC*

Transport

Gallaher Ltd., Trains of the World, set of 48, 1937.
Grade 2 £28-32
Grade 1 £42-48 *ONS*

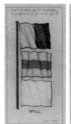

International Tobacco Co. Ltd., International Code of Signals, set of 50, 1934.
Grade 2 £10-14
Grade 1 £20-25 *ACC*

W.D & H.O. Wills, Famous British Liners, set of 30, 1935.
Grade 2 £70-75
Grade 1 £140-150 *ACC*

Continental Trade Cards

The following cards were issued in OXO products all over Europe in several languages, always using the same artwork.

Liebig, Horse Drawn Vehicles, set of 6, 1897.
£50-75 *ACC*

Liebig, War Ships, Series 1, set of 6, 1897.
£20-30 *ACC*

Comics

If you are thinking of starting a collection of comics, a good rule is to focus on a particular company, character or artist and to concentrate on collecting everthing to do with that aspect before widening your scope.

It is important to remember that the price ranges shown in this book are just a guide and that the true value of a comic is what it is worth to you. However, do bear in mind two points: Firstly, British comics tend to be cheaper than American comics at present but given the astronomical price growth in recent years, this margin may soon narrow. Secondly, condition is vital so do steer away from damaged or brown, brittle comics. You will never be able to read the latter without bits falling off and in two years or so, you will be the proud owner of a bag of paper chips.

The last decade or two has seen the introduction of the comic speculator. Childhood memories can have a hard cash value. The only good to come from this is that at least comics are now appearing on the market instead of ending up in waste paper drives, which was the fate of millions of back issues!

Action, No. 27, D.C. Comics, 1940.
£180-200 *NOS*

All Select, No. 4, Timely, 1944.
£80-100 *NOS*

The Kinema, No. 312, Amalgamated Press, 1926. **£5-8** *NOS*

Crackers, No. 266, Amalgamated Press, 1934.
£8-10 *NOS*

Boys and Girls, Associated Newspapers, 1936.
£5-8 *NOS*

Superman, No. 12, D.C. Comics, 1941.
£200-225 *NOS*

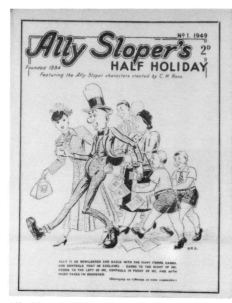

Ally Sloper's Half Holiday, No. 1,
Ally Sloper Publications, 1949.
£3-5 *NOS*

Young Allies, No. 13,
Timely, 1944.
£70-80 *NOS*

The Champion, Volume III,
No. 21, 1895.
£8-10 *NOS*

Big Shot, No. 52, Columbia
Comic Corporation, 1945.
£8-12 *NOS*

The Rover, No. 1131,
D.C. Thompson, 1946.
£1-3 *NOS*

The Wizard, No. 1023, featuring Wilson, D.C.
Thompson, 1943. **£3-5** *NOS*

Comet, No. 24, J.B. Allen,
1947.
£1.50-2.50 *NOS*

Sun, No. 1, J.B. Allen, 1947.
£7-10 *NOS*

The School
Friend, No. 1,
The first Bessie
Bunter story,
Fleetway
Publications,
1919.
£40-50 *NOS*

Lion, No. 115,
Amalgamated Press,
1954.
£1.50-2.50 *NOS*

The Hotspur, No. 786,
D.C. Thompson, 1951.
£3-4 *NOS*

Ghost Rider, No. 11, M.E.,
1953.   **£18-22** *NOS*

Green Lantern, No. 24,
D.C. Comics, 1960.
£100-125 *NOS*

Girl, Volume VIII,
No. 18, Hulton
Press, 1959.
£1-2 *NOS*

Family Star, No. 542,
D.C. Thompson,
1947.
£1-2 *NOS*

The Hornet, No. 369,
D.C. Thompson,
1970.
£1-2 *NOS*

Boyfriend, No. 116, City
Magazines, 1961.
£1.50-2.50 *NOS*

Pluck, No. 2, L. Miller,
1955.
£1.50-2.50 *NOS*

Romeo, D.C. Thompson,
1970.
50p-£1 *NOS*

Adventure, No. 174, D.C. Comics,
1952.
£40-50 *NOS*

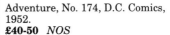

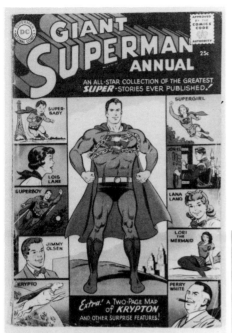

Giant Superman Annual, No. 1,
D.C. Comics, 1960.
£60-80 *NOS*

Al Capps Shmoo, No. 5,
Toby Press Inc., 1950.
£35-45 *NOS*

Toytown, No. 1, Williams
Pub. & Dist., 1972.
£2-3 *NOS*

The Hotspur, Nos. 792,
795 and 799, D.C.
Thompson, 1952.
£2.50-3.50 each *NOS*

Dandy and Nutty, No. 2292, D.C.
Thompson, 1985.
50p-£1 *NOS*

Ovaltiney's, No. 105, Target
Publications, 1937.
£5-8 *NOS*

Misty, Holiday Special,
1980.
£2-3 *NOS*

The Rover, Nos. 1134, 1136, 1143, 1145, 1146 and 1151, D.C. Thompson, 1946.
£1-3 each *NOS*

Princess, I.P.C., 1963.
£5-7.50
NOS

Jinty, No. 1, I.P.C., 1974.
£1-2 *NOS*

All Winners, No. 5, Timely, 1942.
£180-200 *NOS*

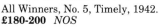

Diana for Girls, No. 19, D.C. Thompson, 1963.
50p-£1 *NOS*

Valiant and Lion, I.P.C., 1974.
£1-2 *NOS*

Sixties newcomer swallows up the fifties title.

Tarzan, No. 1, Byblos Productions, with free gift 'Survival Kit Bag', 1977.
£2-3 *NOS*

Battle, No. 1, I.P.C., 1975.
£1-2 *NOS*

Princess Tina, I.P.C., 1970.
50p-£1 *NOS*

Lindy, No. 1, I.P.C., 1975.
£1-2 *NOS*

The Victor, No. 503, D.C. Thompson, 1970.
£1-2 *NOS*

Princess, I.P.C., 1966.
£1-2 *NOS*

Solo, Nos. 3 and 14, City Magazines/Century 21, 1967.
£2-4 each *NOS*

Diana, No. 159, D.C. Thompson, 1966.
50p-£1 *NOS*

Greetings Cards

An early plastic card, with
felt flowers, 6 by 3.5in
(15 by 9cm).
£13-18 *LB*

A mechanical hand
coloured lithographic
card, by Dean & Son,
and 4 others.
£160-180 *CSK*

Ten hand coloured
engraved valentine
cards, all with
printed humorous
verses, c1855.
£150-175 *CSK*

Magazines

The Aero, Volume I to
VII, nos 1- 122, bound in
7 volumes with indices,
May 25th 1909-May 1913.
£160-180 *ONS*

Cross Reference
Aeronautica

What To Do If It's Catching,
c1930.
£1-1.50 *COL*

Two copies of Aero Modeller, 1957/58. **£1-3 each** *COL*

Flight, an illustrated
weekly journal of aerial
locomotion and transport,
Volume I to VIII, bound
in publisher's cloth with
indices, January 1909-
December 1916.
£575-600 *ONS*

Meccano Magazines, 1957-59.
£1-1.50 each *COL*

1930s manuals.
£50p-£1 each *COL*

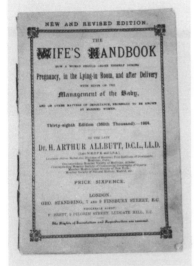

The Wife's Handbook, 7in (18cm)
high. **£3-5** *ROS*

Leach's Wool Embroidery
magazines, with transfers, c1929.
£2-3 each *COL*

Scraps

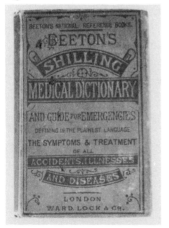

Beeton's Shilling Medical
Dictionary, c1930.
£5-8 *ROS*

A collection in modern photograph album, G. **£100-120** *VS*

Fairgrounds

A Bayol prancing carousel horse, c1900, 56in (142cm) long.
£1,000-1,100 *REL*

A Chanvin fairground pig, c1905, 38in (96.5cm) long.
£400-500 *REL*

A Matthieu carousel camel, c1930, 39in (99cm) long.
£650-750 *REL*

A French papier mâché Revolution figure, 27in (69cm) high. **£180-220** *REL*

A Bayol fairground pig, 29in (74cm) long.
£500-600 *REL*

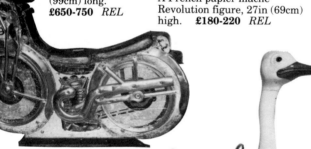

A wood motorcycle.
£80-100 *REL*

A Matthieu fairground duck, 37in (94cm) long.
£900-1,000 *REL*

A French carousel swan by Limonaire, 29in (74cm) long.
£350-400 *REL*

A Matthieu carousel ostrich, 42in (106.5cm) high.
£450-550 *REL*

A French fairground dog, c1930, 33in (84cm) long.
£700-800 *REL*

A French fairground nodding donkey, c1910, 38in (96.5cm) long.
£400-500 *REL*

A painted fairground sign, 40in (101.5cm) high.
£200-225 *REL*

A French carousel cat, 25in (64cm) long.
£400-500 *REL*

A French fairground pig, c1890, 31in (79cm) long.
£450-550 *REL*

A French fairground poodle, c1910, 30in (76cm) long.
£450-550 *REL*

A Devos fairground swan, 31in (79cm) long.
£500-600 *REL*

One of a pair of fairground horses. **£250-350** *REL*

An English fairground clown game.
£200-275 *REL*

A carved wood lady from centre of a carousel, 54in (137cm) high.
£800-900 *REL*

A Bayol fairground cat, c1890, 35in (89cm) long.
£700-800 *REL*

A Tunnel of Love boat.
£200-250 *REL*

A Mexican carousel horse, 37in (94cm) long.
£450-550 *REL*

A French fairground rabbit, by Limonaire, c1890, 37in (94cm) long.
£500-600 *REL*

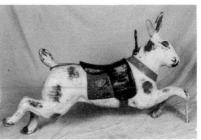

A French carousel rabbit, 34in (86cm) long.
£500-600 *REL*

A French fairground goat, c1890, 23in (59cm) long.
£550-600 *REL*

A pair of painted wood fairground signs, 21 by 27in (53 by 69cm).
£300-350 *REL*

A Devos fairground turkey, 35in (89cm) long.
£700-800 *REL*

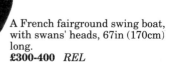

A French fairground swing boat, with swans' heads, 67in (170cm) long.
£300-400 *REL*

A carousel goat, by Cognereaux Marèchal, with brass horns.
£450-500 *REL*

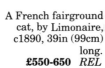

A French fairground cat, by Limonaire, c1890, 39in (99cm) long.
£550-650 *REL*

A Devos carnival carved wood horse, 32in (81cm) long.
£450-550 *REL*

A French carousel donkey, with moving head, 29in (74cm) long.
£350-450 *REL*

A Spanish carousel bull, 54in (137cm) long.
£1,000-1,100 *REL*

Fans

A fan illustrating Aix-les-Bains Les Hôtels Splendide Royal & Excelsior, 10in (25cm) high.
£110-125 *YV*

A brisé fan painted with a cat and a border of mice, the verso with mice by a mousetrap, signed F. Lots, ribbon loose, c1900, 5in (13cm).
£400-450 *C*

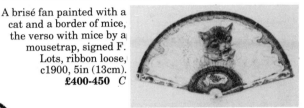

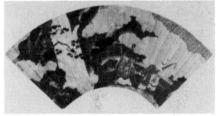

A dismounted fan leaf, painted with a sage and musicians watching a waterfall, Japanese, Kano School, c1700, 19in (48cm) wide, framed and glazed.
£850-900 *C*

A Japanese ivory brisé fan, lacquered in gold with a landscape and volcano, the verso with quail, butterflies and flowers, late 19thC, 10.5in (26cm).
£2,600-2,800 *CSK*

A painted fan with an Assemblage of Gods, the verso with Roman soldiers in a landscape, with carved and pierced mother-of-pearl sticks, English or Flemish, c1765, 11in (28cm).
£925-975 *CSK*

Bought in Moscow in 1888.

A Dutch fan, the leaf painted with an allegory of Love, with carved ivory sticks, c1760, 11in (28cm). **£450-475** *C*

A Japanese ivory brisé fan, gold lacquered with cranes and other birds, the guardsticks decorated with Shibayama work birds and flowers, c1880, 11.5in (29cm). **£3,250-3,500** *C*

A painted fan depicting El Cid defeating the Moors, the verso with a distant view of the battle, ivory sticks pierced and gilt with the arms of Spain, 2 sticks broken, c1750. **£500-550** *CSK*

A lithographic fan, printed with a Turkish scene, the sticks of Mauchline Ware, the guardsticks with scenes of Loch Leven Castle and Castle of Caldwall, some damage, c1860, 11in (28cm). **£575-600** *C*

Le Chat Qui Crie, the silk leaf painted with a cat signed A. Thomasse, embroidered with sequins, horn sticks, some wear, c1905, 9in (23cm). **£1,250-1,350** *C*

A chicken skin fan painted with a view of Rome, the verso with a ruin in the Campagna, ivory sticks, one repaired, c1780, 10.5in (26cm), in contemporary fan box labelled Robt. Clarke, 26 Strand. **£1,750-1,950** *C*

A fan, the leaf painted with a classical scene, the verso with lovers by a monument, the pierced, silvered mother-of-pearl sticks carved, and gilt, c1750, 19thC, 11.5in (29cm) box by Rodien. **£1,400-1,500** *C*

A fan, the leaf painted with figures in 18thC dress, signed E. Chenneviere, tortoiseshell sticks carved and pierced, c1890, 12in (30.5cm), in Duvelleroy box. **£1,250-1,500** *C*

FISHING

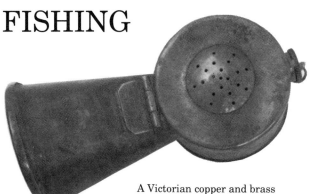

A Victorian copper and brass maggot shute. **£90-100** *EP*

A still life, oil on canvas picture of various fish, dated 1897, 25 by 18in (64 by 46cm).
£400-600 *GHA*

Various novelty items shaped as fish, i.e. butter dishes, ashtrays, bottle openers, etc.
£10-30 each *CPT*

A live bait can, 19thC, 7in (18cm) square. **£35-50** *GHA*

A japanned fly tin, with 6 trays holding 168 gut-eyed salmon flies, by C. Farlow & Co., 8.75 by 5in (22 by 13cm).
£500-600 *GHA*

A willow creel with brass fittings, by C. Farlow, 191 Strand, London, 10in (25.5cm) wide.
£165-185 *GHA*

A Hardy Weroda salmon fly box, with 30 flies, 6.25 by 8in (16 by 20cm) when open.
£80-100 *GHA*

A black japanned fly box, with extra section in the middle, to hold 100 flies, by Malloch of Perth.
£15-20 *JMG*

An antique shell fish scraper net **£50-60** and a galvanised live bait trap. **£70-80** *CPT*

A fishing net, 45in (114cm) long.
£40-60 *GHA*

A wicker creel, 11in (28cm) wide. **£65-85** *GHA*

A silver fish, made in India, c1930, 12in (31cm) long. **£40-50** *JMG*

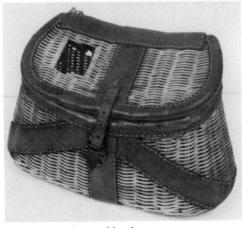

A Scottish wicker and leather creel, 13in (33cm) wide. **£100-120** *GHA*

Two pigskin fly wallets, 7.5 by 5in (19 by 13cm). **£40-60 each** *GHA*

A Hardy wooden pear shaped landing net, with folding knuckle joint, fitted on Hardy extending Greenheart and bamboo shaft. **£175-195** *ND*

A Hardy rosewood box, No. 2, fitted with ivory leaves, 1911. **£200-225** *ND*

A fishing knife, made in Sheffield with silver outside finish, 3.5in (9cm). **£8-10** *JMG*

Two Victorian wooden tackle compendiums: *l.* A wood book type. **£40-45** *r.* Tubular design with detachable inner compartments. **£100-150** *CPT*

A fishing knife, made in Sheffield. **£8-12** *JMG*

An brass line drier, with wooden handle, 19thC, 17.5in (44cm) high. **£165-185** *GHA*

A brown trout mounted in bowfront case, with label 'Killed on Loch Beannoch June 1903', 40in (101.5cm) wide. **£500-600** *GHA*

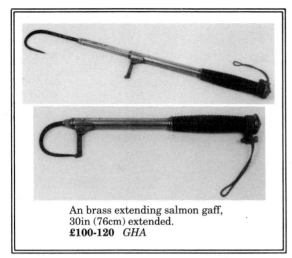

An brass extending salmon gaff,
30in (76cm) extended.
£100-120 *GHA*

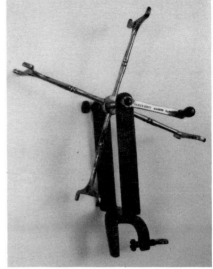

A line drier, with 4 brass arms
and spindle, with 3.5in (9cm)
brass crank stamped Hardy Bros,
Makers Alnwick, set in U-shaped
steel frame with affixed brass
clamp fitting, c1896.
£155-175 *EP*

A plaster cast salmon, J.M.V.
May 1907, Thurso, Caithness,
case 45.5in (115cm) long.
£800-1,200 *GHA*

Two wood priests, 8 and 9.5in (20
and 24cm) long.
£40-60 each *GHA*

A bamboo and brass fishing gaff,
43in (109cm) long.
£20-30 *GHA*

Three roach in bowfront gilt lined
case, by J. Cooper & Sons, 29in
(74cm) long.
£650-700 *ND*

A bowfront case, with gilt edging
and label 'Trout found dying
below Town Mill, Hungerford on
9th June 1914 - 8lb 14oz length
27in', J. Cooper & Sons, 32.5in
(82cm) long.
£500-550 *ND*

A fishing net, with brass fittings
and bamboo, 66in (167.5cm).
£75-100 *GHA*

A pair of Hardy half-moon spirit
flasks, with glass stoppers and SP
caps, 3.5in (9cm) diam., in
maker's leather case.
£225-250 *ND*

Reels
Hardy

A 2¾in Hardy Perfect reel, wide drum, ivorine handle, c1910. **£70-100** *JMG*

A 2½in Hardy Perfect reel, alloy with ivory handle, strap tension regulator, 1896 check. **£800-850** *ND*

A 2¾in Hardy Perfect brass faced trout fly reel. **£750-850** *ND*

A 2¾in Hardy Perfect all brass trout reel, with rod and shaded hand trademark, ivory handle, Pat. Nos. 18373 - 612, strapped tension screw, dished drum with central well and large and small perforations, nickel silver rim and pillars, brass ball bearings in open race. **£1,000-1,250** *EP*

FURTHER READING

Fishing Tackle, A Collectors Guide, Graham Turner, Ward Lock

A 2⅝in Hardy Perfect transitional brass reel. **£2,650-2,850** *ND*

A 6in Hardy Longstone Dorado reel, known as 'General Harrison Pattern', ratchet check action, brake indicator and dial, brass ribbed foot, stamped Pat. No. 272409. **£425-450** *ND*

A 3¼in Hardy The Field reel, alloy with ivorine handle and smooth brass foot, c1900. **£180-200** *ND*

A 3in Hardy brass reel, with
small Hardy name on face and
Edinburgh, probably 1880s,
£80-100 *JMG*

A 5in Hardy Silex No. 2
brass sea fishing reel.
£200-300 *JMG*

*Not shown in Hardy's
catalogues.*

A 3in Hardy Super Silex casting
reel, with twin black handles,
white indicator dial, ivorine check
handle and grooved brass foot, in
leather bag and maker's box.
£220-250 *EP*

*The 3in Super Silex reel was
discontinued c1939.*

A 3⅝in Hardy Cascapedia reel,
with ebonite front and backplates,
nickel silver rims, the backplate
having knurled check adjuster
with 7 red marked settings with
on and off ratchet control.
£4,000-4,500 *EP*

*This reel was made for export
between 1932 and 1939.*

A 2⅝in Hardy 'Field' alloy trout fly reel, with fixed check, ivorine handle, brass drum, pillars and foot.
£360-400 *EP*

This is the smallest 'Field' reel made.

A 4⅝in Hardy Ebona sea reel, with central milled nut controlling brake pressure, twin horn handles and circular line guide attached to foot.
£175-200 *EP*

A 3⅝in Hardy Perfect early silent check trout fly reel, with ivorine handle, strapped tension screw, and brass foot, in maker's box.
£1,000-1,200 *EP*

The early silent Perfect reel was made from 1908 to 1910.

A 3¼in Hardy The Special Perfect reel.
£150-200 *JMG*

A 4in Hardy Perfect brass faced salmon fly reel, with rod and hand trademark, strapped tension screw with turks head locking nut, ivorine handle, brass foot and 1905 check.
£200-220 *EP*

A 3¾in Hardy Uniqua Spitfire model reel, from World War II, manufactured by Jimmy Smith.
£80-100 *JMG*

A 2⅞in Hardy Uniqua Pup Mark II telephone latch reel.
£65-75 *GHA*

A collection of 5 Bakelite centre pins, including a Gyrex, Allcocks Aerialite and Modernite Pixie.
£5-20 each *CPT*

A 4in Hardy Perfect brass faced reel with ivorine handle, hand trademark, 1896.
£500-600 *GHA*

A 3¾in Hardy Uniqua reel, with ivorine handle and wide drum, c1912.
£40-50 *JMG*

A 2⅞in Hardy Perfect duplicated MkII reel.
£80-90 *GHA*

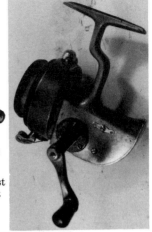

A 4½in Hardy Megstone wood reel, 1920s. **£70-100** *JMG*

A Hardy The Jock-Scott spinning reel, possibly late 1940s. **£100-130** *JMG*

A Hardy 'The Altex' reel, first model with unusual curve at the bottom of the body. **£200-250** *JMG*

A 4½in Hardy Perfect brass faced salmon fly reel, with rod and hand trademark, nickel silver centre engraved 'Hardy's Patent Alnwick', strapped tension screw, inscribed 'W.H.S'. Cutler 2, ivorine handle, brass foot, 1905 check. **£425-450** *EP*

A Hardy Altex No. 2 MkIII reel. **£55-65** *GHA*

A 2½in Hardy Hercules all brass reel, with rod and hand trademark. **£300-400** *GHA*

General

A Howban Birmingham sidecasting alloy reel, twin handles and sliding line guide.
£160-180 *ND*

A 4½in Carter of London drum reel, by Walter Dingley.
£40-60 *JMG*

Dingley left Hardy's in 1910 and started his own business.

A 4½in G. Little of London reel, marked 'Makers to HRH Prince of Wales', 1880s.
£40-50 *JMG*

A 3¼in Ocean City Automatic reel, American, modern.
£20-30 *JMG*

A 3in Chevalier Bowness & Bowness brass reel, with ivory handle, 1880s.
£40-60 *JMG*

A 3¼in Edward Vom Hofe of America reel, patented 1902.
£60-80 *JMG*

Three freshwater spinning multipliers:
Top. Record 1550. **£85-95**
Bottom l. Youngs Gildex. **£20-25**
Bottom r. Hardy Elarex. **£25-30**
CPT

A Farlow Billiken multiplier reel, with counterbalanced crank, ivorine handle, in maker's oak box with compartment containing 5 spare vanes. **£700-720** *EP*

A 4in rosewood and brass plate reel, with ivory handle.
£200-220 *GHA*

A 4¾in Ogden Smith wide drum sea fishing reel.
£40-60 *JMG*

A 3¾in Malloch of Perth Sun & Planet fly reel, designed for use on the river Tay.
£60-80 *JMG*

Walt Disney, Fantasia, 1940,
9in (22.5cm) high.
£2,600-2,800 *CNY*

Walt Disney, Tinkerbelle, from Peter
Pan, 1953, 11in (28cm) wide.
£7,000-7,500 *CNY*

Walt Disney, Make Mine Music:
Peter and the Wolf, 1946, 9.25in
(23cm) wide. **£2,000-2,500** *CNY*

Walt Disney, Lady & The Tramp
Visit the Zoo, 1955, 29.5in (75cm)
long. **£9,500-10,000** *CNY*

Walt Disney, So Dear To My
Heart, The Nativity Scene, 1949.
£1,300-1,500 *CNY*

Walt Disney, The Pointer, 1939,
11in (28cm) long.
£3,000-3,500 *CNY*

l. Warner Bros, Rabbit Seasoning,
watercolour on paper, 1952, 32.5in
(82cm) long. **£5,700-5,900** *CNY*

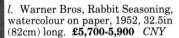

Walt Disney, Fantasia,
1940, 9in (22.5cm) long.
£8,500-9,000 *CNY*

Walt Disney, 101 Dalmations,
1961, 18in (46cm) long.
£6,400-6,600 *CNY*

A poster by Jules Chéret, 2 sheets joined, linen backed, damp stain, worn on folds, repaired, 1894, 96in (243.5in) high. **£450-475** *BBA*

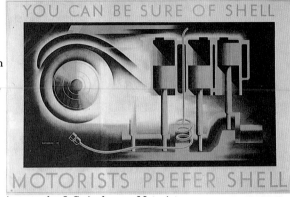

A poster by J. S. Anderson, Motorists Prefer Shell, 1935. **£1,750-1,950** *BBA*

A poster by Abram Games, c1941, fold marks, 30in (76cm) high. **£350-400** *BBA*

A Saville Lumley poster. **£550-575** *BBA*

A poster by E. Kealey, 29.5in (75cm) high. **£300-350** *BBA*

A poster by Eller, some damage, c1935. **£550-575** *BBA*

A poster by Jules Chéret, 2 sheets joined, backed, some damage and minor repairs, 1890, 90in (228in) high. **£450-470** *BBA*

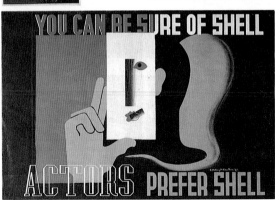

A poster by Edward McKnight Kauffer, some damage, c1935. **£2,100-2,250** *BBA*

Italy For Your Holidays, by Austin Cooper, McCorquodale & Co., 1934. **£850-875** *BBA*

Travels in Space on your Doorstep, by Clifford and Rosemary Ellis, 1937. **£400-425** *BBA*

Münchener Festsommer 1935, by Ludwig Hohlwein, 47.5in (121cm) high. **£200-225** *BBA*

Norwich, It's Quicker By Rail, by Claude Muncaster, Gilmour & Dean, c1935. **£360-380** *BBA*

Frankfort O/M Via Harwich, by Fred Taylor, Vincent Brooks, Day & Son Ltd., c1935. **£230-250** *BBA*

Barbados, Outposts of Empire, Post Office. **£180-200** *BBA*

To The Far East, Canadian Pacific White Empress Route, c1936. **£275-295** *BBA*

Favorites, Business prizes go only to those who earn them. Let's Deserve, by Willard Frederick Elmes. **£300-325** *BBA*

Central Australia, Outposts of Empire, Post Office. **£120-130** *BBA*

Double Indemnity,
Paramount, 1944.
£1,700-1,900   *CNY*

Son of Frankenstein, Universal, 1939,
41in (104cm).   **8,200-8,400**   *CNY*

She Married Her Boss,
Columbia, 1935.
£1,900-2,100   *CNY*

Warner Bros., 1938, 81in (205.5cm)
£11,500-12,500   *CNY*

Universal, 1954, 41in (104cm).
£2,700-2,900   *CNY*

Warner Brothers, 1941, 41in
(104cm).   **£3,200-3,500**   *CNY*

Gun Crazy, United Artists,
1950.   **£2,700-2,900**   *CNY*

Casablanca, Warner
Brothers, 1943, 11in
(28cm).
£2,900-3,100   *CNY*

King Kong, RKO, 1933, 81in
(205.5cm).   **£33,000-35,000**   *CNY*

The Other Man, Triangle-Keystone, 1916, 41in (104cm).
£1,400-1,500 *CNY*

The Virginian, Paramount, 1929, 41in (104cm).
£3,700-3,900 *CNY*

Citizen Kane, RKO, 1941, 41in (104cm).
£12,500-12,800 *CNY*

Out West, Paramount-Arbuckle, 1918, 41in (104cm)
£3,100-3,300 *CNY*

The Master of Mystery, Octagon Films, 1919, 41in (104cm). **£9,500-10,500** *CNY*

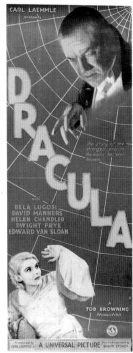

Dracula, Universal, 1931.
£19,000-20,000 *CNY*

The Wolf Man, Universal, 1941, 41in (104cm). **£11,000-12,000** *CNY*

The Devil Is A Woman, Paramount, 1935, 41in (104cm).
£9,500-9,700 *CNY*

The Wild One, Columbia, 1954, 41in (104cm). **£510-530** *CNY*

Gentlemen Prefer Blondes, 20th Century Fox, 1953, 81in (205.5cm). **£820-850** *CNY*

Atom Man versus Superman, Columbia, 1950, 81in (205.5cm). **£4,800-5,000** *CNY*

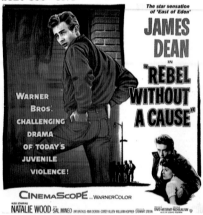

Rebel Without A Cause, Warner Brothers, 1955, 81in (205.5cm). **£2,250-2,500** *CNY*

An American In Paris, MGM, 1951, 81in (205.5cm) **£1,150-1,350** *CNY*

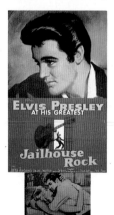

Werewolf of London, Universal, 1935, 36in (91.5cm). **£2,700-3,000** *CNY*

Jailhouse Rock, MGM, 1957, 81in (205.5cm). **£600-700** *CNY*

The War Of The Worlds, Paramount, 1953, 81in (205.5cm). **£3,100-3,300** *CNY*

Destry Rides Again, Universal, 1939, 41in (104cm). **£630-650** *CNY*

A $1,000 bond, for the
Marietta & North Georgia
Railway Company, 1887.
£55-65 *SCR*

Credit Athenien S.A., 1925.
£35-45 *SCR*

Banque Industrielle de Chine.
£30-40 *SCR*

Republic of Estonia, £100
Sterling bond.
£50-60 *SCR*

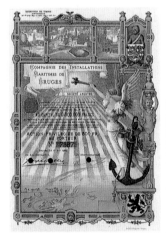

Compagnie des Installations
Maritime de Bruges, the
company formed to construct
the port at Bruges.
£165-185 *SCR*

Four unissued proofs for
Pioneers, W. & A. Churchman's
cigarettes, c1939.
£100-130 *VS*

Barcelona Traction Light &
Power, £20 bond, Waterlow
engraved.
£30-40 *SCR*

An American cigarette
card book, by W. Drake
& Sons, issued 1888.
£30-40 each *ACC*

Four unissued proofs,
Pioneers, W. & A.
Churchman's cigarettes,
c1939.
£80-120 *VS*

A B.O.A.C. advertising fan, c1950, 9in (23cm).
£25-30 *YV*

A Restaurant Frascati, London, advertising fan.
£65-75 *YV*

An Amer Picon advertising
fan, 10in (25cm).
£75-85 *YV*

A Restaurant Toccardi, Paris,
advertising fan, 9in (23cm).
£75-85 *YV*

An Amer Picon advertising
fan, 9.5in (24cm).
£55-65 *YV*

A Tigre, Galeries Lafayette
chromolitho advertising
fan, 9.5in (24cm).
£55-65 *YV*

Reverse side of the Restaurant
Frascati, London, advertising fan,
top right.

A Marie Bryard, Art Deco
advertising fan, 9.5in
(24cm) **£65-75** *YV*

A Carlton Hotel & Restaurant, London,
advertising fan, signed George Redan, 10in
(25cm). **£75-85** *YV*

A Galeries Lafayette advertising fan, 8.5in
(21cm). **£55-65** *YV*

Two onion shaped carafes, c1840, 8.5 and 9in (21 and 22.5cm). **£250-275 each** *Som*

A decanter with lozenge stopper, c1780. **£240-260** *Som*

A spirit decanter, c1810. **£1,800-1,900** *Som*

A decanter, c1815. **£85-95** *Som*

A set of 3 spirit bottles, in a silver plated stand, c1860. **£860-885** *Som*

Two flagons, with cork and metal stoppers, c1830. **£180-250 each** *Som*

Three flagons, with compressed sides and loop handles, c1830. **£160-200** *Som*
r. A pair of spirit bottles, c1800. **£500-550** *Som*

A pair of roemer type wine glasses, 1830, 4in (10cm). **£180-190** and a single roemer type wine glass, with heavy milled prunted knop and hollow ribbed foot, c1800, 5.25in (13cm). **£180-190** *Som*

A triple twist wine glass, the round funnel bowl on a stem with a canary coloured central cable, an inner spiralling opaque white thread and an outer laminated ply, c1770, 6in (15cm). **£8,000-8,500** *Som*

A green faceted glass wine glass, with gilded decoration, 5.75in (14cm). **£400-500** *CB*

Four green wine glasses, c1830, 4 to 5.25in (10 to 13cm). **£60-85 each** *Som*

An engraved roemer, c1680, 5.5in (14cm). **£600-700** *CB*

A wine glass, with bell bowl on a plain stem and plain folded conical foot, c1750, 7in (17.5cm). **£320-350** *Som*

A wine glass, with incised twist stem, c1760, 5.25in (13.5cm). **£850-900** *Som*

An export type wine glass, c1760, 5.5in (14cm). **£600-650** *Som*

A light green export type wine glass, with double ogee bowl, c1760. **£950-1,000** *Som*

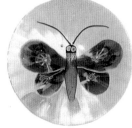

A Baccarat butterfly weight, on star cut base, mid-19thC. **£1,250-1,500** *C*

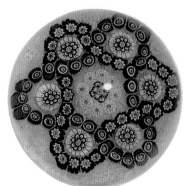

A Baccarat garlanded pompom weight, star cut base, bruised, mid-19thC. **£2,000-2,250** *C*

A Baccarat millefiori weight, mid-19thC, 3in (8cm) diam. **£850-950** *C*

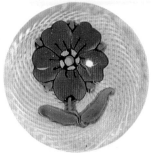

A Clichy fruit weight, mid-19thC, 2.75in (7cm) diam. **£1,500-1,750** *C*

A Clichy garlanded patterned millefiori weight, mid-19thC, 3in (8cm) diam. **£850-900** *C*

A St. Louis red pelargonium weight, mid-19thC, 2.75in (6.7cm) diam. **£1,400-1,600** *C*

A Clichy close millefiori weight, bruised and chipped, mid-19thC. **£1,250-1,500** *C*

A Clichy faceted patterned millefiori weight, mid-19thC. **£2,300-2,500** *C*

A St. Louis pink dahlia weight, mid-19thC. **£1,250-1,500** *C*

l. A St. Louis faceted upright bouquet weight, cut with a window and 3 rows of printies, mid-19thC, 3in (8cm) diam. **£1,000-1,250** *C*

l. A St. Louis weight, set in a white ground, with 4 radiating panels, mid-19thC, 3in (8cm) diam. **£6,000-6,500** *C*

A 'Wrockwardine' jug, with marvered decoration, c1810, 8.5in (22cm). **£650-680** *Som*

A cut glass scent bottle, c1850, 5in (12.5cm). **£100-200** *CB*

Three scent bottles: *l.* c1830, *c.* c1780, *r.* c1840. **£150-400 each** *Som*

l. A splatter type, clear cased, scent bottle, c1830. **£850-900** *r.* A double ended scent bottle, c1880. **£180-200** *Som*

A blue dish with flat diamond cutting, unmarked silver rim, c1780, 3.5in (9cm). **£600-620** *Som*

A clear scent bottle, with cut green overlay, embossed silver mount, c1860. **£275-300** *Som*

An early 'Nailsea' crown glass inkwell, c1820, 2.5in (6cm) high. **£60-70** *Som*

A glass vase, possibly French, c1800. **£120-140** *Som*

Three clear glass scent bottles, c1820, *l.* with silver mount, *c & r.* with gold mounts. **£450-500 each** *Som*

An amethyst cream jug and sugar basin, probably North Country, c1810, jug 4.5in (11.5cm). **£400-430** *Som*

l. A green scent bottle, c1880. **£100-120** *r.* A flat blue scent bottle, with gilt decoration, c1780, 4.5in (11.5cm). **£750-800** *Som*

A sugar comport and cover, c1800, 5.5in (13.5cm). **£600-620** *Som*

A cased glass biscuit barrel, possibly Boulton & Mills, c1900. **£265-285** *CB*

A pair of Victorian vaseline glass vases. **£60-90** *CB*

A cranberry glass posy vase, c1880, 3in (8cm). **£30-50** *CB*

Two opaque flasks, with enamelled decoration, c1760. **£650-680 each** *Som*

A French opaline glass vase, c1850. **£1,000-1,200** *CB*

An opaque glass flask, c1760. **£800-1,000** *Som*

A Victorian vaseline glass vase. **£80-120** *CB*

A pair of cornucopia vases, on marble and alabaster bases, c1840. **£950-980** *CB*

Cranberry glass oil bottles. **£70-80** *PCh*

A cranberry glass celery vase, c1880. **£100-150** *AMH*

A pair of glass tazzas, c1900. **£550-600** *CB*

A Stourbridge night light, c1900. **£80-100** *CB*

An opalescent wrythen glass jug and bowl, c1890, jug 4in (10cm) high. **£100-160** *CB*

A Mary Gregory glass box, 3in (7.5cm) diam. **£100-200** *CB*

Three hyacinth vases. **£20-40 each** *CB*

A carnival glass vase, in ripple pattern, 10in (25cm) high. **£65-70** *TS*

A hand painted glass ashtray. **£40-45** *HEW*

Wax fruit/still life arrangements under glass, English, c1870. **£50-150 each** *CB*

A selection of hyacinth vases, 4 to 7.5in (10 to 19cm). **£20-50 each** *CB*

A pressed glass bowl, c1894. **£35-40** *AMH*

Below: A Murano glass vase, 8in (20cm) high. **£30-35** *ROW*

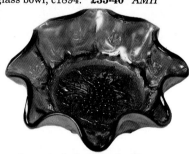

A carnival glass bowl with grapes, 7.25in (19cm) diam. **£45-50** *TS*

A selection of hyacinth vases, c1870, 5 to 8.5in (13 to 21cm) high. **£40-50 each** *CB*

r. An Orange Tree carnival glass bowl, 8.5in (21cm) diam. **£65-70** *TS*

A selection of silvered glass 'Witches Balls'.
£40-60 each *CB*

A 1950s vase, 5.5in (14cm)
high.
£10-20 *ASA*

A Gallé cameo
glass vase,
c1900, marked.
£2,000-2,500
S(AM)

A Gallé cameo
glass vase,
marked, c1910.
£1,500-1,750
S(AM)

A 1960s glass vase,
11.5in (29cm) high.
£20-30 *ASA*

A Continental glass vase, with
enamelled decoration, 10.25in
(26cm) high. **£90-100** *ING*

A selection of 'Witches Balls', 3 to 18in (8
to 46cm) diam. **£40-300 each** *CB*

r. An Austrian streaked glass lemonade set,
with 5 glasses, c1900, jug 10in (25cm) high.
£150-200 *ASA*

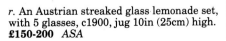

A Scottish silver and agate brooch, with citrine centre, c1850, 2in (5cm) diam.
£250-280 *BWA*

A gold oval pavé set half pearl locket pendant, 19thC.
£1,100-1,200 *CSK*

A gold and diamond oval locket, with central diamonds, 19thC.
£700-800 *Bea*

A 15ct gold, peridot and seed pearl pendant brooch.
£450-500 *Bea*

A gold, silver and diamond pavé set brooch, 19thC.
£2,200-2,500 *Bea*

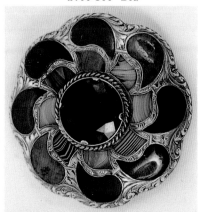

A Scottish silver and agate brooch, with Cairngorm centre, c1850, 2in (5cm) diam.
£225-275 *BWA*

A carved coral bull's head brooch, 19thC. **£350-400** *CSK*

A gold mounted agate and diamond pendant, 19thC. **£850-900** *CSK*

A gold and emerald pendant.
£300-350 *CSK*

A gold, silver and diamond brooch, 19thC.
£850-950 *Bea*

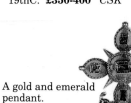

A Scottish silver and agate brooch, with Cairngorm centre, c1860.
£125-150 *BWA*

GLASS

A hand blown blue eye glass, English, c1840, 2.75in (7cm).
£60-80   *CB*

A spiral vaseline specimen vase, c1880, 7.75in (19cm).
£25-30   *WAC*

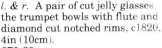

l. & r. A pair of cut jelly glasses, the trumpet bowls with flute and diamond cut notched rims, c1820, 4in (10cm).
£70-80
c. A syllabub glass, with pan top and notched rim, facet cut foot, c1820, 4in (10cm).
£25-35   *Som*

l. A jelly glass, c1800, 4.5in (11cm).
£30-35
c. A bonnet glass, c1750, 3in (8cm).
£40-50
r. A rib moulded jelly glass, c1750, 3.75in (9cm).
£40-50   *Som*

A Victorian opaline hand painted glass vase, 10.5in (26cm).
£30-35   *ING*

Two dwarf ales, the conical bowls engraved with hops and barley, c1800, 4.5 and 5in (12.5 and 13cm).
£65-70 each   *Som*

A Bohemian cased glass egg cup set, mid-19thC, 6.5in (16cm) diam.
£55-65   *WAC*

Two toddy lifters, c1820, 5.5 and 7.5in (14 and 18.5cm).
£85-95   *Som*

Two rummers, c1820.
£60-75 *Som*

l. A dry mustard pot, with loose hollow lid, c1800, 6in (15cm).
£65-75
c. A toddy lifter, c1830, 7in (18cm).
£85-95
r. A pepper, with rib moulded body, on square lemon squeezer foot, brass cap, c1810, 4in (10cm).
£65-75 *Som*

Two Victorian crackle glass jugs, 3.75in (9cm). **£10-15**
6in (15cm). **£25-30** *FMN*

A water jug, with prism cut neck, notched rim and strap handle, c1840, 7in (17.5cm).
£150-170 *Som*

A Bristol blown blue drinking glass, c1840, 4.75in (12cm).
£80-100 *CB*

A glass boot, 3in (8cm).
£50-80 *CB*

A Stourbridge double overlay cruet, c1880, 2.5in (6cm).
£40-50 *WAC*

A glass trumpet, c1900, 8in (20.5cm).
£40-45 *TS*

A Victorian sardine dish, with
silver plated stand. **£30-40** *TRU*

An English opaque
glass vase, 6in
(15cm).
£25-30 *WAC*

A pink opaline vase,
10.5in (26cm).
£25-35 *WAC*

A pair of cut salts, the oval bodies
with slice cutting and crenellated
rims, on moulded diamond lemon
squeezer feet, c1800, 3in (7.5cm).
£180-200 *Som*

Two Victorian custard cups, 2.5
and 3.5in (7 and 9cm).
£10-15 *Som*

A Mary Gregory blue hyacinth
vase, 6in (15cm).
£55-65 *WAC*

A cut glass wig stand,
early 19thC, 7in (17cm).
£35-45 *WAC*

An English opaline mug,
c1830, 3in (8cm).
£150-200 *CB*

Two Victorian green glass jugs, with lily of the valley pattern and gilt rims, 5.5in (14cm). **£45-50 each** *TS*

A hand blown specimen vase, c1910, 3in (8cm). **£10-15** *TS*

A Stourbridge cased jug, 6in (15cm). c1880, **£55-65** *WAC*

A pair of Victorian opaline glass vases, with gilding and jewelled decoration. **£25-30** TS

A Victorian glass vase, small chips, 3.5in (9cm). **£20-30** *WAC*

Two Victorian crackle glass vases, 4.5 and 7in (11 and 18cm). **£20-25 each** *FMN*

A pair of hand painted green glass tankards, 6in (15cm). **£15-20** *TS*

A pair of glass door knobs, with glitter inside, 3in (8cm).
£20-25 *TS*

l. An ovoid bowl rummer, with short stem and conical foot, c1810, 4.5in (11.5cm).
£45-55
r. An ovoid bowl rummer, engraved 'S. Marrion', with floral decoration and a bird in flight, c1820, 5in (12.5cm).
£85-95 *Som*

A Thomas Webb cameo glass scent bottle, the stopper with embossed silver outer cover, moulded mark, assay mark for Birmingham 1888, 6in (15cm).
£650-680 *Bea*

A pressed glass commemorative bowl, Queen Victoria's silver jubilee, 7in (18cm).
£20-25 *TS*

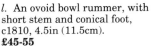

A green glass lamp reservoir.
£25-30 *TS*

Cross Reference
Commemorative
Ceramics
Royal Memorabilia

A Victorian blue glass posy bowl.
£30-35 *TS*

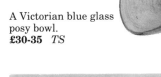

A gilded 'frigger', 'I Love a Sailor', 14in (36cm) long.
£100-180 *CB*

A red glass cornucopia, with gilding, c1880, 7in (18cm).
£20-25 *TS*

Cranberry Glass

A Victorian cranberry cut glass decanter, 10.75in (27cm) high. **£75-95** *AA*

An early Victorian heavy cranberry glass perfume bottle, 4in (10cm). **£60-70** *AA*

A late Victorian cranberry bowl, with silver plated stand, 6.5in (16cm) high. **£60-70** *AA*

A Victorian flower vase épergne, on original mirror back, 12in (31cm) high. **£150-200** *AA*

A cranberry glass ice plate, c1860, 6.5in (16cm) diam. **£50-55** *AMH*

A cranberry glass powder bowl, c1880, 4in (10cm) diam. **£100-135** *AMH*

A Mary Gregory cranberry glass vase, 4in (10cm). **£75-85** *FMN*

A cranberry glass stein, with pewter hinged lid, decorated in Mary Gregory style with a Norseman warrior, with 3 beakers, late 19thC. **£400-450** *GAK*

A shaded cranberry glass beaker, in silver holder, hallmarked Birmingham 1928, 4in (10cm). **£35-45** *AA*

Decanters

A Victorian cut
glass decanter,
9in (23cm).
£35-40 *TS*

Four decanters, c1810, 6.5 to 8in (17 to 20.5cm).
£80-90 each *Som*

A tapered decanter, the body
engraved with leaf pattern and
alternate birds and springs in
between loops and bows, bevelled
lozenge stopper, c1780, 9in
(23cm).
£250-280 *Som*

An emerald green decanter, with
lily of the valley pattern in white,
c1885, 13in (33cm).
£85-90 *TS*

A three bottle silver plated
tantalus. **£150-160** *LF*

A pair of vase shaped decanters,
with diamond and slice cut
bodies, foot rings star cut
underneath, pouring lips and
spire stoppers, c1880, 10.5in
(26.5cm).
£100-110 *Som*

l. & r. Two Victorian Stourbridge claret jugs.
c. A claret jug, l9thC, 12in (31cm).
£200-225 each *P(S)*

Paperweights

A French glass sulphide portrait paperweight, with crystallo ceramic bust of Queen Victoria, set on a blue and white spiral cushion, 3in (7.5cm). **£625-650** *Bea*

For a further selection of paperweights, please refer to Miller's Collectables Price Guide, Volume IV.

Pressed Glass

A brown cloud glass vase-on-stand, 5in (12.5cm) high. **£45-50** *TS*

A John Northwood thread glass bowl, c1880, 5.5in (14cm) diam. **£45-50** *TS*

John Northwood invented the machine that does this threading.

> **Cross Reference**
> Colour Section

A Davidson's amethyst cloud glass tray, c1922, 14in (36cm) wide. **£45-60** *TS*

A pressed glass sugar bowl, 5.5in (14cm) diam. **£8-10** *TS*

A Davidson's jet glass match striker, 3in (7.5cm). **£10-15** *TS*

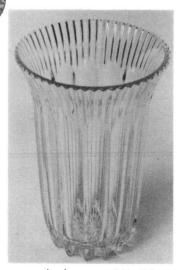

A celery vase, 6.5in (16cm). **£15-20** *TS*

A Sowerby blue glass bowl, marked, 13in (33cm) wide. **£25-30** *TS*

Art Nouveau

A pair of Daum enamelled perfume bottles, with applied silver mounts. **£1,000-1,200** *ABS*

A Daum cameo glass vase, with applied decoration, c1900. **£5,500-6,000** *ABS*

A cream hand painted vase, c1900, 14in (35.5cm). **£85-90** *TS*

A Müller cameo glass lamp, c1910. **£5,000-6,000** *ABS*

Cross Reference
Lighting

A Daum cameo and enamelled vase, c1900. **£2,000-2,500** *ABS*

A Gallé triple overlay cameo glass vase. **£1,500-2,000** *ABS*

A miniature Daum cameo and enamelled vase. **£850-900** *ABS*

A blue glass vase, with raised decoration, slight damage, c1900, 10.75in (27cm). **£55-65** *TS*

A Loetz vase, with applied handles, Austrian, c1900. **£900-1,000** *ABS*

Lalique

Two René Lalique opalescent bowls:
Top. 'Ondines Ouverte', wheel cut mark, and stencilled No.380, after 1921, 8in (20.5cm) diam.
£660-700
Bottom. Stencilled mark, 14.5in (37cm) diam.
£1,900-2,000 *S*

A René Lalique perfume bottle, 'Pan'.
£800-1,000 *ABS*

A René Lalique lamp, 'Gros Poissons Vagues', the bronze base fitted for electricity, engraved mark, after 1922, 15.5in (39.5cm).
£2,400-2,500 *S*

Cross Reference
Automobilia

A René Lalique mascot, 'Tête d'Aigle', moulded mark, after 1928, 4.5in (11cm).
£800-825 *S*

A René Lalique figure, 'Suzanne', engraved and moulded mark, c1925, 9in (23cm).
£9,000-9,500 *S*

Carnival Glass

An Imperial Art Glass bowl, 6.25in (16cm) diam.
£45-50 *TS*

A commemorative plate, 'Independence Hall', 1950s, 8in (20.5cm) diam.
£25-30 *TS*

A comport, 7in (17.5cm) high.
£35-45 *TS*

A Davidson marigold basket,
c1930, 7in (17.5cm) diam.
£15-20 *TS*

A Northwood amethyst basket
weave comport, with plain
interior, 5in (12.5cm) high.
£60-70 *TS*

A marigold glass bowl, 8.75in
(22cm) diam.
£25-35 *WAC*

A Northwood strawberry and
basket weave comport, with
twisted stem, 7in (17.5cm).
£45-50 *TS*

An amethyst glass bowl, 7.5in
(19cm) diam.
£30-40 *WAC*

A green glass bowl, 8.5in (21cm)
diam.
£45-55 *WAC*

A Northwood
green Good
Luck bowl,
9in (23cm)
diam.
£85-95 *TS*

A blue peacock
and grape bowl,
with bearded
berry back,
8.75in (22cm)
diam.
£75-85 *TS*

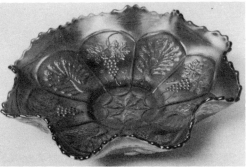

A marigold sugar bowl, 5.25in
(13cm) diam.
£15-20 *TS*

20th Century Glass

A Wiener Werkstätte hand painted beaker, c1908.
£250-300 *ABS*

A Wilhelm Wagenfeld for Vereinigte Lausitzer Glaswerke A.G., 'Kubus-Geschirr', storage containers with two-handled tray, marked, 1938, tray 16.5in (42cm) wide. **£2,000-2,250** *S*

A glass tazza, on a chrome base, c1930, 9in (23cm). **£75-80** *TS*

A Venetian glass clown, slight damage, 14in (36cm) high.
£40-45 *WAC*

A toothpick holder, hand painted with a snipe, 3.5in (9cm) high.
£18-20 *AMH*

An Art Deco amber glass dressing table set, c1930, 13in (33cm).
£30-35 *TS*

An Italian glass vase, 1960s, 6.5in (16cm) high. **£20-30** *ASA*

A Kosta vase, designed by Vicke Lindstrand, c1959, 4.5in (11cm) high.
£150-170 *KAC*

An American glass bowl, with amethyst rim, c1930, 6in (15cm) diam. **£15-20** *TS*

Gramophones

A Columbia early open works phonograph, with 3 cylinders, 14in (36cm) long. **£160-185** *BWA*

A Decca gramophone and needles, 16 by 12in (41 by 31cm). **£60-75** *BWA*

An HMV mahogany table gramophone, records and needles, spring guaranteed, c1935, 18.5 by 15.75in (47 by 40cm). **£125-155** *BWA*

A gramophone, by The Standard Talking Machine Co., of Chicago, original condition, c1900, 19in (48cm) long. **£450-475** *BWA*

The first models had Finch turntables and no tone arm, i.e. the soundbox connected directly to the horn. The winding handle was removed before playing and 78 rpm records could be played, but the centre hole had to be enlarged - 10in records had not been invented.

A portable Academy 'Nippy' gramophone, 13 by 9in (33 by 23cm). **£45-55** *BWA*

Gramophone Needle Tins

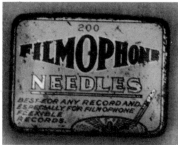

A Filmophone needle tin.
£12-14 *NF*

Gramophone needles were in use in the UK from about 1900 until the 1950s, but they continued to be made and used overseas. The most sought after needles are pre-WWI.

Gramophone needle tins are principally collected for their rarity of design and, as ever, condition is of paramount importance. Slight differences in design and wording on seemingly identical tins are also of interest to the collector.

Aero-Needles.
£45-55 *NF*

Rifanco Elephant needles.
£18-20 *NF*

An HMV aluminium needle tin.
£15-20 *NF*

The 4 most common needle tins, Embassy, Columbia, Songster and HMV.
£4-6 each *NF*

Golden Pyramid needle tin.
£18-22 *NF*

A Columbia Duragold needle tin. **£4-6** *NF*

Cross Reference
Tins
Signs & Advertising

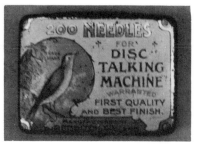

A needle tin for Disc Talking Machine.
£25-30 *NF*

Hatpins & Hatpin Holders

A Victorian elephant hatpin, 9in (23cm).
£15-20 *AA*

A Bakelite and paste Art Deco hatpin, 7in (18cm).
£20-25 *AA*

A silver and amber glass golf club hatpin, c1905, 10in (25cm) long.
£35-40 *AA*

In 1914 the length of hatpins was restricted. They had been made up to 24in long and were considered to be dangerous.

An Edwardian hatpin holder, 4.75in (12cm) high. **£30-40** Hatpins **£5-30 each** *AA*

An Art Nouveau porcelain hatpin holder, 4.5in (11cm) high.
£35-40 *AA*

Inkstands

A silver inkstand, inscribed 'South Leeds General Election 1906 to Dr & Mrs Hawkyard, A Souvenir from Sir John & Lady Walton', Chester 1904, maker James Jay, 9.5 by 6.75in (24 by 17cm).
£600-800 *AMH*

A boat shaped silver inkwell, with single faceted glass bottle, hinged silver lid, Sheffield 1906.
£175-185 *GAK*

A silver plated golfing inkstand, English, late 19thC, 8in (20cm) wide.
£450-475 *S*

> **Cross Reference**
> Golf

247

An agate and ormolu inkwell, in the form of an oil lamp, 19thC, 6in (15cm) wide.
£180-220 *BWA*

A silver plated ram's horn desk stand, fitted with 2 lidded ink pots modelled as mesh patterned golf balls, 21in (53cm) wide.
£350-370 *C(S)*

A silver capstan inkwell, with reed and tie decoration to base and lid, Sheffield 1905.
£130-140 *GAK*

A silver capstan inkwell, Birmingham 1926, base 3in (8cm) diam.
£55-65 *TRU*

JEWELLERY

A Bohemian gilded brass filigree necklace, with green glass stones, c1920. **£30-40** *AA*

An Edwardian coral necklace, 16in (41cm) long.
£20-25 *AA*

A white metal and enamel pendant, c1930.
£10-20 *ASA*

l. An early Victorian 15ct gold, ruby, diamond and pearl ring.
£250-275
c. A Victorian 18ct gold, ruby and diamond gypsy set ring.
£295-325
r. An Edwardian 18ct gold, pearl and tourmaline ring, Birmingham 1912.
£150-165 *FMN*

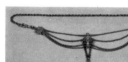

A gold bangle, set with 11 graduated opals and 20 diamonds, one opal replaced.
£1,200-1,300 *SWO*

A Victorian rope chain necklace.
£70-100 *ASA*

A simulated pearl and paste baguette necklace, c1935. **£30-40** *AA*

A 9ct gold, amethyst and seed pearl pendant, 1in (2.5cm) diam. **£90-110** *FMN*

An Edwardian silver, seed pearl and paste pendant, 3in (8cm). **£90-120** *FMN*

A Victorian 9ct gold, peridot and pearl Art Nouveau style pendant, 1.5in (4cm). **£150-165** *FMN*

An Edwardian 9ct rose gold bracelet, Chester 1907. **£190-225** *FMN*

A Victorian 9ct gold, peridot and pearl Art Nouveau style pendant, 1.5in (4cm). **£185-200** *FMN*

An opaline glass and crystal necklace, c1940, 28in (71cm) long. **£25-35** *AA*

A Victorian filigree gilded brass necklace, with pink paste stones. **£35-40** *AA*

An Art Deco frosted amber glass necklace, c1920. **£25-35** *AA*

An Edwardian paste necklace, with faceted glass stones in brass setting. **£25-30** *AA*

A gold bracelet set with semi-precious stones. **£120-180** *ASA*

Brooches

A Victorian 15ct gold, pearl and aquamarine brooch, 1in (2.5cm) high.
£295-350 *FMN*

A Victorian mosaic on silver brooch, 1in (2.5cm) diam.
£40-45 *FMN*

A Victorian 18ct gold bar brooch, set with seed pearls.
£80-90 *TRU*

An O.B.E. enamel brooch.
£70-75 *PAR*

An Edwardian mosaic brooch, 1.75in (5cm) wide. **£30-40** *FMN*

A Victorian mosaic brooch, with carved mother-of-pearl centre, 1.25in (3cm) wide.
£40-45 *FMN*

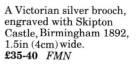

A Victorian silver brooch, engraved with Skipton Castle, Birmingham 1892, 1.5in (4cm) wide.
£35-40 *FMN*

A silver mounted agate brooch.
£30-40 *ASA*

> **Cross Reference**
> Militaria

A North Devon Hussars tortoiseshell and silver brooch.
£50-55 *PAR*

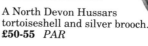

A gilt metal brooch. **£30-50** *ASA*

A 15ct gold brooch, the dove of Peace carrying a branch set with 3 seed pearls.
£140-150 *HSS*

An Arts & Crafts brooch, set with
shell, c1920, 4in (10cm).
£150-175 *DID*

An aquamarine and seed pearl
bar brooch, 1920s, 2in (5cm) long.
£130-140 *FMN*

Art Nouveau Jewellery

A French 18ct gold brooch, by
Emile Vernier, c1900, 1.5in (4cm).
£275-300 *DID*

A Murrle Bennet & Co. enamel
and sterling silver bracelet,
c1900. **£225-250** *DID*

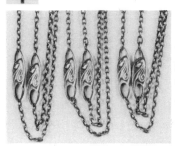

A Murrle
Bennet & Co.
silver long
guard.
£245-275
DID

Mexican Jewellery

A silver pendant.
£50-80 *ASA*

An enamel necklace, c1950.
£235-250 *DID*

A white metal and onyx square panel and link
bracelet, Antonia Pineda, 1940s. **£100-150** *CSK*

A silver pendant, set with a semi-precious stone, c1900.
£70-100 *ASA*

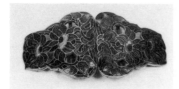

A metal and enamel buckle.
£15-30 *ASA*

Cross Reference
Buckles

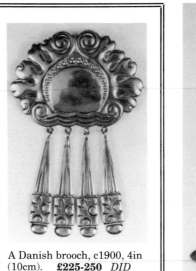

A Danish brooch, c1900, 4in (10cm). **£225-250** *DID*

A 9ct gold pendant, with mother-of-pearl centre and fresh water pearl drop, 2in (5cm) long. **£75-95** *AA*

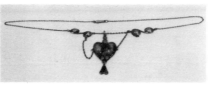

A silver and enamel necklace.
£120-200 *ASA*

A Murrle Bennet & Co. silver and enamel pendant, 2.25in (6cm).
£250-275 *DID*

A Murrle Bennet & Co. 18ct gold opal ring, c1900.
£180-200 *DID*

A Murrle Bennet & Co. gold locket, c1900.
£375-400 *DID*

A 15ct gold and opal brooch, English, c1900.
£200-225 *DID*

A silver, enamel and mother-of-pearl brooch.
£50-80 *ASA*

Liberty

A buckle, by A. Knox for Liberty & Co., c1900.
£300-350 *DID*

A silver and pearl brooch, by Oliver Baker for Liberty & Co., 1in (3cm). **£200-250** *DID*

An enamel butterfly locket, by A. Knox for Liberty & Co., c1900.
£380-400 *DID*

An Arts & Crafts pearl and turquoise brooch, 2.75in (7cm).
£135-150 *DID*

A Liberty & Co. ruby and enamel on silver pendant, c1900, 1.5in (4cm).
£200-250 *DID*

A silver and enamel Liberty & Co. brooch, c1900, 1in (3cm).
£140-175 *DID*

Art Deco Jewellery

A pair of base metal ear clips, 1.25in (3cm). **£5-7** *COL*

A simulated jade bracelet, c1930.
£15-20 *ASA*

A silver ring, set with turquoise and mother-of-pearl.
£50-80 *ASA*

A three-sectional white metal buckle, with central green glass feature. **£25-45** *ASA*

A silver and turquoise bracelet. **£120-180** *ASA*

An amber leaf shaped brooch.
£5-15 *ASA*

A silver chain necklace, with green stone pendant, c1920.
£25-30 *AA*

Bog Oak Jewellery

Cuff Links

A pair of 9ct gold cuff links, Birmingham 1939.
£65-70 *FMN*

A pair of enamel and mother-of-pearl cuff links.
£40-45 *JBB*

A pair of Connemara marble cuff links.
£25-32 *JBB*

A pair of earrings, with 9ct gold wires. **£40-45** *PR*

A pair of Edwardian gold plated on brass cuff links, engraved with swallows.
£25-30 *FMN*

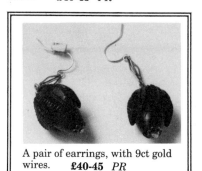

A pair of earrings, with 9ct gold wires. **£40-45** *PR*

A pair of Edinburgh silver cuff links. **£40-45** *JBB*

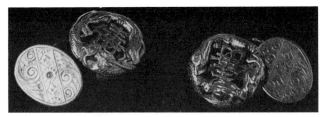

A pair of Oriental silver gilt cuff
links. **£50-55** *JBB*

A pair of dyed mother-of-pearl in
metal cuff links.
£30-40 *JBB*

A pair of Art Deco enamel cuff
links. **£25-30** *JBB*

A pair of silver cuff links,
Birmingham 1902.
£35-40 *JBB*

A pair of silver and enamel rose
shaped cuff links.
£35-40 *JBB*

A pair of agate cuff links.
£30-35 *JBB*

A pair of enamel on brass cuff
links, c1930. **£30-35** *FMN*

A pair of 9ct gold engraved cuff links,
c1960. **£60-70** *FMN*

A pair of 9ct gold cuff links,
Birmingham 1944.
£60-65 *FMN*

A pair of 18ct white gold with
diamonds cuff links.
£400-425 *JBB*

Two pairs of gold plated
on brass cuff links, with
horses and Scottie dogs,
c1940.
£12-14 each pair *FMN*

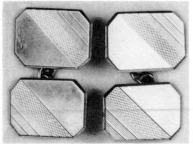

A pair of silver cuff links, c1930.
£25-30 *FMN*

Costume Jewellery

A selection of costume jewellery.
£18-70 each *JBB*

A cabochon and pearl on gilt
parrot's head brooch, from Oscar
de la Renta's Fashion Show.
£225-250 *MAS*

A Trifari eagle's head
brooch, with white and
blue paste decoration
and marquise red
paste eye.
£150-160 *CSK*

A cut glass and gilt leaf design
bracelet, by Schiaparelli, 1940s.
£150-175 *MAS*

A silver and agate bracelet, made by Napier, 1950s.
£100-125 *MAS*

A Pennino coppered white metal spray brooch, with central imitation aquamarine cluster, and a gilt white metal ribbon scroll brooch, with circular purple, red and white paste decoration.
£175-185 *CSK*

A Trifari ballerina white paste brooch, with imitation moonstone face, and a Boucheron imitation cabochon, amethyst and white paste star brooch.
£110-120 *CSK*

A silver and enamel butterfly brooch.
£50-80 *ASA*

A pair of metal ear clips, 1930.
£3-5 *COL*

A silver dancing couple brooch, 1940s.
£30-35 *TRU*

A French heart shaped paste and pearl brooch, c1940.
£65-75 *MAS*

A silver ballerina brooch, 1940s. **£25-30** *TRU*

A silver and enamel butterfly brooch.
£40-80 *ASA*

American Costume Jewellery

A gilt and paste mask brooch, 1940s. **£80-90** *MAS*

A gilt swirl brooch, 1940s. **£70-80** *MAS*

A gilt and paste bird brooch, designed by Schlumberger for Trifari, 1940s. **£240-250** *MAS*

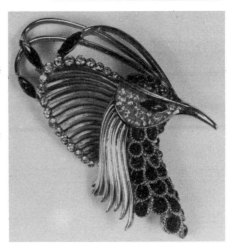

A rhodium plated paste and pearl peacock brooch. **£75-95** *MAS*

A silver gilt brooch, marked Jomaz, 1940s. **£170-180** *MAS*

A gilt and paste rooster brooch, by Napier, 1940s. **£140-150** *MAS*

An enamel and paste on gilt spray brooch, by Coro, 1940s. **£140-150** *MAS*

A rhodium plated lantern brooch, unsigned, 1940s. **£90-100** *MAS*

Jet Jewellery

A Whitby jet necklace with turquoise pendant drop.
£40-45 *PR*

A Whitby jet bracelet, with gold relief. **£45-55** *PR*

A Whitby jet bracelet.
£40-45 *PR*

A Whitby jet necklace, with diamanté clasp, 14.5in (37cm) long.
£80-90 *PR*

A Whitby jet short necklace, with cross, 10in (25cm) long. **£45-50** *PR*

A pair of Whitby jet earrings, on 9ct gold drop wires.
£40-45 *PR*

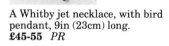

A Whitby jet necklace, with bird pendant, 9in (23cm) long.
£45-55 *PR*

A Whitby jet serpent bracelet.
£45-50 *PR*

A pair of Whitby jet earrings.
£25-30 *PR*

A pair of Whitby jet long drop earrings, on gold wires.
£45-50 *PR*

A Victorian jet necklace. **£90-100** with matching bracelet. **£60-65** and earrings. **£30-35** *PR*

A Whitby jet bead necklace, with original clasp, 13in (33cm) long. **£80-90** *PR*

A Victorian necklace, possibly vulcanite, with Whitby jet cross, 16.5in (42cm) long. **£65-75** *PR*

A Whitby jet long rope of beads with cross. **£55-70** *PR*

A Whitby jet link necklace, with original clasp, 11in (28cm) long. **£30-36** *PR*

Name Brooches

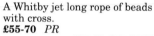

A silver name brooch, Matilda, with raised heart, Chester 1897, 1.5in (4cm) long. **£60-65** *FMN*

A silver name brooch, Mercy Ellen, CD & FD Birmingham 1896, 1.5in (4cm) long. **£50-55** *FMN*

A silver Mizpah brooch, Chester 1889, 1in (2.5cm) diam. **£45-55** *FMN*

A silver name brooch, Lydia, Chester 1898, 1.75in (5cm) long. **£60-65** *FMN*

A silver buckle name brooch, Alice, W.J.H. registered design, Birmingham 1897, 1.5in (4cm) long. **£60-65** *FMN*

A silver name brooch with gold edges, Sarah, Chester 1893, 1.75in (5cm) long. **£60-65** *FMN*

Scottish Jewellery

A double heart brooch, the centre symbol has romantic association with Mary Queen of Scots, c1860, 2.75in (7cm) wide. **£80-100** *BWA*

A silver and grey agate brooch, c1860. **£150-175** *BWA*

A Victorian Luckenbooth brooch, set with Perthshire agates, the centre symbol has romantic association with Mary Queen of Scots, 2.25in (6cm) high. **£150-175** *BWA*

A Celtic style silver brooch, c1930, 1.75in (5cm) diam. **£12-15** *TRU*

A silver brooch, set with agate and citrine star centre, c1850, 1.75in (4cm) diam. **£120-150** *BWA*

A Luckenbooth silver double heart brooch, c1850, 2.5in (6cm). **£70-80** *BWA*

Luckenbooth brooches were given as good luck and betrothal presents and 18thC examples often have inscriptions.

A silver and agate fouled anchor brooch, 3in (8cm) high. **£125-130** *BWA*

A Luckenbooth double heart engraved brooch, c1850, 2.75in (7cm) high. **£70-80** *BWA*

Jukeboxes & Slot Machines

● Jukeboxes from the 1940s (the 'Golden Age') have remained static in price during the past year.

● Jukeboxes from the 1950s (the 'Silver Age') have shown a steady 10-20% increase in value over the last 12 months.

The Wurlitzer model 2000 was introduced in 1956 to celebrate the company's centennial year. It was the first 200 selection model from the Wurlitzer factory.

A Wurlitzer model 2000 jukebox, with 200 selections of 45rpm records and rotary turning pages, fully restored, 55.5in (140cm) high. **£5,500-6,500** *CSC*

A Chantal Meteor 200 jukebox, with 200 selections of 45rpm records, c1959, restored, 59in (150cm) high. **£6,000-6,500** *CJS*

The Chantal was the only jukebox made in England.

A Wurlitzer model 1100, with 24 selections of 78rpm records, fully restored, 58in (147cm) high. **£7,500-8,500** *CSC*

Model 1100 was most colourful of all Wurlitzer jukeboxes. The use of facet cut clear plastic pilasters over revolving multi-coloured cylinders caused it to be more vivid. The Gothic shaped dome offered clear visibility to the mechanism. This was the last jukebox that Paul Fuller designed for the company.

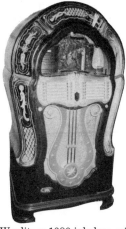

A Wurlitzer 1080 jukebox, with 24 selections of 78rpm records, c1947, fully restored, 59in (150cm) high. **£9,500-9,800** *CJS*

A Seeburg KD200 jukebox, with 200 selections, rotating selection drum and automobile like fins, c1957, fully restored, 56.5in (143cm). **£3,000-3,500** *CJS*

The Seeburg model KD200 was produced in 1957.

An AMI Continental jukebox, with domed glass porthole revealing the record changer, c1962, fully restored, 65in (165cm). **£3,000-3,250** *CJS*

An AMI Continental II jukebox, fully restored, 65in (165cm) high. **£3,250-3,850** *CSC*

The AMI Continental II of 1962 was the last of the classics from AMI. Available as either a 100 or 200 selection 45rpm machine it was once found in many English coffee bars.

A Rock-Ola Commando jukebox, with bird's-eye maple veneers and illuminated red and yellow front glasses, with 20 selections of 78rpm records, fully restored, 1942, 72.25in (183cm) high. **£14,000-16,000** *CSC*

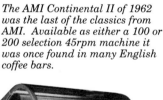

A Rock-Ola 1446 Comet jukebox, fully restored, 53in (135cm) high. **£3,500-4,250** *CSC*

The Rock-Ola model 1446 Comet was the 45rpm model for 1954. The capacity of 120 selections are housed within a carousel and the corresponding titles are hidden away on a rotary selection drum.

A Seeburg model V200 jukebox, 45rpm, fully restored, 56.5in (143cm) high. **£5,400-6,300** *CSC*

A Wurlitzer model 600 jukebox, with 20 selections of 78rpm records, fully restored, 54in (137cm) high. **£5,000-6,000** *CSC*

The Wurlitzer model 600 was introduced in August 1938 and was one of the early models that incorporated illuminated plastics.

Slot Machines

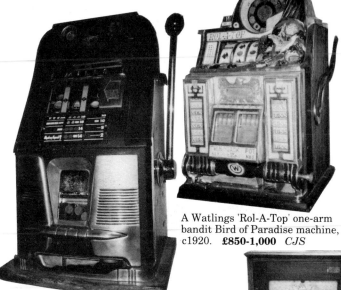

A Bryans 'Elevenses' penny play 'Allwin' machine, c1965, 18 by 14in (46 by 36cm). **£195-395** *CJS*

A Watlings 'Rol-A-Top' one-arm bandit Bird of Paradise machine, c1920. **£850-1,000** *CJS*

A Mills 'High Top' one-arm bandit, with escalator and jackpot, c1960. **£275-475** *CJS*

A Circle Skill cigarette vending machine, 1928. **£250-350** *CJS*

A Mills 'Black Cherry' one-arm bandit, c1920. **£650-850** *CJS*

A National brass till. **£275-300** *MR*

A Jennings 'The Governor' Indian head one-arm bandit, c1960. **£350-750** *CJS*

A William IV officer's gilt
shoulder belt plate of the
Grenadier Guards.
£300-325 *WAL*

A Victorian officer's
gilt and silver helmet
plate of The Prince of
Wales's Volunteers, in
very good condition.
£110-120 *WAL*

An officer's 1869 pattern gilt
and silver plated shako plate
of the 4th Royal Lancashire
Light Infantry Militia.
£130-150 *WAL*

An officer's silver plated
copper shoulder belt
plate, East Lothian
Yeomanry Cavalry,
c1795. **£300-325** *WAL*

A Georgian officer's gilt
and silver plated shoulder
belt plate of The 3rd Foot
Guards.
£525-575 *WAL*

An Irish officer's silver
coloured shoulder belt
plate of the Dublin
Volunteers, c1795.
£450-485 *WAL*

A Georgian officer's
gilt and silver plated
shoulder belt plate of
the Coldstream
Regiment of Foot
Guards, c1795.
£350-375 *WAL*

An officer's 1812 pattern
diestruck copper gilt
shako plate of the
Yorkshire Militia.
£235-250 *WAL*

An Irish officer's
copper gilt shoulder
belt plate, c1795.
£350-375 *WAL*

l. An officer's gilt and
silver plated shoulder
belt plate of The First
Regiment of Foot
Guards, c1795.
£750-775 *WAL*

An officer's gilt and silver
plated shoulder belt plate
of The Highland Light
Infantry, post-1902.
£260-280 *WAL*

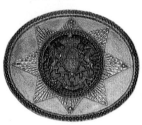

An Irish officer's silver
plated copper shoulder
belt plate of the
Walworth Infantry,
c1795.
£450-485 *WAL*

l. An officer's gilt and
silver plated shoulder
belt plate of the
Coldstream Guards,
c1835.
£450-475 *WAL*

A painted wood bass drum of the Royal Horse Guards, bearing Royal Arms with George V Cypher, maker's plate George Potter & Co., Aldershot. **£300-350** *WAL*

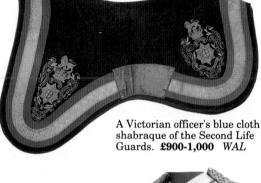

A Victorian officer's blue cloth shabraque of the Second Life Guards. **£900-1,000** *WAL*

An officer's sabretache of the 11th Hussars, c1850. **£2,500-2,750** *CSK*

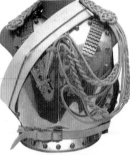

A post-1902 Household Cavalry trooper's plated cuirass. **£425-475** *WAL*

An officer's steel cuirass of the Household Cavalry, steel with leather and velvet, early 19thC. **£1,600-1,750** *WAL*

l. A Georgian Lieutenant General's scarlet coatee, with embroidery and gilt buttons, c1825. **£900-1,000** *WAL*

r. A Victorian officer's scarlet cloth shabraque of the Royal Horse Guards, with embroidery. **£450-500** *WAL*

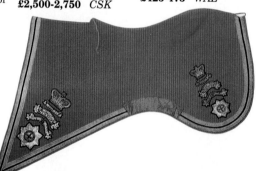

l. A copper powder flask embossed as entwined dolphins. **£300-350** *WAL*

A Victorian officer's blue cloth shabraque of the 1st (Royal) Dragoons, with embroidery. **£600-675** *WAL*

r. An officer's sabretache flap of the 9th Queen's Royal Lancers, c1840 **£1,500-1,750** *CSK*

A Victorian officer's full dress sabretache of the 7th Queen's Own Hussars, 11.75in (30cm) high. **£1,000-1,100** *CSK*

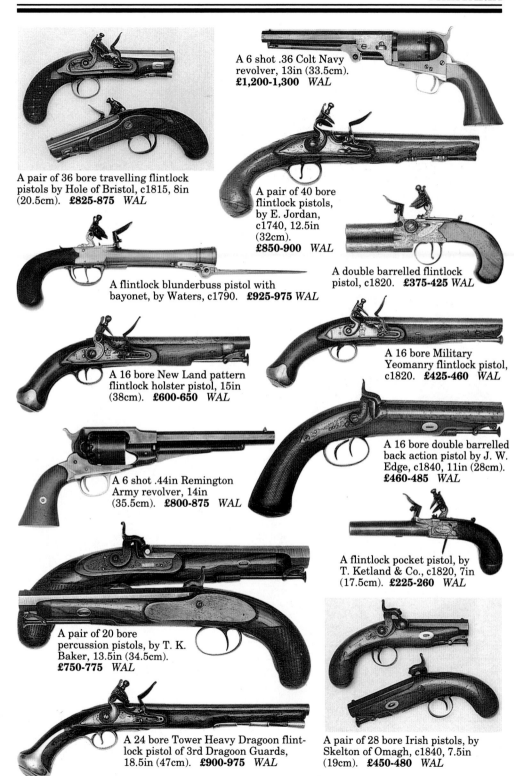

A pair of 36 bore travelling flintlock pistols by Hole of Bristol, c1815, 8in (20.5cm). **£825-875** *WAL*

A 6 shot .36 Colt Navy revolver, 13in (33.5cm). **£1,200-1,300** *WAL*

A pair of 40 bore flintlock pistols, by E. Jordan, c1740, 12.5in (32cm). **£850-900** *WAL*

A flintlock blunderbuss pistol with bayonet, by Waters, c1790. **£925-975** *WAL*

A double barrelled flintlock pistol, c1820. **£375-425** *WAL*

A 16 bore New Land pattern flintlock holster pistol, 15in (38cm). **£600-650** *WAL*

A 16 bore Military Yeomanry flintlock pistol, c1820. **£425-460** *WAL*

A 6 shot .44in Remington Army revolver, 14in (35.5cm). **£800-875** *WAL*

A 16 bore double barrelled back action pistol by J. W. Edge, c1840, 11in (28cm). **£460-485** *WAL*

A flintlock pocket pistol, by T. Ketland & Co., c1820, 7in (17.5cm). **£225-260** *WAL*

A pair of 20 bore percussion pistols, by T. K. Baker, 13.5in (34.5cm). **£750-775** *WAL*

A 24 bore Tower Heavy Dragoon flintlock pistol of 3rd Dragoon Guards, 18.5in (47cm). **£900-975** *WAL*

A pair of 28 bore Irish pistols, by Skelton of Omagh, c1840, 7.5in (19cm). **£450-480** *WAL*

A Victorian officer's silver plated helmet of the Royal Horse Guards.
£2,300-2,500 *WAL*

An officer's bearskin of the Irish Guards, with St. Patrick's blue hackle feather plume on right.
£450-475 *WAL*

An officer's bearskin of the Grenadier Guards, with hair plume on left.
£600-650 *WAL*

An officer's helmet of the East Devon Volunteer Cavalry, 1812 pattern black leather with horsehair mane, c1820.
£2,100-2,200 *CSK*

A Victorian officer's silver plated helmet of the 1st Royal Dragoons.
£1,200-1,300 *WAL*

An 1843 pattern officer's helmet of the 3rd Dragoon Guards, burnished gilt skull, lined with leather.
£3,300-3,500 *CSK*

An officer's bearskin of the Coldstream Guards, with scarlet hackle feather plume on right.
£450-475 *WAL*

An Indian helmet Khula Khud, the one piece bowl chiselled overall with flowering foliage, twin plume sockets, sliding nasal bar, and tall top spike, c1800.
£780-950 *WAL*

An Elizabeth II officer's silver plated helmet of The Life Guards, with white hair falling plume.
£1,100-1,250 *WAL*

A post-1902 officer's silver plated helmet of The Life Guards, with white hair falling plume.
£1,850-2,000 *WAL*

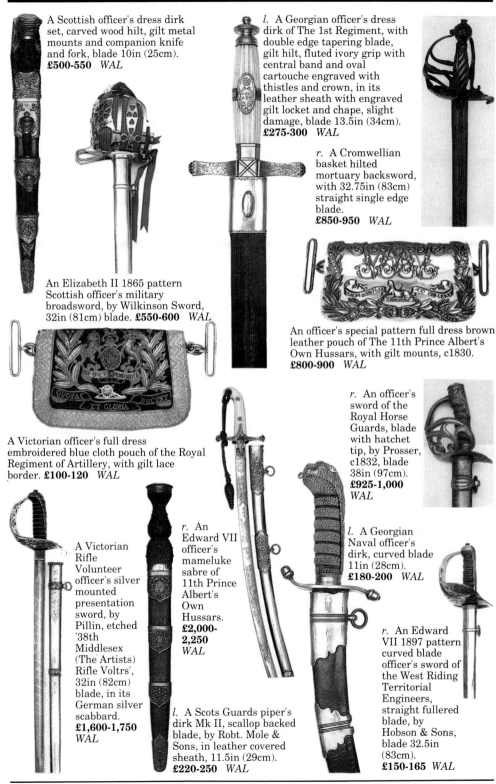

A Scottish officer's dress dirk set, carved wood hilt, gilt metal mounts and companion knife and fork, blade 10in (25cm). **£500-550** *WAL*

l. A Georgian officer's dress dirk of The 1st Regiment, with double edge tapering blade, gilt hilt, fluted ivory grip with central band and oval cartouche engraved with thistles and crown, in its leather sheath with engraved gilt locket and chape, slight damage, blade 13.5in (34cm). **£275-300** *WAL*

r. A Cromwellian basket hilted mortuary backsword, with 32.75in (83cm) straight single edge blade. **£850-950** *WAL*

An Elizabeth II 1865 pattern Scottish officer's military broadsword, by Wilkinson Sword, 32in (81cm) blade. **£550-600** *WAL*

An officer's special pattern full dress brown leather pouch of The 11th Prince Albert's Own Hussars, with gilt mounts, c1830. **£800-900** *WAL*

A Victorian officer's full dress embroidered blue cloth pouch of the Royal Regiment of Artillery, with gilt lace border. **£100-120** *WAL*

r. An officer's sword of the Royal Horse Guards, blade with hatchet tip, by Prosser, c1832, blade 38in (97cm). **£925-1,000** *WAL*

A Victorian Rifle Volunteer officer's silver mounted presentation sword, by Pillin, etched '38th Middlesex (The Artists) Rifle Voltrs', 32in (82cm) blade, in its German silver scabbard. **£1,600-1,750** *WAL*

r. An Edward VII officer's mameluke sabre of 11th Prince Albert's Own Hussars. **£2,000-2,250** *WAL*

l. A Georgian Naval officer's dirk, curved blade 11in (28cm). **£180-200** *WAL*

l. A Scots Guards piper's dirk Mk II, scallop backed blade, by Robt. Mole & Sons, in leather covered sheath, 11.5in (29cm). **£220-250** *WAL*

r. An Edward VII 1897 pattern curved blade officer's sword of the West Riding Territorial Engineers, straight fullered blade, by Hobson & Sons, blade 32.5in (83cm). **£150-165** *WAL*

A Canton plate, depicting 'The Drunken Poet', c1830, 10in (25cm) diam. **£100-120** *BOW*

Sumida figures, Meiji period, Japanese, c1900, largest 8in (20cm) high. **£60-70 each** *BOW*

A Kutani vase, Meiji period, c1880, 8.75in (22cm) high. **£70-80** *BOW*

An Arita dish, from the Fukagawa factory, Orchid mark, Japanese, c1870, 8.5in (21cm) diam. **£60-70** *BOW*

A Satsuma Imperial style vase, Edo period, c1830. **£120-140** *BOW*.

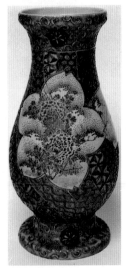

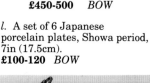

A pair of Japanese Imari vases, Edo period, c1820, 10.75in (27cm) high. **£450-500** *BOW*

l. A set of 6 Japanese porcelain plates, Showa period, 7in (17.5cm). **£100-120** *BOW*

A Satsuma vase, mid-19thC, 12in (30.5cm) high. **£150-160** *BOW*

A Satsuma 15 piece tea set, Tai-Sho period, c1915, teapot 6in (15cm) high. **£250-280** *BOW*

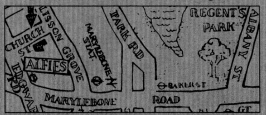

An Excelda gramophone, Swiss, 1931. **£140-180** *NF*

A Nirona gramophone, German, 1924. **£250-300** *NF*

A Mikiphone, Swiss, 1924. **£250-300** *NF*

A Bing Kiddyphone, German, 1930. **£180-220** *NF*

A Peter Pan gramophone, British, c1926. **£200-250** *NF*

A Pixie Grippa, by Perephone, London, 1924. **£150-200** *NF*

A Peter Pan gramophone with telescopic horn, British, 1923. **£200-250** *NF*

A Bing Pygmyphone, German, 1924. **£100-150** *NF*

An Acme miniature portable, by Nissan, c1950. **£220-280** *NF*

A Gamanette tinplate gramophone, German, 1930. **£200-250** *NF*

A tinplate gramophone, German, c1925. **£200-250** *NF*

A Chad Valley gramophone, c1950. **£100-150** *NF*

A Pixiephone, from US Zone, Germany, c1947. **£150-200** *NF*

A Bingola gramophone, German, 1928. **£150-200** *NF*

A Colibri gramophone, c1930. **£150-200** *NF*

200 Winner gramophone needles. **£12-15** *NF*

Kosmos Extra gramophone needles. **£20-25** *NF*

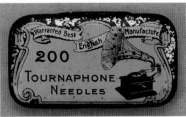

200 Tournaphone needles. **£18-22** *NF*

'Embassy' Radiogram gilded needles. **£14-18** *NF*

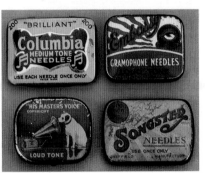

The four most common gramophone needle tins. **£4-6 each** *NF*

A circular tin of Columbia gramophone needles. **£35-40** *NF*

A tin of Submarine gramophone needles. **£45-50** *NF*

A tin of Tudor gramophone needles. **£10-12** *NF*

200 Decca gramophone needles. **£8-10** *NF*

HMV Tungstyle gramophone needles. **£18-20** *NF*

A circular tin of Dominion gramophone needles. **£30-35** *NF*

HMV Triple-tone needles. **£30-35** *NF*

A tin of Verona gramophone needles. **£18-22** *NF*

A Wurlitzer 1700, 104 selections of 45rpm, 1954, fully restored, 55.5in (141cm) high. **£4,500-5,500** *CSC*

A Wurlitzer 2000 Centennial model, 200 selections, restored, c1956, 56in (142cm) high. **£5,500-6,000** *CJS*

A Seeburg 148, 20 selections of 78rpm, restored, 57in (144.5cm). **£4,000-4,500** *CSC*

A Rock-Ola 464, c1976, 46in (116.5cm) high. **£900-1,200** *CJS*

A Wurlitzer 1015, c1946, 60in (152cm) high. **£10,500-12,000** *CSC*

A Seeburg 8800 Hitone, 1941, 63in (160cm) high. **£5,000-6,000** *CSC*

A Wurlitzer 1050 Nostalgia model, limited edition, the last 'American' Wurlitzer made, 58in (147cm) high. **£5,000-5,500** *CJS*

A Wurlitzer 750, 24 selections of 78rpm, 1941, 56in (142cm) high. **£10,000-11,000** *CSC*

A Rock-Ola 1422, 20 selections of 78rpm, fully restored, 1946, 58in (147cm) high.
£5,500-6,250 *CSC*

A Wurlitzer 1800, 104 selections of 45rpm, c1955, 55in (139.5cm) high. **£3,000-4,000** *CJS*

A Wurlitzer 10 cassette jukebox, c1974, 42in (106.5cm) high.
£1,200-1,800 *CJS*

A Rock-Ola 1428, 20 selections of 78rpm, c1948, 58in (147cm) high. **£5,500-6,000** *CJS*

An AMI model I, with curved glass windscreen, fully restored, c1958.
£3,250-3,750 *CJS*

A Seeburg V200, 200 selections of 45rpm, c1955, 56.5in (143cm) high.
£5,200-5,800 *CJS*

An AMI model A, 40 selections of 78rpm, restored, 1946, 68in (172.5cm) high.
£5,000-6,000 *CSC*

A Rock-Ola Tempo I, c1959, 60in (152cm) high.
£3,000-3,500 *CJS*
This machine featured on T.V. 'Jukebox Jury' programme

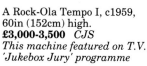

An illustrated record, 'Mademoiselle' by Chris Denver, c1930. **£30-40** *HEW*

A Mura Phone wall telephone, by G.E.C., c1950, 9in (23cm) high. **£225-275** *NOW*

An illustrated record, playing a selection from 'A Bedtime Story'. **£30-40** *HEW*

A green Ericsson 300 Series telephone, with drawer. **£250-300** *NOW*

A selection of Coronet Midget cameras, 2.5in (6.5cm) high, black **£40-50**, coloured **£80-120 each** *NOW*

A Binatone Canberra radio, c1960, 10in (25cm) high. **£22-25** *COL*

An illustrated record, playing 'Don't Blame Me', by Betty Bolton, c1930. **£30-40** *HEW*

A Neo Phone, with drawer, c1945. **£300-500** *NOW*

An illustrated record, playing 'Unless', by the Odonians Dance Orchestra. **£30-40** *HEW*

An illustrated record, 'Hold Your Man', c1930. **£30-40** *HEW*

An illustrated record, playing 'Pardon Madame', c1930. **£30-40** *HEW*

A telephone in working order, c1930. **£40-60** *WAC*

A military style stage jacket, worn by Michael Jackson during the 1984 Victory tour.
£3,300-3,500 *CSK*

A devil's costume, comprising a catsuit and horned helmet, worn by Alice Cooper on stage c1970.
£1,400-1,500 *CSK*

Madonna's crucifix pendant, Virgin Tour brochure, 1985, 3 photographs and a letter of authenticity.
£3,900-4,000 *CSK*

Derek and the Dominos D-35 Martin acoustic guitar, serial No. 263874.
Est. £5,700-8,500 *S(NY)*

A piece of a guitar smashed by Jimi Hendrix at the Monterey Pop Festival, c1967.
£5,000-5,500 *S(NY)*

Prince's custom-made perspex cane filled with translucent fluid and various shaped pieces of glitter, used on stage during the Purple Rain World Tour, 1984-85.
£1,200-1,300 *CSK*

Jimi Hendrix's Gibson Les Paul electric guitar, Serial No. 56043.
Est. £17,000-19,000 *S(NY)*

Derek and the Dominos electric guitar, 1966.
Est. £2,800-4,000 *S(NY)*

Elton John's racoon coat, worn on his 1984 World Tour. **£3,100-3,250** *CSK*

John Lennon's Hofner Compensator steel string acoustic guitar, 1960s.
£19,000-20,000 *S(NY)*

Jimi Hendrix's Hagstrom 8-string electric bass guitar, 1967.
Est. £3,500-4,500 *S(NY)*

A 1960s PVC vanity case, 10in (25.5cm) wide. **£8-10** *FAB*

A group of Dam trolls, 1961-65, 6 to 12in (15 to 30.5cm). **£10-30 each** *FAB*

A psychedelic table lamp, 1960s, 10in (25cm) high. **£20-25** *FAB*

The first Rave magazine, 1964. **£15-20** *FAB*

A 1928 Mercedes Benz barometer, 1960s. **£8-12** *FAB*

A pair of platform sole shoes, 1970s. **£6-8** *FAB*

A 1960s paperweight, 3.25in (8cm) diam. **£5-8** *FAB*

A nest of 3 tables, made in U.K. **£40-50**
Four melamine cups and saucers. **£8-10** *FAB*

A copy of Vogue, September 1964. **£8-10** *FAB*

A Japanese musical cocktail set, 10in (25cm) high. **£60-70** *FAB*

A melamine dish, Harry Shaw Coaches, c1960, 5in (12.5cm) long. **£5-7** *FAB*

An enamel sign, 18in (45.5cm) high.
£100-150 *K*

A Bovril chromolithograph die-cut show card, 19in (48.5cm). **£60-80** *ACh*

A Hudson's Dry Soap chromolithograph, c1900, 18in (45.5cm). **£150-200** *ACh*

A Fry's Chocolate Cream Egg box label, c1930, 8.5in (21cm) square. **£25-35** *ACh*

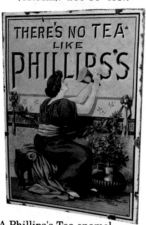

A Phillips's Tea enamel sign, c1900, 48in (122cm) high. **£300-400** *ACh*

A Pelaw Metal Polish transfer printed tinplate sign.
£180-250 *K*

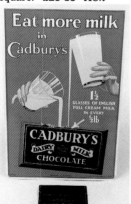

A Cadbury's paper window bill and wrapper, c1938.
£20-25 *ACh*

A tinplate advertisement for Pritchard's Health Salt Headache Drink.
£100-150 *K*

A large advertisement for Cooper's Powder Dip.
£175-200 *K*

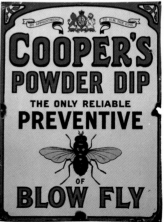

A chromolithograph die-cut show card, c1920s. **£60-70** *ACh*

A transfer printed tinplate finger plate. **£150-200** *K*

A dummy paper wrapped biscuit tin, 1917-1920, 9.5in (24cm) square. **£30-40** *ACh*

A Spa Chocolates Squirrel Brand box, c1930, 12.5in (32cm) wide. **£20-30** *ACh*

A McVitie & Price's sample biscuit tin, 3.25in (8cm) diam. **£20-25** *ACh*

A chromolithograph dummy salmon package, c1920, 13.5in (35cm) high. **£40-60** *ACh*

A Coleman's shop size toffee tin, 8in (20.5cm). **£30-40** *ACh*

An unopened packet of Rinso, c1930, 5.5in (14cm) high. **£10-15** *ACh*

A Terry's chocolate show card, c1950, 8in (20cm) high. **£18-20** *ACh*

Kitchenalia

An early copper traveller's kettle, with fold-over handle, 5in (13cm) diam.
£30-35 *PAR*

A red and white plastic recipe box.
£5-6 *AAM*

A string cutter, c1930, 7in (18cm) wide.
£35-40 *COL*

Menu Holders, 1920s, 4in (10cm) long.
£15-20 each *HEW*

A marmalade cutter, by Follows & Bate Ltd., Manchester, c1900.
£25-30 *ING*

A set of 6 painted plywood napkin holders, 1930s.
£15-20 *CSA*

A pair of old bellows, leather renewed.
£90-95 *AL*

A 'Star' vacuum cleaner, 51in (130cm) long.
£20-28 *TRU*

A copper kettle, 11in (28cm) high.
£65-70 *COL*

A pair of thistle pickle forks, Birmingham 1946, 4.5in (11cm) long.
£30-40 *TVA*

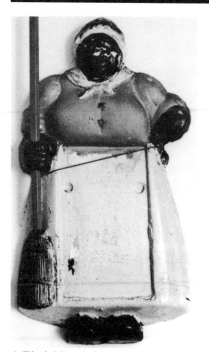

A copper pan, with brass handles, 15in (38cm) diam. **£260-270** *PAR*

A 'Black Mama' plaster kitchen notepad holder, 1930s, 10.5in (26cm) high. **£2-4** *TRU*

A copper and wrought iron stand, 34in (86cm) high. **£80-90** *AL*

A Rippingille's oil stove, c1890, 18.5in (47cm) wide. **£185-200** *AL*

A copper grog bucket, with swing top handle and fixed side handle, 19thC, 10in (25cm) diam. **£250-275** *PAR*

A copper pan and cover, with brass handles, 9in (23cm) diam. **£45-50** *PAR*

A spherical clear glass bowl fly catcher, on 3 feet, with applied ring round lip damaged. **£30-35** *BBR*

A copper stove cover, c1880, 36in (92cm) high. **£250-300** *AL*

Gas Cookers

A 'Puritan' No. 502 double hot plate, by the Florence Co., USA, the front tap rail with 2 brass taps, c1890. **£75-150** *CSK*

A brass nursery gas wall light bracket with boiling ring, c1885. **£110-150** *CSK*

The boiling ring would have been used for heating the baby's milk.

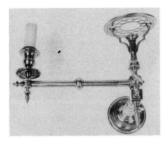

A grey enamel No. 1 'Bungalow' cooker on cast iron stand, by The Foundry Co. Ltd., Elmscott Warwick, with cast iron sides and back, 3 brass taps for 2 boiling rings and grill, c1912. **£35-100** *CSK*

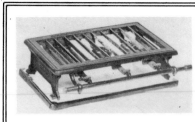

A 'Talbot' hot plate, by Fletcher Russell & Co., with front tap rail for 2 burners and turnover grill, drop-in bar-type grid and white enamel base plate, c1897.
£270-300 *CSK*

Formerly in the Segas Museum, Old Kent Road Depot.

The 'Great Duck' portable deflector cooker, of sheet steel with 4 cast iron cabriole feet, 3 boiling rings, the oven, deflector oven and hotplate, c1915, 32.5in (82cm).
£155-255 *CSK*

A French blue enamel table gas cooker, 'Le Standard No. 3', by Et. Brachet & Richard, drop-down door with porcelain handle, 4 brass taps for 3 boiling rings, grill and top boiler, side tap for oven, boiling rings missing, c1900.
£110-150 *CSK*

A 'Davis Wee Cooker', by the Davis Gas Stove Co., London, with 4 brass butterfly taps for 2 boiling rings, one grill and oven, on original stand, c1898.
£660-760 *CSK*

A Main cooker, No.52, with removable burners and cast one-piece grid, c1905, 28.75in (73cm) high.
£110-200 *CSK*

Originally hired out by the Gas Light & Coke Company at 1/9d per quarter.

A 'Metropolitan' No. 211 double gas range, by the Davis Gas Stove Co., London, with 8 taps and cast plate rack, burners and grill plates missing.
£210-250 *CSK*

Two gas cookers by John Wright & Co.:
l. No. 552, with loose white enamel crown plate and cast iron oven, c1910. **£155-255**
r. A 'Eureka' No. 405, with front tap rail for 2 rack type boiling burners and grill, fixed white enamel crown plate and enamel back and sides to oven, c1907, 21.5in (54cm) high.
£385-450 *CSK*

A French amber enamel table gas cooker, 'Le Vatel' type 400, by Lilor Paris, with 6 brass taps to feed oven burner, 2 grill burners and 3 boiling burners, door to oven and oven spit, c1915. **£825-900** *CSK*

A gas range, Model 140 New Pattern, by Richmond & Co., Warrington & London, with original copper hot water urn and gas attachment, side tap rail with 6 brass taps for 5 boiling burners and grill and brass side tap for oven, 1897.
£1,100-1,500 *CSK*

Installed from new at the cost of £12 13s 6d in 1897 at G. Austin & Sons cow keepers and dairymen, 39 Brayard Road, Peckham SE15, in their milk processing room. Taken out of service Oct. 26 1989.

A circular gas cooker, by Hare & Co., with single wrought iron boiling ring on top and another in oven base, 38in (97cm) high.
£1,100-1,500 *CSK*

Formerly in the Segas Museum, Old Kent Road Depot.

A Fletcher Russell 'Celebrity' copper disc hot water heater with bracket, c1905.
£70-100 *CSK*

Keys

A 'Kater' cooker on stand, by The British Gas Appliance Co., 3 brass taps feeding the side boiling ring, grill and oven burners and turnover grill, c1907. **£105-150** *CSK*

Two Art Nouveau style pedestal table boiling burners, c1905.
£125-150 *CSK*

A selection of keys, 2 to 4.25in (5 to 11cm) long.
£8-18 each *OD*

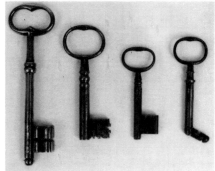

A selection of keys, 3.25 to 5.5in 8 to 14cm) long. **£6-22 each** *OD*

Lighting

A frosted wall light, possibly Lalique, 6 by 11in (15 by 28cm). **£80-150** *ASA*

An English coral satin glass oil lamp, c1880, 20in (51cm) high. **£400-500** *CB*

An Art Nouveau brass and bronze lamp, 29in (74cm) high. **£150-200** *ASA*

A copper table lamp, 1960s, 16.75in (42cm) high. **£18-22** *COL*

A Victorian oil lamp with marble stand, 29in (74cm) high. **£200-300** *ASA*

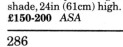

A brass lamp with a globe shade, 24in (61cm) high. **£150-200** *ASA*

A pair of gilt metal wall lights. **£250-300** *ASH*

A cream marbled with gold Anglepoise lamp, made by Herbert Terry & Sons Ltd., Redditch, c1940. **£20-30** *ROW*

A chinoiserie lamp, with replacement shade, 1930s, 60in (152cm) high.
£275-295 *ROW*

A crystal glass table lamp, 15in (38cm) high.
£100-200 *ASA*

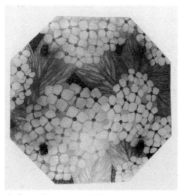

A domed octagonal hanging ceiling shade, decorated with pink and blue hydrangeas on green foliage, by Löys Lucha, c1929, 23in (59cm) diam, with triple silk suspension cords.
£950-1,000 *RID*

A pair of Venetian and overlaid glass lustres, hung with prism drops, one repaired, 9.5in (24cm).
£200-250 *GAK*

A pair of Victorian red painted metal oil filled Christmas candles, with green painted holly pattern, 8in (20cm) high.
£28-32 *ROW*

A Venini clown lamp, 23.5in (60cm) high.
£100-200 *ASA*

A domed octagonal hanging ceiling shade, decorated with yellow, blue and white flowers with peacock centres, by Löys Lucha, 1930s, 23in (59cm) diam, with triple silk suspension cords.
£1,000-1,100 *RID*

A copper table lamp, filled with oil and wax, heat from bulb melts wax to give volcanic effect, 1960s, 16.25in (41cm) high.
£15-18 *COL*

An Art Nouveau spelter figure table lamp, signed at base, 'Ch Perron', Verde Antico base, 26in (66cm). **£240-260** *GAK*

A silver plated Corinthian column oil lamp, with cut glass font, 32in (81cm). **£285-300** *GAK*

An Art Nouveau wrought iron and glass ceiling light. **£300-400** *ASA*

Luggage

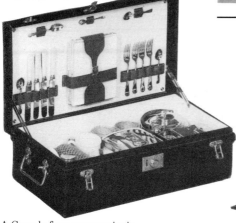

A Coracle four-person picnic set, the leathercloth case with fitted interior holding kettle and burner, cups, glasses, plates, cutlery, food boxes and other accessories, 1920s-30s, 22.5in (57cm) wide. **£1,320-1,500** *S*

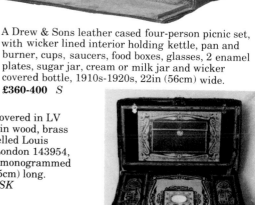

A Drew & Sons leather cased four-person picnic set, with wicker lined interior holding kettle, pan and burner, cups, saucers, food boxes, glasses, 2 enamel plates, sugar jar, cream or milk jar and wicker covered bottle, 1910s-1920s, 22in (56cm) wide. **£360-400** *S*

A lady's trunk, covered in LV material, bound in wood, brass and leather, labelled Louis Vuitton, Paris, London 143954, lock no. 019412, monogrammed L.LL, 40in (101.5cm) long. **£1,250-1,400** *CSK*

A leather covered trunk, with card and leather fittings, mid-19thC, 31in (79cm) wide. **£100-120** *TRU*

METALWARE

Arts & Crafts and Art Nouveau

A Liberty Tudric pewter tumbler holder, designed by Archibald Knox, 2.5in (6cm) high, with glass. **£50-60** *HEW*

An Art Nouveau copper plant holder, 12.5in (31cm) long. **£30-35** *OD*

A WMF pin tray, 4.5in (11cm) diam. **£70-80** *NCA*

A Tudric pewter tray, for Liberty & Co., No. 025, c1902, 18 by 13in (46 by 33cm). **£90-100** *ROW*

A copper vase, by Roycroft, USA, 9.5in (24cm) high. **£250-280** *NCA*

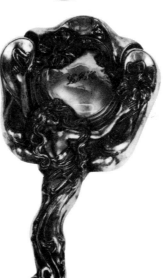

An Art Nouveau initialled silver plate hand mirror, 10.5in (26cm) long. **£75-85** *HEW*

A pair of copper and brass wall vases, 9in (23cm) high. **£15-20** *OD*

A pewter jardinière, 4.25in (11cm) high. **£50-60** *HEW*

A Cymric matchbox holder, 2.5in (6cm) long. **£80-100** *NCA*

A Newlyn copper tray, 5.5in (14cm) diam. **£30-40** *NCA*

An Arts & Crafts copper framed mirror, 21 by 17in (53 by 43cm). **£70-75** *ROW*

A Newlyn copper tray, 5.25in (13cm) square. **£40-45** *NCA*

A Newlyn copper tray, 4.25in (11cm) diam. **£40-45** *NCA*

An Art Nouveau pewter smoking lady wall plaque, 7in (18cm) wide. **£40-45** *HEW*

Brass

A Victorian brass crumb scoop, with ebony handle. **£25-30** *TRU*

A Victorian brass shoe horn, 9in (23cm) high. **£30-35** *OD*

Cross Reference
Candlesticks

A brass trivet, 6in (15cm) diam. **£18-20** *ROW*

Four brass candlesticks:
l. A French domed cylindrical base and tall slender stem, c1600, 8in (20cm). **£475-500**
c. Dutch bell shaped base with mid-drip pan and baluster stem, 17thC, 5.5in (14cm). **£475-500**
r. A pair of candlesticks, each with petal base and knopped stem, c1750, 7.25in (18.5cm). **£250-275** *S(S)*

Two brass vestas:
l. An eagle's head, 2.25in (5cm)
£70-75
r. An owl wearing a top hat, 2in (5cm).
£60-65 *GAK*

A selection of brass door knockers, Victorian Dartmoor pixie, the others 1920s, 3 to 5in (8 to 13cm) long.
£18-22 each *ML*

A pair of painted brass bookends depicting the Cutty Sark. **£40-50** *TRU*

> **Cross Reference**
> Smoking

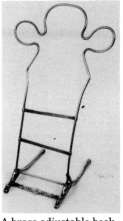

A brass adjustable book rest, 15in (38cm) high.
£35-45 *AMH*

A solid brass backplate from a cash register, 13 by 8.5in (33 by 21cm). **£10-15** *ROW*

Bronze

Two bronze mortars:
l. Decorated in relief with 2 beaded lugs, twin handles, initialled 'T.I.', 'A.I.' and a cross, 17thC, 5.5in (14cm). **£375-400**
r. With 4 loop handles, late 16thC, 6.5in (16cm).
£225-250 *S(S)*

A bronze urn and cover by Moigney, 8.5in (21cm) high.
£120-130 *TRU*

Copper

An Edwardian coal box, with brass finial, handles and feet, 18in (46cm) high. **£90-100** *ROW*

Door Stops

Ally Sloper and Mrs Sloper, 11.75in (30cm) high. **£250-350** *PC*

Characters from a comic strip which appeared in a weekly humorous magazine Judy, in August 1867.

Mr Punch, c1870, 12.5in (32cm) high. **£100-150** *PC*

An early cast iron door stop, 16in (41cm). **£40-50** *PAR*

A cast iron lion, 6in (15cm) high. **£25-30** *ROW*

A cast iron lion, 9.25in (23cm) long. **£35-40** *ROW*

Jesus and the Woman of Samaria, c1865, 10in (25cm) high. **£100-150** *PC*

Pewter

A Queen Anne tavern pot, by William Hux, William III capacity mark, ownership initials H.I. to handle, touch in base O.P. 2498, restored, c1705, 5in (13cm).
£3,500-3,750 *S(S)*

A Sheffield pewter musical tankard, plays Marching through Georgia, 6in (15cm) high. **£50-100** *PC*

A pair of chalices, with engraved inscription dated 1736, 6.25in (16cm).
£950-1,000 *S(S)*

A William III beaded tazza, c1690, 8.75in (22cm) diam.
£300-325 *S(S)*

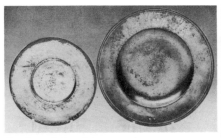

Two broad rim plates:
l. Continental, by Claude Morant, 9in (23cm), **£275-295**
r. By George Smith, initialled IM, touch adverso O.P. 4347, c1681, 12in (31cm).
£500-550 *S(S)*

A pair of baluster stem candlesticks, each with canted rectangular dished base, early 18thC, 6.25in (16cm).
£350-375 *S(S)*

A porringer with anchor mark flanked by initials to base, inscribed John Archer died 1740, c1680, 5in (13cm) diam.
£410-440 *S(S)*

A Queen Anne tavern pot, ownership initials EH to handle, and later engraved cartouche, c1705, 5in (13cm). **£1,500-1,600** *S(S)*

Two reeded rim bowls, both c1690, 14 and 15in (36 and 38cm) diam. **£300-350 each** *S(S)*

A Jersey lidded measure, by John De St Croix, with touch under lid and ownership SDC to handle, c1780, 10.75in (27cm). **£300-325** *S(S)*

Silver

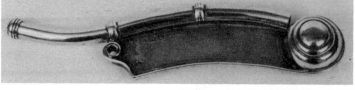

A bosuns whistle, London 1798, T. Streeter, 4.5in (11cm) long. **£500-600** *AMH*

An Edwardian silver mounted prayer book, London 1904, 5.5 by 2.75in (14 by 7cm). **£80-90** *TRU*

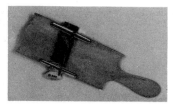

A silver and ivory cucumber slicer, made by Phipps & Robinson, London 1795, 8.5in (21cm) long. **£1,200-1,400** *AMH*

A tea infuser frame, London c1830, 3in (8cm) diam. **£80-100** *AMH*

The muslin bag was fixed into the holes around the ring.

A pair of boxed napkin rings, Birmingham 1926. **£50-60** *TRU*

A snuff box, Birmingham 1873. **£210-230** *TRU*

A gentleman's hair brush, with engine turned silver back. **£12-15** *TRU*

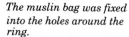

An apple corer and fruit knife, Birmingham 1831, 6.5in (16cm) long. **£550-650** *AMH*

Two baby's rattles:
l. Birmingham 1894, 2.5in (6cm).
r. Birmingham 1902, 3.5in (9cm)
long.
£50-60 each *HOW*

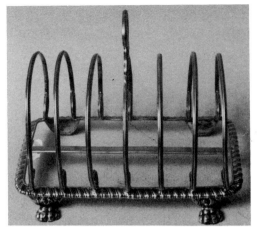

A George III toast rack, Sheffield
1819, 6.5in (16cm) long.
£225-275 *TRU*

A cigar case,
5.5in (14cm) long.
£60-70 *TRU*

Cross Reference
Smoking

A pair of chased sugar tongs,
Sheffield 1906, 6in (15cm).
£20-25 *ROW*

A George III oval teapot, with
ivory handle, by James Young,
1790, with contemporary plain
oval stand, by Elizabeth Jones,
1791, 21oz together.
£500-525 *GAK*

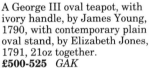

A set of 12 Edwardian dessert
knives and forks, with ivory
handles, Sheffield 1903.
£250-270 *TRU*

A set of 6 silver and enamel
teaspoons, Birmingham 1934.
£80-90 *TRU*

A silver topped jar, Birmingham
1913.
£25-30 *TRU*

Four Victorian oval salts, with pierced sides, complete with liners, Chester 1896.
£30-35 *GAK*

A Victorian two-handled octagonal tea tray, with presentation inscription, made by Elkington & Co. Ltd., London 1890, 154oz, complete with original oak case.
£1,500-1,600 *RBB*

An oval pap boat, with offset pourer, by Andrew Fogelberg, London 1798. **£125-150** *GAK*

A 4-piece tea service, by Mappin & Webb, Sheffield 1933, 55oz.
£660-700 *GAK*

A Victorian toast rack of 7 hoop design, with central ringlet carrying handle, London 1874, 9oz. **£120-140** *GAK*

An Edwardian cream jug, with hammered finish, Birmingham 1902.
£70-80 *TRU*

A pair of cast silver salt frames complete with blue glass liners, Sheffield 1892, 5oz.
£225-250 *GAK*

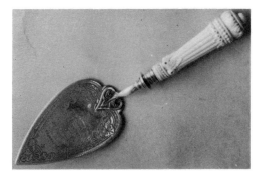

A Victorian presentation trowel, engraved with an inscription dated 1894, ivory handle, Sheffield 1893.
£140-160 *GAK*

A silver plated cocktail shaker.
£25-30 *TRU*

An Edwardian 3-piece silver tea set, the sugar bowl and cream jug internally gilded, London 1911/13, approx. 30oz together.
£500-550 *GAK*

A pair of sugar tongs, Sheffield 1905, 6.5in (16cm).
£20-25 *ROW*

A George II two-handled porringer with hollow handles, marked for London 1755, maker Henry Brind, 5in (13cm) high, 16oz.
£825-850 *GAK*

A pair of George III silver goblets, bearing a crest, London c1773, 16oz.
£550-575 *GAK*

| Cross Reference |
| Drinking |

A stud box, hallmarked Birmingham 1912.
£900-1,000 *S*

Originally belonged to Harry Vardo, together with 2 postcards, one depicting Harry Vardon with trophy, the other depicting trophies.

A Charles II two-handled porringer, with maker's mark A.R. Mullet, engraved with initials, 2.75in (7cm) high, 3.75oz.
£500-550 *P(L)*

A silver mounted hip flask, Sheffield 1932, 4.5in (11cm) high.
£90-100 *TRU*

A sauceboat, Birmingham 1934.
£70-80 *TRU*

Silver Plate

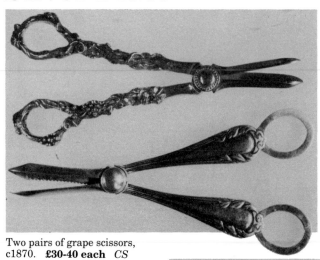

Two pairs of grape scissors,
c1870. **£30-40 each** *CS*

A Continental electro plated
centrepiece, early 20thC.
£500-525 *DaD*

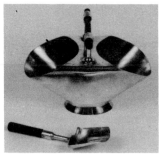

A sugar basin and shovel,
design attributed to Christopher
Dresser, 6in (15cm).
£150-200 *ZEI*

Spelter

A locket containing butterfly seal.
£5-15 *ASA*

A mirror with alabaster base,
1930s, 12in (31cm) high.
£180-200 *HEW*

A bronzed spelter figure
clock ornament with
mariner and ship's
wheel, 27in (69cm).
£175-200 *GAK*

A pair of figures,
labelled 'L'Orage'
par Bruchon,
19in (48cm) high.
£100-125 *ROW*

A pair of figurines depicting seated
Roman warriors on horseback
escorting slaves, on rectangular
matching plinths, 19thC, 17in (43cm) high.
£185-200 *GH*

A figure by Lorenzl, 8.25in (21cm)
high.
£200-250 *HEW*

MILITARIA
General

A framed advertising display of Eley's Sporting Ammunition, 25 by 31in (64 by 79cm).
£850-875 *WAL*

A French officer's iron campaign bed, mounted in ormolu, signed Desouches, late 18thC, 68in (172.5cm) long.
£7,600-8,600 *S(NY)*

According to Harding Collection records, this bed was used by Napoleon Bonaparte during the Egyptian Campaign of 1798.

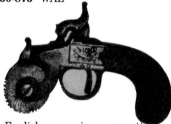

An English percussion eprouvette, signed S. Nock, minor damage, c1825, 5.5in (14cm).
£300-350 *ASB*

A flintlock eprouvette, measuring wheel with 15 divisions, walnut stock, brass trigger guard and pommel, 18thC, damaged, 14in (36cm) long. **£450-475** *HSS*

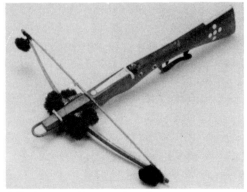

A German sporting crossbow for a child, late 18thC, fitted with later string and woollen tassels, 17.5in (44cm). **£650-700** *S(NY)*

A model of a field gun and limber, with bronze barrel, minor restorations, 19thC, 24.25in (62cm). **£1,100-1,500** *S(NY)*

Richard Simkin, Officers and Men of the 15th (King's) Hussars, 1768-1884, signed, watercolour heightened with white, unframed, 18.75 by 13.25in (48 by 34cm).
£450-475 *S*

The 15th Light Dragoons raised in 1759 and first commanded by Colonel George Augustus Eliott became known as the 15th (or the King's) Regiment of (Light) Dragoons in 1766. In 1807, in common with other light dragoons, they were called hussars. The title was simplified in 1861 to the 15th (The King's) Hussars. In 1920 they amalgamated with the 19th Hussars (Queen Alexandra's Own) and in 1933 the regiment became the 15th/19th King's Royal Hussars.

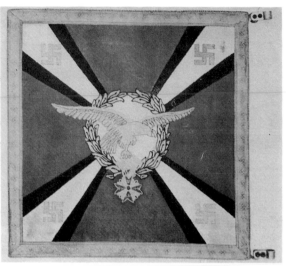

A square car pennant of the Commander-in-Chief of the Luftwaffe Reichsmarschall Göring, minor stains.
£225-250 *WAL*

No provenance, probably good post-war copy.

A brass powder and shot measure, scales to 2oz and 5 drams, c1800, 6in (15cm).
£160-180 *WAL*

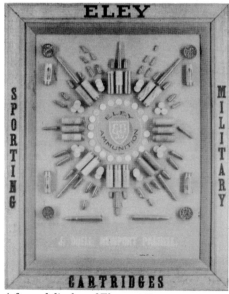

Richard Simkin, The Royal Irish Fusiliers at Dublin Castle, signed watercolour, 14.5 by 21.5in (37 by 54cm). **£750-800** *S*

A framed display of Eley sporting and military cartridges.
£2,000-2,400 *S(S)*

Richard Simkin, Officers and Men of the 2nd Dragoon Guards Queen's Bays, 1687-1914, signed, watercolour heightened with white, unframed, 21.25 by 14.25in (54 by 36cm).
£500-550 *S*

A German horseman's hammer, grip replaced, early 17thC, 21in (53cm).
£1,100-1,500 *S(NY)*

A framed advertising display of Eley's sporting cartridges, 24.5 by 30.5in (62 by 77cm). **£950-1,000** *WAL*

Badges

An other rank's brass glengarry badge of the R Anglesey Light Infantry Militia.
£60-70 *WAL*

A pre-1922 cast pouch or belt badge of the 3rd Skinner's Horse.
£80-90 *WAL*

A Victorian officer's gilt and silver plated glengarry badge of The Gloucestershire Regt., with original velvet, some wear, c1895.
£90-100 *WAL*

An other rank's white metal cap badge of the 1st Voluntary Battalion The Lancashire Fusiliers. **£70-80** *WAL*

A Boer War brass slouch hat badge of Marshall's horse.
£100-110 *WAL*

A Victorian officer's embroidered forage cap badge of the Essex Regt, some wear to velvet.
£90-100 *WAL*

A pre-1947 officer's silver cap badge of the 16th Light Cavalry, London 1926.
£140-150 *WAL*

A pre-1922 other rank's die struck cap badge of the 119th Infantry (The Mooltan Regt).
£170-190 *WAL*

An officer's cap badge of The Oxfordshire Light Infantry, hallmarked Birmingham 1903.
£85-95 *WAL*

A pre-1922 other rank's die struck brass puggaree badge of the 1st Brahmans, brooch pin.
£65-75 *WAL*

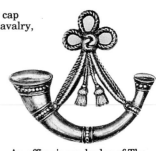

A pre-1922 silver cap badge of the 4th Rajputs, hallmarked Birmingham 1916.
£210-225 *WAL*

A pre-1903 officer's silver plated cap badge of the 2nd Bengal Lancers and a cast brass 2 BL title.
£110-120 *WAL*

A silver cap badge of the Liverpool Pals, hallmarked London 1914.
£85-95 *WAL*

As given by the Earl of Derby to each recruit joining before 16.10.1914.

A cap badge of The King's Shropshire Light Infantry, gilt initials.
£60-70 *WAL*

A gilt cap badge of the Westminster Dragoons IY, brooch pin.
£70-80 *WAL*

A silver cap badge of the Liverpool Pals, hallmarked London 1914.

An officer's cap badge of the Prince Albert Volunteers, by Scully, Montreal.
£95-100 *WAL*

A pre-1922 other rank's cast white metal puggaree badge of the 84th Punjabis, brooch pin.
£100-110 *WAL*

A pre-1947 officer's silver cap badge of the 1st Madras Pioneers, Birmingham 1926.
£170-180 *WAL*

An officer's cap badge of The Royal Armoured Corps, hallmarked Birmingham 1942.
£95-110 *WAL*

A Victorian officer's Maltese Cross puggaree badge of the 31st Punjab Infantry, hallmarked Birmingham 1892.
£290-310 *WAL*

An officer's cap badge of The South Wales Borderers, hallmarked Birmingham 1942.
£110-120 *WAL*

An officer's puggaree badge of the 16th Punjab Regt., Birmingham 1925.
£110-125 *WAL*

An officer's cap badge of the Kings Own Royal Lancaster Regt., Birmingham 1935.
£130-150 *WAL*

A pre-1903 other rank's cast brass badge of the 9th Bengal Artillery, slide fastening.
£150-170 *WAL*

A silver cap badge of the Somersetshire Light Infantry, Birmingham 1906.
£110-125 *WAL*

An officer's cap badge of the 90th Punjabis, hallmarked Birmingham 1907.
£110-125 *WAL*

Gorgets

A Georgian officer's universal pattern gilt gorget.
£130-150 *WAL*

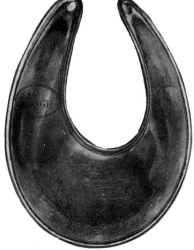

A Georgian officer's copper gorget of the Omagh Corps, retaining traces of gilt.
£140-160 *WAL*

Helmet Plates

A Dragoon Guards officer's 1834 pattern gilt helmet plate, slight damage.
£110-125 *WAL*

A Victorian officer's helmet plate of the Ordnance Stores Department.
£170-180 *WAL*

A post 1902 officer's gilt helmet plate of The Royal Artillery.
£60-75 *WAL*

A Victorian cadet's gilt helmet plate of the Royal Military College.
£75-85 *WAL*

A Victorian officer's gilt and silver plated helmet plate of The Hampshire Regiment.
£140-150 *WAL*

A post 1902 other rank's white metal helmet plate of the 13th (Kensington) County of London Regiment.
£60-70 *WAL*

A Victorian officer's blackened white metal helmet plate of a Voluntary Battalion The Royal Irish Rifles.
£250-270 *WAL*

Shoulder Belt Plates

Bayonets

An Austrian M 1849 Augustin rifle sword socket bayonet, blade 23in (59cm).
£120-140 *WAL*

A George III officer's silver gilt rectangular shoulder belt plate of The 25th (Kings Own Borderers) Regiment.
£575-600 *WAL*

This pattern is not mentioned by Parkyn and was evidently worn about the Waterloo period and preceded the better known special scrolled pattern with slide.

A Georgian officer's die struck copper gilt oval shoulder belt plate of the St Martin's Loyal Volunteers, gilt rubbed.
£150-170 *WAL*

A second pattern sword bayonet 1843 pattern, for the Sappers & Miners carbine, socket marked '15.C.92', blade 24.5in (62cm),.
£120-130 *WAL*

A Georgian other rank's rectangular brass shoulder belt plate of The 58th (Rutland) Regiment.
£225-250 *WAL*

Daggers

An officer's gilt and silver plated rectangular shoulder belt plate of The 96th Regiment, with original leather liner.
£225-250 *WAL*

A pre-1855 officer's gilt rectangular shoulder belt plate of The Royal Artillery.
£240-260 *WAL*

A Soviet army officer's dagger, blade 7.5in (19cm).
£80-90 *WAL*

A Nazi land customs officer's dagger, by Paul Weyersberg.
£375-400 *WAL*

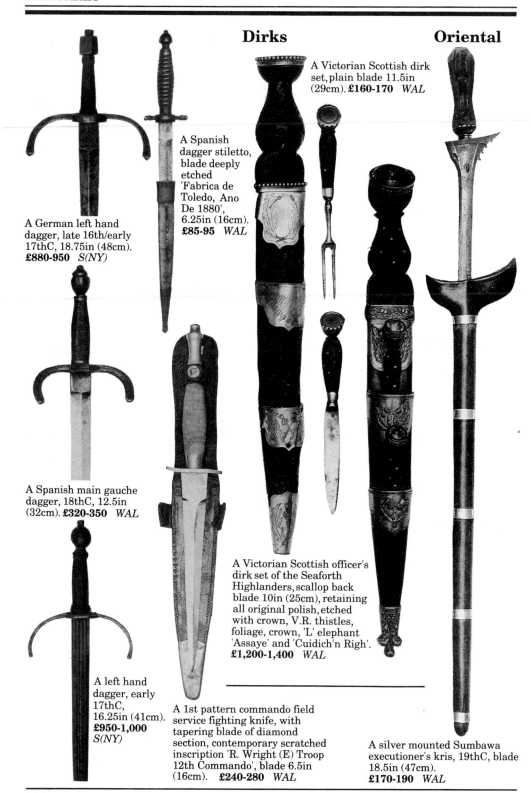

Dirks

Oriental

A Victorian Scottish dirk set, plain blade 11.5in (29cm). **£160-170** *WAL*

A German left hand dagger, late 16th/early 17thC, 18.75in (48cm). **£880-950** *S(NY)*

A Spanish dagger stiletto, blade deeply etched 'Fabrica de Toledo, Ano De 1880', 6.25in (16cm). **£85-95** *WAL*

A Spanish main gauche dagger, 18thC, 12.5in (32cm). **£320-350** *WAL*

A Victorian Scottish officer's dirk set of the Seaforth Highlanders, scallop back blade 10in (25cm), retaining all original polish, etched with crown, V.R. thistles, foliage, crown, 'L' elephant 'Assaye' and 'Cuidich'n Righ'. **£1,200-1,400** *WAL*

A left hand dagger, early 17thC, 16.25in (41cm). **£950-1,000** *S(NY)*

A 1st pattern commando field service fighting knife, with tapering blade of diamond section, contemporary scratched inscription 'R. Wright (E) Troop 12th Commando', blade 6.5in (16cm). **£240-280** *WAL*

A silver mounted Sumbawa executioner's kris, 19thC, blade 18.5in (47cm). **£170-190** *WAL*

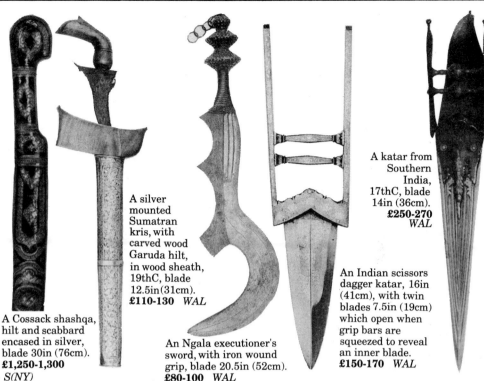

A Cossack shashqa, hilt and scabbard encased in silver, blade 30in (76cm). **£1,250-1,300** *S(NY)*

A silver mounted Sumatran kris, with carved wood Garuda hilt, in wood sheath, 19thC, blade 12.5in(31cm). **£110-130** *WAL*

An Ngala executioner's sword, with iron wound grip, blade 20.5in (52cm). **£80-100** *WAL*

A katar from Southern India, 17thC, blade 14in (36cm). **£250-270** *WAL*

An Indian scissors dagger katar, 16in (41cm), with twin blades 7.5in (19cm) which open when grip bars are squeezed to reveal an inner blade. **£150-170** *WAL*

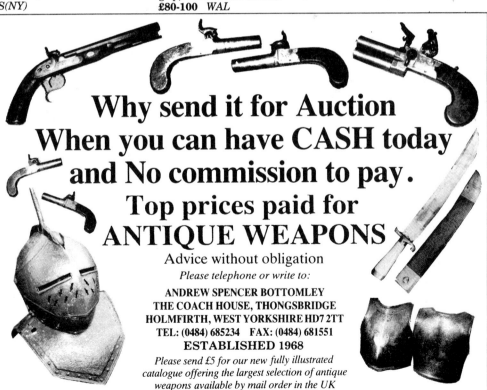

Swords

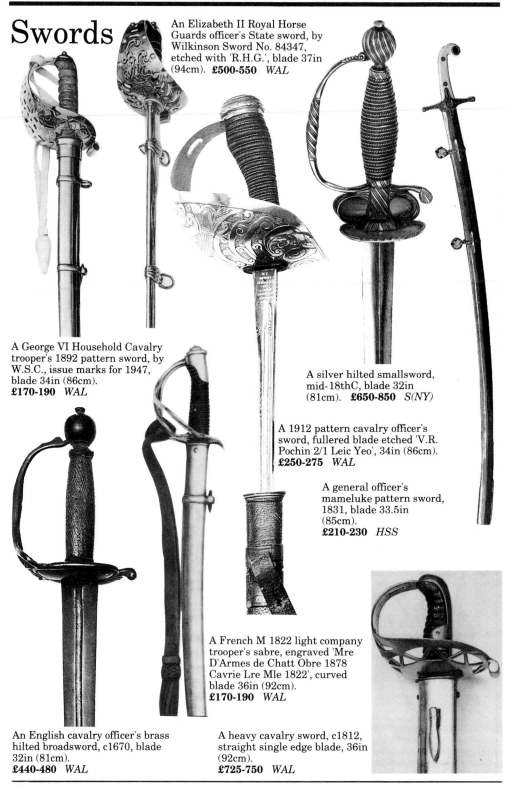

An Elizabeth II Royal Horse Guards officer's State sword, by Wilkinson Sword No. 84347, etched with 'R.H.G.', blade 37in (94cm). **£500-550** *WAL*

A George VI Household Cavalry trooper's 1892 pattern sword, by W.S.C., issue marks for 1947, blade 34in (86cm). **£170-190** *WAL*

A silver hilted smallsword, mid-18thC, blade 32in (81cm). **£650-850** *S(NY)*

A 1912 pattern cavalry officer's sword, fullered blade etched 'V.R. Pochin 2/1 Leic Yeo', 34in (86cm). **£250-275** *WAL*

A general officer's mameluke pattern sword, 1831, blade 33.5in (85cm). **£210-230** *HSS*

A French M 1822 light company trooper's sabre, engraved 'Mre D'Armes de Chatt Obre 1878 Cavrie Lre Mle 1822', curved blade 36in (92cm). **£170-190** *WAL*

An English cavalry officer's brass hilted broadsword, c1670, blade 32in (81cm). **£440-480** *WAL*

A heavy cavalry sword, c1812, straight single edge blade, 36in (92cm). **£725-750** *WAL*

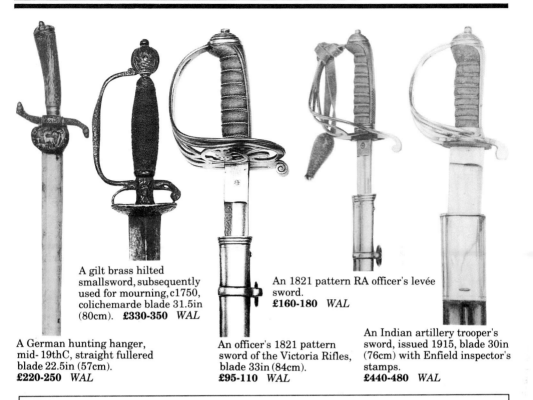

A gilt brass hilted smallsword, subsequently used for mourning, c1750, colichemarde blade 31.5in (80cm). **£330-350** *WAL*

An 1821 pattern RA officer's levée sword. **£160-180** *WAL*

A German hunting hanger, mid- 19thC, straight fullered blade 22.5in (57cm). **£220-250** *WAL*

An officer's 1821 pattern sword of the Victoria Rifles, blade 33in (84cm). **£95-110** *WAL*

An Indian artillery trooper's sword, issued 1915, blade 30in (76cm) with Enfield inspector's stamps. **£440-480** *WAL*

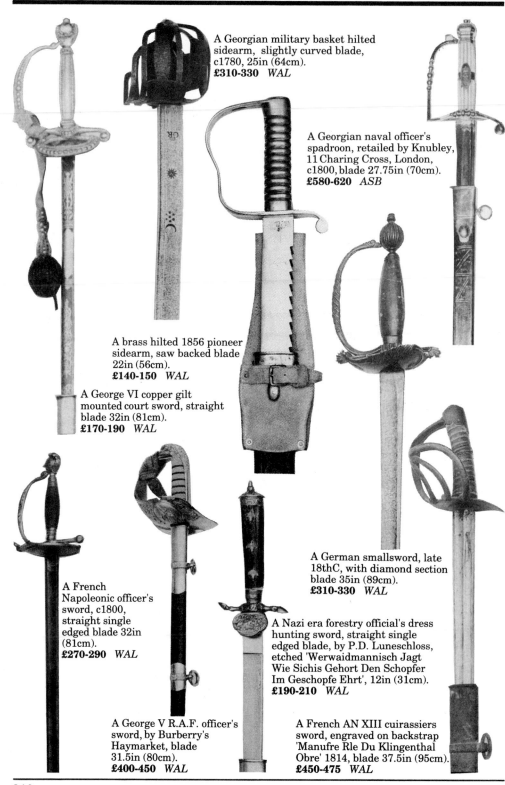

A Georgian military basket hilted sidearm, slightly curved blade, c1780, 25in (64cm).
£310-330 *WAL*

A Georgian naval officer's spadroon, retailed by Knubley, 11 Charing Cross, London, c1800, blade 27.75in (70cm).
£580-620 *ASB*

A brass hilted 1856 pioneer sidearm, saw backed blade 22in (56cm).
£140-150 *WAL*

A George VI copper gilt mounted court sword, straight blade 32in (81cm).
£170-190 *WAL*

A French Napoleonic officer's sword, c1800, straight single edged blade 32in (81cm).
£270-290 *WAL*

A German smallsword, late 18thC, with diamond section blade 35in (89cm).
£310-330 *WAL*

A Nazi era forestry official's dress hunting sword, straight single edged blade, by P.D. Luneschloss, etched 'Werwaidmannisch Jagt Wie Sichis Gehort Den Schopfer Im Geschopfe Ehrt', 12in (31cm).
£190-210 *WAL*

A George V R.A.F. officer's sword, by Burberry's Haymarket, blade 31.5in (80cm).
£400-450 *WAL*

A French AN XIII cuirassiers sword, engraved on backstrap 'Manufre Rle Du Klingenthal Obre' 1814, blade 37.5in (95cm).
£450-475 *WAL*

Medals

A naval general service medal 1793-1840, dated 1848, with one bar 'Java', awarded to Amos Batron.
£275-295 *HSS*

An RAF cross and bar group for World War II and Korea.
£1,500-1,750 *CAA*

Awarded to a Squadron Leader, complete with pilot's wings and miniatures.

A World War I C.G.M. pair, awarded to Able Seaman E.J. Moore, R.N., Conspicuous Gallantry Medal, Geo. V (A.B., English Channel, 19 Feb. 1918), British War Medal, 1914-1918 (A.B., R.N.). **£1,100-1,500** *S*

Approximately 110 Conspicuous Gallantry Medals were awarded to Naval and Royal Marine Personnel for W.W.I.

A Shackleton Expedition Polar Medal pair, awarded to an Albert Medallist Petty Officer 1st Class H.E. Wild, R.N., Polar Medal 1904, 1 clasp, Antarctic 1914-16, in silver (H.E.Wild, In Charge of Stores, Aurora), Messina Earthquake, 1908, small silver medal.
£4,250-4,750 *S*

Approximately 32 such Polar Medals for Shackleton's Trans-Antarctic Expedition, 1914-1916, the Messina Earthquake Medal was for services aboard H.M.S. Lancaster.

A World War II C.G.M. group for
operation agreement, Sergeant J.
Povall, Royal Marines, C.G.M.
Geo. VI (T./Cpl., R.M.), impressed
naming, fixed suspension, 1939-
45 Star, Africa Star, War Medal,
Royal Marine Meritorious Service
Medal, Geo. VI (Sgt., C.G.M.,
28.2.1951), R.N. Long Service and
Good Conduct Medal, Geo.VI
(Mne., R.M.), this one stamped
'replacement'.
£5,500-6,000 *S*

A George Cross (exchange
E.G.M.) group, awarded to Able
Seaman G.W. Harrison, Royal
Navy, George Cross, 1914-15 Star
(A.B., R.N.), British War Medal,
Victory Medal, 1939-45 Star,
Atlantic Star, Africa Star,
Defence Medal, War Medal, R.N.
Long Service and Good Conduct
Medal, Geo. V.
£3,000-3,500 *S*

*Approximately 112 Empire
Gallantry Medal recipients were
entitled to an exchange George
Cross at the time of the latter
award's institution in 1940.*

An Egypt Campaign C.G.M.
group, awarded to Sergeant H.
Henry, Royal Marine Light
Infantry, Conspicuous Gallantry
Medal, Vic., second type
(Corporal, R.M.L.I.) officially
impressed in large block capitals,
Egypt Campaign, 1882, rev.
dated, 1 clasp, Tel-el-Kebir
(Corpl., R.M.L.I.), Royal Naval
L.S. & G.C., Vic., 1.25ins. type
(Sergt., R.M.L.I.), Khedive's Star,
dated 1882.
£3,750-4,250 *S*

*Approximately 250 Conspicuous
Gallantry Medals have been won
by Naval or Royal Marine
Personnel since the award's
institution in 1855, but only about
40 of these to the latter body, 10 of
them for the Egyptian operations
of 1882-85.*

A Davison's pewter medal for
Trafalgar, 1805, as struck for
crew members of H.M.S. Victory.
£1,300-1,400 *S*

An O.B.E., Military Cross group, awarded to a Lt.. Colonel who was Deputy Director of Supply and Transport for India. **£500-650** *CAA*

A World War II Distinguished Service Order group. **£700-800** *CAA*

Awarded to a naval Commander for sinking 3 enemy submarines.

A Boulton's medal for Trafalgar, 1805, specimen striking. **£600-650** *S*

A Waterloo June 18th 1815 medal, awarded to George Cooper, 3rd Batallion of Grenadier Guards, with ribbon and a note of the family provenance. **£250-275** *HSS*

A Royal National Institution for the Preservation of Life from Shipwreck (R.N.L.I.), awarded to Mr Richard Eddy, voted 19 March 1834, Silver Medal, Bust of George IV, reverse Lifesaving Scene, with second award boat, with integral loop and ring suspension. **£800-900** *S*

An early K.C.B., K.H. group awarded to Admiral Sir Robert Smart, R.N., The Most Honourable Order of the Bath (K.C.B.), Military Division, The Royal Guelphic Order of Hanover (K.H.) Military Division, Naval General Service, 1793, 2 clasps, Algiers (1328), Navarino (1142) (Lieut., R.N.), Germany, Prussia, Order of the Red Eagle, Knight's breast badge in gold and enamels. **£5,000-5,500** *S*

A Zulu War and Arctic Exploration pair, awarded to Ab Seaman J. Pearson, R.N., South Africa 1877, 1 clasp, 1879 (A.B., H.M.S. Shah), a later impressed issue, c1890, Arctic Discoveries, 1875-76 (A.B., H.M.S. Alert). **£1,500-1,750** *S*

Approximately 170 such Arctic Medals issued, 63 of these to H.M.S. Alert.

Uniforms

A Victorian goat hair sporran, with silver mounts, 20in (51cm) long.
£350-450 *BWA*

A Victorian officer's brown leather Voluntary Rifles. pouch of the Isle of Man
£110-130 *WAL*

A Victorian Volunteer Artillery officer's full dress shoulder belt and embroidered pouch.
£65-85 *WAL*

An officer's brown leather shoulder belt and pouch of the 27th Punjab Infantry.
£400-440 *WAL*

A Captain's full dress blue tunic, with scarlet facings of a Bengal Lancers Regiment.
£260-280 *WAL*

Headdress

A Victorian officer's blue cloth spike helmet of The Bedfordshire Regiment.
£370-390 *WAL*

A Victorian officer's full dress embroidered pouch of the Queen's Own Glasgow Yeomanry, blue cloth.
£300-350 *WAL*

A 1902-8 other rank's busby grey cloth of the Queen's Westminster Rifle Volunteers.
£220-250 *WAL*

A post 1902 officer's silver plated helmet of the 1st Royal Dragoons.
£950-975 *WAL*

A Royal Horse Artillery other rank's busby.
£150-175 *WAL*

A Victorian officer's silver plated helmet of the Second Life Guards.
£1,750-1,950 *WAL*

A post 1902 officer's blue cloth spike helmet of The Worcestershire Regiment.
£420-450 *WAL*

An Italian Marines shako, label inscribed 'Chaco Italian Army', c1910.
£150-170 *WAL*

A German Gothic sallet, c1480, 8.75in (22cm) high.
£2,350-2,750 *S(NY)*

An officer's bearskin of the Scots Guards.
£425-450 *WAL*

A comb morion, single piece construction, brass rivets restored, plume holder lacking, late 16thC.
£800-900 *S*

Pistols

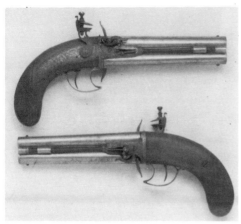

A pair of flintlock turn-over pistols, unsigned, English or Flemish, c1825, 12in (31cm).
£1,600-2,000 *S(NY)*

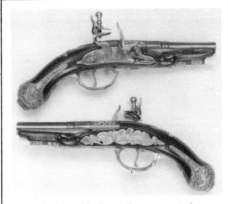

A pair of Italian silver mounted ebony stocked flintlock pistols, late 18thC, barrels and locks refinished, 9in (22cm).
£2,500-3,000 *S(NY)*

The decoration on the barrels is probably the work of Tortiglione, c1835.

A 16 bore British New Land Pattern flintlock pistol, c1810, barrel 9in (23cm).
£380-420 *ASB*

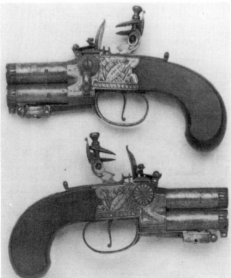

A pair of English flintlock boxlock over-and-under tap action pocket pistols, by Mortimer, London, Birmingham proof marks, c1820, 6in (15cm).
£1,400-1,800 *S(NY)*

A Queen Anne style cannon barrelled boxlock flintlock pocket pistol, by Collis of Oxford, barrel 7.25in (18cm).
£375-400 *WAL*

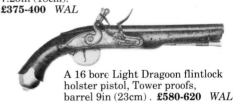

A 16 bore Light Dragoon flintlock holster pistol, Tower proofs, barrel 9in (23cm). **£580-620** *WAL*

A Queen Anne type brass flintlock travelling pistol, boxlock action, by Parkes of London, c1775, .56 brass barrel proof marked London, 12in (31cm). **£525-550** *L*

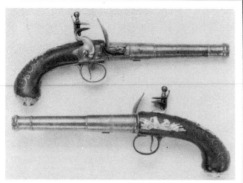

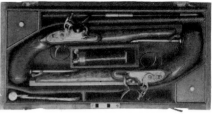

An English cased pair of flintlock officer's pistols, by Blissett, London proof marks, c1820, 13.5in (34cm).
£1,750-2,200 *S(NY)*

A pair of English silver mounted flintlock turn-off pistols, by Stanton, London proof marks and foreigner's mark, London silver hallmark and maker's mark of Jeremiah Ashley, c1750.
£2,000-2,500 *S(NY)*

Jonathan Stanton was apprenticed to his uncle William Turvey in 1739 and elected Master of the Gunmaker's Company in 1765.

A boxlock flintlock pistol, 18thC, 5in (13cm) steel turn-off barrel.
£550-580 *HSS*

A Persian flintlock blunderbuss pistol, c1860, barrel 8.5in (21cm).
£240-260 *WAL*

A .56 sea service flintlock belt pistol, Tower proved, barrel 12in (31cm) . **£775-825** *WAL*

A pair of 16 bore officer's percussion travelling pistols, by Hamburger & Co. London, c1830. **£900-950** *HSS*

An English cased pair of flintlock coat pistols, by H.W. Mortimer & Son, Gunmakers to His Majesty, 89 Fleet Street, c1810, 8.5in (21cm).
£2,000-2,500 *S(NY)*

A brass framed and barrelled boxlock flintlock pocket pistol, 6.75in (17cm), barrel 2in (5cm).
£175-185 *WAL*

A 22 bore percussion holster pistol by Harvey of Plymouth, 11in (28cm), octagonal twist barrel 6.25in (16cm).
£300-330 *WAL*

A 6-shot .28 E Whitney patent single action percussion pocket revolver, No. 1421, 7.5in (19cm), barrel 3.5in (9cm).
£400-425 *WAL*

An English 70 bore Cooper's patent 6-shot self cocking bar hammer percussion pepperbox revolver, by Reilly, London, c1855, barrel 3.5in (9cm).
£1,200-1,400 *ASB*

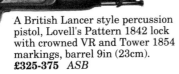

A 24 bore percussion travelling pistol, by Wood of Worcester, converted from flintlock, 9.5in (24cm), octagonal barrel 5in (13cm).
£290-320 *WAL*

A British Lancer style percussion pistol, Lovell's Pattern 1842 lock with crowned VR and Tower 1854 markings, barrel 9in (23cm).
£325-375 *ASB*

A gold plated pinfire revolver, 12mm 6-shot, 10.75in (27cm) long.
£775-800 *L*

Believed to be the property of Napoleon III.

A 6-shot .44 Remington Army single action percussion revolver, No. 73082, 13.5in (34cm), octagonal barrel 8in (20cm).
£550-600 *WAL*

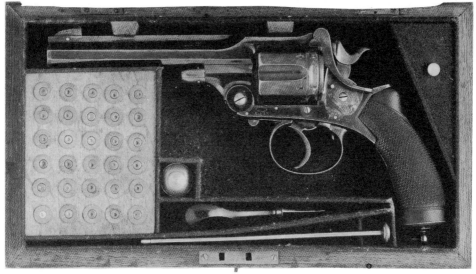

A Wm Moore & Grey .450/.455/.476 Tranters patent double action revolver, No. 5023, 6-shot fluted cylinder, 6in (15cm) barrel, original finish, in fitted oak case. **£900-950** *S(S)*

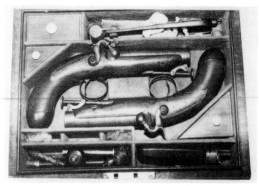

A pair of Irish 15 bore percussion pocket pistols, signed Harris, Dublin, c1840, barrels 4in (10cm).
£1,500-1,700 *ASB*

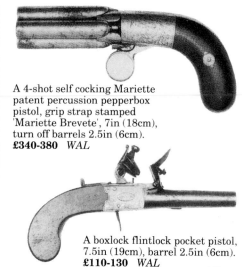

A 4-shot self cocking Mariette patent percussion pepperbox pistol, grip strap stamped 'Mariette Brevete', 7in (18cm), turn off barrels 2.5in (6cm).
£340-380 *WAL*

A boxlock flintlock pocket pistol, 7.5in (19cm), barrel 2.5in (6cm).
£110-130 *WAL*

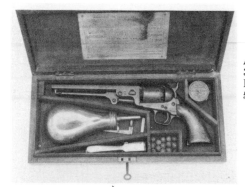

A cased English Colt navy, 36 calibre, No. 35761, barrel has London address, some tools.
£525-575 *L*

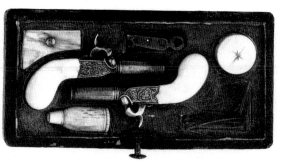

A 30 bore English percussion pocket pistol, retailed by Field, Oxford, c1840. **£300-350** *ASB*

A cased 12-shot pinfire 7mm revolver, serial No. 39602, in original condition. **£400-450** *L*

A cased pair of miniature percussion pistols, small paper label inscribed in script 'Pistols used in the duel between Count Swaggeras and M Bomastis', c1840, barrel .5in (2cm) long, 4mm bore. **£2,250-2,500** *S*

Rifles, Muskets & Shotguns

An India pattern flintlock musket and bayonet, c1800, musket 55in (140cm), bayonet 21.5in (54cm).
£800-850 *S*

A flintlock double barrelled fowling piece, by Charles Moore, with 30in (76cm) browned damascus barrels.
£800-900 *EP*

A 16 bore British flintlock cavalry carbine, guard with regimental marking RC CH E41, dated 1797, barrel 20.25in (51cm).
£580-600 *ASB*

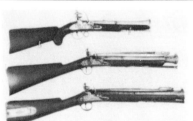

Three blunderbusses:
Top. An English H.E.I.C. flintlock, c1800, 25in (64cm).
£1,100-1,200
Centre. A brass barrelled flintlock with spring bayonet, by Twigg, London, late 18thC, 30in (76cm). **£850-900**
Bottom. An Irish iron barrelled flintlock with spring bayonet, by McDermot, Dublin, c1800, 31.5in (80cm).
£850-900 *S*

A cased percussion double barrelled 2-groove game rifle, serial No.6092, 39 bore, the rib inscribed J. Purdey, Oxford Street, London, 30in (76cm) browned and sighted twist barrels, case 34in (86cm) long. **£5,750-6,000** *S*

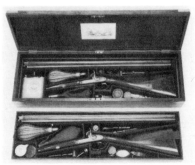

A percussion muzzle loading shotgun, by J. Purdey, with 29.5in (65cm) browned damascus barrels.
£2,200-2,400 *EP*

A cased pair of percussion double barrelled sporting guns, 16 bore with ribs inscribed W. Dooley 11 Ranelagh Street, Liverpool, c1849, 30in (76cm) browned twist barrels, case 33in (84cm) long.
£5,500-6,000 *S*

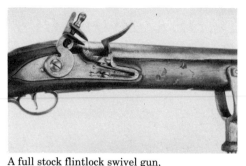

An Alexander Henry .500 black powder express double rifle, with 28in (71cm) barrels.
£800-900 *EP*

A full stock flintlock swivel gun, signed Columbell on lock and barrel, 72in (183cm) overall, barrel 54in (137cm), **£700-750** *L*

Columbell was a gunmaker to the Ordnance, 1756, also EIC 1716, capp to Garrett Johnson 1712, trading from Parliament Street West 1763.

Trench Art

● Refers to all those domestic items produced by the armed forces during periods of inactivity, to pass the time and to give away as keepsakes.

● Made from whatever materials were to hand, often spent brass shell cases or bullets.

● Shell cases turn up as ingenious containers which often had intricate, hand worked patterns on the sides.

● Others were made into curios, such as miniature brass peaked caps or miniature coal buckets.

● Another example of trench art is seen where soldiers cut out a rectangle from a khaki shirt and inked in a scene or a rhyme. These would serve as personal greeting 'cards' at Christmas or on birthdays.

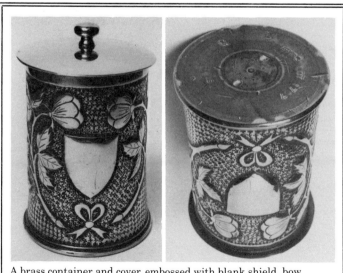

A brass container and cover, embossed with blank shield, bow and floral swags, WWI, 6in (15cm) high. **£80-90** *PAR*

A hand punched pattern container, made from shell casing, WWI.
£30-35 *PAR*

Miniature Furniture

An inlaid mahogany linen press, mid-19thC, 15in (38cm) wide.
£3,000-3,500 *S(NY)*

A rosewood bookcase cabinet, late 19thC, 17in (43cm) wide.
£2,200-2,500 *S(NY)*

A chinoiserie gilt decorated black japanned bowfront cabinet, early 19thC, 10.25in (26cm) wide.
£700-900 *S(NY)*

Cross Reference
Dolls House Furniture & Accessories

An inlaid walnut chest of drawers, 18thC, 13in (33cm) wide.
£760-850 *S(NY)*

A George II style inlaid walnut bureau, with fitted interior, 19thC, 10in (25cm) wide.
£2,800-3,200 *S(NY)*

A Victorian tip-up table, 3in (8cm) high.
£40-45 *TRU*

An inlaid mahogany bowfront chest of drawers, early 19thC, 14.25in (36cm) wide.
£950-1,200 *S(NY)*

Money Boxes

A 'Mason Bank' mechanical bank, by Shepard Hardware Company, c1887, 7.25in (18cm) long.
£5,700-8,500 *S(NY)*

A cast iron 'Trick Pony' mechanical bank, coin retainer missing, by Shepard Hardware Company, c1885, 7in (18cm) long.
£570-600 *S(NY)*

A 'Dentist' mechanical bank, by J. & E. Stevens Company, spring broken, c1885, 9.5in (24cm) long.
£7,000-7,500 *S(NY)*

Place coin in the dentist's pocket, press lever at his feet, the dentist extracts a tooth and the patient falls backwards depositing the coin in the gas bag. The patient falls backwards in the chair throwing his arms up.

A cast iron 'New Creedmore Bank' mechanical bank, by J. & E. Stevens Company, c1877, 10in (25cm) long.
£200-250 *S(NY)*

A 6d money box which when full contains £1 for a wireless licence, 2.25in (6cm) high.
£3-4 *TRU*

A treacle glaze money box in the form of a lady's head, mid-19thC, 4.25in (11cm) high.
£40-45 *OD*

A 'Boy Scout' mechanical bank, by J. & E. Stevens Company, c1912.
£8,200-9,000 *S(NY)*

A cast iron 'Mule Entering Barn' mechanical bank, by J. & E. Stevens Company, c1880, 8.5in (21cm) long.
£1,200-1,500 *S(NY)*

Lock the mule into position and place coin between the hind legs, pushing lever activates the mule to kick the coin into the barn and a dog appears simultaneously.

A brass and mahogany
money box, c1880, 10.5in
(26cm) long.
£200-300   *AMH*

A 'Called Out Bank' mechanical
bank, by J. & E. Stevens
Company, c1900, 9in (23cm) high.
£5,200-5,500   *S(NY)*

'Paddy and the Pig' mechanical
bank. by J. & E. Stevens
Company, c1882, 8.5in (21cm)
high.
£1,900-2,200   *S(NY)*

A 'Professor Pug Frog's Great
Bicycle Feat' mechanical bank, by
J. & E. Stevens Company, c1892.
£6,300-7,000   *S(NY)*

*Place the coin over rear bicycle
wheel, turning the centre crank
makes the frog spin, depositing
the coin.*

A 'Santa Claus at Chimney' cast
iron mechanical bank, by Shepard
Hardware Company.
£650-750   *CNY*

325

Musical

An 'Aslanian' bird's-eye maple concert harp, 72in (182.5cm).
£1,300-1,500 *ALL*

Mechanical Music

A French musical automaton of a girl holding a tray, Leopald Lambert, Jumeau head stamped in red Deposé, Tête Jumeau, Bte S.G.D.G., 14, late 19thC, with original tune sheet, 18in (46cm) high.
£1,700-2,200 *S(NY)*

An 'Odeon' piano accordion, c1940, 16in (41cm) wide.
£40-50 *TRU*

A giltwood and painted harp, by Sebastian Erard, London.
£1,700-1,900 *DA*

An HMV portable gramophone in black rexine suitcase style case.
£60-70 *PAR*

> **Cross Reference**
> Gramophones

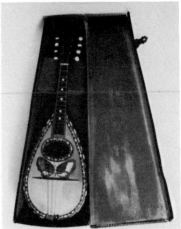

A mandolin, inlaid with a butterfly in tortoiseshell, mother-of-pearl and ivory, with case.
£80-90 *TRU*

A Gallanti Super Dominator accordion, in black and white chrome mounted Art Deco case, with rexine carrying case.
£340-380 *DA*

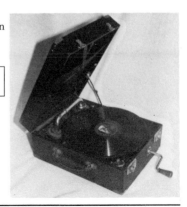

Night Lights

Two night lights:
l. A ceramic turret, with Greener base, badly matched,
r. A Spode lighthouse, 5in (12.5cm).
£25-30 each PC

A cobalt blue Queen Mary head figural night light, base embossed Eclipse Lamp, Rd No 566724, British Made, 4.25in (11cm) high.
£170-180 *BBR*

A porcelain night light holder, 8.75in (22cm) high.
£40-50 PC

Oriental

A carved hardwood bear, 6.25in (16cm) high.
£65-75 *TRU*

A Mongolian style coconut and white metal mounted snuff bottle, the stopper inset with coral and malachite, 3.25in (8cm) high.
£250-300 *CSK*

A Japanese jubako (picnic box) in Arita blue and white porcelain, c1900, 11in (28cm) high.
£100-120 *BOW*

These are still used particularly during celebrations.

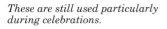

A carved hardwood lion, chipped, 13in (33cm) long.
£40-50 *TRU*

A Chinese ivory carving of a locust and bunch of cherries on a lettuce, 9.75in (24cm) long, with plush box.
£600-650 *CSK*

Cross Reference
Militaria

A Japanese court sword or tachi, signed Seki No Ju Kani Tono Hira Kumi Tsokuru, c1890.
£1,200-1,500 *CAA*

A Korean rectangular box, decorated in mother-of-pearl, damaged, 17th/18thC, 9.75in (24cm) long.
£225-250 *CSK*

A Chinese crocidolite (blue tiger's eye) snuff bottle and stopper, carved as a turtle, 3.25in (8cm) long.
£190-210 *CSK*

A Japanese articulated bronze model of a crayfish, 6 claws missing, 17in (43cm) long with antennae.
£220-250 *CSK*

For a further selection of snuff bottles see Miller's Collectables Volume IV pages 334-336

A Chinese bamboo cylindrical brushpot, chipped, 6.25in (16cm) high.
£1,300-1,400 *CSK*

A Japanese black lacquer circular dish, inlaid in ivory, mother-of-pearl and bone, 21in (53cm) diam.
£450-475 *CSK*

Oriental Ceramics

A pair of Japanese Kutani figures, decorated in green, gold, black and red, mid-19thC.
£180-220 *BOW*

A Chinese blue and white meat platter, made for export to Europe, Chien Lung period, 1770, 16in (41cm) wide.
£250-280 *BOW*

A Japanese hors d'oeuvre set, 12in (31cm) diam, with hand painted box.
£85-95 *RFA*

An Arita soup bowl and cover, in blue, white, red and gold pattern, c1900, 5.5in (14cm) diam.
£30-35 *BOW*

A Chinese blue and white planter, depicting precious objects, mid-19thC, 7.25in (18cm) wide.
£70-80 *BOW*

Two Chinese blue and white wine cups, depicting Li Tai Po, the drunken poet with children, marked Yung Cheng, late 18thC, 2.5in (6cm) high.
£70-80 *BOW*

A Chinese blue and white plate, made for export to Europe, Chien Lung period, c1770, 9in (23cm) diam. **£40-50** *BOW*

A Chinese porcelain tea caddy, Chien Lung period, c1780, 4in (10cm) high.
£80-90 *BOW*

A Chinese soup bowl, famille rose colours, early 1900, 4.5in (11cm) diam. **£30-40** *BOW*

A Cantonese blue and white moon or pilgrim flask, c1875, 24in (62cm) high.
£500-550 *BOW*

A copy of a Ming design, used for keeping water.

Oriental Metalware

A Chinese silver dish, with dollar in base, c1930, 3.5in (9cm) diam.
£12-14 *BOW*

A Chinese silver mug, with good luck character, c1900, 2.5in (6cm) high.
£45-50 *BOW*

A Japanese silver temple gate pepper, c1920, 2.5in (6cm) high.
£30-35 *BOW*

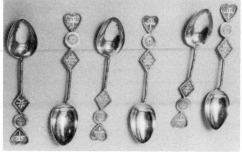

A Japanese silver maple leaf dish, c1920, 8in (20cm) wide. **£45-50** *BOW*

A set of Chinese silver teaspoons, c1900, 5in (13cm) long. **£50-60** *BOW*

Osbornes & Wax Pictures

The Weavers, Canterbury, 8 by 6in (20 by 15cm).
£12-18 *FMN*

A Georgian wax portrait of a gentleman, in gilt frame with circular mount.
£170-180 *DA*

For a further selection of waxed pictures see Miller's Collectables Volume IV pages 469-472

Andrew Lumisden Esq., a profile portrait on a black oval ground, inscribed, signed and dated Tassie F 1784, gilt metal frame, 3 by 2.5in (8 by 6cm).
£325-350 *MCA*

Andrew Lumisden (1720-1801), a prominent Jacobite, became private secretary to Prince Charles Edward Stuart and was present at Culloden

Llanberis Pass, 5.75 by 7.75in (14 by 19cm).
£20-25 *JMC*

Paperweights

A granite paperweight with silver and citrine handle, 5.5in (14cm) wide.
£120-150 *BWA*

For a further selection of paperweights please see the Glass Section

Papier Mâché

A pair of red dishes, with gold stars, 6.5in (16cm) diam. **£25-30 each** *AI*

Cross Reference
Writing

A shell dish, 12in (31cm) wide.
£25-30 *AI*

A tray, 12.5 by 10in (32 by 25cm).
£20-28 *AI*

A pin tray, 5.75in (14cm) diam.
£10-12 *AI*

A tray, 10in (25cm) diam.
£20-26 *AI*

A papier mâché mirror, 9in (23cm) high.
£60-70 *AI*

A papier mâché on copper bowl, 10in (25cm) diam.
£60-70 *AI*

Patch Boxes

Patch boxes are tiny ornate containers used to hold beauty patches or beauty spots. These patches, as well as being fashionable in the 18thC, were often used to cover pox marks and scars.

A silver and agate patch box with the word EDINA, short for Edinburgh, on the lid, 1.5in (4cm) high. **£180-200** *BWA*

Photograph Frames

An English silver photograph frame, with blue velvet easel back, modern, 11.75in (30cm) high. **£180-190** *CNY*

An English silver photograph frame, with blue velvet easel back, modern, 12in (31cm) high. **£285-300** *CNY*

An English silver double photograph frame, with blue velvet easel back, modern, 12.25in (31cm) wide. **£165-175** *CNY*

Photographic Pictures

These photographic pictures are glass photographic negatives that have been hand coloured or painted on the reverse. This method of producing very attractive and colourful pictures was popular between 1840 and 1870.

Roman potters, 14.25 by 12in (36 by 31cm). **£95-115** *AA*

These pieces illustrate how these paintings on glass negatives are produced. Once broken they are irreparable.

The figure of a girl, 21 by 16.75in (53.5 by 43cm). **£110-125** *AA*

Playing Cards

A portrait of a lady, 9.5 by 8.5in (24 by 22cm). **£90-95** *AA*

Police

A double pack of Aircraft playing cards, 1950s. **£5-6** *COB*

For a further selection of playing cards see Miller's Collectables Price Guide Volume IV, pages 349-350.

A Metropolitan Special Constabulary hat, 1936. **£28-30** *COL*

A silver Metropolitan Special Constabulary First Aid Competition badge, Birmingham 1938. **£20-22** *COL*

A Metropolitan Police, Driving School, Hendon, Certificate, 1949, 10.25 by 12.25in (26 by 31cm). **£10-12** *COL*

A silver Metropolitan Special Constabulary medal, Beckenham, c1935, in original box. **£15-18** *COL*

Portrait Miniatures

A Victorian brass tipstaff, with 2-piece crown soldered to body and turned ebony handle, 9.5in (24cm). **£100-150** *WAL*

A young gentleman wearing a blue coat over a white waistcoat and stock, by Savinien-Edome Dubourjal, signed and dated 1829, 3.5in (8.5cm) high. **£820-860** *C(G)*

Two ladies, after Plimer, in décolleté dresses, 19thC, 2.75in (7cm) high. **£375-400** *CSK*

Posy Holders

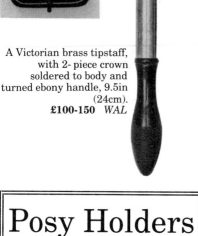

A Russian cornet shaped posy holder, engraved with a presentation inscription and name in German enclosed by flowers and foliage, with chain attached, c1900, 6.5in (16cm). **£325-375** *CSK*

For a further selection of posy holders see Miller's Collectables Price Guide, Volume I, page 305.

A lady in a white dress with forget-me-nots in her hair, with a bright-cut gilt metal mount, after François Hall, 19thC, 2in (5cm) high. **£725-775** *CSK*

A lady in a blue dress and lace bonnet with blue ribbons, German School, 19thC, 2.5in (6cm) high. **£150-175** *CSK*

An officer with grey hair and a red coat, in a gilt wood frame, mid-18thC, 3 by 2.25in (7.5 by 5.25cm). **£340-360** *P(S)*

A lady, set in the lid of a tortoiseshell box, French School, 19thC, 2.5in (6.5cm) diam. **£440-480** *CSK*

Postcards

Raphael Tuck, In the Forest, 9336 complete, a set of 6, G. **£28-32** *VS*

Bridlington Lifeboat with Motor Tractor, by Photochrome, corner crease, G. **£30-35** *VS*

Raphael Tuck, Educational Series, embossed, butterflies, No. 8 complete, set of 12, VG. **£45-50** *VS*

Ellam, Russo-Japanese War, comedy, Hildesheimer 5243 complete, set of 6, VG. **£50-55** *VS*

Raphael Tuck, Empire, 243-254 complete, Battleships, set of 12, VR. **£60-65** *VS*

H. Willebeek Le Mair, Children's Pieces of Schumann, complete, published by Augener, set of 12, VG-EX. **£65-70** *VS*

Cats, C.W.F., 793 complete, slight album corner, marks, set of 6, G. **£55-60** *VS*

Cross Reference
Ephemera
Autographs

Theodore Roosevelt, an ink caricature on postcard, signed by Roosevelt to top edge, some light staining and postal cancellation to image, FR. **£90-95** *VS*

Dogs, chromos, series 53, published by Misch & Stock, set of 3, G-VG. **£22-25** *VS*

Tenterden Station, Kent, slight album corner marks, VG-EX. **£20-25** *VS*

Southend-on-Sea, Steam Lifeboat, set of 3, G. **£28-30** *VS*

Margaret Tarrant, Months of the Year, complete, some with album corner marks, set of 12, G. **£40-60** *VS*

The Elizabeth Simson lifeboat and Crew at Gorleston, VG. **£15-18** *VS*

Japan, Imperial Government Railways, views with embossed Art Nouveau surrounds, set of 3, VG. **£18-20** *VS*

New Zealand Railway Stations, black and white and coloured, set of 6, G-VG. **£28-30** *VS*

Cameroons, German Period, set of 4, G. **£18-22** *VS*

London Suburbs, Stations by Spalding, G-VG, set of 7. **£65-70** *VS*

Billericay Station by Spalding, set of 3, G-VG. **£25-30** *VS*

Advertisements, a scarce set of Aviation/Balloons, from Au Bon Marché, Aviation in the Year 2000, slight scuffing, set of 8, G. **£65-70** *VS*

Crete, an unusual selection, including the 1911 Deputies, all sepia, set of 13, G-EX. **£38-42** *VS*

Paddle Steamer Adverts for Cosens, set of 6, G. **£60-65** *VS*

USA, Quanah, Acme & Pacific Railway Co., including Red Indian, trains, etc., set of 8, VG. **£40-45** *VS*

Political, Gruss von der Maifeier, 'Freedom, Equality, Brotherhood', workers and interior of blacksmith's shop, EX. **£15-18** *VS*

Great Yarmouth Lifeboat, black and white return of Lifeboat after Skylark Disaster, set of 4, G-VG. **£30-35** *VS*

First Train in Tickhill Station, 1908, slight corner knock, VG. **£25-30** *VS*

Titanic, by Batchelder Bros., signed to reverse by B. V. Dean, survivor, VG. **£28-30** *VS* **£40-70** **unsigned** *VS*

Lifeboats at the SS Lugano Fire, by Judges, postally used 1906, VG. **£22-25** *VS*

Louis Wain

Tucks, Mascot, Series 3, 3553, The Contented Mascot, VG.
£40-70 *VS*

Tucks, Mascot, Series 3, 3553, The Meal-time Mascot, VG.
£40-70 *VS*

Tucks, Mascot, Series 3, 3553, The Skipping Mascot, VG.
£40-70 *VS*

C.W.F. Series 598, cats heads, complete, postally used, set of 6, G-VG.
£120-130 *VS*

C.W.F., 453 complete, set of 6, VG.
£110-120 *VS*

Tucks Mascot, Series 3, 3553, The Runner's Mascot, VG.
£40-70 *VS*

C.W.F. 484 complete, 2 postally used, set of 6, G-VG.
£80-85 *VS*

Tucks, Stripes to the Front, 8716, EX.
£30-35 *VS*

Tucks, Cheer Up, 8826, postally used, G-VG.
£16-18 *VS*

Tucks, Theatre Cats, 3896 complete, nos. 3885- set of 12, G.
£250-260 *VS*

Advertisement, Jacksons Hats and Boots, Cricket Game, postally used 1912, corner crease, G.
£130-140 *VS*

Write-Aways, green back, including Cricketer, Bathing, Fishing, set of 11, VR. **£130-140** *VS*

Advertisement for Jackson Boots, postally used 1908, corner crease, G.
£48-52 *VS*

Posters

Motoring

Edwin Calligan, Plas Newydd, 1936.
£170-180 *BBA*

Tristram Hillier, Tourists Prefer Shell, 1936. **£550-575** *BBA*

Cross Reference
Railway Posters
Shipping Posters

Wartime

Britian Needs You At Once, WW1, 29.5 by 19.5in (75 by 49.5cm).
£65-75 *BBA*

Abram Games, Danger, Don't Touch, J. Weiner Ltd., for H.M.S.O., c1941, 40 by 25in (101.5 by 63.5cm).
£170-180 *BBA*

Your Country's Call, Isn't This Worth Fighting For, 29.5 by 19.5in (75 by 49.5cm). **£425-450** *BBA*

Lewitt-Him, Think Twice Before Making Any Trunk Call, 1943, 28 by 36in (71 by 91.5cm).
£140-150 *BBA*

Baron Low, Everyone Should Do His Bit, Enlist Now, WW1, 29.5 by 19.5in (75 by 49.5cm).
£130-150 *BBA*

Radios & Televisions

A Mullard Master 3 radio, c1928,
21in (53cm) wide.
£75-80 *HEG*

A Pye mains radio, c1931,
18.5in (47cm) high.
£150-170 *HEG*

A G.E.C. BC3235 all electric
AC model radio, with wood
case and Bakelite grill,
c1931, 18in (46cm) high.
£150-170 *HEG*

A B.T.H. loudspeaker, 15in
(38cm) high, c1931.
£50-60 *HEG*

A McMichael super range
portable 4 radio, 1931.
£100-120 *HEG*

A Decca battery radio, c1940,
12.5in (31cm) wide.
£25-30 *COL*

A Marconiphone Model P20B
portable radio, c1948, 6.5in
(16cm) wide.   **£20-30** *HEG*

A B.T.H. speaker, c1928, 23in
(53cm) high.
£40-60 *HEG*

A Sobell cream Bakelite
portable radio, c1948, 8.5in
(21cm) high.   **£60-70** *HEG*

An Ekco U75 Consort Bakelite
radio, c1948, 14in (36cm) wide.
£60-80 *HEG*

A G.E.C. BC4750 radio, c1945, 22in (56cm) wide. **£70-80** *HEG*

This model was also produced with a TV screen in the centre.

A Premier Bakelite radio, made from a kit, c1948, 11.5in (29cm) wide. **£50-60** *HEG*

A Pye 200 Bakelite electric radio, 1948, 13in (33cm) wide. **£60-80** *HEG*

A Braun portable valve radio, c1955, 8.5in (21cm) wide. **£40-50** *HEG*

EARLY WIRELESS & TELEVISION SETS WANTED
SOME EXAMPLES OF TYPES AND PRICES PAID

MARCONI MULTIPLE TUNER
£2,000

W.W.I. TRENCH RECEIVER
£700

GEC° PHONE 2 VALVE

£400

HMV MARCONI TELEVISION

BAIRD TELEVISOR
£1,500

ERICSSON 4 VALVE
£800

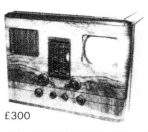

£300

ALL OTHER EARLY WIRELESS/TELEVISION SETS WANTED.
ALSO HORN GRAMOPHONES, PHONOGRAPHS, TELEPHONES ETC.
MR. YATES, THE HEWARTHS, SANDIACRE, NOTTM. NG10 5NQ 0602 393139

A wartime civilian radio, made from cheapest materials, available, 1944.
£75-85 *HEG*

An Ever Ready portable painted perspex case, c1946, 14in (36cm) high.
£50-60 *HEG*

A Philco Model 527 People's Set Bakelite radio, c1936, 16.5in (42cm) high.
£250-300 *HEG*

An Ekco transistor battery radio, 1950s, 8in (20cm) wide.
£12-15 *COL*

An Ekco A22 radio, c1945, 14in (36cm) high.
£250-300 *HEG*

An Ultra Model R906 snakeskin covered radio, c1952, 14.5in (37cm) wide.
£60-80 *HEG*

A KB Model FB10 cream Bakelite 'toaster' radio, 1950, 9.5in (24cm) wide.
£80-90 *HEG*

A French Reela L'Empereur radio, green and gold metal, c1955, 21.5in (54cm) wide.
£100-120 *HEG*

An Ultra Coronation Twin Bakelite portable radio, battery and mains, 1953, 11.5in (29cm) wide.
£50-60 *HEG*

A Pye personal transistor radio, with original box and instructions, c1958, 6in (15cm) wide. **£30-40** *HEG*

A Philips Philetta gold plastic electric radio, c1955.
£50-60 *HEG*

Novelty Radios

A Keiller of Dundee tin, in the shape of a radio, 7.5in (19cm) wide. **£10-15** *HEG*

A Bambi portable radio, c1960, 5in (13cm) wide.
£20-30 *HEG*

A Minifon wire recorder, with watch microphone, West German, c1955.
£100-150 *HEG*

A boat radio, c1970, 11in (28cm) wide.
£30-40 *HEG*

An Adam & Eve radio, made in Hong Kong, c1972, 8in (20cm) high.
£30-40 *HEG*

A Radio Rex novelty toy, with original box and instructions, c1935, 6.5in (16cm) high.
£50-60 *HEG*

When you call 'Rex' the dog jumps out of the kennel.

A microphone radio, made in Hong Kong, c1989, 10.5in (27cm) high.
£15-20 *HEG*

Television

A Bush 22in (56cm) TV, c1950, 15in (38cm) high.
£200-250 *HEG*

A Bush Model TV12B, BBC Birmingham only, 1949.
£180-200 *RR*

A Bush Model T18, 12in (31cm) TV/Radio, 1938.
£500-600 *RR*

A Marconiphone Model 707, 7in (18cm) TV/Radio, 1937.
£900-1,200 *RR*

A Pye Model VT4, BBC/ITV 12in (31cm) table model TV, 1954.   **£75-95** *RR*

A Bush Model TV85 BBC/ITV 17in (43cm) table model TV, with Belling Lee 'Golden V' antenna aerial.
£30-50 *RR*

A Baird Televisor, 30-line electro-mechanical television, 1930.
£1,500-1,700 *RR*

A Pye Model T102, 9in (23cm) table model TV, 1947.   **£100-130** *RR*

TV Related Toys

A set of BBC Television Toys, 1959, a mobile control room, extending mast and roving eye vehicles.
£250-300 *RR*

A German papier mâché tobacco box, 19thC, 5.25in (13cm). **£2,100-2,300** *CSK*

An ivory box, depicting Leda and the Swan, 2.5in (6cm) diam. **£420-450** *CSK*

A Stobwasser papier mâché tobacco box, early 19thC, 5.5in (14cm) diam. **£3,000-3,250** *CSK*

A papier mâché snuff box, 19thC, 4in (10cm) diam. **£200-250** *CSK*

A papier mâché snuff box, with painted lid, 3.25in (8cm) long. **£60-70** *PC*

A German papier mâché snuff box, 19thC, 3.75in (9cm) diam. **£2,400-2,600** *CSK*

A tortoiseshell lined papier mâché snuff box, 3.5in (9cm) diam. **£950-1,000** *CSK*

A silver snuff box, London 1881, 4in (10.5cm) long, 6oz 15dwt. **£1,100-1,250** *S*

A silver snuff box, by Rawlings & Summers, London 1843, 3.75in (9.5cm) long. **£400-450** *S*

A George I silver tobacco box, 3.75in (10cm) long. **£2,000-2,500** *S*

A German papier mâché snuff box, the cover printed and painted, mid-19thC, 3.5in (9cm) wide. **£180-200** *CSK*

l. A papier mâché snuff box, early 19thC, 3.5in (9cm) wide. **£2,100-2,300** *CSK*

A papier mâché snuff box, early 19thC, 4in (10cm) diam. **£450-500** *CSK*

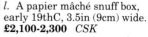

A pair of circular salts, by R. & S. Garrard, London 1907, 14oz. **£240-260** *AAR*

Two George II wine labels, c1740. **£220-230** *S*

A pair of George III wine labels, London 1812. **£125-150** *S*

A silver punch bowl, by William Comyns & Sons, London 1896, 10in (25cm) diam, 64oz. **£1,500-1,700** *AAR*

A vinaigrette, Birmingham 1843, 1.5in (3.5cm) long. **£1,500-1,600** *S*

Two wine labels, London 1821 and 1834. **£250-280** *S*

A silver gilt etui, c1720, 7.75in (19cm) long. **£1,200-1,400** *S*

A Victorian silver sugar basket, London, 1877, 8oz. **£240-260** *AAR*

A pair of George III silver gilt wine labels, London 1811. **£1,500-1,600** *S*

Companion silver gilt wine label to 'Port' label *above right*.

Three William IV wine labels, c1835. **£225-250** *S*

A pair of pierced silver salts, by E. J. & W. Barnard, London 1842, 5.5oz. **£280-300** *AAR*

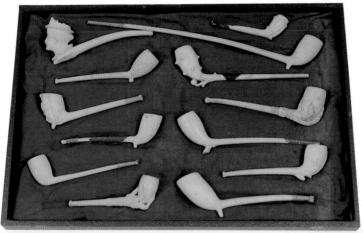

A selection of Shropshire clay pipes, c1900.
£150-200 each *ACh*

A Wedgwood match striker, 3.75in (9.5cm).
£45-55 *PC*

A boot match striker, 2.25in (6cm) high.
£15-30 *PC*

A brass vesta box, decorated with a bird print, 1.75in (4.5cm) high.
£25-30 *PC*

A silver mounted Meerschaum and amber cheroot holder, 19thC.
£2,300-2,500 *S*

l. A ceramic match striker, 3.5in (9cm) high.
£25-30 *OD*

A Russian cigarette and vesta case, gilt lined, 4in (10cm) high.
£475-500 *CSK*

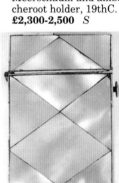

A mother-of-pearl vesta box, 2in (5cm) high.
£40-50 *PC*

r. A German papier mâché cigar case, painted with a portrait of Prince Albert of Saxe Coburg, c1840, 5.25in (13cm) high.
£1,400-1,500 *CSK*

An agate and silver plated vesta box, 2in (5cm) high.
£35-40 *PC*

347

A complete set of 176 Cracker Jack baseball cards, 1915.
£56,000-60,000 *S(NY)*

Joe Di Maggio's auto-graphed game used bat, 1941.
£10,000-11,000 *S(NY)*

1887 Detroit Baseball Club Team cabinet. **£3,200-3,500** *S(NY)*

A complete set of 66 Topps Super Baseball cards, mint condition, 1969.
£2,500-3,000 *S(NY)*

Roger Maris' 1961 All-Star base-ball bat, and his personal bat.
£14,000-16,000 *S(NY)*

59 '144 Series' Cracker Jack cards, 1914. **£3,000-3,500** *S(NY)*

Honus Wagner, Sweet Caporal Cigarettes, c1910.
£125,000+ *S(NY)*

Eddie Plank, Sweet Caporal Cigarettes, c1910.
£11,000-12,000 *S(NY)*

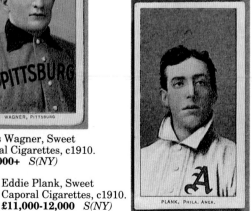

1951 Bowman, No.253 Mickey Mantle, mint condition.
£8,000-8,500 *S(NY)*

A complete set of 340 Topps baseball cards, near mint condition, 1956.
£3,500-4,500 *S(NY)*

Willie Mays' San Francisco Giants jersey, 1965.
£12,000-12,500 *S(NY)*

Joe Di Maggio's game worn spikes, 1941.
£4,000-4,500 *S(NY)*

The Syracuse Stars Imperial Team cabinet, 1888.
£6,000-6,500 *S(NY)*

Don Drysdale's Dodgers flannel jersey, 1958. **£2,000-2,500** *S(NY)*

1963 New York Yankees World Series ring.
£5,000-6,000 *S(NY)*

Madonna's baseball uniform.
£4,000-4,500 *S(NY)*

Ty Cobb's game worn jersey, c1922. **£47,000-50,000** *S(NY)*

Joe Di Maggio's New York Yankees uniform, 1941.
£58,000-60,000 *S(NY)*

Ted Williams' Boston Red Sox jersey, 1966. **£6,000-6,500** *S(NY)*

Chicago Baseball Club, 1888, features Cap Anson.
£7,000-7,500 *S(NY)*

Sandy Koufax' Los Angeles Dodgers jersey, 1963.
£8,000-9,000 *S(NY)*

An unused 'Cormorant' golf ball, by G. Brodie Breeze. **£475-525** *C(S)*

An unused gutta ball, by Andrew Patrick, c1860. **£7,800-8,000** *C(S)*

A smooth gutta golf ball, c1850. **£1,750-1,850** *C(S)*

A long nosed mid spoon, by Tom Morris, c1885. **£2,100-2,500** *S*

A Wm. Park long transitional driver, with beech head and hickory shaft, c1890. **£575-625** *S*

A track iron, stamped Kilrymont, c1860. **£1,500-1,600** *C(S)*

A black-smith made track iron, c1790. **£21,000-22,000** *C(S)*

A long nosed driver, by McEwan, c1870. **£1,800-1,900** *C(S)*

A baffing spoon, by McEwan, c1870. **£3,100-3,300** *C(S)*

A feathery golf ball, by J. Gourlay, c1835. **£5,500-6,000** *S*

A feathery golf ball, 1845, 1.6in (4cm) diam. **£2,500-2,750** *S*

A large feathery golf ball, 19thC. **£2,100-2,250** *S*

A Ludwig Sandison (Aberdeen) long nosed putter, c1885. **£1,600-1,800** *S*

A feathery golf ball, mid-19thC. **£1,700-1,800** *S*

A long nosed spoon, by Tom Morris, c1885. **£3,500-3,750** *S*

An R. Forgan & Son driver, with Prince of Wales feathers stamp, c1885. **£1,250-1,350** *S*

An Urquhart Patent adjustable iron, stamped Mitchell Manchester, c1905. **£1,100-1,200** *S*

A Gourlay feathery golf ball, c1840.
£2,600-2,750 *S*

A feathery golf ball, mid-19thC.
£1,500-1,600 *S*

A 'hoe' design putter, with shortened hickory shaft, stamped R. Forgan & Son, St. Andrews, c1900.
£1,600-1,750 *S*

An Anderson patent cross head crescent shaped iron, c1895.
£1,000-1,100 *S*

A feather filled golf ball, c1840.
£2,100-2,250 *C(S)*

A red painted feather filled golf ball, c1840.
£2,750-2,950 *C(S)*

A T. Alexander feather ball, c1830, 2in (4.6cm) diam.
£8,900-9,500 *S*

A Sir W. H. Dalrymple hammer cross head patent golf club, c1892, and 2 other 20thC clubs.
£2,500-2,750 *S*

A Coste Jeu de Mail hardwood iron bound club, French, mid-18thC.
£10,500-11,500 *S*

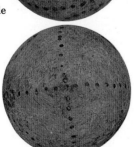

Six Jeu de Mail hardwood balls, French, mid-18thC, various sizes.
£1,600-1,750 *S*

A Robert Simpson driver, c1885.
£1,000-1,100 *S*

A Thomas Dunn short spoon, c1875.
£2,100-2,300 *S*

351

A Doulton Burslem wall plaque, painted with a panel of a golfer and his caddy, 14in (36cm). **£3,600-3,800** *C(S)*

A bronze figure of The Rt. Hon. A. J. Balfour, c1894, 16.5in (42cm). **£3,000-3,300** *S*

A red playing coat, the brass buttons engraved L.G.C., for Leicestershire Golf Club, c1890. **£950-1,000** *C(S)*

A Royal Doulton Crombie Series Ware bowl, c1925. **£1,200-1,300** *S*

A Foley miniature crested china golfing jug, early 20thC, 1.5in (4cm). **£140-150** *S*

A Copeland Spode stoneware decanter, 18in (46cm). **£1,500-1,600** *C(S)*

A Lenox silver mounted golfing jug, American, signed E. A. Delan, hallmarked silver rim and spout, some damage, c1898, 14.5in (37cm). **£2,400-2,600** *S*

l. A Lenox silver mounted three-handled cup, c1900. **£4,000-4,500** *S*

A Burntsfield Links West End Golfing Club silver medal, c1850, uninscribed. **£1,200-1,300** *S*

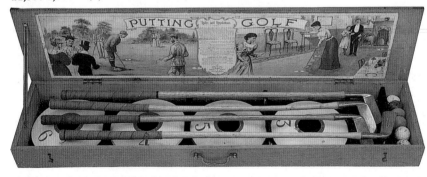

A boxed putting set, c1900. **£1,800-2,000** *S*

Railways

A British Railways
'totem' station sign.
£100-150 *SRA*

A Great Eastern Railway
station lamp top, 32.5in
(82cm) high.
£250-275 *ONS*

A Pullman pen holder.
£10-15 *COB*

An early number plate.
£300-400 *SRA*

A selection of oval engraved free
passes for the Great Northern
Railway, 19thC.
£85-95 each *DN*

An early 'Trespassers Will Be Prosecuted' sign.
£100-150 *SRA*

A cast iron Sheffield & Midland Railway sign.
£500-600 *SRA*

l. An LMS Railway lamp, c1930.
£30-35
r. A SR Railway lamp, c1930.
£20-25 *COB*

A 5in gauge
live steam
locomotive.
£4,500-5,000
SRA

A Great Eastern Railway
mahogany mantel clock, inscribed
Beaven London. **£485-500** *ONS*

A selection of early railway timetables.
£60-80 *SRA*

Nameplates

Bonnie Dundee, No. 2059,
finished in blue, 66in (167cm)
long.
£5,200-5,500 *ONS*

A Great Western Railway
nameplate.
£4,500-5,000 *SRA*

A London & North Western
Railway nameplate, 1904.
£2,500-3,000 *SRA*

A LMSR Jubilee Class cast brass
nameplate No 5571, together with
a photograph of locomotive, 20in
(50cm) long. **£4,000-5,000** *ONS*

Osprey, No. 2031, finished in red,
slight damage, 41in (104cm) long.
£4,500-5,000 *ONS*

A London Midland & Scottish
Railway nameplate.
£13,500-14,000 *SRA*

Scottish Union No. 2025, finished
in blue, 71.5in (181cm) long.
£5,000-5,500 *ONS*

Sea Eagle, No. 2039, finished in
red, slight damage.
58in (147cm) long.
£4,800-5,000 *ONS*

Kestrel, No. 2030, finished in red, 43.5in
(110cm) long. **£4,500-4,800** *ONS*

A London & North Eastern
Railway nameplate.
£12,000-14,000 *SRA*

Railway Posters

First in the Field, New West Country Engines, by Leslie Carr, published by Southern Railway, 1945.
£225-250 *ONS*

Winter Sunshine Southern Electric, McCorquodale & Co. Ltd. for Southern Railway, 1935, 40 by 25in (102 by 64cm).
£190-210 *BBA*

Scot Passes Scot, LMS poster.
£350-400 *SRA*

A Great Western Railway poster.
£400-450 *SRA*

Dresden via Harwich, by Fred Taylor, John Waddington Ltd. for LNER, c1930, 50in (127cm) long.
£240-260 *BBA*

An LMS poster of Loch Awe.
£200-250 *SRA*

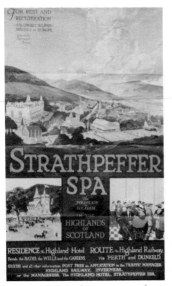

A Highland Railway poster of Strathpeffer Spa.
£250-300 *SRA*

C.W. Taylor, Explore East Anglia, Vincent Brooks, Day & Son Ltd. for L.N.E.R., c1935, 40 by 25in (102 by 64cm).
£120-130 *BBA*

Austin Cooper, Paris for the Weekend, Waterlow & Sons Ltd. for Southern Railway, 1934, 40 by 25in (102 by 64cm).
£750-800 *BBA*

Rojan, Kew Gardens, The Baynard Press for Southern Railway, 1937, 40 by 25in (102 by 64cm). **£320-340** *BBA*

Scarborough, by Fred Taylor.
£225-250 *ONS*

British Railways Locomotives, by A. N. Wolsternholme, published by the British Transport Commission, views of 21 various locomotives of early BR period including electric, turbine, diesel and steam engines, 51in (129.5cm) wide.
£330-350 *CSK*

George Massiot Brown, While you Sleep, London-Paris by Train-Ferry, The Baynard Press for Southern Railway, 1937, 40 by 25in (102 by 64cm).
£275-300 *BBA*

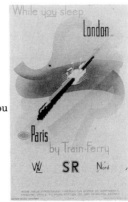

Gwen Raverat, St. John's Bridge, Cambridge, Vincent Brooks, Day & Son Ltd. for L.N.E.R., c1935, 40 by 25in (102 by 64cm).
£180-200 *BBA*

Viola Gardner, Trunks In Advance, Waterlow & Sons Ltd. for Southern Railway, 1934, 40 by 25in (102 by 64cm).
£125-145 *BBA*

Skegness Is So Bracing, by John Hassall for GNR, 1908, 80in (201cm) high.
£480-520 *ONS*

London Transport

A Great Western Railway poster of Cornwall. **£400-450** *SRA*

Margaret Calkin James, Kenwood, Dangerfield Printing Co. Ltd., 1935, 40 by 25in (102 by 64cm).
£165-185 *BBA*

Frederick Charles Herrick, The Riches of London: Touching, The Baynard Press, 1927, 40 by 25in (102 by 64cm).
£165-185 *BBA*

Tom Eckersley, London Transport Services, Public Enquiries, J. Weiner Ltd., 1945, 25 by 18.5in (64 by 47cm).
£85-90 *BBA*

Edward Bawden, Regent's Park, Curwen Press, 1936, 40 by 25in (102 by 64cm).
£320-350 *BBA*

Rock & Pop

A Columbia Records album, Born To Run, signed by Bruce Springsteen and The E Street Band in black felt pen, c1984.
£400-425 *CSK*

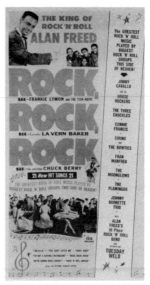

An original 3-sheet poster from the 1957 film 'Rock, Rock, Rock'.
£630-680 *S(NY)*

The Animals pen and ink autographs, on The Hotel George Washington stationery, 1965.
£630-680 *S(NY)*

The Animals signed the stationery at the hotel where they were staying at the time of the concert.

An advertising poster for Jerry Lee Lewis at the Tower Ballroom, New Brighton, May 1962, 30 by 20in (76 by 51cm).
£775-800 *S*

Prince's black matador style stage jacket.
£1,600-1,700 *CSK*

Accompanied by a letter from the vendor stating that Prince wore the jacket in Holland during his Parade Tour and that he threw it into the crowd during the song Kiss at the Rotterdam, Ahoy, August 19th 1986.

A Premier chrome plated snare drum, snare missing, with autographed letter signed Rick Buckler of The Jam.
£585-625 *CSK*

A concert poster for The Supremes at the Lincoln Center, Diana Ross, Florence Ballard and Mary Wilson, 1965, 37.5 by 24.5in (95 by 62cm) framed.
£2,000-2,500 *S(NY)*

A Fender Pro-Amp amplifier, serial no. 57118, the valve combo with one speaker 15in (38cm) diam., brown rexine covering and beige cloth grille, 2 Normal/Vibrato inputs.
£7,500-7,750 *S*

It is a matter for conjecture as to whether this particular amplifier may have been used by the Beatles: they were certainly using Fender equipment in the late 60s and John Lennon is pictured with a similar amplifier.

A BTR 2.A/M recording console from the Abbey Road Studios, serial no. 4465, 1950s, 31.5in (80cm) wide.
£575-600 *S*

A British Record Industry Award, Stand and Deliver, inscribed Best Selling Single 1981, Second Place Awarded to Adam and The Ants, 13 by 9in (33 by 23cm) framed.
£70-80 *CSK*

A harmonica, M. Hohner, Marine Band harp, used by Bob Dylan in his first appearance at Gerdis Folk City, and throughout the summer of 1961.
£2,200-2,500 *S(NY)*

A black and white photograph of a German group signed on the reverse by the Jimi Hendrix Experience, in black felt tip pen, creased, 8 by 10in (20 by 25cm).
£575-600 *S*

The signatures were obtained when the Experience played at the Jaguar Club, Scala, Herford on 28th May, 1967, the vendor was a member of the Other Fire and played regularly at the club from 1963-67.

A pair of Keith Moon's bass drumskins, as used in the film 'Tommy', 1974.
£2,200-2,300 *S*

A pair of Eric Clapton's shoes: turquoise leather stage shoes, by Terry de Havillard, London.
£1,200-1,300 *CSK*

Boy George's clown costume, in purple and silver lamé, 1980s.
£600-650 *S*

Donated by Boy George to raise money for the charity Shelter.

Guitars

A Gretsch Chet Atkins 6120 archtop electric guitar, serial no. 35400 in an orange finish, with hardshell case, 1960.
£1,650-1,850 *CSK*

A new Fender Squier Telecaster solidbody electric guitar, serial no. M2124601, in a cream finish, signed and inscribed 'Love God' Prince, in blue felt pen.
£2,600-2,800 *CSK*

A Mexican guitar, , signed by all 4 Beatles, strings missing, with case, c1965.
£6,300-6,800 *S(NY)*

A Kramer Axe solidbody electric guitar, serial number A5145, with black finish, signed and numbered 118/1000 by Gene Simmons, in hardshell case, 1980.
£3,500-3,700 *CSK*

A Rickenbacker 335 semi-acoustic electric guitar, serial no. 2V237, in a sunburst finish, 1958.
£1,100-1,200 *CSK*

The Beatles

Two customised flight bags:
l. A B.E.A. black canvas bag, 1964, 9.5 by 13.75in (24 by 35cm).
£1,200-1300
r. A T.W.A. red plastic bag, 1965, 12in (31cm) high.
£1,800-2,000 *S*

A wood bass promotional drum, from Sgt Peppers Lonely Hearts Club Band, 28in (71cm) diam.
£1,800-2,200 *S(NY)*

A John Lennon autograph and caricature, blue felt tip pen on paper, inscribed 'Give Peace A Chance' love John Lennon 69, 3.25 by 4.75in (8 by 12cm).
£1,800-2,200 *S(NY)*

An advertising poster proof, September 16, 1964, for a City Park Stadium, New Orleans, La., Beatles concert, 22 by 13.75in (56 by 35cm).
£1,250-1,450 *S(NY)*

Elvis Presley

A 14ct gold ring with oval tiger's eye in a Florentine finish.
£5,100-5,300 *S(NY)*

A biography from a programme book, inscribed 'To Bill my respect Elvis Presley', matted and framed. **£760-800** *S(NY)*

A concert poster proof, August 9, 1956, for Pontchartrain Beach, New Orleans, LA., 22 by 13.75in (56 by 35cm).
£1,800-2,200 *S(NY)*

Queen

A black wet-look two-piece stage suit, with maker's printed label Fred Spurr stitched inside, worn by Freddie Mercury on stage, c1979. **£2,800-2,900** *CSK*

A presentation 'gold' disc, 'We Are The Champions', signed on the reverse by Peter Brown, 14.25 by 10.25in (36 by 26cm), framed.
£650-675 *CSK*

A purple plush velvet suit, worn by Keith Richards c1972.
£800-825 *CSK*

Rolling Stones

A German tour poster for Hamburg, Ernst-Merck-Halle, April 1st, 1967, 23 by 32.75in (59 by 83cm), together with 2 other tour programmes.
£3,000-3,100 *CSK*

Film Memorabilia

Charleton Heston's shirt from Ben Hur, oatmeal coloured cotton blouse with light blue embroidery, Western Costume Co., Hollywood, MGM, 1959.
£450-550 *S(NY)*

A Universal Studios, Paul Newman's costume from Butch Cassidy and the Sundance Kid, label inscribed 2471//P. Newman, mounted in a display case, , 1969.
£4,800-5,000 *S(NY)*

Sets of lobby cards:
Top: Three The Adventures of Robin Hood, First National Re-issue, Errol Flynn, Basil Rathbone, Olivia de Havilland.
£150-175
Bottom: Eight The Fighting 69th, Warner Bros., 1940, James Cagney, Pat O'Brien, George Brent.
£250-275 *Bon*

Cross Reference
Colour Review

A Wizard of Oz costume, emerald green felt jacket with cream coloured appliqué and blue/green brocade, MGM, 1938.
£2,000-2,200 *S(NY)*

Worn by one of the inhabitants of Emerald City.

A Hanna-Barbera Studios gouache on multi-cel setup applied to a watercolour production background, The Flintstones, A Night on the Town, 1960s, 7.5 by 9.5in (19 by 24cm).
£570-600 *CNY*

A Walt Disney Studios gouache on full celluloid applied to a watercolour production background, Pooh Gets Ready for Bed, 9 by 12in (23 by 31cm).
£1,100-1,300 *CNY*

A Walt Disney Studios, gouache on partial celluloid applied to a Courvoisier airbrush background, Jiminy Cricket, Pinocchio, 1940, 9.5 by 8in (24 by 20cm).
£1,800-2,200 *CNY*

E.T.

Two plastic and metal key rings, 1.75 and 2.5in (4 and 6cm) high. **30-40p each** *PC*

Two E.T. Hugglets vinyl lapel clip-ons, 3.5 and 4in (9 and 10cm) high. **£1-2 each** *PC*

An E.T. Spaceship board game, 17 by 9in (43 by 23cm). **£10-15** *PC*

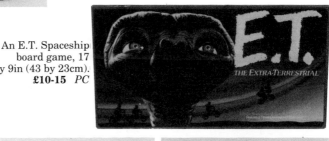

A grey pottery E.T. money box, 5in (13cm) high. **£3-5** *PC*

A talking E.T. figure, c1984, 10in (25cm) high. **£10-15** *PC*

A battery operated grey E.T. vinyl Bendy Toy, his finger lights up red, 6in (15cm) high. **£10-15** *PC*

A grey pottery E.T. figure, 5in (13cm) high. **£4-6** *PC*

A grey pottery E.T. jug, with hand painted black features, 4.25in (11cm) high. **£4-6** *PC*

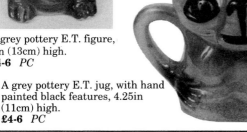

A grey E.T. mug, 4.25in (12cm) high. **£4-6** *PC*

Royal Memorabilia

A silver Jubilee holder, with pull-out photographs of King George V and Queen Mary, 1935, 1.25in (3cm) square.
£12-15 *ROS*

A Davenport blue and white plate, with George III in the centre surrounded by agricultural implements.
£400-425 *SCW*

An Edward VIII unused carved foundation stone, 11.5 by 8.5in (29 by 21cm).
£40-45 *OD*

A tin tray to commemorate the marriage of H.R.H. Prince Charles and Princess Diana, 1981. **£2-3** *WAC*

> **Cross Reference**
> Ceramics
> Commemorative Ware

A bronze King Edward VIII wall plaque, 9in (23cm) diam. **£90-110** *COB*

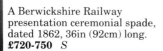

A Paragon mug with a portrait of Prince Charles aged 4 years, produced at the time of his mother's Coronation, 1953.
£100-110 *SCW*

A Berwickshire Railway presentation ceremonial spade, dated 1862, 36in (92cm) long.
£720-750 *S*

The first turf of the Berwickshire Railway was cut with this spade by Lady Campbell, Tuesday 14th October, 1862.

A Mayer's cyclamen pink loving cup, with multi-colour underglaze print of Edward and Alexandra to commemorate their wedding in 1863, 5in (13cm) high. **£700-725** *SCW*

Ten chromo plated illustrations from a Wills hard back book to commemorate Queen Victoria's Diamond Jubilee, June 22nd 1897.   **£160-180** *VS*

Scales, Balances & Weights

A Royal Copenhagen plate, commemorating the 40th Jubilee of King Christian IX, the father of Queen Alexandra.   **£150-160** *SCW*

A set of 10 brass bell weights, stamped Oxon, 19thC, 14lb-1oz.
£450-475 *CSK*

A black enamelled and lacquered brass electric balance, signed Lord Kelvins' Patents Electric Balance No. 694, James White Glasgow and London, 22in (56cm) wide.   **£240-260** *CSK*

A beam balance jockey scale, by W. & T. Avery & Co., Birmingham, with leather covered wood seat, c1900, base 71.5in (180cm) wide.
£3,000-3,250 *CSK*

A set of 6 Wedgwood china weights.
£660-720 *SUF*

A set of 5 Burmese bronze 'chicken' weights, and a companion set of 6 'duck' weights.   **£275-300** *CSK*

365

Scientific Instruments

A Thatcher's rotary calculator, by Keuffel & Esser, New York, No. 4012, with instructions on baseboard and mahogany case with label in lid, 24in (61cm) wide.
£575-600 *CSK*

A boxwood nocturnal dial, index arm and rotating disc stamped with lunar and solar scales, with two projecting lugs inscribed 'G' and 'L' for Great and Little Bear, the reverse with points of the compass, 18thC, 10in (25cm) high.
£1,500-1,700 *HSS*

An oxidised and lacquered brass aneroid barometer, signed J. Goldschmid à Zurich No. 445, in fitted leather covered case, 6in (15cm) wide.
£420-450 *CSK*

A lacquered brass barograph, unsigned, in a glazed mahogany case with chart drawer, 15in (38cm) wide.
£600-625 *CSK*

A pocket barometer with case, by Negretti & Zambra, with inches, millibars and feet, c1880, 3in (7.5cm) diam.
£80-100 *BWA*

A child's Magic Lantern, German, made for Gamages, with coloured strips and slipping slides, in original box.
£100-120 *HEG*

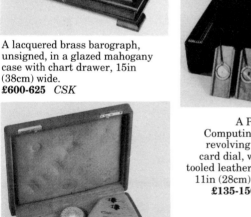

A Palmer's Computing Scale, revolving printed card dial, with gilt tooled leather border, 11in (28cm) square.
£135-150 *CSK*

A Curta Type 1 calculator, sectioned for display with separate components, in fitted case, by Contina, Liechtenstein.
£650-700 *CSK*

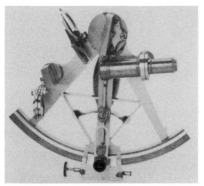

A lacquered brass diamond frame sextant, by Troughton & Simms London Platina 3523, in fitted mahogany case, 13.5in (34.5cm) wide. **£550-575** *CSK*

A Slater's Improved Armillary Sphere, late 19thC, overall height 13in (33cm). **£650-675** *C*

A Persian Celestial globe, unsigned, 19thC, stand probably later, overall height 12in (30cm). **£1,900-2,200** *C*

The inclusion of planetary positions makes this sphere unique among Islamic celestial globes.

Globes

A metal celestial globe, probably Indo-Persian, unsigned and undated, overall height 11in (28cm). **£2,250-2,500** *C*

A miniature terrestrial globe in English, by Rand McNaley & Co., 5in (13cm) high. **£110-130** *CSK*

A terrestrial pocket globe, by Jacob and Halse, London, 1809, 3in (7cm) diam. **£1,600-1,800** *C*

A Geographic Educator terrestrial globe, American, with track of the trans-Atlantic flights of Lindbergh and Chamberlain dividing into 7 sections containing jig-saw puzzles of the Continents, one piece missing, 11in (28cm) high. **£225-250** *CSK*

A New Portable Terrestrial Globe, by John Betts, London, collapsing globe, c1860, 15in (38cm) diam. **£400-440** *C*

The first issue of the Betts umbrella globe; Betts died c1863, and the publication of the globe was taken up by George Philip & Son in 1880.

A 'sphere terrestre' children's game, by R. Barbot, published for the Ministère de l'Instruction Publique, the globe on a Paris prime meridian, decorated with the paper flags of 24 nations and tracks of the principal steamship routes, in original box with instruction sheet, overall height 11in (28cm). **£1,200-1,400** *C*

Microscopes

A mahogany slide cabinet of 21 drawers with bone handles, with many slide preparations, 19thC, 14.5in (37cm) high. **£1,100-1,200** *CSK*

An oxidised and lacquered brass microscope, signed W. Watson & Son, 313 High Holborn, London, No. 6641, with accessories, c1900, 13in (33cm) high. **£500-550** *CSK*

A lacquered brass compound binocular microscope, signed on the stand J. B. Dancer, optician, Manchester, No. 407, 19thC, in mahogany case, 18in (45.5cm) high. **£950-1,100** *C*

Surveying

A brass surveying compass, signed S. Thaxter & Sons, Boston, with maker's trade label, in fitted mahogany case, 19thC, 15.5in (39.5cm) wide, with tripod. **£220-240** *CSK*

A lacquered brass theodolite, signed Cary London, in fitted mahogany case with accessories, late 18th/early 19thC, 9in (22.5cm) wide. **£1,100-1,250** *CSK*

A lacquered brass surveyor's cross, signed W. & T. Gilbert, London, in mahogany case, 19thC, 5in (12cm) wide. **£480-520** *CSK*

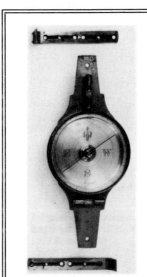

A lacquered brass surveying compass, signed W. & L. E. Gurley, Troy, N.Y., in fitted mahogany case with maker's trade label, 16.5in (42cm) wide. **£275-295** *CSK*

Telescopes

A four draw telescope, unsigned, object glass 1in diam., shagreen covered outer body tube cover, 18thC, 12.5in (32cm) long closed. **£850-900** *C*

A lacquered brass 3in refracting telescope, signed Newton & Co., 41.25in (105cm) long body tube, in fitted mahogany case with accessories, 19thC. **£1,750-1,850** *C*

A lacquered brass 2.25in refracting portable telescope, signed Cary London Francis E. James from A.H.H. 1903, 29in (74cm) body, in fitted mahogany case. **£1,500-1,600** *C*

A 3in reflecting telescope, signed on the back plate, James Short London, c1747, in mahogany veneered oak carrying case. **£1,850-1,950** *CSK*

A brass 2in reflecting telescope, unsigned, simulated fishskin covered, 14in (35.5cm) long body tube, late 18thC, in oak case. **£775-825** *CSK*

Stereoscopes

A Brewster pattern walnut stereoscope. **£150-160** *HEG*

A wood Sunscope, folds down to fit into card box, with boxed views, 1920. **£140-160** *HEG*

A Jules Rickard stereoscopic slide projector, contained in a fitted case together with slides, spectacles and spare bulbs. **£220-240** *HSS*

A stereoscopic viewer and cards, c1860. **£250-300** *LBL*

A Holmes viewer, with wood body, and 12 cards, 1895. **£35-45** *HEG*

A collection of stereo cards of South Africa, 1900. **£50-60** *BBA*

A Holmes viewer, with aluminium body, and 12 cards, 1905. **£35-45** *HEG*

A talking View-Master stereoscope, with Flipper story and music, c1960. **£10-12** *HEG*

A boxed set of 100 Boar War stereograms, 1901. **£100-120** *HEG*

A Camerascope, the cards given with Army Club cigarettes, c1920s. **£20-30** **Cards 40p a pair** *HEG*

A Stitz Auto illuminated viewer, 1960s. **£45-55** *HEG*

A novelty Vistascreen stereoscope, with boxed stereograms, c1950. **£15-20** *HEG*

A View-Master stereoscope, with 3 picture reels, 1954. **£8-10** *HEG*

Medical Instruments

A burnished steel tooth key, with claw and chequer grip ivory handle, and 2 shaped elevators with chequer grip bone handles.
£220-240 *CSK*

A Millikin & Lawley half-disarticulated human skeleton.
£75-85 *HCH*

A pharmacist's brass table for folding powder papers, 19thC, 2.75in (7cm) wide.
£20-30 *MRT*

A hearing trumpet.
£100-110
BWA

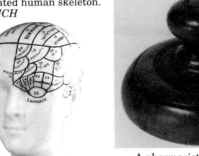

A pharmacist's boxwood pill rounder, 19thC, 3in (8cm) diam.
£25-35 *MRT*

A porcelain phrenological bust, impressed mark by F. Bridges Phrenologist, 19thC, 5.5in (14cm) high.
£650-675 *CSK*

A hearing trumpet, 11.5in (29.5cm) long.
£100-140 *BWA*

A 13 second glass pulse taker, in boxwood case, 19thC, 7in (18cm) long.
£35-45 *MRT*

A surgeon's amputation set, signed Laundy, in fitted velvet lined mahogany case, large bone saw missing, c1800, 16in (41cm) wide.   **£675-725** *CSK*

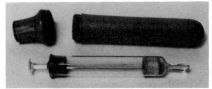

A glass syringe, in boxwood case, 19thC, 9in (23cm) long.
£35-45 *MRT*

A surgeon's silver plated bullet prober, mid-19thC, 9.5in (24cm) long.   **£40-50** *BWA*

A male contraceptive device, of animal membrane, with printed satirical scene, inscription 'Voila mon choix', and thread and silk tie, French, early 19thC, 8in (20cm) long. **£3,500-4,000** *CSK*

Male contraceptives were first alluded to in the 11thC by a Greek writer Antoninus Liberalis. In the 16thC Gabriel Fallope suggested the use of a 'fine linen bag' and a preparation of astringent herbs. Colonel Cundum is said to have invented the dried gut of sheep worn by men in the act of coition to prevent venereal infection c1700.

A Dr. Nelson inhaler, 9.5in (24cm) high. **£25-30** *ROS*

A brass adjustable leg splint, with foot support, with locking screw, 19thC, 20in (51cm) high. **£125-150** *CSK*

A pharmacist's rosewood handled poultice iron, 19thC, 11.5in (29.5cm) long. **£20-30** *MRT*

A hanging lifesize instructional print of a human skeleton, flanked by sectional illustrations, on paper, some tears, 76in (193cm) long. **£150-175** *CSK*

A pharmacist's turned boxwood double-ended powder measure, late 19thC, 3.5in (9cm) high. **£35-45** *MRT*

Spectacles

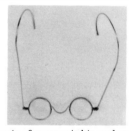

A pair of ring-sided spectacles, c1750. **£160-180** *BWA*

A pair of surgeon's binocular glasses. **£40-45** *BWA*

A pair of Chinese lacquered frame spectacles, brass cased folding bridge, possibly 18thC, 4.5in (11.5cm) wide. **£720-750** *CSK*

A pair of Golding spectacles, with a tortoiseshell case, 19thC, 7.5in (19cm) long. **£100-140** *BWA*

A pair of silver sunglasses, c1824. **£80-95** *BWA*

Scripophily

A bearer share in S. A. André Citroën, with cars round the border, c1936. **£32-35** *SCR*

A gold mining share in Mines D'Or de Kilo Moto, a Belgian Congo company, nationalised without compensation, red and black, 1944. **£5-6** *SCR*

A share certificate of the Mediterranean Electric Telegraph Company, which linked Sardinia with the European mainland, black and white, 1854. **£110-120** *SCR*

These companies achieved their objectives by laying cable under the sea. John Brett, who signed the share, was one of the most successful engineers in this field, having laid the Dover-Calais cable and later, using Brunel's SS Great Eastern, the Atlantic cable.

A Chinese Government loan re-organisation certificate, engraved by Waterlow, 1913. Brown **£12-15** Blue **£32-35** *SCR*

A £100 bond for the Kingdom of Roumania, with vignette of the castle on which Dracula stories are based, engraved by Waterlow, blue and black, 1929. **£32-35** *SCR*

A share certificate for The London & New Zealand Exploration Company, formed to invest in and raise capital for New Zealand mining companies, English and French text, green and beige, 1896. **£32-35** *SCR*

Akcionarsky Pivovar Na Smichove, a share in Czech brewer of Pils, multi-coloured, 1937. **£145-150** *SCR*

The buildings still exist but are now almost derelict.

A $1000 bond for the Kingdom of Bulgaria, issued under the 1928 Stabilisation Loan, engraved by Bradbury Wilkinson. **£72-75** *SCR*

A Certificate of Education, 1907, 11.5in (29.5cm) wide. **£2-3** *COL*

America

A $10,000 registered bond for New York Central Rail Road Company, blue, 1913. **£10-12** *SCR*

A $1,000 bond issued by the State of Ohio, for Cleveland Short Line Railway Company, brown, 1911. **£10-12** *SCR*

A Cincinnati Indianapolis St Louis & Chicago Railway Company $1,000 bond, one of only 7,500 issued, green and black, 1880. **£38-40** *SCR*

A California Diamond Oil Company, share issued in San Francisco incorporated under the laws of Arizona, green and black, 1905. **£12-15** *SCR*

A Providence & Worcester Railroad Company share, green and black with orange printed 'seal', c1957. **£8-10** *SCR*

A Chicago, Burlington & Quincy Railroad share, red and black, c1900. **£23-25** *SCR*

A State of Kansas bond, issued by the Osage City Bank on behalf of the State, repayable in gold, One of 750 issued, engraved by the St Louis Banknote Company, brown, 1882. **£28-30** *SCR*

A Beech Creek Railroad Company bond, brown and black, 1892. **£28-30** *SCR*

A $1,000 West Shore Railroad Company bond, red and black, c1918. **£8-10** *SCR*

Canada

A Canadian Collieries (Dunsmuir) Ltd. share certificate, registered in Toronto, green and black, c1913. **£10-12** *SCR*

A share certificate of West Canadian Oil & Gas Ltd., registered in Calgary, blue and black, 1959. **£6-8** *SCR*

Great Britain

A Liverpool Sewage Utilization Company certificate, black and white, c1868. **£23-25** *SCR*

A British Gas Light Co., share certificate, 1825. **£270-275** *SCR*

A General Screw Steam Shipping Company share certificate, 1852. **£32-35** *SCR*

A Claridge's Hotels share certificate, orange, yellow and black, 1921. **£68-70** *SCR*

India

An Rs500 India General Navigation & Railway Company Ltd. debenture, engraved by Waterlow, green and black, 1915. **£15-18** *SCR*

A Savana Industrial and Financial Company, Pondichery, India certificate, brown, 1952. **£12-15** *SCR*

Mexico

A Compania Mexicana de Petroleo 'El Tigre' bearer share with coupons attached, green and black with printed revenue stamps, 1929. **£16-18** *SCR*

A Negociacion Agricola 'La Sautena' share in Mexican hacienda located on the Texas border, green, red and black, 1907. **£52-55** *SCR*

South Africa

A share certificate of The South African Irrigation & Investment Co., black and white with red overprint, 1863. **£32-35** *SCR*

Russia

A St Petersburg Land & Mortgage Co. Ltd. £100 debenture, engraved by Waterlow.
£62-65 *SCR*

A New Russia Company Ltd. First Mortgage Debenture, engraved by Waterlow, blue, 1910.
£23-25 *SCR*

The company formed in 1869 by John Hughes, a Welsh expatriate recruited by the Tsar to recreate the steel town of Merthyr Tydfil in Russia. The result was Donetz, originally known as Hughesovska.

Spain

A SA Minas Del Tesorero bearer share, issued in Madrid, green and black, 1907. **£38-40** *SCR*

A certificate of La España Industrial textile company, black, 1854. **£16-18** *SCR*

Insurance Policies

A Law Accident Insurance Society Ltd. employers' indemnity policy, damaged, 1909, 21in (53cm) long.
£4-6 *COL*

An Atlas Assurance Company Ltd. insurance policy, 1908, 20in (51cm) long.
£8-11 *COL*

A Royal Exchange Assurance insurance policy, 1911, 20in (51cm) long.
£10-14 *COL*

Sewing

A brass thimble.
£3-5 *AA*

A Regency mahogany and foliate inlaid sewing box, with tray, sewing implements and small ivory dishes, 9.25in (23cm) wide.
£450-500 *CSK*

A Naumann sewing machine, without cover, 20 by 10.5in (51 by 26cm).
£12-14 *AL*

An advertising box for Coats threads.
£100-115 *LBL*

A Winselmann Titan sewing machine, without cover, 16 by 9in (41 by 23cm).   **£20-25** *AL*

Two silver thimbles:
r. Chester 1918.
l. London 1927.
£17-20 each *AA*

A sewing machine inside its box, 19 by 9.25in (48 by 23cm).
£25-30 *AL*

A tin sewing box, painted jade green, with internal brass lift-out section, divided as illustrated on the lid, early 20thC.
£50-60 *ROW*

A Victorian novelty pin cushion, applied with various coloured agates, Birmingham, 3.5in (9cm).
£200-250 *CSK*

A Singer sewing machine, with cover.
£25-30 *AL*

A metal tape measure, early 20thC, 2in (5cm) high.
£80-98 *AMH*

Shipping

A brass ship's bell, 'Commodore', English, inscribed on one side, c1880, 15in (38cm) diam.
£350-375 *S*

A Siebe Gorman & Company diver's helmet, early 20thC, 18in (46cm) high.
£1,050-1,150 *S*

An oak brass bound ship's wheel, 30in (76cm) diam.
£150-175 *PCh*

A wood casket encrusted with a wide variety of sea shells, English, mid-19thC, 11.5in (29cm) wide. **£250-275** *S*

A ship's oil can, c1930, 5in (13cm) high.
£8-10 *COL*

The diameter measures the same as height so that when filled it cannot fall over.

A Merchant Navy pennant, 1940s, 24in (62cm) long.
£25-30 *COB*

A Royal Navy sailors' document case, c1840. **£30-35** *COB*

Two sailors' arm badges, pre-WWII. **£5-8** *COB*

A white canvas covered circular lifebuoy, R.M.S. Titanic, Liverpool.
£1,800-2,000 *ONS*

A pair of Barbadian shell pictures, mid-19thC, 8.25 and 9in (21 and 23cm) wide each.
£1,850-1,950 *S*

A Norwegian pattern rotary foghorn, in stained pine case, French and English instructions, late 19thC, 23in (59cm) long.
£450-480 *S*

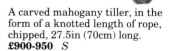

A carved mahogany tiller, in the form of a knotted length of rope, chipped, 27.5in (70cm) long.
£900-950 *S*

Lanterns

A Russian ship's lamp, c1960.
£50-60 *DHO*

A Sestrel ship's binnacle compass, on mahogany and oak base, English, 1930s, 56in (142cm) high.
£1,000-1,100 *S*

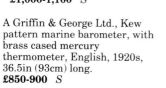

A Griffin & George Ltd., Kew pattern marine barometer, with brass cased mercury thermometer, English, 1920s, 36.5in (93cm) long.
£850-900 *S*

Two ship's lanterns, Port and Starboard, 24.5in (62cm) high.
£100-155 *GRF*

A copper ship's lamp, c1850, 23in (59cm) high.
£100-120 *DHO*

A ship's Port lamp, c1940, 21.5in (54cm) high.
£50-60 *DHO*

Shipping Ephemera

A passenger list for a Cunard Cruise, 1933.
£7-8 *COB*

A selection of shipping companies sailing lists, 1930s-60s.
£10-15 each *COB*

A Cunard brochure, 1950s.
£5-6 *COB*

An advertising booklet, The World's Wonder Ships. **£4-5** *COB*

Two photographs of the SS Titanic, 8 by 10in (20 by 25cm) each.
£5-6 each *COB*

An Admiralty book of lost or damaged vessels during WWII, 1947.
£15-20 *COB*

A selection of shipping companies matchboxes. **£1-2 each** *COB*

A publicity brochure for the Orient Line, 1948.
£6-7 *COB*

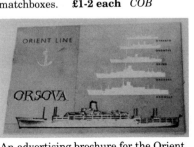

An advertising brochure for the Orient Line, 1950s. **£5-6** *COB*

A sailing list for the White Star Line, 1928.
£8-10 *COB*

Menus

A Canadian Pacific Line menu,
1935. **£6-7** *COB*

A Cunard Line menu, 1930s.
£4-5 *COB*

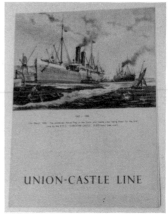

A Union-Castle Line menu,
1950s. **£5-6** *COB*

Posters

A black and white advertising
poster for John Brown &
Company, Ltd., 1915.
£10-15 *COB*

A Richard Beck poster for Orient
Line Cruises, The Baynard Press,
1937, 40 by 25in (101.5 by 64cm).
£160-180 *BBA*

A Charles
Dixon poster,
Union-
Australasian
Line to New
Zealand and
Australia.
£100-120
ONS

An advertising
poster for
Cook's, The
Wise Traveller
Has Friends
Everywhere.
£110-130
ONS

A P Irwin Brown poster for LMS
Express & Cunard Liner, Royal
Scot alongside Aquitania, 1924.
£3,250-3,500 *ONS*

A broadsheet for an early Isle of
Wight Regatta, 1835.
£35-40 *COB*

Cross Reference
Posters
Railway Posters

*This is believed to be the first
poster published by the LMS after
the grouping in 1924.*

Sixties & Seventies

Two Melamine dishes, 1960, larger advertising 5in (13cm) long, **£3-5** and small **£2-3** *FAB*

A 'donkey' cruet set, made in Hong Kong, 1960s.
£2-3 *FAB*

A 'Babycham' cruet set, 1960, 6.5in (16cm) high.
£2-4 *FAB*

A black and yellow cruet set, 1960s, 1.5in (4cm) high.
£3-5 *FAB*

A liqueur bottle and box, decorated by Dali, c1971, 12.5in (32cm) high.
£100-120 *KAC*

A tin, 1960s, 7in (18cm) high.
£3-5 *FAB*

A plastic cruet set, made in Hong Kong, 1960, 2.5in (6cm) high, with box.
£3-5 *FAB*

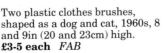

A pair of blue and grey Permaware ashtrays, 4.25in (11cm) wide.
£3-5 *FAB*

Two plastic clothes brushes, shaped as a dog and cat, 1960s, 8 and 9in (20 and 23cm) high.
£3-5 each *FAB*

A 'Fuzz Puppy' tissue box cover, with original tissues, American, 1970s, 8in (20cm) high.
£5-8 *FAB*

A pair of red and black
Permaware ashtrays, c1960,
4.25in (11cm) long.
£3-5 *FAB*

A green and orange 'Gonk',
1960s, 14in (36cm) high.
£8-10 *PC*

A set of coasters, with cocktail
recipes, early 1960s.
£3-5 *FAB*

A Pifco electric foot massager,
shown at 1961 Ideal Home
Exhibition.
£8-10 *FAB*

A Morphy-Richards hair dryer, in
original box, 1960s.
£8-10 *FAB*

A G Plan red plastic clock,
c1970, 10.5in (26cm) high.
£6-8 *FAB*

Mary Quant knitting patterns.
£1-2 each *FAB*

A Sparklets soda syphon,
with original box, c1970.
£6-8 *FAB*

Lambretta touch up paint and
stand, early 1960s, 19in (48cm)
high.
£200-250 *FAB*

Three Lord Nelson's pottery
containers, 5 to 7.5in
(13 to 19cm) high.
£3-5 each *FAB*

A copy of Vogue, April 1964.
£8-10 *FAB*

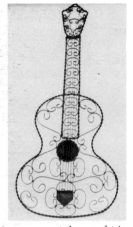

An ornamental wrought iron guitar, 1960s, 29.5in (75cm) long. **£8-10** *FAB*

A Crossroads Special book, autographed by the cast, c1970. **£10-12** *FAB*

A set of different coloured egg cups, 1960s.
£4-5 the set *FAB*

A Royal Copenhagen bottle vase, 1960s, 11in (28cm) high. **£70-90** *KAC*

A plastic Britvic pineapple ice bucket, 1960s, 12in (31cm) high. **£12-15** *FAB*

A pair of kitchen storage tins, 1970s, 5.5in (14cm) high. **£2-3** *FAB*

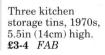

An Armitage Shanks ceramic advertising ashtray, to mark 150 year anniversary. **£4-6** *FAB*

Three kitchen storage tins, 1970s, 5.5in (14cm) high.
£3-4 *FAB*

A smoker's stand, 1970s, 21in (53cm) high.
£8-10 *FAB*

60s & 70s Ceramics

A Piazza ware ceramic jug, black and red on white ground, by M.J. Wood, 1960s, 9in (23cm) high.
£8-10 *FAB*

A Crown Devon ceramic jug, black, red and grey on a mottled ground, 1960, 7in (18cm) high.
£10-15 *FAB*

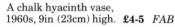

A chalk hyacinth vase, 1960s, 9in (23cm) high. **£4-5** *FAB*

A Crown Devon vase, Memphis, designed by Colin Melbourne, 1960s, 6in (15cm) high.
£40-50 *FAB*

Two Beswick ceramic items, black and white with yellow interior, vase 7in (18cm) high.
£12-15
dish 6.25in (16cm) wide.
£8-10 *FAB*

A brown and white jug, by Arthur Wood, 1960s, 9.5in (24cm) high.
£8-10 *FAB*

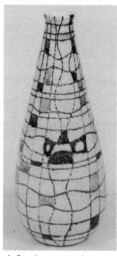

A foreign ceramic vase, 1960s, 8in (20cm) high.
£6-8 *FAB*

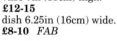

A Midwinter cup and plate set, Cannes, designed by Hugh Casson, 9.25in (23cm) wide.
£5-8 *FAB*

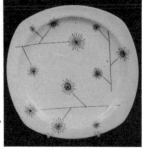

A Midwinter plate, Cannes, designed by Hugh Casson, 7.5in (19cm) diam. **£3-4** *FAB*

A Midwinter plate, Flower Mint, designed by Jessie Tait, c1960.
£5-6 *FAB*

A Homemaker plate, Woolworths from 1957-61, 9in (23cm) diam. **£6-8** *FAB*

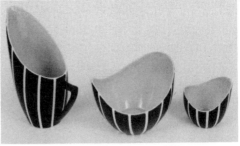

Three items of Hornsea ware, black and white with yellow interiors, 1960s, 2.25 to 5.5in (6 to 14cm) high. **£3-5 each** *FAB*

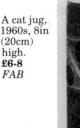

A cat jug, 1960s, 8in (20cm) high. **£6-8** *FAB*

A ceramic bowl, coloured grey and yellow, late 1950s, 11in (28cm) wide. **£12-15** *FAB*

A Troika pottery cylinder vase, 1960s, 14.5in (37cm) high. **£60-80** *KAC*

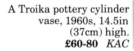

A ceramic cat, 1960s, 14in (36cm) high. **£6-8** *FAB*

60s & 70s Costume

A Carnaby Street Mina smock, coloured red, white and blue, 1960s. **£10-12** *FAB*

A Mary Quant designed Alligator blue check raincoat, 1960s. **£50-60** *FAB*

A Delamare PVC raincoat, 1960s. **£30-40** *FAB*

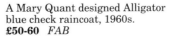

Cross Reference
Textiles

A jacket, The Jam pop group, could be bought by mail order from the Musical Express, late 1970s.
£40-50 *FAB*

A pair of Levi flared jeans, c1960.
£35-40 *FAB*

A psychedelic coat, 1960s.
£25-35 *FAB*

A kaftan, coloured pink, black, turquoise and blue, 1960s.
£8-10 *FAB*

A pair of cork soled sandals, 1960s. **£4-8** *FAB*

Two pairs of stockings, Lucky Charm and Strümpfe, 1960s.
£8-12 *FAB*

A Donovan cap, in blue and green Welsh tweed, 1960s.
£6-8 *FAB*

A turquoise suede synthetic fur trimmed coat. **£20-25** *FAB*

A suede mesh bag, with metal handles, 1960s, 18in (46cm) long.
£2-3 *FAB*

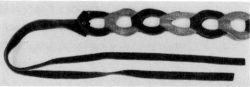

Two leather belts, 1960s.
£2-3 each *FAB*

A brown and beige leather tie belt, 1960s.
£2-3 *FAB*

60s & 70s Furniture

A psychedelic magazine rack, c1960, 12in (31cm) wide.
£5-8 *FAB*

A green Habitat chair of Swedish design, early 1970s.
£15-25 *FAB*

An occasional table, 1960s, 13.5in (34cm) diam. **£5-8** *FAB*

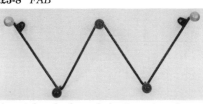

A metal and coloured plastic coat rack, 1960s, 18in (46cm) wide. **£5-6** *FAB*

A daisy shaped compressed cardboard table, with purple top and green base, 1960s, 52in (132cm) diam.
£85-100 *FAB*

60s & 70s Glass

An art glass vase, c1960, 12in (30.5cm) high.
£20-30 *FAB*

Three red, yellow and blue Murano cased glass pieces, largest 9in (22.5cm) high **£10-15**, small 3.5in (9cm) wide **£4-6** *FAB*

A green glass fish, c1960, 7in (17.5cm) high.
£3-5 *FAB*

A blue and green Murano glass bowl, c1960, 6in (15cm) diam.
£10-12 *FAB*

Cross Reference
Glass

A yellow cased glass vase, 1960s, 20in (51cm) high.
£10-15 *FAB*

60s & 70s Jewellery

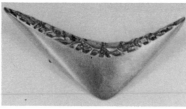

A pewter brooch by Caret, c1960
£10-12   *FAB*

A 'Top of the Pops' pendant,
1970.   **£3-5**   *FAB*

A silver pendant,
1960s.
£15-20   *FAB*

Three stainless steel pendants, 1960s, 2
to 3in (5 to 7cm) long.   **£3-8 each**   *FAB*

A filigree metal bangle, c1960s,
2in (5cm) diam.   **£3-5**   *FAB*

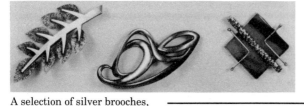

A selection of silver brooches,
c1960, 1.75 to 2.5in (4 to 6.5cm)
long.   **£15-20 each**   *FAB*

60s & 70s Lamps

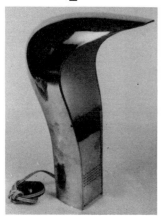

Cross Reference
Lighting

A set of 3 purple
hanging lamps,
c1970.
£10-15   *FAB*

An orange plastic
lampshade,
c1970, 9in
(23cm) high.
£3-5   *FAB*

A Lamperti lamp, by Casati and
Ponzio, 1960s, 13in (33cm) high.
£100-120   *KAC*

A lava lamp, c1960, 17in (43cm)
high.
£25-30   *FAB*

60s & 70s Stainless Steel

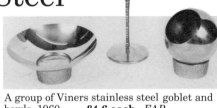

A group of Viners stainless steel goblet and bowls, 1960. **£4-6 each** *FAB*

A set of Viners stainless steel spoons in a box and a 3-piece cutlery set, 1960. **£5-6 each set** *FAB*

Two pairs of stainless steel candle holders, 1960, 2 and 3in (5 and 8cm) diam. **£3-5 a pair** *FAB*

A 7-piece stainless steel party set, 3.5in (9cm) diam., with box. **£4-6** *FAB*

A set of Trentway stainless steel napkin rings, in box, made exclusively for Boots, 1960. **£4-5** *FAB*

A chrome Ronson table lighter, lined in blue, 1960s, 3in (8cm) high. **£10-12** *FAB*

A satin steel dish, 1960, 20in (51cm) long. **£6-8** *FAB*

60s & 70s Toys

Two Chad Valley kaleidoscopes, 7.5 and 13.5in (19 and 34cm) long. **£2-6 each** *FAB*

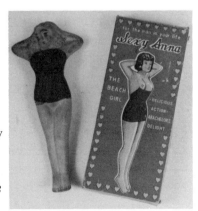

A Sexy Anna, The Beach Girl, with box, 1960, 6in (15cm) high. **£5-10** *FAB*

A three-dimensional executive toy, as seen on TV in 'Blake's Seven', 1970s, 8in (20cm) high. **£10-15** *FAB*

Cross Reference
Toys

Smoking

A cigar cabinet, for restoration, 19thC, 16.5in (42cm) wide.
£60-65 *TRU*

A Craven 'A' cork tipped Virginia cigarette tin, 'Made specially to prevent sore throats'.
£4-5 *ROW*

A tobacco rasp, with maker's mark J.M. in script, dated 1703, 2.75in (7cm) long.
£750-800 *S*

Cross Reference
Ceramics

A cast iron match holder, in the form of a Turk, 6in (15cm) high.
£400-500 *BWA*

A Staffordshire pottery tobacco jar, 19thC, 5in (13cm) high.
£50-55 *TRU*

A late Victorian cigarette holder, mouthpiece cracked, with case. **£55-65** *WW*

A silver match holder, c1930.
£20-30 *ASA*

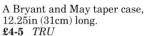

A Bryant and May taper case, 12.25in (31cm) long.
£4-5 *TRU*

An Art Deco silver and enamel extending cigarette holder. **£30-60** *ASA*

Cigarette Cases

A chromium plated petrol fuelled table cigarette lighter, in the form of a jet fighter aeroplane, 1950s, 9.5in (23.5cm) long.
£60-80 *HSS*

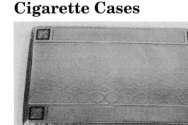

A silver cigarette case, c1930.
£30-50 *ASA*

A commemorative silver and enamel cigarette case, base inscribed R.M.S. 'Empress of China' (H.M. Armed Cruiser) Launched By Lady Northcote Barrow in Furness, 25th March 1891, scratched and chipped, hallmarked Chester 1890, 3.25 by 4.25in (8 by 10.5cm).
£825-975 *S*

A highly decorated silver cigarette case. **£20-40** *ASA*

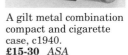

A gilt metal combination compact and cigarette case, c1940.
£15-30 *ASA*

A Bakelite cigarette container, the doors swing open to reveal cigarettes, 7in (18cm) high.
£18-20 *COL*

A simulated tortoiseshell cigarette case, with watch set into the lid. **£30-50** *ASA*

A white metal and enamel cigarette case, c1930.
£15-25 *ASA*

Pipes

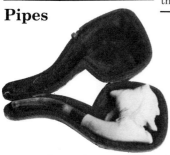

A Meerschaum clay pipe, the bowl carved in the form of the Devil, 19thC, 5in (13cm) long.
£140-150 *TRU*

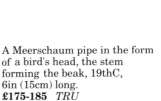

A silver mounted Meerschaum pipe, with amber stem, 7in (18cm) long.
£150-160 *TRU*

A Meerschaum pipe in the form of a bird's head, the stem forming the beak, 19thC, 6in (15cm) long.
£175-185 *TRU*

A Bavarian carved stained horn and wood pipe base, 19thC, 20in (51cm).
£80-100 *MJB*

Vesta Cases

A silver line engraved vesta case, Birmingham 1912, 1.75in (5cm) wide.
£25-30 *TRU*

An engraved silver vesta case, Birmingham 1920, 1.75in (5cm) wide. **£35-40** *TRU*

An engraved silver vesta case, Birmingham 1915, 1in (3cm) wide. **£20-22** *TRU*

A silver vesta case set with agate thistles, c1880, 1.75in (5cm) long. **£80-90** *BWA*

A silver vesta case, Birmingham 1919, 1.75in (5cm) wide. **£30-35** *TRU*

A fluted silver vesta case, with taper case to side, London 1890, 1.5in (4cm) wide. **£55-60** *TRU*

A leather vesta case, c1890, 2.5in (6cm) long. **£60-75** *AMH*

A plain silver vesta case, Birmingham 1873, 1.25in (3cm) wide. **£35-40** *TRU*

Snuff Boxes

A carved wood Scottish snuff figure, early 19thC, 29in (74cm) high. **£1,750-1,850** *B*

A nickel plated snuff box, the lid engraved 'Hugh Bennett', 3in (8cm) wide. **£18-20** *TRU*

A selection of Scottish snuff mulls, in wood, ivory and horn, with silver mounts and dedications, 2.25 and 2.5in (5 and 6cm). **£300-500 each** *BWA*

Spoons

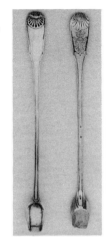

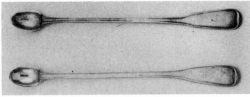

A pair of thread pattern salt spoons, moulded with shells and armorial engraved, Toulouse c1770, 6.75in (16.5cm) long, 50gr.
£1,110-1,150 *S(Mon)*

A pair of French salt spoons, with reeded borders and armorial engraved, 18thC, 6.25in (15.5cm) long, 36gr.
£420-450 *S(Mon)*

A pair of Georgian engraved gold plated serving spoons, London 1810.
£125-150 *AA*

Caddy Spoons

Three caddy spoons, by Hilliard & Thompson, Birmingham c1860. **£200-260** *AMH*

A caddy spoon, by E. Morley, London c1795, 3in (8cm).
£180-225 *AMH*

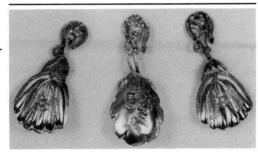

A caddy spoon, maker G.F., London 1878.
£100-135 *AMH*

A silver caddy spoon, London 1820, 3.5in (9cm) long.
£60-70 *AMH*

A caddy spoon, Hester Bateman, London 1787, 2.5in (6cm) long.
£250-300 *AMH*

A filigree silver caddy spoon, c1795, 2.5in (6cm) long.
£200-225 *AMH*

A silver caddy spoon by Lias & Wakely, London 1878, 4in (10cm) long.
£100-125 *AMH*

A caddy spoon, by H. Hyams, London 1866, 3.5in (9cm) long.
£200-230 *AMH*

A caddy spoon, maker W.M., Edinburgh 1878, 4in (10cm) long.
£200-225 *AMH*

Sport

A set of 50 cards Parkhurst Ice Hockey, 1957/58, featuring players from Montreal and Toronto. **£1,000-1,200** *S(NY)*

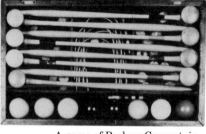

A game of Parlour Croquet, in original mahogany box, 14.5in (37cm) long. **£330-360** *CSK*

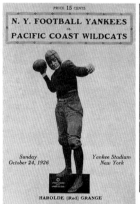

A pair of lignum vitae bowling balls, the inset ivory disc with owner's initials and number of ball. **£30-40** *PAR*

An Eton Royal Football Club cap, 1913-14. **£60-65** *COB*

American Football

A jersey worn by Joe Namath, New York Jets, c1967. **£2,850-3,000** *S(NY)*

A complete run of 24 Superbowl programmes, 1967-1990. **£1,150-1,250** *S(NY)*

A group of 4 football programmes of matches all played in New York, 1929-1931. **£350-400** *S(NY)*

A jersey worn by Merlin Olsen, L.A. Rams, early 1970s. **£775-875** *S(NY)*

Twenty Seven unused football matchbooks, in mint condition, 1930s-1940s. **£220-250** *S(NY)*

Baseball

A 1927 Pirates World's Series Press Pin.
£820-850 *S(NY)*

A 1955 World Series Phantom Press Pin at Comiskey Park.
£820-850 *S(NY)*

A piece of Joe DiMaggio's wedding cake, wedding and reception invitations and a newspaper cutting, November 19, 1939.
£700-750 *S(NY)*

At the wedding of Joe DiMaggio and actress Dorothy Arnold in San Francisco, guests were given wedding cake wrapped in cellophane to take home. This piece is exactly as it was given in 1939, with 2 bisque columns and a rose from the cake.

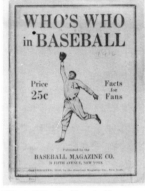

Who's Who in Baseball magazine, published by Baseball Magazine, soft cover, 1916.
£200-240 *S(NY)*

An Adirondack bat used by Mike Schmidt during his first MVP season in 1980, 170A, No.20 on knob.
£450-500 *S(NY)*

An Adirondack bat used by Willie Mays, No.302.
£1,800-2,200 *S(NY)*

Willie Mays hit 660 home runs during his career.

A Brooklyn Dodgers autographed baseball, with 28 signatures on an official National League ball, 1947.
£820-850 *S(NY)*

A 1912 World's Series ticket stub, for New York vs Boston Game 3, at Fenway Park in Boston.
£450-550 *S(NY)*

A sterling silver season pass for Cincinnati Ball Park, 1902.
£2,500-3,000 *S(NY)*

An Al Simmons cigar box, c1930.
£630-680 *S(NY)*

Basketball

A set of 72 Bowman basketball cards and memorabilia, 1948.
£2,900-3,100 *S(NY)*

A Scott's Potato Chips basketball card of George Mikan, 1950, 4in (10cm) high.
£2,750-3,000 *S(NY)*

These regionally issued basketball cards are extemely rare, very few are known and the Mikan card may well be the rarest of all basketball cards.

A Topps basketball poster ruler, a complete set of 23, c1969.
£475-500 *S(NY)*

No.5 was not issued.

Boxing

A Jake Kilrain, 'Champion Pugilist of the World' silk boxing scarf.   **£1,800-2,000** *S(NY)*

A brass snuff box depicting John Heenan and Thomas Sayers in their famous bout for the boxing championship of the world, 1860.
£500-700 *S(NY)*

Cross Reference
Snuff Boxes

A poster for the Louis/Schmeling fight, 1936, 22in (56cm) high.
£700-900 *S(NY)*

Cricket

Yorkshire Cricket (Lord Hawke), a chromolithograph by Spy, 1892, 12 by 7in (31 by 18cm), mounted.
£280-320 *CSK*

Gubby Allen's photograph album, chiefly of sporting teams and fixtures during his time at Eton (1915-21) and Cambridge (1922-23), containing 51 photographs.
£2,800-3,200 *DN*

The Australians 1888, a commemorative printed silk handkerchief, depicting the Australian IX of 1888, 16in (41cm) sq.
£260-280 *CSK*

Curling

A curling stone, with an iron ring, c1830, 8.5in (21.5cm) high. **£70-80** *LBL*

A box of curling stones, stamped J. C. Forgan, with removable handles. **£350-450** *LBL*

Bonnor Stood Still at the Crease, Lord Sherman Keeping Wicket, by Lucien Davis, RI, signed, 9 by 6in (23 by 15cm). **£225-250** *Bon*

A pair of presentation curling stones, with ivory handles, c1895. **£250-300** *LBL*

Golfing

A brass gutty golf ball mould for the Trophy dimple pattern golf ball, stamped John White & Co., Edinburgh, numbered 1917/3657, 3in (8cm) diam. **£800-850** *C(S)*

A Doulton Lambeth stoneware golfing jug, relief moulded showing Lost Ball, Putting and Driving scenes, c1905, 7.5in (19cm) high. **£750-775** *S*

An Elkington bronze trophy figure of Harry Vardon after Ludlow, early 20thC. **£1,250-1,500** *S*

Twelve unused Cestrian gutty balls, mostly wrapped, made by the Telegraph Manufacturing Co. Ltd., Helsby, Cheshire, in original cardboard box, c1898. **£3,250-3,500** *S*

A silver plated golfing desk piece, late 19thC, 6in (15cm) high. **£480-500** *S*

A Verulam Golf Club brass captain's prize, presented to Samuel Ryder, depicting Abe Mitchell in the centre of a circular tray, 1927, 5.75in (14.5cm) diam. **£475-500** *S*

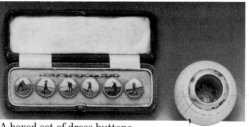

A boxed set of dress buttons, depicting golfers in various positions, together with a spelter figure of a golfer, and a Doulton Lambeth ceramic golf ball matchstriker, c1900.
£650-675 *S*

A metal golf ball marking machine, stamped Chamber's patent No. 18712-10.
£375-400 *C(S)*

A silver plated golfing inkwell, c1890, 11in (28cm) wide. **£700-750** *S*

An unused silver score book, originally belonged to Harry Vardon, engraved H.V., hallmarked Birmingham 1906, 4.5in (11cm) high.
£1,600-1,700 *S*

Three boxes of the Colonel patented Blue Ring cardboard tees. **£550-575** *C(S)*

Golf Clubs

A McEwan long nosed putter, with beech head and hickory shaft, c1880.
£550-580 *S*

A Dalrymple's Patent brass and wood dual lofted club, stamped Sir W. Dalrymple's Patent, 34.
£2,750-3,000 *C(S)*

A rut iron head, shaft missing, c1865, hosel 5in (12.5in).
£600-625 *S*

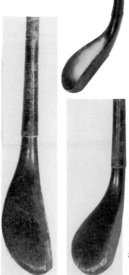

A mammoth niblick, by Cochrane of Edinburgh, stamped Fortnum & Mason, Piccadilly, London. **£725-750** *C(S)*

A Transitional scared head play club, by Robert Forgan.
£550-580 *C(S)*

A scared head long nosed putter, the head stamped T. Morris, the shaft reduced.
£350-380 *C(S)*

A blacksmith-made lofter, with dished hand hammered face, c1870.
£975-1,025 *C(S)*

A mid-iron with pierced and sparred face, the head stamped 4, the shaft inscribed 'W', stamped W. Wilson, Maker, St Andrews.
£3,750-4,000
C(S)

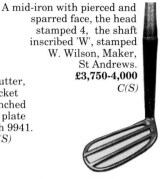

A patented putter, with short socket and hand punched face, the sole plate stamped Legh 9941.
£875-925 *C(S)*

A Sterling silver Walter Hagen putter, inscribed Silver Putters Sweepstakes, with ebonised shaft.
£450-480 *C(S)*

A brass headed Centro putter by Gibson of Kinghorn, head stamped John Henry Patent No. 1559.
£425-450 *C(S)*

Golfing Ephemera

The Royal and Ancient Game of Golf, by H. H. Hilton, numbered 239/900.
£850-875 *S*

Rules of the Royal and Ancient Golf Club St Andrews with alphabetical list of members, 1888.
£350-375 *S*

Three golf books and a letter from A. G. Tait, comprising: Hutchinson British Golf Links, numbered 169/250, Taylor on Golf, 1902, and F. G. Tait a Record, by J.L. Low, 1900.
£1,300-1,400 *S*

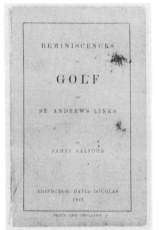

Reminiscences of Golf on St Andrews Links, by James Balfour, printed by David Douglas, Edinburgh, 1887.
£1,600-1,800 *S*

The Banff Golf Club Bazaar, Edinburgh 1895, by J. P. Grant.
£680-720 *S*

A cartoon, How To Get A Good Tip Out Of The Golfer, 1913, 18 by 14.5in (46 by 37.5cm).
£50-55 *AMH*

Stanhopes

Stanhopes are small trinkets or souvenir items made from a variety of materials such as bone, metal, wood, plastic or plaster. Each contains a tiny microscope lens invented in the latter half of the 18thC by the 3rd Earl Stanhope, after whom Stanhopes were named. Mounted within each lens is a minute early 'transparency' usually depicting from one to a dozen different views of a popular tourist resort or other place of interest. Others commemorate important events such as exhibitions, or contain a portrait of a famous person. It was in 1853, not long after the invention of photography, that David Brewster first had the idea of placing one of these micro-photographs within a piece of jewellery, thus producing the first Stanhope.

From the 1860s until well into the 20thC a great variety of objects were manufactured, mainly in the UK and France, the earliest examples being rings and brooches. Those most commonly found today date from the

1890s and later, and include pens, pencils, paper knives, crosses, sewing aids, miniature binoculars and a variety of gold and silver charms. More scarce, but still available to the diligent searcher, are such items as smokers' requisites, perfume bottles, bookmarks and whistles. The early pieces of jewellery and any object containing more than one Stanhope are much harder to find.

The most interesting images are views of any place outside the UK or France, royalty, maps, nudes and marriage vows. The number of views shown on any one Stanhope is normally 1, 5, 6 or 8, but up to 12 can be found. Quite scarce and worth looking for are hand tinted images. Those seen are often of English seaside resorts tinted blue, pink or lilac with varying degrees of skill.

Although Stanhopes were still being produced as late as the 1960s their popularity died out after WWI, owing probably to the general loss of interest suffered by any novelty with the passing of time.

A needle case with a view of Exposition de 1867, 3.5in (9cm) long.
£40-50 *AMH*

An American advertising penknife, with a horse picture, 3.25in (8.5cm) long.
£40-60 *PC*

An étui, with memory of Andover, incomplete, 4.25in (11cm) long.
£25-35 *PC*

A red cut glass scent bottle, with a silver metal top, and a view of Birchington-on-Sea, 2in (5cm) high. **£45-60** *PC*

A vesta vase, with compass and views of walks, memory of Knighton.
£55-65 *PC*

A rifle pencil, 6in (15cm) long.
£35-45 *PC*

A thimble, with a view
of Shakespeare, 1in
(2.5cm) high.
£35-45 *PC*

Three acorn thimble holders, 2.5
to 2.75in (6 to 7cm) high.
£35-45 each *PC*

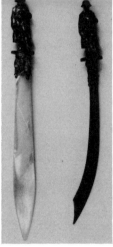

A watch, .75in (2cm) diam.
£35-45 *PC*

An Indian head, with
view of Niagara Falls,
3in (7.5cm) high.
£35-45 *PC*

Two Napoleon paper
knives, longest
mother-of-pearl, 6in
(15cm) long.
£25-35 each *PC*

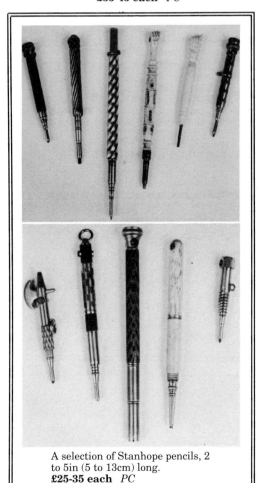

A prayer book, with a view
of The Marine Parade,
Lowestoft, 1in (2.5cm)
high. **£30-40** *PC*

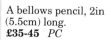

A bellows pencil, 2in
(5.5cm) long.
£35-45 *PC*

A selection of Stanhope pencils, 2
to 5in (5 to 13cm) long.
£25-35 each *PC*

A pair of scissors, with views of London, with case 2in (5cm) long. **£45-55** *PC*

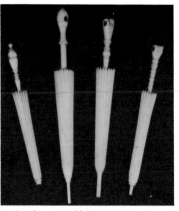

A selection of bone parasols, 4 to 5.25in (10 to 13cm) long. **£30-35 each** *PC*

Four binocular Stanhopes: Eiffel Tower, .75in (2cm), Brighton, 1in (2.5cm), Dumfries, 1in (2.5cm), Linton & Lynmouth, 1in (2.5cm) long. **£15-20 each** *PC*

A thimble holder in a nutshell case, with '2002' view, 2in (5cm) long. **£45-55** *PC*

A metal ring with a naughty picture. **£80-90** *PC*

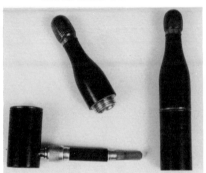

A bottle/pipe with dice, made for the Franco British Exhibition, London, 1908, with a view of Edinburgh, 5.5in (14cm) long. **£40-50** *PC*

A needlework box with 2 drawers, 4in (10cm) wide. **£85-100** *PC*

A silver metal bracelet. **£50-60** *PC*

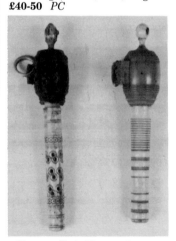

Two needle holders and tape measures, 4.25 to 4.5in (11 to 12cm) long. **£35-40 each** *PC*

A miniature pipe, 2in (5cm) long. **£35-45** *PC*

An egg cup, with a view of Rheinfall, 3in (7.5cm) high. **£35-45** *PC*

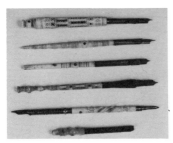

A selection of Stanhope pens, 3.75 to 6in (9 to 15cm) long.
£15-25 each *PC*

A selection of paper knives, 4.5 to 9in (11.5 to 23cm) long.
£15-25 each *PC*

A brass letter opener with magnifying glass, 6.5in (16.5cm). **£50-60** *PC*

Two German pipes, 4.5in (11.5cm) and 3.25in (8cm) long.
£35-45 each *PC*

A Cinematographe prayer book with views of clothed figures, when squeezed the clothes are removed, .75in (2cm) high.
£75-85 *PC*

A penknife with 6 views of Clacton-on-Sea, 2.25in (6cm) long.
£35-45 *PC*

A bottle/pipe for the Franco British Exhibition, London, 1908. **£20-25** *BWA*

Two shakers, probably sand to blot ink, with views of Jerusalem in Arabic, 4in (10cm) high.
£35-45 each *PC*

A selection of Stanhope pens with paper knives, 7 and 8in (18 and 20cm) long.
£15-25 each *PC*

A bottle/pipe, for the Imperial International Exhibition, London, 1908 and 1909, 5.5in (14cm) long.
£40-50 *PC*

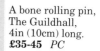

A Foto Kino, with different views when handle is turned. **£75-85** *PC*

A bone rolling pin, The Guildhall, 4in (10cm) long.
£35-45 *PC*

Taxidermy

A badger's head.
£85-95 *EB*

Two pheasants in a glass case,
37in (94cm) wide.
£150-200 *GHA*

Two kingfishers,
mounted in a flat
fronted case, 10.5in
(26cm) high.
£80-120 *GHA*

A fox with a partridge, mounted
in a flat fronted cabinet, 19thC,
42in (106.5cm) wide.
£250-300 *GHA*

A pike's head, 20lb weight.
£70-80 *EB*

A pike, caught at Tring,
Hertfordshire, by L. H. Holmes,
on 11 March 1908, 9lbs 8oz,
mounted in a bow fronted case,
40in (101.5cm). **£600-800** *GHA*

| **Cross Reference** |
| Fishing |

A vixen in a flat fronted case,
probably by Hutchinson,
Aberystwyth.
£250-270 *ND*

A grouse in a glass case.
£100-110 *EB*

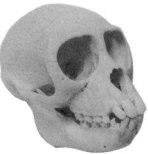

A monkey's skull.
£18-20 *EB*

A monkey's head made into a
paperweight.
£60-65 *EB*

A squirrel on a log.
£55-65 *EB*

Tea Caddies

An inlaid mahogany and cross-banded tea caddy, mid-19thC, 11.75in (30cm) wide.
£100-120 *PCh*

A Victorian oval tea caddy, with hinged half lid and small ivory handle.
£80-90 *LF*

A Regency rosewood crossbanded and brass inlaid tea caddy, with fitted interior, 13.5in (34.5cm) wide. **£100-120** *PCh*

A Regency mahogany tea caddy, c1810. **£400-600** *WA*

Teapots

A Gibson's black and gold teapot, 7in (17.5cm) high. **£30-35** *OD*

Tea Making

A Victorian black glazed teapot, restored, c1880, 10in (25cm) wide. **£20-25** *OD*

A tea blender's tasting jug, c1900, 2.5in (6.5cm) high. **£10-12** *OD*

A treacle glazed stoneware Toby teapot, c1820, 8in (20cm) high. **£70-80** *OD*

An Aylesford Priory teapot, c1960, 10.5in (26.5cm) high. **£25-30** *OD*

A Hobb's infuser, by R. H. Plant & Co., design reg. 1885, 4in (10cm) diam. **£10-12** *OD*

An Etruscan style teapot, 7.5in (19cm) high. **£12-18** *OD*

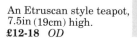

An underglaze brown printed teapot, c1840, 12.5in (31cm) high. **£70-75** *OD*

A black and gilt teapot, 6.25in (16cm) high. **£20-25** *OD*

A puce yellow lustre teapot and lid, with blue transfer print, c1840, 6.5in (16.5cm) high. **£30-35** *OD*

A miniature drab coloured stoneware teapot, with moulded decoration, c1840. **£30-35** *OD*

A Cyples teapot, damaged, c1810, 5.5in (14cm) high. **£60-65** *OD*

A Royal Worcester brown teapot, c1965, 4.5in (11.5cm) high. **£8-10** *OD*

Cross Reference
Ceramics

A yellow glaze teapot, William Fishley-Holland, c1930. **£20-22** *OD*

A Staffordshire Pottery limited edition Batman teapot and cover, 8in (20cm) high. **£50-60** *PC*

A Wade green teapot, with purple, pink and yellow decoration, 6.5in (16.5cm) high. **£5-8** *OD*

A Lovatt's Potteries Ltd. green teapot, 5.5in (13.5cm) high. **£10-12** *OD*

A Tudric pewter teapot with fibre handle, Liberty & Co., c1905, 4in (10cm) high. **£45-50** *OD*

An Art Deco copper teapot, with a ceramic lining, 6in (15cm) high. **£30-35** *OD*

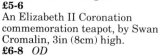

A Festival of Britain tea caddy, 1951, 4in (10cm) high. **£5-6**
An Elizabeth II Coronation commemoration teapot, by Swan Cromalin, 3in (8cm) high. **£6-8** *OD*

A transfer printed anti-tannic tea infuser pot, by Marshalls Patent, c1910, 5.5in (14cm) high. **£30-35** *OD*

Telephones

An Ericsson ivory telephone, c1940s.
£180-240 *NOW*

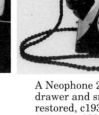

A Neophone 200 Series, with drawer and small ringer, restored, c1930-50.
£75-115 *NOW*

A Neophone on a bell box, c1940.
£100-130 *NOW*

A Bakelite red telephone, c1945.
£350-500 *BHE*

A royal blue telephone, 1938, in working order.
£75-85 *BGA*

An Ericsson 300 Series telephone, with drawer, and a call exchange button.
£70-90 *NOW*

A double-sided Public Telephone sign, c1930.
£150-200 *BHE*

An ATM Monophone, as used on the Hull Corporation telephone system.
£125-175 *NOW*

An Ericsson 300 Series telephone, c1937-59.
£60-85 *NOW*

A Bakelite ivory telephone, c1945.
£250-375 *BHE*

A K6 telephone kiosk, c1935.
Restored. **£1,250-1,500**
Unrestored. **£425-475**
BHE

An Ericsson 'cobra' phone, ringer missing, 1950s.
£10-35
NOW

A City of London Police Public Call Post telephone, c1930.
£5,000-6,500
BHE

A Metropolitan Police Public Call Post telephone, c1935.
£4,000-5,000 *BHE*

A Bakelite green 300 Series telephone, c1945. **£350-500** *BHE*

Toy Telephones

A toy telephone bank, 13in (33cm) high.
£30-35 *NOW*

A toy candlestick telephone, 6in (15cm) high.
£20-35 *NOW*

A toy telephone and money box, with slot under the handle, 3.5in (9cm) high.
£15-20 *NOW*

A toy coin box telephone money bank, 7in (18cm) high.
£35-40 *NOW*

A toy candlestick telephone, 9.5in (24cm) high.
£25-45 *NOW*

A red toy telephone, with clockwork ringer, operated by handset cradle, 7in (18cm) wide.
£25-30 *NOW*

Miniature 300 Series telephones, available in blue, red and cream 1.5in (4cm) high.
£5-10 each *NOW*

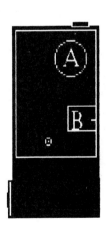

TEXTILES

A woolwork picture, after
George Morland, early 19thC,
22 by 15in (55 by 37.5cm).
£175-185 *DN*

A wool printed Paisley pattern
shawl, predominantly cream and
red, slight damage, 19thC.
£120-130 *PAR*

An early Welsh checked wool
blanket, purple and blue on
cream ground, hand cut and
blanket stitched.
£50-60 *CHA*
*Large rolls of this material were
made then cut in lengths.*

A set of 5 lace edged mats,
painted with music hall dancers,
19thC.   **£80-100** *TVA*

An orange ostrich feather fan,
with diamante handle, 1920s,
28in (71cm) long.
£40-50 *LB*

A pair of
pictures,
silk work
on metal.
£140-150
AI

Babywear

A hand painted moiré silk cover
for Baby Book, unused, c1930.
£12-16 *AA*

A young girl's dress and jacket of
tartan silk, labelled Spécialité
pour Enfant, Mme Fontaine
Duclos, 4 rue Mondovi, 4 Paris,
c1865.
£225-250 *CSK*

A very fine lawn baby's dress.
£30-40 *PAR*

An antique silk toddler's dress, with hand made lace.
£55-65 *PAR*

A very fine lawn toddler's dress.
£25-35 *PAR*

A Victorian silk baby's gown, with hand made lace.
£90-100 *PAR*

A pair of Oriental baby's shoes.
£15-25 *PAR*

A Victorian fine lawn baby gown.
£30-40 *PAR*

A pair of Victorian baby's shoes.
£40-45 *PAR*

A French silk hand made baby's dress. **£40-45** *PAR*

A cotton lawn christening robe, with lace trimming, 44in (112cm) long.
£60-80 *LB*

Beadwork

A beaded handbag, c1925, 8in (20cm) wide. **£8-12** *COL*

A beaded pin cushion, a WWI sweetheart gift, 7.5in (19cm) long. **£28-30** *TS*

A beaded bag, with handles, c1925, 8in (20cm) wide. **£8-10** *COL*

A beaded pin cushion, 3.75in (9cm) square. **£15-20** *LB*

A pair of Regency wrist bracelets, finely beaded on silk in flower designs, with ormolu and chalcedony clasps, 7in (18cm) long. **£150-250** *TOR*

Costume

A late Victorian burgundy velvet gown, with bustled skirt, 56in (142cm) long. **£200-250** *LB*

An ivory satin evening dress, the back trained with bows, c1870. **£85-95** *CSK*

A gentleman's cotton dressing gown, c1815. **£2,250-2,350** *CSK*

A pair of kid gloves, English, c1610. **£1,600-1,700** *CSK*

A folding top hat, with original box. **£50-60** *AL*

Head Scarves

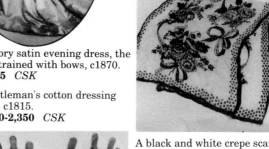

A black and white crepe scarf. **£4-6** *LB*

A floral silk crepe head scarf. **£6-8** *LB*

Dressmaking Patterns
Handbags & Purses

Vogue patterns for evening wear, 1950s. **£4-6 each** *COL*

A sequinned evening bag, c1930, 5.5 by 6.5in (14 by 16cm). **£8-10** *BGA*

A Simplicity pattern, 1950s. **£4-6** *COL*

A black beaded bag, c1920, 8.5in (21cm) wide. **£8-12** *COL*

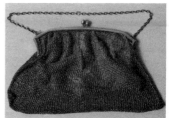

A silver mesh evening purse, Birmingham 1913, 6oz. **£30-40** *TRU*

Rug Fragment Covers

A Kurdish rug fragment cushion, 19thC, 19in (48cm) wide. **£60-75** *SAM*

A mahogany stool, with antique Shahsavan jajim fragment top, 25in (64cm) wide. **£350-450** *SAM*

An amboyna wood stool, inlaid with ebony, maple and burr yew, with Qashqai tribal bag face South West Persian top, 24in (61cm) wide. **£800-1,200** *SAM*

Two cushions of Shahsavan Tribal kelim fragments, c1900, 16in (41cm) square. **£45-55 each** *SAM*

A Qashqai tribal produce bag, filled with down to provide a bolster cushion, 19thC, 41in (104cm) long. **£250-350** *SAM*

A Shahsavan bedding bag, turned upside down and used as either a seat or table, c1900, 39in (99cm) long. **£400-600** *SAM*

Samplers

A finely worked Continental sampler, by Anna Pagand, showing animals, birds and plants, 19thC, 15.5 by 10in (39 by 25cm), unframed. **£150-175** *PAR*

A needlework sampler, by Alison Clunie, in Birmingham frame, 1830, 22 by 23in (56 by 59cm). **£450-500** *LBL*

A woolwork sampler, by Margaret Kearton, 1853, 24 by 23in (62 by 59cm). **£475-500** *DN*

Tiles

A display of fireplace tiles. **£30-40** *GRF*

A set of 12 tiles, stamped De Morgan, Merton Abbey, turquoise ground with daisy pattern. **£1,200-1,300** *LRG*

A Mintons ship tile, by Moyr Smith, 6in (15cm) square. **£25-28** *NCA*

A Mintons tile, Oranges, 6in (15cm) square. **£25-30** *NCA*

A set of 6 C.H. Brannam tiles, depicting fish, each 6in (15cm) square. **£480-500** *NCA*

> **Cross Reference**
> Art Nouveau

A selection of fireplace tiles. **£8-10 each** *GRF*

A Wedgwood tile, 1890s, 9in (23cm) square. **£30-35** *COB*

Sets of 6 fireplace tiles. **£40-60 the set** *GRF*

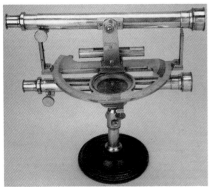

A Belgian brass theodolite, signed Brand Frères Opticiens du Roi, Bruxelles, 19thC, 13in (33cm) high. **£775-800** *C*

A lacquered brass binocular microscope, 19thC. **£675-700** *C*

A bone woman paper knife figurine, 19thC, 5in (12.5cm). **£500-550** *CSK*

A Dutch brass and fruitwood Cuff-type monocular microscrope, 18thC, 22in (56cm) high. **£2,750-3,000** *C*

An electric dental drill, with Edison motor, c1880, 11in (28cm) long. **£750-850** *BWA*

A pair of Nuremburg nose spectacles. **£2,750-3,000** *CSK*

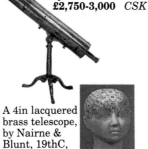

A 4in lacquered brass telescope, by Nairne & Blunt, 19thC, 25.5in (65cm) long. **£900-950** *C*

An ivory cane handle, 19thC, 2.5in (6.5cm). **£1,400-1,600** *CSK*

A brass monocular microscope, 19thC. **£1,400-1,600** *C*

A Cuff-type microscope, mid-18thC, 17in (43.5cm) high. **£3,400-3,600** *C*

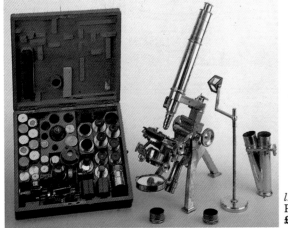

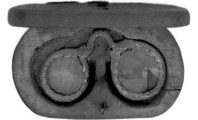

A pair of Nuremburg single wire nose spectacles, German, 17thC, in original wooden case. **£4,200-4,400** *CSK*

l. A brass No. 1 monocular microscope, by Powell & Lealand, 1877, 19in (49cm) high. **£6,500-7,000** *C*

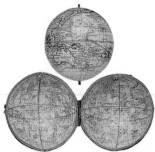

A terrestrial globe, by Charles Smith & Son, c1834, 3.75in (9.5cm) diam. **£2,400-2,600** *C*

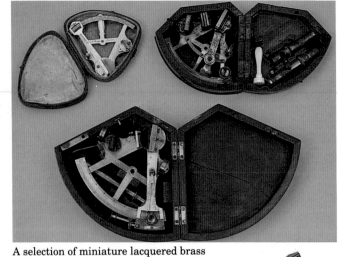

A selection of miniature lacquered brass sextants, 19thC, largest 6in (15cm) wide. **£1,000-1,800 each** *C*

A boxwood and mahogany octant, American, 1778, 19.5in (49.5cm) wide. **£2,200-2,500** CSK

A pocket globe, by Newton & Son, c1831, 3in (8cm) diam. **£1,600-1,700** *C*

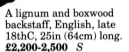

A lignum and boxwood backstaff, English, late 18thC, 25in (64cm) long. **£2,200-2,500** *S*

An ebony and brass octant, 12in (30.5cm). **£550-600** *CSK*

A brass and ebony octant, 14.5in (37cm). **£650-700** *CSK*

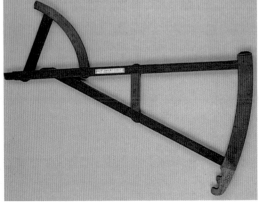

A 'Davis' backstaff, by F. Blow, London, 18thC, 23.5in (60cm) wide. **£2,900-3,100** *C*

An 'A' frame sextant, 19thC, 6.5in (16.5cm) wide. **£550-600** *CSK*

A pocket globe, by N. Lane, c1833, 3in (7.5cm) diam. **£1,800-1,900** *C*

A J.H. Dallmeyer 2 by 4in box camera, with lens. **£2,750-3,000** *CSK*

A Marion & Co., half-plate tropical reflex camera, No. M907, with a Ross, London Homocentric 8.5in f6.3 lens No. 140661. **£3,000-3,400** *CSK*

A London Stereoscopic Co., with Goerz Dagor lens. **£1,100-1,250** *CSK*

A London Stereoscopic Co., quarter plate camera, with Black Band lens, No. 17147 and maker's plaque. **£825-875** *CSK*

A Thornton-Pickard quarter plate Folding Ruby camera, with a Dallmeyer Stigmatic f6 6.4in lens No. 137707. **£1,250-1,350** *CSK*

A Stereoscopic Co., Parvex De Luxe camera. **£1,250-1,400** *CSK*

A London Stereoscopic Co. quarter plate Artists Reflex camera No. S132. **£3,100-3,300** *CSK*

A Simons & Co. 35mm Sico camera, No. 52. **£4,500-5,000** *CSK*

A Nouvel Appareil Gaudin daguerreotype camera outfit, signed A. Gaudin, Rue Montmartre, 76, Paris, contained in a wood box with brass handle, hinged lid and side panels. **£18,000-20,000** *CSK*

A 6.5 by 3in mahogany body and brass bound stereoscopic hand and stand camera, A. Adams & Co., London, with a pair of Ross Homocentric f6.3 5in lenses, and plate. **£2,500-2,750** *CSK*

A 45 by 107mm mahogany body Royal Mail Stereolette camera, W. Butcher & Sons. **£1,000-1,100** *CSK*

r. A 35mm walnut body cinematographic camera/projector, Lumiére, France. **£12,750-13,250** *CSK*

A 9 by 12cm boxform Anschütz camera, C. P. Goerz. **£3,500-3,750** *CSK*

l. A quarter plate mahogany body patent Optimus detective camera, Perken, Son & Rayment. **£1,100-1,250** *CSK*

A 6 by 9cm boxform patent Anschütz camera, C. P. Goerz. **£3,250-3,750** *CSK*

A floor standing Sapho stereoscope, Royal Novelty Co. **£3,000-3,300** *CSK*

A 6 by 13cm Stereo Sigriste camera, S. O. L./J.G. Sigriste, Paris. **£6,750-7,250** *CSK*

A 2.5 by 2.5in Ford's Tom Thumb camera, Max Jurnick, U.S.A. **£8,250-8,750** *CSK*

r. A 6 x 9cm collapsable Spido strut camera, Gaumont, Paris. **£500-550** *CSK*

A wood and aluminium 'Perfecscope', made in the U.S.A., c1895.
£50-70 *BBA*

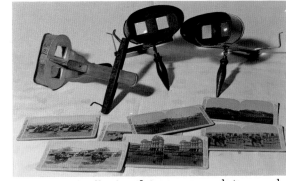

A collection of stereoscopes and stereo cards.
£50-70 each *BBA*

A Napier coffee maker, c1850, 10.5in (26.5cm) high.
£400-450 *BWA*

A Senior Monarch gramophone, c1908.
£1,200-1,450 *BWA*

A praxinoscope and musical box, E. Reyauld, Paris, 8.5in (21.5cm) drum. **£7,800-8,500** *CSK*

l. An early type wood stereoscope, possibly mahogany, c1885.
£90-135 *BBA*

r. An all aluminium stereoscope, made in the U.S.A.
£50-70 *BBA*

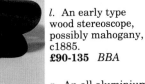

A wood and brass stereoscope, with magnifying glass, c1865.
£300-350 *BBA*

TARTAN WARE

A MacFarlane box containing playing cards, c1890, 3.5in (9cm) high. **£150-200** *LBL*

A Mauchline family photograph album, c1885, 8.5in (21.5cm) long. **£300-350** *LBL*

A Tartan ware card case, 4.5in (11.5cm) long. **£100-125** *LBL*

Two novels with McKenzie and Drummond Tartan ware covers. **£600-700 each** *LBL*

A plaid box, c1885, 3.5in (9cm) long. **£90-100** *LBL*

A Mauchline ware money box, 4in (10cm) long. **£65-75** *LBL*

A darning mushroom, c1885, 3.5in (9cm) high. **£40-50** *LBL*

Four Tartan ware napkin rings. **£20-25 each** *LBL*

A book mark, 9in (22.5cm) long. **£80-110** *LBL*

A tub/pot, 3in (7.5cm) high. **£30-35** *LBL*

A Stuart stamp box with drawer, c1850, 1.25in (3cm) wide. **£100-120** *LBL*

A Stuart string holder, c1845, 4in (10cm) high. **£300-400** *LBL*

A Mauchline ware jewellery box, 6in (15cm) wide. **£100-125** *LBL*

A Maclean spectacle case, 5.5in (14cm) long. **£100-110** *LBL*

Four large napkin rings, 2in (5cm) diam. **£35-45 each** *LBL*

A quilt, probably Durham. **£100-125** *AI*

A beaded bag, c1925,
£35-40 *HEW*

A beaded bag, 7in
(17.5cm) long.
£30-40 *LB*

A Regency beadwork wrist bracelet,
6in (15cm) long. **£25-75** *TOR*

Two late Victorian beadwork cushions,
18in (45.5cm) long. **£100-120** *LBL*

An Art Nouveau panel,
c1890, 37in (94cm) long.
£45-60 *STK*

A patchwork quilt, c1840, 72in
(182.5cm). **£550-600** *LBL*

A pair of Regency beaded bracelets,
7in (17.5cm) long. **£150-350** *TOR*

A sampler in a rosewood frame,
c1820, 21in (53.5cm) long.
£650-700 *LBL*

A Regency embroidered velvet wrist
bracelet, with ormolu clasp, 7in
(17.5cm) long. **£25-65** *TOR*

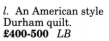

A glass beadwork
embroidered cushion,
c1880. **£80-120** *STK*

l. An American style
Durham quilt.
£400-500 *LB*

An Edwardian broderie anglaise and lace christening gown. **£75-100** *LB*

A 1920s gold and bronze lace dress. **£120-130** *ACL*

A nurse's uniform, with pinafore, c1915. **£50-60** *ACL*

A 1960s mini dress, 37in (94cm) long. **£45-50** *CLA*

A 1950s boned corselette **£20-25** and a net petticoat. **£12-15** *CLA*

A crepe dress, with braid trim and utility label, c1940, 45in (114cm) long. **£50-60** *CLA*

A 1940s red Cross uniform, 42in (107cm) long. **£40-50** *ACL*

An Ayrtia worked baby gown and cap, c1870. **£250-300** *LB*

A baby's christening gown, hand tucked and trimmed with ribbon and lace, c1870. **£200-250** *LB*

r. A Mary Quant mini dress, 32in (81cm) long. **£30-40** *CLA*

A builder's half model of The SS Duke of Fife, by the Ailsa Ship Building Co., Troon, in original glazed case, 76in (194.5cm) long. **£4,250-4,500** *CSK*

A detailed builder's half model of the barque Torridon, built by Paul Hall & Co., Aberdeen, 1865, 81.5in (206cm) long. **£7,250-7,500** *CSK*

A builder's model of The SS St. Magnus, built for the North of Scotland, Orkney & Shetland Steam Navigation Co. Ltd., by Paul Russell & Co., Aberdeen, 63in (160cm) long. **£12,500-13,500** *CSK*

A French prisoner-of-war boxwood model of a 100-gun man-of-war, 13in (33cm) long, on original oval rosewood base and later domed cover. **£13,500-14,000** *CSK*

Embessage of Newcastle, built for Hall Brothers Steam Ship Co., by Joseph Thompson & Sons Ltd., Sunderland, 1935, 54in (137cm) long. **£4,500-5,000** *CSK*

A model of the motor 'Pair' fishing vessel Lirana of San Sebastian, built by Paul Russell & Co., Aberdeen, 21.5in (54.5cm) long, in contemporary glazed mahogany case. **£5,750-6,250** *CSK*

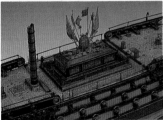

A boxwood model of HMS Victory, c1806, 18in (46cm) long. **£12,500-13,500** *S*

A Bassett Lowke one-eighth inch scale model of the steam ship Great Britain, 48in (122cm) long, in presentation glazed display case. **£5,000-5,500** *S*

A Märklin tinplate circus set, controlled by gyroscopic action. **£10,250-10,500** *CNY*

An airship musical roundabout, possibly French, c1915. **£1,800-2,000** *CNY*

An American National wood, tin and brass pedal car, c1910. **£5,700-5,900** *CNY*

A biplane circling a hangar, by Cardini, Italy, c1925, 14in (35.5cm) high. **£1,100-1,300** *CNY*

A Nomura Toys tinplate Fokker tri-motor plane, Japanese, c1930. **£3,250-3,500** *S*

A Doll and Cie ferris wheel ride, 13.5in (34cm) high. **£2,500-2,700** *CNY*

A Märklin tinplate carousel, c1910, 16in (41cm) diam. **£48,000-50,000** *S*

An acrobat, German, c1905, 15in (38cm) high. **£3,250-3,500** *S*

A Bing De Dion tinplate car, German, c1907, 8.25in (21cm) long. **£1,400-1,600** *CSK*

A tinplate saloon car, German, c1910, 10in (25cm) long. **£2,000-2,250** *S*

A Fischer Bleriot monoplane, German, c1910, 9.5in (24cm) long. **£2,000-2,500** *S*

A Radiguet tinplate and copper steam battleship, 'Inflexible', French, c1895. **£6,300-6,700** *CNY*

426

A Märklin tinplate phaeton, German, c1910, 11.5in (29cm) long. **£10,000-11,000** *S*

A Carette tinplate landaulette, with clockwork motor, c1910, 12.5in (32cm) long. **£6,000-6,500** *S*

A lithographed tinplate roadster, with clockwork motor, German, c1925, 10in (25cm) long. **£775-850** *S*

A French tinplate horse-drawn open double decker tram, c1890.
£41,000-43.000 *CNY*

A Bing tinplate racing car, with clockwork motor some restoration, c1904, 11.5in (29cm) long. **£8,750-9,000** *S*

A tinplate phaeton, c1885, 20in (51cm) long. **£13,000-14,000** *CNY*

A Märklin tinplate motor car, German, c1910, 8.5in (21.5cm) long. **£4,500-5,000** *S*

A Carette lithographed tinplate French double deck motor omnibus, German, c1910, 11.5in (29cm) long. **£12,500-13,500** *S*

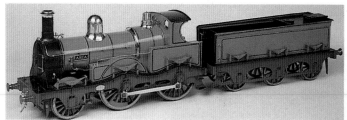

A 5in gauge model of the London, Chatham & Dover Railway 2-4-0 locomotive and tender 'Asia', by E. V. Fry, 52in (132cm) long.
£2,300-2,500 *C*

A Märklin Gauge III steam 4-4-0 locomotive and tender, with 2 carriages, 'The Tsar's Train', some damage, c1905, 28in (71cm) long.
£15,500-16,500 *S*

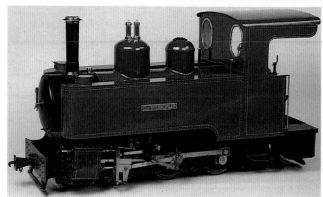

A 2.25:12in scale 5in gauge model of the Fowler 0-6-0 side tank locomotive, 'The Wild Fowler', built from drawings by W. Fidler, c1964, 47in (119.5cm) long.
£2,250-2,500 *C*

A Bing gauge I 4-6-2 Pacific clockwork locomotive and tender, control leavers to cab, c1920, 27.25in (69cm) long.
£1,250-1,500 *S*

A Märklin Gauge I 4-6-0 clockwork experiment locomotive, G 1021, with a six-wheeled tender, c1925, 23in (59cm) long.
£1,800-2,000 *S*

An exhibition standard gauge O two rail electric model of the LNER Class VI 2-6-2 side tank locomotive, No. 2908, built by J. S. Beeson, fitted with Westinghouse vacuum pump, 11.25in (28.5cm) long, showtrack and glazed case.
£2,250-2,500 *C*

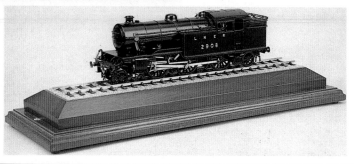

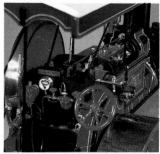

A scale model of a Burrell single cylinder 2-speed, 3 shaft, 10 ton road roller of 1922, built by G.D. McLeman, 14.25in (36cm) long. **£6,800-7,000** *C*

A Märklin painted tinplate refreshment trolley, 9in (23cm) long. **£2,000-2,500** *CNY*

A detailed scale model of the twin cylinder Foden steam wagon of 1912, Reg. No. M4441, built by G.D. McLeman, 16in (41cm) long, with display base and glazed cover. **£6,750-7,000** *C*

A detailed 7mm fine scale 2-rail electric model of GWR Castle Class 4-6-0 locomotive and tender, built by J.S. Beeson. **£7,250-7,500** *CSK*

r. A detailed model of the LNER Ivatt Class C1 4-4-2 Atlantic locomotive and tender, built by J.S. Beeson. **£5,500-6,000** *CSK*

l. A 7mm fine scale 2-rail electric model of the LMS Rebuilt Royal Scot 4-6-0 locomotive and tender, built by J. Brierley, 17.75in (45cm) long. **£3,500-3,750** *CSK*

r. A French Trix diecast 'Nord' 4-4-0 locomotive No. 68374 and 8-wheel bogie tender, **£1,500-1,600** a Trix 'Nord' bogie coach,**£350-400** and a Trix 'Nord' baggage car, all items 1936. **£550-600** *CSK*

A Märklin clockwork tinplate 'District Railway' bogie, c1906, **£6,050-6,500** and Station, Cat. Ref. 2023, c1910. **£2,400-2,600** *CSK*

A brass and wrought iron model of a twin oscillating cylinder condensing paddle engine. **£4,750-5,000** *C*

A Märklin hand painted railway station, c1910. **£12,000-13,000** *CNY*

r. A Dessin tinplate floor train, with paper label DE.S. **£7,000-7,500** *S*

A Märklin 3-rail electric 2-8-2 LNER locomotive, No. 2001, and matching 8-wheel tender, Cat. Ref. L70/12920, c1938. **£8,500-9,000** *CSK*

A Hornby clockwork type 51 locomotive, tender, 2 passenger and one brake coach and track, c1940. **£100-150** *STK*

A Märklin hand painted 4-4-2 locomotive and 6-wheel tender, with reverse, brake and speed control, c1904. **£1,750-2,000** *CSK*

r. A Bing gauge 1 4-6-0 clockwork locomotive, 'Sir Sam Fry', No. 423, together with 6-wheel tender, 24in (61cm) long. **£2,000-2,250** *S*

A Coronation Street jigsaw, c1960.
£10-15 *COB*

Toy tractor, 5.5in (14cm) high,
c1950, **£100-120**, and small
Matchbox tractor. **£8-10** *NOW*

A centaur carousel, by Anderson,
41in (104cm) long. **£900-1,000** *REL*

A Mickey Mouse speaking
toy, 5in (13cm) high.
£15-20 *COL*

A celluloid Mickey Mouse
riding Pluto toy, Japanese,
c1932, 7.75in (19cm) long.
£4,800-5,000 *CNY*

A Minnie Mouse carousel figure,
37in (94cm) high. **£450-500** *REL*

Fantasia poster, 1940, 41in
(104cm) high.
£3,200-3,400 *CNY*

A Märklin automaton, c1910,
11in (28cm) high.
£5,500-6,000 *CNY*

A Lincoln pedal car, restored, c1935,
45in (114cm) long.
£5,200-5,500 *CNY*

A Mickey Mouse watch, by
Ingersoll, c1930, hands
missing. **£50-60** *COB*

A tinplate castle, probably German, 42in (106.5cm) long. **£2,600-3,000** *CNY*

A Marusan Ford Sedan, Japanese, c1950, good condition, 13in (33cm) long. **£1,900-2,100** *S*

A boxed set of German bisque head aviator figures, c1920. **£3,200-3,500** *CNY*

A Märklin castle, with revolving moat, 13in (33cm) high. **£2,200-2,500** *CNY*

A Toschi Ferrari Grand Prix racing car, Italian, c1959, 22in (56cm) long. **£2,400-2,600** *S*

A Chad Valley double deck Carr's biscuit tin bus, 10in (25cm) long. **£1,100-1,300** *S*

A Märklin hand painted kitchen, c1900, 37in (94cm) long. **£5,800-6,200** *CNY*

A Märklin pull-along water tanker, c1912, 22.5in (57.5cm) long. **£11,500-12,000** *CNY*

A Spanish boxed tinplate toy, c1964, 8.5in (21cm) high. **£50-60** *ACh*

A Märklin pond, c1900, 16in (41cm) diam. **£1,100-1,500** *CNY*

Boxed sets of Meccano aeroplane construction kits. **£300-500 each** *CNY*

A Mettoy musical jack-in-the-box, c1960, 6in (15cm). **£100-120** *ACh*

Tins, Signs & Advertising

Advertising

An O-Cedar Mop advertisement, c1940, 6.5in (16.5cm) diam.
£4-6 *COL*

A Wrigley's PK Chewing Gum machine.
£80-90 *WEL*

An Atora chromolithographed die cut show card, 15in (38cm) wide.
£20-30 *ACh*

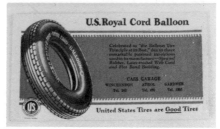

A U.S. Royal Cord Balloon advertisement blotter card, 6.5in (16.5cm) wide.
£6-8 *AAM*

A Gold Flake Cigarettes shop advertising pack, pre-war, 12in (30.5cm) high.
£8-10 *COB*

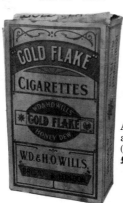

A Be-Ro Self Raising Flour advertising card, drawing signed VH, c1950, 12in (30.5cm) high.
£20-25 *ACh*

An Ever Ready Alldry Radio shaped standing display, with hinged platform for radio, 38.5in (97cm) wide.
£65-70 *ONS*

A cigarette cabinet, c1900, 33in (84cm) high.
£145-160 *BBR*

Cross Reference
Golf

Two Penfold plaster advertising figures, late 1930s, 20.5in (52cm) high.
With Pipe. **£500-550**
Without Pipe. **£265-285** *S*

A Mitchell's Gold Medal Cigarettes display cabinet.
£400-450 *SRA*

A Dewar's Perth Whisky 'classic' coaster, W.T. Copeland & Sons, Stoke-on-Trent, 6.25in (16cm) diam.
£210-240 *BBR*

A Dunville's Old Irish Whisky card advertisement, white lettering on orange background, 20.5in (52.5cm) wide.
£28-32 *BBR*

Cross Reference
Drinking

An optician's wall hanging shop front clock, 50in (127cm) high.
£90-125 *REL*

A Compo advertising card.
£100-120 *SRA*

A Capstan hardboard advertisement and stand for outside a shop, c1950, 32in (81cm) high.
£40-50 *ACh*

An Ever Ready standing three dimensional four-section display, 40in (101cm) high.
£55-60 *ONS*

Packaging

A Persil box made from recycled paper, c1940.
£10-15 *ACh*

A plaster display cow from a butcher's shop, 60in (152cm) long.
£400-500 *REL*

A Monkey Brand soap packet, c1920, 5in (14cm) wide. **£5-6** *ACh*

A cardboard matchbox sized chocolate box, c1890. **£10-12** *COB*

Paper Bags

A paper bag advertising Ibcol, c1955, 7in (18cm) wide. **50p-70p** *COL*

A Chiesmans' paper bag, c1955. **50p-70p** *COL*

A confectionery bag from Sheerness, c1950. **50p-70p** *COL*

A Borax packet, c1930, 5.5in (14cm) wide. **£3-4** *ACh*

An Oxydol soap powder packet, c1940, 6.5in (16.5cm) wide. **£10-15** *ACh*

A selection of soap powder boxes, 1920-30, largest 5.5in (14cm) high. **£3-12 each** *ACh*

Signs

A Melox enamel sign, c1930.
£15-25 *COB*

A Budweiser metal advertising sign, 1970s. **£25-30** *COB*

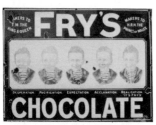

A Fry's Chocolate enamel advertising sign.
£300-350 *SRA*

A Jenner Bros Ltd. sign from a taxi cab, 9.5in (24cm) wide.
£8-10 *COL*

A Grosvenor Studio sign from a taxicab.
£15-16 *COL*

Prices are affected by condition.

An Angus F. Gunn Ltd. sign from a taxi cab. **£10-12** *COL*

A metal sign from a taxi cab, 9.5in (24cm) wide.
£12-14 *COL*

An Oxo window poster, framed and glazed, c1930, 12.5in (32cm) high.
£35-45 *ACh*

An enamel sign for Wincarnis Wine Tonic, 73in (185cm) high.
£450-500 *REL*

A Ogston's Toilet Soaps celluloid coated chromolithographed sign, framed and glazed, c1890, 23.5in (60.5cm) high.
£70-100 *ACh*

A brass firescreen, c1930.
£25-30 *COB*

Cross Reference
Drinking

Pub Signs

A painted iron pub sign, 42in (106.5cm) high.
£35-40 *REL*

A painted wood pub sign, 36in (92cm) high.
£50-60 *REL*

A glass sign from an Irish pub, 66in (167.5cm) high.
£900-1,000 *REL*

A painted iron pub sign, 42in (106.5cm) high.
£40-45 *REL*

A painted wood pub sign, 36in (92cm) high.
£40-45 *REL*

Tins

A Carters Seidlitz Powders tin, c1920, 5in (12.5cm) high.
£20-25 *ACh*

A McVitie & Price biscuit tin, decorated with Victoria Cross Episodes, 5.5in (14cm) wide.
£85-95 *Bea*

Toiletries

A silver gilt and red glass double-ended scent bottle, 5in (13cm) long, in fitted case.
£200-250 *BWA*

Two silver topped and blue glass double-ended scent bottles, 4in (10cm) long.
£125-150 each *BWA*

A silver powder brush holder, made for Selfridges, Birmingham 1937, 2.5in (6cm) long.
£40-50 *AMH*

A baby's brush and comb set, Birmingham silver hallmark, 1927, in original box, 3 by 4in (8 by 10cm).
£35-40 *AA*

A Bilston blue enamel etui, c1780, 3.75in (9cm) long.
£900-1,200 *RdeR*

A silver comb case, with engine turned decoration, c1930.   **£10-20** *ASA*

Powder Compacts

A black enamel and silver powder compact.   **£30-50** *ASA*

An Art Deco white metal and enamel compact.
£5-15 *ASA*

A silver and enamel compact, c1930.
£30-45 *ASA*

A combination compact and lipstick holder.
£10-20 *ASA*

A Continental silver enamel compact, with gilded interior and back, c1920.
£250-325 *AA*

An Art Deco white metal and enamel compact.
£10-20 *ASA*

Razors

A Rolls Autostrop razor, with case, 6in (15cm) long.
£6-7 *TRU*

A box of 7 'Days of the Week' razors.
£60-75 *PAR*

A Valet razor, without box.
£1-2 *TRU*

A razor case, 3.5in (9cm) long.
£3-4 *ROS*

Tools & Farm Implements

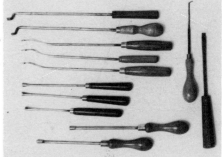

A set of 12 piano adjuster's tools, late 19thC.
£45-55 *MRT*

A selection of Silversmith's burnishers, 19thC.
£1-3 each *MRT*

Two ebony and brass levels, 19thC, plain 10in (25cm) long. **£18-22** and fancy 12in (31cm).
£30-40 *MRT*

Blacksmith's Tools

A blacksmith's swage. **£5-10** *PLO*

A blacksmith's plater. **£5-10** *PLO*

A box of English nickel silver drawing instruments, the lift-out tray with ivory rules, late 19thC, 6.5 by 11in (16 by 28cm).
£150-200 *MRT*

A horse tooth rasp, 25in (64cm) long.
£12-15 *PLO*

A blacksmith's hot set.
£5-10 *PLO*

A pair of blacksmith's tongs.
£6-10 *PLO*

Two hot sets.   **£10-15** *PLO*

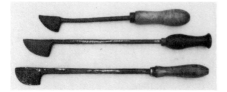

Irons for firing tendons on horses,
14 to 17in (36 to 43cm) long.
£15-20 each *PLO*

*This practise is now illegal in
England.*

A blacksmith's hammer.
£5-10 *PLO*

Bookbinder's Tools

Two bookbinder's centre tools,
19thC, 1 and 2.5in (2.5 and 6cm)
wide.
£10-20 each *MRT*

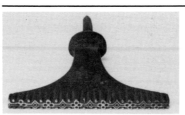

A brass decorative pallet, used to
apply gilt decoration to leather
bindings, 19thC, 3in (8cm).
£20-30 *MRT*

Two ornamental rolls, 19thC, 2
and 3.5in (5 and 9cm) diam.
£30-50 each *MRT*

A bookbinder's
beech plough,
19thC, 18in (46cm).
£35-45 *MRT*

Farm Implements

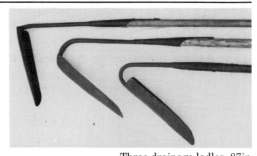

Three drainage ladles, 87in
(221cm) long.
£15-20 each *PLO*

Three dyke spades and handles,
97in (246cm) long.
£35-40 each *PLO*

A clay spade, 43in (109cm) long.
£20-30 *PLO*

A thatcher's eaves knife, 62in (157cm) long.
£20-30 *PLO*

A post hole digger 36in (92cm) long.
£15-20 *PLO*

A shearing hook, used for thatching hay and straw.
£5-10 *PLO*

A hayrick knife, 58in (147cm) long.
£12-20 *PLO*

Two cast iron seats for farm machinery.
£40-50 each *PLO*

Two cross cut saws, 65in (165cm) long.
£15-20 each *PLO*

A thatcher's comb or rake, 40in (102cm) long.
£12-20 *PLO*

A land drain pipe cleaner, 68in (173cm) long.
£12-15 *PLO*

A pair of wood and leather clogs.
£15-20 *PLO*

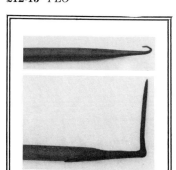

A rabbiting spade with hook for lead on ferret, 90in (229cm) long.
£30-40 *PLO*

A ditching spade, c1920, 42in (107cm) long.
£35-50 *PLO*

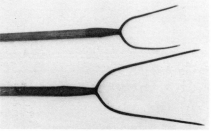

Two pitchforks, the large one for loading hay onto a wagon, 69in (175cm) long, the small one for stable use, with more blunted ends.   **£12-15 each** *PLO*

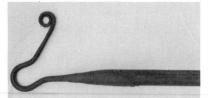

A shepherd's crook, c1900.
£35-50 *PLO*

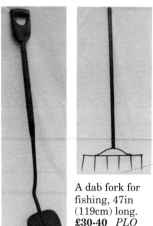

A turf spade, c1900,
83in (211cm) long.
£20-30 *PLO*

A selection of garden and sheep
shears, 12in (31cm) long.
£4-5 each *PLO*

*The difference between garden
and sheep shears is that the ends
of the blades on the garden shears
have sharp points; sheep shears
more blunted ends.*

A dab fork for
fishing, 47in
(119cm) long.
£30-40 *PLO*

A short handled turfing spade,
56in (142cm) long.
£15-20 *PLO*

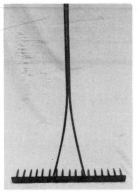

A Hampshire hay rake, 72in
(183cm). **£25-30** *PLO*

*The shape of the handle tells the
area of its origin.*

A wooden cart jack, late 19thC,
30in (76cm) long.
£40-50 *PLO*

A digging iron, 5in (13cm) long.
£6-10 a pair *PLO*

*This iron was strapped to the boot
to protect the foot when digging.*

A cast iron cart jack, 32in
(81cm) long. **£40-50** *PLO*

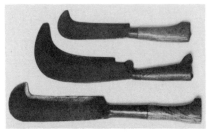

Three billhooks of various
makes, c1900, 13 to 18in
(33 to 46cm) long.
£10-20 each *MRT*

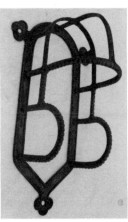

A cast iron bridle rack.
£20-30 *PLO*

A weeding tool, 47in (119cm) long.
£30-40 *PLO*

A large dock
or thistle fork.
£5-15 *PLO*

A gin trap, 12in
(31cm) long.
£4-5 *PLO*

Rules

An ivory proof slide rule, for
calculating the strength of, and
duty payable on, alcoholic drink,
c1900, 6in (15cm).
£40-50 *MRT*

A folding boxwood barrel
measuring rule, c1900, 24in
(61cm). **£30-40** *MRT*
*This rule gives a direct reading of
barrel contents and is intended
only for small barrels, pins,
firkins etc.*

An ivory folding rule, 19thC, 12in
(31cm). **£40-50** *TRU*

A Rabone four-fold boxwood rule
with level, c1920, 36in (92cm).
£25-35 *MRT*

Woodworking Tools

A mitre plane, by Buck, c1850,
9in (23cm) long.
£230-250 *MRT*

A small size lock mortice chisel,
early 20thC, 16in (41cm) long.
£20-25 *MRT*

A selection of carving
tools, various dates, 8 to
11in (20 to 28cm) long.
£4-8 each *MRT*

A cast iron, rosewood filled 1.5in
(29cm) wide shoulder plane,
c1870, 8in (20cm) long.
£35-45 *MRT*

Two joiner's ebony and brass
squares, mitre 13.5in (34cm).
£25-35 and square, 7.5in (19cm).
£6-8 *MRT*

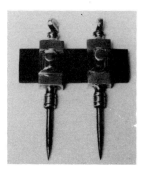

A rosewood handled timber
scribe, 19thC, 9in (23cm) long.
£25-35 *MRT*

Two large brass carpenter's
trammel heads, 19thC,
7in (18cm) long.
£30-40 *MRT*

Two small brass carpenter's trammel heads, 19thC, 4in (10cm) long.
£25-35 *MRT*

Two craftsman made bow saws, beech 21in (53cm) long. **£25-35** boxwood, 12in (31cm) long.
£60-70 *MRT*

An Ultimatum brace, by William Marples, c1880, 14in (36cm) long.
£125-175 *MRT*

Three router planes: mahogany, 18thC, 8in (20cm). **£80-100**, mahogany, 19thC, 8in (20cm). **£55-65,** and ebony, 19thC, 3in (8cm). **£45-55** *MRT*

A beech rounding plane, by Varvill & Son, c1850, 9in (23cm) long.
£35-45 *MRT*

A brass and ebony mortice gauge, c1910, 8in (20cm) long.
£25-35 *MRT*

Two rosewood and brass boat levels, by Edward Preston, Birmingham, 19thC, 6 and 9in (15 and 23cm) long.
£15-35 each *MRT*

Three boxwood thumb planes: c1880, 2in (5cm) long, **£50-60**, compassed, 3.5in (9cm) long, **£30-40**, and compassed, 5in (13cm) long. **£20-30** *MRT*

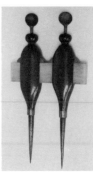

Two mahogany trammel heads, with iron points and screws, c1860, 11.5in (29cm) long.
£80-100 *MRT*

A boxwood carver's maul, 19thC, 4in (10cm) diam.
£35-45 *MRT*

Two moulding planes:
l. mid-19thC, by Moseley, 9.5in (24cm) long. **£10-15**
r. by Loveage, London, c1745, 10in (25cm) long. **£55-65** *MRT*

An octagon box-handled paring chisel, 19thC, 11.5in (29cm) long.
£18-22 *MRT*

A boxwood cutting gauge, late 19thC, 10in (25cm) long.
£10-15 *MRT*

Three beechwood moulding planes, 19thC, 9.5in (24cm) long, 4-irons. **£300-350**, 3-irons. **£125-175**, and 2-irons. **£35-45** *MRT*

Three turnscrews, 19thC, 21 to 25in (53 to 64cm) long. **£10-35 each** *MRT*

Three mortice chisels, late 19thC, 10.5 to 14in (26 to 36cm) long. **£5-12 each** *MRT*

Tortoiseshell

An early Victorian impressed tortoiseshell veneered card case, with a view of Abbotsford. **£125-135** *WW*

Japanese gold lacquer on tortoiseshell napkin rings, c1900. **£25-45** *TOR*

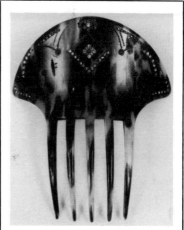

A celluloid tortoiseshell comb, c1905, 5in (13cm) long. **£15-20** *AA*

A tortoiseshell, gold and silver brooch, 1855. **£50-175** *TOR*

A papier mâché snuff box with simulated tortoiseshell top, c1835. **£25-65** *TOR*

A Victorian tortoiseshell veneered card case, with printed glass picture. **£140-150** *WW*

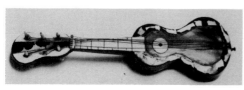

A Neapolitan tortoiseshell veneered guitar, with ivory pegs and mother-of-pearl inlay, 5.5in (14cm). **£20-50** *TOR*

TOYS

A French speaking picture book, c1910, in boxed cover, 12 by 9.5in (31 by 24cm).
£750-800 *S*

A German static electricity 'Humoristic Mystic Box' toy, box applied with print of circus with celluloid cover and 4 balsa wood clown figures that dance when cover is rubbed, 11.75in (29cm), and a Blondin acrobat sand toy, in a wooden case, c1910, 10in (25.5cm) high.
£525-550 *S*

A paster hanging Bonzo, 3in (7.5cm) high.
£5-6 *HEG*

A Panorama 'London to Paris', with wooden stage, cloth curtain, and folding card side flaps, depicting a long train and boat journey between London and Paris in watercolours on paper, hand operated on 2 rolls, late 19thC, 12in (31cm) wide, in original wooden box.
£625-650 *S*

A Spider-Man toy camera for 126 cartridges, c1978, 5.25in (13cm) wide. **£10-15** *HEG*

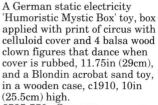

A tinplate wind-up Punch and Judy show, 7 by 7.5in (18 by 19cm).
£25-30 *HEG*

A William Britains mechanical footrace toy, in original wooden box with Milliken & Lawley retailer's label, English, late 19thC.
£5,500-6,000 *S*

An American painted wood-jointed Bimbo cat figure, c1935, 9in (22.5cm) high.
£270-300 *CNY*

A Mr McGregor battery operated toy, in original box, 11in (28cm) high. **£40-60** *NOW*

A French 'Jeu d'Ovide' metamorphic toy, with details of head profile altered by series of turned wooden knobs mounted alongside the image, in a card case, early 20thC, 16in (41cm) wide.
£600-650 *S*

A celluloid pull toy, stamped 'Germany' under trolley, c1900, 10in (25cm) wide.
£150-250 *STK*

A Mighty Mouse Home Movie, Mother Goose's Birthday Party, in original box, 5.25in (13cm) wide.
£10-12 *COL*

Diecast Toys

A child's sit-on toy, c1960.
£10-15 *COB*

A Dinky Paris Autobus, in original box, 5.5in (12.5cm) long.
£40-45 *HEG*

Four Corgi Mini Cooper rally cars, c1960, in original boxes.
£600-650 *N*

Three Corgi toy cars: Chitty-Chitty Bang Bang, James Bond's Aston Martin, and Pcpeye's Paddle Wagon.
£100-125 the set *PCh*

A Meccano Dinky Toys French aeroplane set, 61Z, c1930, lacking box lid. **£825-875** *S*

Two Dinky Trojan vans.
£100-120 *SWO*

A Corgi Batman set, No. 40, including Batmobile, figures, Bat-boat and trailer and Batcopter, in original display box. **£160-180** *WAL*

A Dinky Thunderbird 2, No.101, in original display box.
£200-225 *WAL*

Disney

A Mickey Mouse battery powered car, c1960.
£10-15 *COB*

Two Mickey Mouse finger puppets, 3.75in (9cm) high.
£3-4 each *COL*

Meccano

Two Mickey and Minnie Mouse figures, c1930, 9 and 10in (22.5 and 25cm) high. **£70-100 each** *NOW*

A Meccano Aeroplane No 0 Constructor Set, finished in Service Grey, in original blue wartime packing box, with instructions, propeller broken, 1941. **£385-400** *CSK*

A French Mickey Mouse balance toy, lithographed paper on metal figure, the tail used as a counter weight, 11.5in (29.5cm) high. **£130-150** *S(NY)*

A painted wooden Emerson Mickey Mouse radio, c1935, 7.5in (18.5cm) high. **£700-750** *CNY*

A Meccano tinplate Aeroplane Constructor kit, Outfit No. 0, in green and cream, in box, with instructions, incomplete, c1934. **£160-180** *DN*

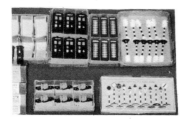

Rocking Horses

- J (Jervis) Collinson has always been a small family business in the city of Liverpool. Started in 1836, they produced a variety of coloured horses until 1850 when Queen Victoria visited the factory riding a dapple grey horse after which they only produced grey rocking horses. Collinson horses were unmarked until 1981, since when a gold plate has been applied to the front of the stand base.

- Baby Carriages Ltd. was founded by members of the Collinson family in about 1884 in Liverpool. They produced a variety of rocking horses, toy horses and carts until 1958.

- G. & J. Lines produced rocking horses from their factory in the Caledonian Road between 1850 and 1931 and claimed to be the largest toy factory in Britain. Their trademark was a metal disc stamped with a thistle.

- F. H. Ayres were located at Aldersgate in London and produced high quality toys and sports goods as well as rocking horses from 1864. If Ayres horses are marked, there is a stamped plate under the belly or a small plaque on the swing top. They had ceased production of these high quality horses by 1940.

- Patterson Edwards were established in 1892 in the Old Kent Road by H.S. Jarvis. In 1955 the trademark LEEWAY was adopted for all their rocking horses and prams.

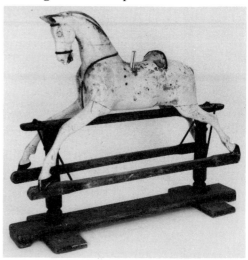

A Victorian carved pine rocking horse, with original paint, on turned supports and stand. **£450-500** *LRG*

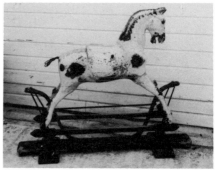

A rocking horse, on a carriage spring safety stand, by F. H. Ayres, c1907, 54in (137cm) long. **£1,800-2,000 when restored** *STE*

A rocking horse, by F. H. Ayres, c1900, 72in (182.5cm) long.
**£1,900-2,100 in good condition
with original paint
£1,200-1,300 in poor condition
or badly restored** *STE*

A rocking horse by G. & J. Lines, c1911, 31in (79cm) long.
**£1,500-1,600 in good condition,
£400-500 in poor condition or
badly restored** *STE*

FURTHER READING
*The Rocking Horse, A History of
Toy Horses*, by Patricia
Mullins, New Cavendish Books

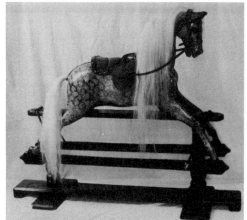

A Victorian dapple grey rocking
horse, on a safety stand, with
replacement real horsehair mane
and tail and hand made hand
dyed tack, paintwork restored and
reglazed.
£1,200-2,500 *WA*

A rocking horse, by G. & J. Lines, not original paint, c1910, 81in (205.5cm) long.
£1,600-1,700 if original or well restored
£1,000-1,100 in poor condition *STE*

A rocking horse, by F. H. Ayres, made for Gamages, London, c1900, 52in (132cm) long.
£1,800-2,000 *STE*

A Bauer Krause rocking horse, German, fully restored, 46in (116.5cm) long. c1920
£800-900 in good condition
£100-200 in poor condition *STE*

A rocking horse, by Leeway, London, c1955, 35in (89cm) long.
£300-400 in original condition,
£500-600 if larger *STE*

A rocking horse, by Collinson, original paint, c1940, 50in (127cm) long.
£700-800 restored
£100-200 in poor condition *STE*

A rocking horse, by Baby Carriages of Liverpool, original paint, c1910, 37in (94cm) long.
£900-1,000 in good condition or restored larger £1,300-1,400 £300-400 in poor condition or badly restored *STE*

Not to be confused with Collinsons of Liverpool, which are inferior quality and have studs for eyes. Baby Carriage horses are very well made with glass eyes and some have a transfer on the centre of the stand, 'B.C.C. Rambler Liverpool'.

A Triang rocking horse, on a light varnished beech stand, with identification marks, round disc on front, triangle on rear of base, Triang written in red, original paint, new saddle blanket, c1939, 34in (86cm) long.
£1,100-1,300 in good condition, £300-400 in poor condition
STE

Soldiers & Figures

A Johillco Silver Jubilee Set, in original presentation box, some damage, 1935. **£185-200** *CSK*

A Britain's No. 44F Country Cottage, with a Greenhouse, cold frame, lawn mower, swing, trellis and trees, in original box. **£540-560** *S(S)*

A selection of Rose Miniatures, Military figures: *l*: Indian Army, Queen's Own Corps of Guides. **£100-110** *r*: Indian Army, Sikhs. **£90-110** *WAL*

A Britain's for CFE or Charterhouse CIV Supply Wagon. **£550-575** *CSK*

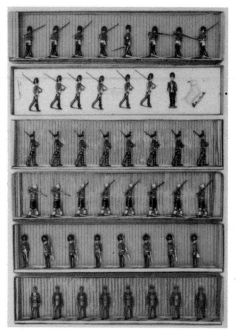

A Pre-War set No. 7, The Royal Fusiliers, City of London Regiment. **£90-100**
A Set No. 74, Royal Welsh Fusiliers, 23rd Foot with mascot ram. **£100-110**
A pre-war Set No. 212, The Royal Scots/The Royal Regiment. **£160-180**
A pre-war Set No. 114, The Queen's Own Cameron Highlanders, in kilted tropical dress. **£140-160**
A pre-war Set No. 205, The Coldstream Guards, at the salute. **£120-140**
A pre-war set No. 240, The Royal Air Force. **£350-375** *WAL*

A collection of figures formed as a Circus Display and Big Top, 'Reynolds's Model Circus', by various makers, probably 1950s. **£1,600-1,700** *CSK*

Cinema Favourites, 3 Felix the Cats, in original box, and 2 'Pets Stores' toy grocery shops, some parts missing. **£325-350** *CSK*

Stuffed Toys

A Dean's rag book Dismal Desmond, c1920, 4.75in (12cm) high. **£40-50** *NOW*

A Chad Valley articulated Bonzo, c1920, 9.5in (24cm) high. **£100-150** *NOW*

A Steiff black mohair and plush poodle on wheels, c1910, 17.25in (44cm) long. **£750-775** *S*

Teddy Bears

A Merrythought Golly, c1950, tear on trousers, 35.5in (90cm) high. **£375-400** *S(S)*

An articulated Felix The Cat, c1920, 11in (28cm) high. **£75-100** *NOW*

A Stevenson growler bear, with glass eyes, stuffed with wood shavings, limited edition of 100, 23in (59cm) high. **£150-200** *STE*

A well loved teddy bear, c1930, 16in (41cm) high. **£100-125** *PAR*

A Merrythought Cheeky teddy bear, label on one foot. **£60-75** *PAR*

A hand sewn teddy bear, by Anita Oliver, 1in (2.5cm) high. **£30-35** *CD*

A Chiltern bear, 14in (35.5cm) high. **£130-150** *PAR*

'Lukas' an English pale golden plush covered teddy bear, with brown glass eyes, and a photograph of him with Miss Rebecca Ridgway preparing for the British Cape Horn Kayak Expedition, 1992, 10in (25cm) high. **£25-30** *CSK*

A Chad Valley teddy bear, pads replaced, 13in (33cm) high. **£120-130** *PAR*

A Chad Valley teddy bear, with label on one foot, 10in (25cm) high. **£60-75** *PAR*

A pair of early German teddy bears, pre-1920, 8in (20cm) high. **£180-200 each** *PAR*

A straw-filled teddy bear, possibly Herman, 1950s, 14in (36cm) high. **£200-240** *PAR*

A Chad Valley straw-filled teddy bear, with button in ear and label on foot, a small hump on the back, c1930, 27in (68.5cm) high. **£500-550** *PAR*

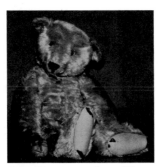

A German cream mohair teddy bear, 'Wispa', maker unknown, 10in (25cm) high. **£300-400** *TEM*

A Steiff cone nose bear, 'Mr Chump', apricot colour, with blank ear button, c1905, 28in (71cm) high. **£3,000-3,500** *TEM*

A teddy bear with a waistcoat, 1930s, 20in (51cm) high. **£120-145** *PAR*

'Jed', a teddy bear, origin unknown, with boot button eyes, 12in (31cm) high.
£100-120 *TEM*

An English teddy bear, 'Big Brother', gold with black leather pads, c1950, 24in (61cm) high.
£100-150 *TEM*

Two Steiff teddy bears, c1910:
A large golden plush covered, with growler and button in ear, pads recovered, 13in (33cm) high.
£925-950
A small white plush bear with brown glass eyes, button in ear and rattle in tummy, wear to plush, c1910, 5in (13cm) high.
£400-425 *CSK*

An English straw-filled teddy bear, late 1930s, 10in (25cm) high. **£80-95** *PAR*

A Chad Valley straw-filled teddy bear, with button under the chin, 25in (64cm) high.
£300-350 *PAR*

A Steiff 'Edward' silver blonde bear, pre-1907, 24in (61cm) high.
£1,200-1,800 *TEM*

Tinplate

An articulated tinplate fish, 8in
(20cm) long.
£15-20 *HEG*

A Superman tinplate lunch box,
1978, 8in (20cm) wide.
£20-25 *HEG*

A green tinplate trunk, 2.75in
(7cm) wide. **£4-7** *HEG*

A Märklin hand painted tinplate
steam driven water trough, in
yellow and brown with a green
base, c1904, 12.5in (31cm) long.
£950-1,200 *S(NY)*

*A similar toy is illustrated in the
1904 Märklin catalogue no. 4231.*

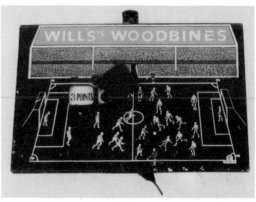

A Wills's football game, c1930, 6
by 4in (15 by 25cm).
£12-15 *HEG*

A German lithographed tinplate
mechanical fairground ride toy,
'The Whip', 1920s, 8.75in (22cm)
wide, in original lithographed box.
£1,700-1,800 *S*

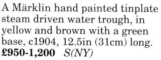

A tinplate monkey on a
stick, 19in (48cm) long.
£15-18 *COL*

A Chad Valley tinplate money
box, 5.5in (14cm) high.
£15-20 *HEG*

Cross Reference
Money Boxes

A tinplate toy tambourine, hand painted, c1920, 8.5in (21cm) diam.
£20-25 *PSA*

A Paya tinplate motorcyclist, with HP monogram, numberplate I-804 and chrome exhaust which emits sparks as the bike moves, small rust patch, c1930, 11in (28cm).
£1,650-1,750 *S*

A Japanese electric tinplate car, 12.5in (32cm) long.
£65-70 *COL*

A Marusan electric tinplate Cadillac sedan, c1951, 12.5in (32cm) long.
£1,850-2,000 *S*

A German tinplate motorcycling family, by Tipp & Co., lacking headlamp, c1930, 9.5in (24cm).
£1,500-1,650 *S*

A Burnett tinplate armoured car, lithographed in grey, with clockwork motor driving rear wheels, c1915, 7.5in (19cm) long.
£500-550 *S*

A Marusan friction drive tinplate Ford sedan, finished in yellow and white, 13in (33cm) long.
£6,200-6,500 *S*

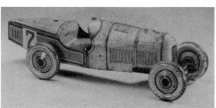

A tinplate and clockwork racing car, by Tipp & Co., probably based on the Alfa-Romeo P2, in silver and grey, driver missing, 19.25in (49cm).
£380-400 *S(S)*

A Wells grandfather clock, 8in (20cm) high.
£40-50 *HEG*

A Shuco painted tinplate 6080 construction turntable fire escape, with 4-section extending ladder, firemen and 1 wheel nut missing, 1950s, 10.5in (26cm) long.
£625-650 *CSK*

A Günthermann lithographed tinplate 'Captain Campbell's Blue Bird' record car, in sea green, c1930, 20in (51cm) long, in original worn box.
£1,550-1,650 *S*

A green tinplate 'Clikka' frog, 3in (8cm) wide.
£1-2 *HEG*

Two somersaulting tinplate boys, 4in (10cm) wide.
£4-5 *HEG*

A Mettoy Minor tinplate typewriter, c1950, in original box, 10.5in (26cm) wide.
£20-22 *COL*

A tinplate musical box, 7.5in (19cm) high.
£8-10 *HEG*

A clockwork tinplate tractor, in working order, c1950, 8.5in (21cm) long.
£30-40 *BGA*

A sand bucket, 4.5in (11cm) high.
£6-7 *COL*

A boxed matchbox Jumbo, c1940, 4.25in (11cm) long.
£150-200 *NOW*

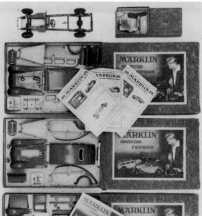

A group of Märklin constructor car toys, 1930s, chassis 14in (36cm) long.
£4,750-5,000 *S*

A tinplate globe, 1.5in (4cm) diam.
£2-3 *HEG*

A tinplate pecking bird, 2.75in (7cm) wide.
£10-12 *HEG*

A Chad Valley tinplate double deck Greenline bus, lithographed green, with yellow roof, as a No.721 Aldgate and Brentwood service, 10in (25cm) long.
£1,100-1,250 *S*

Trains

A display model of a 3.5in (9cm) gauge 2-4-2 tank locomotive No.112, powered by an electric motor to all wheels, finished in MR green livery, in glazed case. **£1,100-1,200** *S(S)*

A French Hornby brake van, 6in (15cm) long. **£80-85** *NOW*

A Hornby Series LNER Special electric Pullman train set, c1935, all in original box. **£2,800-3,000** *CSK*

A 3.5in (9cm) gauge model of the SR King Arthur Class 4-6-0 locomotive and tender No.777 'Sir Lamiel', built by J M Proud, with carrying boxes, instructions, firing irons, boiler certificate valid to 10.10.86, 10 by 50.25in (25 by 128cm). **£2,400-2,600** *CSK*

A Hornby Paris Lyons Marseilles engine, 0-4-0 gauge, 6.75in (17cm) long. **£135-170** *NOW*

A Bing gauge I 'Sydney' 4-4-0 clockwork locomotive and tender, in Great Western green, restored, 22.75in (58cm) long. **£820-850** *S*

A Bing gauge III spirit fired live steam model 4-4-0 locomotive and tender, No. 7093, 'King Edward' repainted black, 27in (69cm) overall. **£475-500** *Bea*

A Hornby clockwork train set, with tank engine, LMS, 1930s. **£150-250** *STK*

A Trix portable train set, in original fitted wooden case with special inserts, apparently unused, case 21in (54cm) long. **£550-575** *CSK*

A Märklin 'Disaster' hut, 'exploding' when door is pushed or fired on, with spring mechanism and cap detonator, c1905. **£840-860** *CSK*

Treen

A clerk of works lignum vitae coring ball, for rolling through drains to test, 6in (15cm) diam. **£40-50** *MRT*

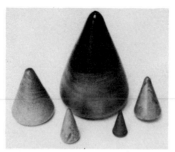

A selection of plumber's lignum vitae turnpins, 1 to 4in (3 to 10cm) diam. **£1-15 each** *MRT*

A selection of plumber's lignum vitae bobbins, .75 to 2.5in (4 to 6cm) diam. **£1-8 each** *MRT*

Two boxwood cartridge filling devices, 19thC, 7.25 and 8.5in (18 and 21cm) long. **£75-95 each** *MRT*

A boxwood cartridge crimper, 19thC, 6.5in (16cm) long. **£40-50** *MRT*

Mauchline Ware

Mauchline (pronounced Mochlin) is a small Scottish town near Ayr, which gave its name to this very collectable range of decorative Scottish souvenir ware.

The industry was it is peak during the 1860s and continued until 1933 when the box works burnt down, effectively ending production.

A vast array of goods were produced, sent to all corners of the U.K. and the Commonwealth, providing a rich area for today's collectors.

A luggie, a drinking vessel, with print of Burns Monument, 3.5in (9cm) diam. **£55-65** *LBL*

A razor hone, 10in (25cm) long. **£70-80** *LBL*

A rolling pin with print of Sea View Isle of Wight, 6.5in (16cm) long. **£25-35** *LBL*

A Mauchline ware and papier mâché card box, 4.5in (11cm) long. **£80-90** *LBL*

Three napkin rings. **£25-30 each** *LBL*

A string holder with print of Holyrood Palace, 3.5in (9cm) high. **£45-55** *LBL*

A table/money box, with print of Edinburgh From The Calton Hill, 4.75in (12cm) long. **£55-65** *LBL*

A snuff box, with hidden hinge, 3.5in (9cm) long. **£45-55** *LBL*

Tartan Ware

A card case with cards, 'Miss Florence Danby', 4.25 by 3in (11 by 8cm). **£65-70** *AI*

A cannister with lid, 3.25in (8cm) high. **£22-28** *AI*

A box, 5 by 3in (13 by 8cm). **£55-60** *AI*

A napkin ring, 2in (5cm) diam. **£22-25** *AI*

A rolling pin, for sealing letters, 6.75in (17cm) long. **£25-30** *AI*

A Caledonian Tartan ware stamp box, 1.75in (5cm) diam. **£70-80** *LBL*

A counter, 3 by 2in (8 by 5cm). **£70-75** *LBL*

A Stuart Tartan ware pin cushion, 2in (5cm) wide. **£80-100** *LBL*

A cribbage box, 4.75 by 3in (12 by 8cm). **£28-32** *AI*

Typewriters

An Oliver portable typewriter, in black crackle finish case.
£12-14 *TRU*

A Corona portable typewriter, the case finished in green enamel.
£25-30
TRU

A Blickensderfer No. 5 portable typewriter.
£75-85 *HCH*

Walking Sticks

A convertible steel walking/shooting stick, with leather covered handle.
£25-30 *ROW*

A carved bone cudgel, 25in (64cm) long.
£175-200 *PCh*

A mechanical donkey's head walking stick, probably German, the collar engraved 'Brigg London', on knotted wood shaft, late 19thC.
£1,100-1,200 *S*

The spelter head with button eyes drops its jaw and pricks its long ears at the touch of a button on the gilt collar.

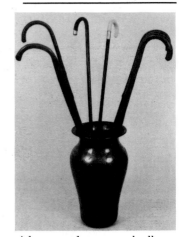

A hammered copper umbrella stand, c1900, 16.5in (42cm) high.
£45-50 *ROW*

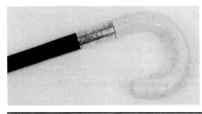

An ivory handled silver mounted ebony cane, Birmingham 1918.
£120-130 *ROW*

A wooden stick with silver tip, Birmingham 1923.
£35-40 *ROW*

Watches

An American nickel cased pocket watch, by Elgin.
£50-60 *TRU*

A gentleman's silver cased pocket watch, with English fusee lever movement by J.C. Heselton, Beverley, London, 1857.
£60-70 *TRU*

A small 14ct gold fob watch, with Swiss cylinder movement, c1890.
£80-100 *TRU*

A nickel cased pocket watch, with Swiss lever movement, the dial signed Kay & Co.
£50-60 *TRU*

A gentleman's brass cased pocket watch, with pin pallet lever escapement, 1920s.
£15-25 *TRU*

A silver cased fob watch, with silvered dial and Swiss cylinder movement.
£30-40 *TRU*

A brass cased key wound fob watch, with cylinder escapement, 19thC.
£25-30 *TRU*

A nickel cased 8-day Goliath pocket watch, 3in (8cm) diam.
£80-90 *TRU*

A silver cased fusee lever pocket watch, with silvered dial, by William Gray, Mid Calder, case hallmarked London 1865.
£75-80 *TRU*

A lady's keyless fob watch, with engine turned silver case and Swiss lever movement. **£40-50** *TRU*

A pocket watch, with square pillar movement, lacking outer case, signed Taylor, London, early 18thC. **£140-160** *TRU*

A brass hunter cased pocket watch, with pin pallet lever escapement, made for the Turkish market, 19thC. **£30-40** *TRU*

A leather covered gilt metal (5cm) long. **£250-275** *L*

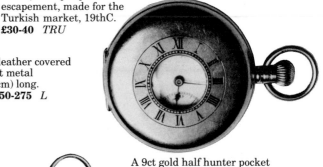

A silver and gold Movado purse watch, with import mark for 1928, and case, maker G.S. **£225-250** *L*

A 9ct gold half hunter pocket watch, with Swiss movement, finished by Benson, Birmingham 1926, 2in (5cm) diam. **£240-280** *TRU*

A silver pair cased verge pocket watch, by Turner & Son, Cliffe, Lewes, London 1875, 2.25in (7cm)diam. **£145-155** *TRU*

A silver pair cased verge pocket watch, by John Lewis, Chalford, Nr Stroud, case hallmarked London 1821, 2.25in (6cm) diam. **£150-200** *TRU*

An 800 standard silver cased hunter pocket watch, jewelled Swiss lever movement, made for the Turkish market, 1.75in (4cm) diam. **£70-80** *TRU*

Wristwatches

A Boucheron white gold wristwatch, 2.5cm square. **£1,500-1,700** *C*

A WWII German airman's wristwatch, by A. Lange & Sohne, 5.5cm diam. **£925-950** *C*

An International Watch Co. pink gold wristwatch, 3.5cm diam. **£1,000-1,100** *C*

A chrome cased rotary wristwatch, in waterproof case, with silvered dial and Arabic numerals, 1930s. **£35-40** *TRU*

A gentleman's silver wristwatch, 1920s. **£65-70** *TRU*

A lady's silver wristwatch, with enamel dial and silver expanding bracelet. **£25-30** *TRU*

A lady's 9ct gold wristwatch, with Swiss 15 jewel lever movement and 9ct gold expanding bracelet. **£50-55** *TRU*

A gentleman's Swiss chronograph wristwatch, with 18ct gold case. **£240-250** *TRU*

A Tourneau gold calendar and moonphase chronograph wristwatch, 3.5cm diam. **£950-975** *C*

A silver wristwatch, with black enamel dial, 1920s. **£55-60** *TRU*

A steel cased wristwatch, with pin pallet movement, 1920s. **£35-40** *TRU*

Omega

A lady's 9ct gold Omega wristwatch, in original Bakelite box, 1930s.
£85-95 *TRU*

A modern 18ct gold calendar quartz Constellation wristwatch, in original presentation case, 3.2cm diam.
£950-975 *L*

An automatic wristwatch, with centre seconds and date aperture, in gold plated case, c1960.
£90-100 *TRU*

Patek Philippe

An 18ct pink gold Calatrava wristwatch, with original black leather strap and pink gold buckle, certificate of origin dated March 1992 and original packaging, 3cm diam.
£4,500-5,500 *C*

An automatic Seamaster 600, professional diver's steel wristwatch.
£225-250 *CSK*

A gentleman's gold automatic Genève date wristwatch.
£225-250 *CSK*

A gentleman's gold wristwatch, 1.5in (3.5cm) diam.
£1,800-2,200 *C*

A gold wristwatch, 1950s, 3 by 3.6cm.
£3,250-3,350 *C*

Piaget

An 18ct gold wristwatch, with gold flexible bracelet and clasp, 2.5cm square.
£1,250-1,500 *C*

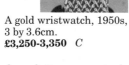

A modern platinum perpetual calendar automatic wristwatch, with original black leather strap and platinum buckle, presentation box with date change tool, certificate of origin, red leather wallet and outer packaging, 3.5cm diam.
£24,000-25,000 *C*

An 18ct gold rectangular wristwatch, with cabouchon winder, 2.5cm square.
£875-925 *C*

Rolex

A lady's gold and diamond set Oyster Perpetual Date-Just chronometer wristwatch, with flexible gold bracelet and deployant clasp, 1in (2.5cm) diam.
£3,500-3,750 *C*

A Prince wristwatch, with vertical rectangular dial, 1920s.
£1,900-2,100 *HSS*

A 9ct yellow gold scientific wristwatch, 3cm diam.
£2,750-3,000 *C*

Swatch Watches

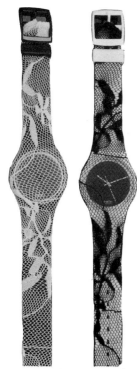

A jelly fish 1985, created by the artist Andrew Logan and produced in a limited edition of 30 pieces.
£1,750-1,950 *C*

Swatch Art Collection, Keith Haring, Models avec Personnages GZ100, Mille Pattes GZ103, Serpent GZ102 and Blanc sur Noir GZ104.
£1,750-1,950 *C*

Keith Haring was already known as a graffiti artist when, in 1985, he was asked to design a Special for Swatch USA. Modele avec personnages was followed by 3 more in autumn 1985. Each piece was produced in a limited edition of 9,999 pieces. The artist died recently in New York.

A jelly fish 1985, created by Andrew Logan and produced in a limited edition of 30 pieces.
£1,650-1,850 *C*

Two USA Specials, velvet undergrounds, No. GZ999.
£8,000-8,500 *C*

Each model produced as one of 500 only in 1985.

These models were commissioned by Swatch for the 1985 Alternative Miss World Contest. Each piece is unique and signed by the artist and was given exclusively to notable guests at this event.

Watch Chains

An American gold plated watch chain, 19thC.
£25-30 *TRU*

Two gold plated single albert watch chains.
£18-25 each *TRU*

A Continental silver albertine watch chain.
£12-18 *TRU*

Two silver curb link watch chains, c1900, 12 and 16in (31 and 41cm) long. **£25-30 each** *TRU*

A Victorian brass watch chain, bar missing.
£5-8 *TRU*

A curb link watch chain, c1900.
£25-30 *TRU*

A Continental silver plated albertine watch chain.
£10-15 *TRU*

Writing Accessories

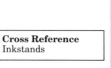

A boxwood pen wiper in the form of a coal scuttle, c1870, 3.5in (8.5cm) wide.
£90-110 *AMH*

An imitation pearl, amber and paste propelling pencil, gold plated end, c1930, 4in (10cm) long.
£20-30 *FMN*

A combined travelling inkwell, vesta case, and 'go-to-bed' taper, c1880, 2in (5cm) high.
£80-110 *AMH*

Cross Reference
Inkstands

Fountain Pens

A Dunhill Namiki gold dust and painted floral decoration lever fill pen, with yellow metal lever and Dunhill Namiki nib.
£450-475 *CSK*

A chased plunger-fill pen, with metal band and Onoto nib, by De La Rue Co.
£60-70 *CSK*

Mont Blanc

A Spider's Web white metal overlaid safety pen, with No.O nib, nib damaged, c1920.
£825-850 *Bon*

Parker

Mabie Todd

A chased barrel eyedropper fill pen, the cap marked 4500, with Swan clip and nib.
£90-100 *CSK*

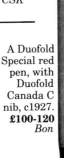

A Duofold Special red pen, with Duofold Canada C nib, c1927.
£100-120 *Bon*

A red Streamline Duofold Special, with twin cap bands and Duofold nib, c1929.
£75-85 *Bon*

Sheaffer

A red veined grey Balance JR pen and pencil set, with feather touch nib, c1930.
£125-145 *Bon*

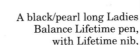

A black/pearl Lifetime pen, with Lifetime Serial Number nib, cap lip cracked, c1928.
£80-90 *Bon*

A black/pearl long Ladies Balance Lifetime pen, with Lifetime nib, c1930.
£70-80 *Bon*

Wahl-Eversharp

A coral red Gold Seal Junior pen and pencil set, with high rollerball clips and Gold Seal flexible nib, c1929, with box.
£300-325 *Bon*

Waterman

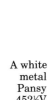

A white metal Pansy 452½V Panel pen, with No. 2 nib.
£80-100 *Bon*

A white metal 452½ Gothic pen, with No. 2 nib, c1925.
£100-125 *Bon*

A plain black lever-fill No. 52 pen, with three 9ct gold bands, in maker's box.
£75-85 *CSK*

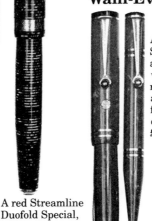

DIRECTORY OF SPECIALISTS

(A&A) Arms & Armour, (A&C) Arts & Crafts, (A&M) Arms & Militaria, (AD) Art Deco, (ADC) Art Deco Ceramics, (ADJ) Art Deco Jewellery, (Ae) Aeronautica, (AN) Art Nouveau, (Au) Automobilia, (B) Boxes, (Ba) Barometers, (BH) Button Hooks, (Bk) Books, (BM) Beer Mats, (Bot) Bottles, (BP) Baxter Prints, (Bu) Buttons, (C) Costume, (Ca) Cameras, (CaC) Card Cases, (CC) Cigarette Cards, (Ce) Ceramics, (Co) Comics, (Cns) Coins, (Col) Collectables, (Com) Commemorative, (Cor) Corkscrews, (D) Doulton, (DHF) Dolls House Furniture, (Do) Dolls, (DS) Display Stands, (E) Ephemera, (F) Fishing, (Fa) Fans, (G&CC) Goss & Crested China, (G), Glass, (Ga) Games, (GC) Greeting Cards, (Go) Golfing, (Gr) Gramophones, (H/HP) Hairdressing & Hat Pins, (I) Inkwells, (J) Jewellery, (Ju) Jukeboxes, (K), Kitchenalia, (L&K) Locks & Keys, (L&L) Linen & Lace, (LB) Le Blond Prints, (M) Metalware, (Ma) Matchboxes, (MB) Money Boxes, (O) Oriental, (OAM) Old Amusement Machines, (P) Pottery, (PB) Perfume Bottles, (PL) Pot Lids, (PM) Papier Mâché, (PMem) Police Memorabilia, (Po) Postcards, (R) Radios, (R&C) Rugs & Carpets, (Ra) Railwayana, (RH) Rocking Horses, (S) Silver, (S&MI) Scientific & Medical Instruments, (SC) Scottish Collectables, (Scr) Scripophily), (Sew) Sewing, (Sh) Shipping, (SP) Staffordshire Pottery, (St) Stereoscopes, (T&MS) Tins & Metal Signs, (T) Textiles, (Ta) Tartanware, (TB) Teddy Bears, (Te) Telephones, (Ti) Tiles, (To) Toys, (TP) Torquay Pottery, (Tr) Treen, (TW) Tunbridge Ware, (TV) Televisions, (W) Watches, (Wr) Writing, (WS) Walking Sticks

LONDON

A. J. Partners (Shelley),
J28 Gray's-in-the-Mews,
1-7 Davies Mews, W1.
Tel: 071-629 7034/723 5363
(ADC)

Abstract, Kensington
Church Street Antique
Centre, 58-60 Kensington
Church Street, W8.
Tel: 071-376 2652
(ADJ)

Academy Costumes Ltd.
(Hire only),
25 Murphy Street, SE1.
Tel: 071-620 0771
(T, C)

Act One Hire Ltd., 2a
Scampston Mews,
Cambridge Gardens, W10.
Tel: 081-960 1456/1494
(T, C)

Andrews, Frank,
10 Vincent Road, N22.
Tel: 081-881 0658 (home)
(G)

Antique Textile Company,
100 Portland Road,
Holland Park, W11.
Tel: 071-221 7730
(T, C)

Anything American, 33-35
Duddenhill Lane, NW10.
Tel: 081-451 0320
(Ju)

Baddiel, Colin, Gray's
Mews, 1-7 Davies Mews,
W1.
Tel: 071-408 1239/081-452
7243
(T)

Baddiel, Sarah,
The Book Gallery, B12
Gray's Mews, 1-7 Davies
Mews, W1.
Tel: 071-408 1239/081-452
7243
(Go)

Bangs, Christopher, SW11.
Tel: 071-223 5676
(M)

Barham Antiques,
83 Portobello Road, W11.
Tel: 071-727 3845
(B)

Barometer Fair, at
Cartographia Ltd.,
Pied Bull Yard, Bury
Place, Bloomsbury, WC1.
Tel: 071-404 4521/4050
(Ba)

Beverley & Beth,
30 Church Street, NW8.
Tel: 071-262 1576
(AD, G)

Blanchard, Sophia,
Alfie's Antique Market,
Church Street, NW8.
Tel: 071-723 5731
(T)

Boston, Nicolaus,
Kensington Church Street
Antiques Centre, 58-60
Kensington Church Street,
W8.
Tel: 071-376 0425
(P)

Bridge, Christine,
78 Castelnau, SW13.
Tel: 081-741 5501
(G)

British Commemoratives,
1st Floor, Georgian
Village,
Camden Passage, N1.
Tel: 071-359 4560
(Com, G&CC)

Brittania, Stand 101,
Gray's Antique Market, 58
Davies Street, W1.
Tel: 071-629 6772
(D)

Button Queen,
19 Marylebone Lane, W1.
Tel: 071-935 1505
(Bu)

Cameron, Jasmin, Stand
J6, Antiquarius, 131-141
King's Road, SW3.
Tel: 071-351 4154
(Wr)

Capon, Patrick, 350 Upper
Street, Islington, N1.
Tel: 071-354 0487/081-467
5722
(Ba)

Casimir, Jack, Ltd.,
The Brass Shop, 23
Pembridge Road, W11.
Tel: 071-727 8643
(M)

Cekay Antiques, Gray's
Antique Market, 58 Davies
Street, W1.
Tel: 071-629 5130
(WS)

Chelsea Lion, Chenil
Galleries, 181-183 King's
Road, SW3
Tel: 071-351 9338
(Do, To)

Chenil Galleries, Enigma
Z2, Pamela Haywood Z3,
Persifage Z5, Forthergill
Crowley D11-12, 181-183
King's Road, SW3.
Tel: 071-351 5353
(T, C)

Childhood Memories,
Teapot Arcade, Portobello
Road, W11.
(Do)

Clark, Gerald, Antiques,
1 High Street, Mill Hill
Village, NW7
Tel: 081-906 0342
(SP)

Classic Collection, Pied
Bull Yard, Bury Place,
WC1.
Tel: 071-831 6000
(Ca)

472

Classic Costumes Ltd..
Tel: 081-764 8858/071-620 0771
(T, C)

Collector's Shop, The,
9 Church Street, NW8.
Tel: 071-706 4586
(D)

Cropper, Stuart, Gray's Mews, 1-7 Davies Mews, W1.
Tel: 071-629 7034
(To)

Dauphin Display Cabinet Co., 118 Holland Park Avenue, W11.
Tel: 071-727 0715
(DS)

David, 141 Gray's Antique Market, Davies Street, W1.
Tel: 071-493 0208
(Cor, K, PMem)

De Fresne, Pierre, 'Beaux Bijoux', Q9/10 Antiquarius, 135 King's Road, SW3.
Tel: 071-352 8882
(ADJ)

Decodence (Bakelite) (Gad Sassower), Shop 13, The Mall, Camden Passage, N1.
Tel: 071-354 4473
(AD)

Dollyland, 864 Green Lanes, Winchmore Hill, N21.
Tel: 081-360 1053
(Do)

Donay, 35 Camden Passage, N1.
Tel: 071-359 1880
(Ga)

Donohoe, L25/7, M10/12 Gray's Mews, 1-7 Davies Mews, W1.
Tel: 071-629 5633/081-455 5507
(S)

East Gates Antiques, Stand G006, Alfie's Antique Market, 13-25 Church Street, NW8.
Tel: 071-724 5650
(G)

Eureka Antiques, Geoffrey Vanns Arcade, 105 Portobello Road, W11.
(Saturdays)
(Ta, CaC, J)

Field, Audrey, Alfie's Antique Market, 13-25 Church Street, NW8.
Tel: 071-723 6066
(L&L)

Fobbister, Rosemary, Stand 28, The Chelsea Antique Market, 245-263 King's Road, SW3.
Tel: 071-352 5581
(PM)

Gallery of Antique Costume & Textiles, 2 Church Street, Marylebone, NW8.
Tel: 071-723 9981
(T, C)

Gee, Rob, Flea Market, Camden Passage, N1.
Tel: 071-226 6627
(Bot, PL)

Georgian Village, 1st Floor, Islington Green, N1.
Tel: 071-226 1571/5393
(Bot)

German, Michael, 38B Kensington Church Street, W8.
Tel: 071-937 2771
(A&A, WS)

Gerwat-Clark, Brenda, Alfie's Antique Market, 13-25 Church Street, NW8.
Tel: 071-706 4699
(Do)

Goldsmith & Perris, Stand 327, Alfie's Antique Market, 13-25 Church Street, NW8.
Tel: 071-724 7051
(S)

Gosh Comics, 39 Great Russell Street, WC1.
Tel: 071-636 1011
(Co)

Harbottle, Patricia, Geoffrey Vann Arcade, 107 Portobello Road, Wll.
(Saturdays)
Tel: 071-731 1972
(Cor)

Harrington Bros., The Chelsea Antique Market, 253 King's Road, SW3.
Tel: 071-352 1720
(Bk)

Heather's Teddys, World Famous Arcade, 177 Portobello Road, W11.
Tel: 081-204 0106
(TB)

Hebbs, Pam, 5 The Annexe, Camden Passage, N1.
(TB)

Hogg, David, S141, Gray's Antique Market, Davies St., W1.
Tel: 071-493 0208
(BH)

Horne, Jonathan, 66B & C Kensington Church Street, W8.
Tel: 071-221 5658
(SP)

Howard, Derek, Chelsea Antique Market, 245-253 King's Road, SW3.
Tel: 071-352 4113
(S&MI)

Howard, Valerie
131E Kensington Church Street, W8
Tel: 071-792 9702
(P)

Ilse Antiques, 30-32 The Vaults, The Georgian Village, Islington, N1.
(Ti)

Jaertelius, Monica, The Mall, Camden Passage, N1.
Tel: 081-546 2807
(Bu)

Jag, Unit 6, Kensington Church Street Antiques Centre, 58-60, Kensington Church Street, W8.
Tel: 071-938 4404
(ADC)

Jessops, 65 Great Russell Street, WC1.
Tel: 071-831 3640
(Ca)

Keith, Old Advertising, Unit 14, 155a Northcote Road, Battersea, SW11.
Tel: 071-228 0741/6850
(T&MS)

King & Country, Unit 46, Alfie's Antique Market, 13-25 Church Street, NW8.
Tel: 071-724 3439
(Go)

Lassalle, Judith, 7 Pierrepont Arcade, Camden Passage, N1.
Tel: 071-607 7121
(Wed & Sat)
(RH)

Latford, Cliff, Photography, G006, Alfie's Antique Market, 13-25 Church Street, NW8.
Tel: 071-724 5650, and at Colchester
Tel: 0206 564474
(Ca)

London Silver Vaults, Chancery House, 53-65 Chancery Lane, WC2.
Tel: 071-242 3844
(S)

Maskerade, Antique Centre, Kensington Church Street, W8.
Tel: 071-937 8974
(J)

Memories, 18 Bell Lane, Hendon, NW4.
Tel: 081-203 1772/202 9080
(Po)

Miller, Jess, PO Box 1461, W6.
Tel: 081-748 9314
(F)

Moderne, Stand 5, Georgian Village, Camden Passage, N1.
(Bu)

Murray Cards (International) Ltd., 51 Watford Way, Hendon Central, NW4.
Tel: 081-202 5688
(E, CC)

New Century, Art Pottery, 69 Kensington Church Street, W8.
Tel: 071-376 2810
(ADC)

Noelle Antiques, S26 Chelsea Antiques Market, 253 King's Road, SW3.
Tel: 071-352 5581
(BH)

Norman, Sue, Stand L4 Antiquarius, 135 King's Road, SW3.
Tel: 071-352 7217
(C)

Old Amusement Machines,.
Tel: 081-889 2213/0782 680667
(OAM)

Oosthuizen, Jacqueline 1st Floor, Georgian Village, Camden Passage, N1.
Tel: 071-226 5393/352 5581
and
23 Cale Street, SW3.
Tel: 071-352 6071
(SP, TP)

Oosthuizen, Pieter G. K., 16 Britten Street, SW3
Tel: 071-352 1094/1493
(A&M)

Ormonde Gallery, 156 Portobello Road, W11.
Tel: 071-229 9800/042482 226
(O)

Past and Present Toys, 862 Green Lanes, Winchmore Hill, N21.
Tel: 081-364 1370
(TB, To)

Past and Present, York Arcade, Unit 5, Camden Passage, N1.
Tel: 071-833 2640
(ADC)

Patrician, 1st Floor, Georgian Village, Camden Passage, N1.
Tel: 071-359 4560/435 3159
(ADC, I, PB)

Pieces of Time, Gray's Mews, 1-7 Davies Street, W1.
Tel: 071-629 2422
(W)

Pinchin, Doug, Dixon's Antique Centre, 471 Upper Richmond Road West, East Sheen, SW14
Tel: 081-878 6788/948 1029
(D)

Powell, Sylvia, Decorative
Arts, 18 The Mall, Camden
Passage, N1.
Tel: 071-354 2977
(Ce)

Pleasures of Past Times,
11 Cecil Court, Charing
Cross Road, WC2.
Tel: 071-836 1142
(Bk, GC)

Relic Antiques, 248
Camden High Street,
NW1.
Tel: 071-485 8072
(K)

Reubens, 44 Honor Oak
Park, Brockley, SE23.
Tel: 081-291 1786
(S&MI)

Rotation Antiques,
Pierrepont Row
Fleamarket, Camden
Passage, N1.
Tel: 071-226 8211
(ADC)

Scripophily Shop,
Britannia Hotel, Grosvenor
Square, W1.
Tel: 071-495 0580
(Scr)

Stateside Comics plc,
125 East Barnet Road, N4
Tel: 081-449 5535
(Co)

Thimble Society of London,
The Bees, S134 Gray's
Antique Market, 58 Davies
Street, W1.
Tel: 071-493 0560
(Sew)

Top Ten Comics,
9-12 St Anne's Court,
Soho, W1.
Tel: 071-734 7388
(Co)

Trio (Theresa Clayton).
Gray's Mews, 1-7 Davies
Mews, W1.
Tel: 071-629 1184
(PB)

Ursula, P16, 15 & 14,
Antiquarius, 135 King's
Road, SW3.
Tel: 071-352 2203
(H/HP)

Vintage Cameras Ltd., 254
& 256 Kirkdale,
Sydenham, SE26.
Tel: 081-778 5416/5841
(Ca)

Walker, Pat, Georgian
Village, Camden Passage,
N1
Tel: 071-359 4560/435 3159
(Do)

West, Mark J., Cobb
Antiques, 39B High Street,
Wimbledon Village, SW19.
Tel: 081-946 2811/540 7982
(G)

Weston, David, Ltd. 44
Duke Street St James,
SW1.
Tel: 071-839 1051/2/3
(S&MI)

White, John, Alfie's
Antique Market, 13-25
Church Street, NW8.
Tel: 071-723 0449
(ADC)

Wilcox, Norman, Alfie's
Antique Market, 13-25
Church Street, NW8.
Tel: 071-724 5650
(R)

Wynyards Antiques, 5
Ladbroke Road, W11.
Tel: 071-221 7936
(Tr)

Yesterday Child, Angel
Arcade, 118 Islington High
Street, N1.
Tel: 071-354 1601/0908
583403
(Do)

Young, Robert, Antiques,
68 Battersea Bridge Road,
SW11.
Tel: 071-228 7847
(P)

Yvonne, K3 Chenil
Galleries, 183 King's Road,
SW3.
Tel: 071-352 7384
(Fa)

Zeitgeist, 58 Kensington
Church Street, W8.
Tel: 071-938 4817
(A&C, AN)

Avon

Barometer Shop, 3 Lower
Park Row, Bristol.
Tel: 0272 272565
(Ba)

Bath Dolls' Hospital &
Teddy Bear Clinic, 2
Grosvenor Place, London
Road, Bath.
Tel: 0225 319668
(Do)

Bristol Dolls' Hospital, 50-
52 Alpha Road, Southville,
Bristol.
Tel: 0272 664368
(Do)

China Doll, The, 31 Walcot
Street, Bath.
Tel: 0225 465849
(Do, DHF)

Dando, Andrew,
4 Wood Street, Bath.
Tel: 0225 422702
(P)

Gibson, Gloria, 2 Beaufort
West, London Road, Bath
BA1 6QB.
Tel: 0225 446646
(B)

Great Western Toys,
Great Western Antique
Centre, Bartlett Street,
Bath.
(To)

Jessie's Button Box,
Great Western Antique
Centre, Bartlett Street,
Bath.
Tel: 0272 299065
(Bu)

Linford, Carr, 10-11
Walcot Buildings, London
Road, Bath.
Tel: 0225 317516
(CaC)

Marchant, Nick, 13 Orwell
Drive, Keynsham, Bristol.
Tel: 0272 865182
(M)

Pugh, Robert & Carol,
Bath.
Tel: 0225 314713
(P)

Saffell, Michael & Jo, 3
Walcot Buildings, London
Road, Bath.
Tel: 0225 315857
(T&MS)

Scott's, Bartlett Street
Antiques Centre, Bartlett
Street, Bath.
Tel: 0225 625335
(Ce)

Somervale Antiques, 6
Radstock Road, Midsomer
Norton, Bath.
Tel: 0761 412686
(G, PB)

Winstone Stamp Company,
S82 Great Western
Antiques Centre, Bartlett
Street, Bath.
Tel: 0225 310388
(CC, Ra)

Bedfordshire

Sykes Christopher
Antiques, The Old
Parsonage, Woburn.
Tel: 0525 290259
(Cor, S&MI, M)

Berkshire

Asquiths of Windsor, 10
George V Place, Thames
Avenue, Windsor.
Tel: 0753 854954/831200
(TB)

Below Stairs, 103 High
Street, Hungerford.
Tel: 0488 682317
(K)

Boxes From Derek
McIntosh, 10 Wickham
Road, Stockcross,
Newbury.
Tel: 0488 38295
(B)

Mostly Boxes, 92 & 52b
High Street, Eton, Windsor.
Tel: 0753 858470
(B, I, TW)

Buckinghamshire
Cars Only, 4 Granville
Square, Willen Local
Centre, Willen, Milton
Keynes.
Tel: 0908 690024
(To)

Foster, A. & E., Little
Heysham, Forge Road,
Naphill.
Tel: 024 024 2024
(Tr)

Neale, Gillian A.,
The Old Post Office,
Wendover.
Tel: 0296 625335
(Ce)

Cambridgeshire

Cambridge Fine Art Ltd.,
Priest House, 33 Church
Street, Little Shelford.
Tel: 0223 842866/843537
(BP)

Cheshire

Avalon, 1 City Walls,
Northgate Street, Chester.
Tel: 0244 318406
(Po)

Dé Jà Vu Antiques,
Hatters Row, Horsemarket
Street, Warrington.
Tel: 0925 232677
(Te)

Dollectable, 53 Lower
Bridge Street, Chester.
Tel: 0244 44888/679195
(Do)

Eureka Antiques,
7a Church Brow, Bowdon.
Tel: 061-926 9722
(CaC, J, Ta)

Nantwich Art Deco &
Decorative Arts, 87 Welsh
Row, Nantwich.
Tel: 0270 624876
(AD)

Rayment, Derek, Antiques,
Orchard House, Barton
Road, Barton, Nr Malpas.
Tel: 0829 270429
(Ba)

Cornwall
Millcraft Rocking Horse
Co., Lower Trannack Mill,
Coverack Bridges, Helston.
Tel: 0326 573316
(To, RH)

Cumbria
Bacchus Antiques,
Longlands at Cartmel.
Tel: 044 854 475
(Cor)

Ceramic Restorers,
Domino Restorations, 129
Craig Walk, Windermere.
Tel: 05394 45751
(Ce)

Derbyshire
Norman King,
24 Dinting Road, Glossop.
Tel: 04574 2946
(Po)

Spurrier-Smith Antiques,
28b, 39-41 Church Street,
Ashbourne.
Tel: 0335 43669/42198
(M)

Devon
Bampton Telephone &
General Museum of
Communication and
Domestic History,
4 Brook Street, Bampton.
(Te)

Hill, Jonathan 2-4 Brook
Street, Bampton.
Tel: 0398 31310
(R)

Honiton Lace Shop,
44 High Street, Honiton.
Tel: 0404 42416
(L&L)

Dorset
Chicago Sound Company,
Northmoor House,
Colesbrook, Gillingham.
Tel: 0747 824338
(Ju)

Lionel Geneen Ltd.,
781 Christchurch Road,
Boscombe, Bournemouth.
Tel: 0202 422961
(O)

Mitton, Mervyn A.,
161 The Albany, Manor
Road, Bournemouth.
Tel: 0202 293767
(PMem)

Old Button Shop,
Lytchett Minster.
Tel: 0202 622169
(Bu)

Old Harbour Antiques, The
Old Bakery, 3 Hope
Square, Weymouth.
Tel: 0305 777838
(Sh)

Yesterday's Tackle &
Books, 42 Clingan Road,
Southbourne.
Tel: 0202 476586
(F)

Essex
Blackwells of Hawkwell,
733 London Road,
Westcliff-on-Sea.
Tel: 0702 72248
(DHF)

East Gates Antiques, 91a
East Hill, Colchester.
Tel: 0206 564474
(G)

G.K.R. Bonds Ltd.,
PO Box 1, Kelvedon.
Tel: 03765 71711
(Scr)

It's About Time, 863
London Road, Westcliff-on-
Sea.
Tel: 0702 72574
(Ba)

R. F. Postcards, 17 Hilary
Crescent, Rayleigh.
Tel: 0268 743222
(Po)

Waine, A., Tweedale, Rye
Mill Lane, Feering,
Colchester.
(ADC)

Old Telephone Co., The
Granary Antiques Centre,
Battlesbridge, Nr.
Wickford.
Tel: 0268 734005
(Te)

Gloucestershire
Acorn Antiques, Sheep
Street, Stow-on-the-Wold.
Tel: 0451 831519
(Ce)

Cotswold Motor Museum,
The Old Mill, Bourton-on-
the-Water.
Tel: 0451 21255
(Au)

Greenwold, Lynn, Digbeth
Street, Stow-on-the-Wold.
Tel: 0451 30398
(J)

Lillian Middleton's
Antique Dolls Shop, Days
Stable, Sheep Street, Stow-
on-the-Wold.
Tel: 0451 31542
(Do)

Park House Antiques,
Park Street, Stow-on-the-
Wold.
Tel: 0451 30159
(Do, DHF, TB)

Samarkand Galleries, 2
Brewery Yard, Stow-on-
the-Wold.
Tel: 0451 832322
(R&C)

Specialised Postcard
Auctions, 25 Gloucester
Street, Cirencester.
Tel: 0285 659057
(Po)

The Trumpet, West End,
Minchinhampton,
Nr. Stroud.
Tel: 0453 883027
(Col)

Hampshire
Art Deco China Centre,
62 Murray Road,
Horndean.
Tel: 0705 597440
(ADC)

Cobwebs, 78 Northam
Road, Southampton.
Tel: 0703 227458
(Ae, Au, Sh)

Evans & Partridge
Auctioneers, Agriculture
House, High Street,
Stockbridge.
Tel: 0264 810702
(F)

Gazelles, 31 Northam
Road, Southampton.
Tel: 0703 235291
(AD)

Goss & Crested China
Ltd., 62 Murray Road,
Horndean.
Tel: 0705 597440
(G&CC)

Millers of Chelsea Ltd.,
Netherbrook House,
Christchurch Road,
Ringwood.
Tel: 0425 472062
(P)

Romsey Medal Centre,
5 Bell Street, Romsey.
Tel: 0794 512069
(A&M)

Toys Through Time,
Fareham.
Tel: 0329 288678
(Do)

Hereford &
Worcester
Barometer Shop, New
Street, Leominster.
Tel: 0568 3652
(Ba)

BBM Jewellery & Coins,
(W. V. Crook), 8-9 Lion
Street, Kidderminster.
Tel: 0562 744118
(I, J, Cns)

Button Museum, Kyrle
Street, Ross-on-Wye.
Tel: 0989 66089
(Bu)

Radiocraft, 56 Main Street,
Sedgebarrow, Nr Evesham.
Tel: 0386 881988
(R)

Hertfordshire
Ambeline Antiques, By
George Antique Centre,
St. Albans.
Tel: 0727 53032/081-445
8025
(H/HP)

Coombs, P., 87 Gills Hill
Lane, Radlett.
Tel: 0923 856949
(Ca)

Forget Me Not, By George
Antique Centre, 23 George
Street, St. Albans.
Tel: 0727 53032/0903
261172
(J)

Oriental Rug Gallery,
42 Verulam Road, St
Albans.
Tel: 0727 41046
(R&C)

Isle of Wight
Nostalgia Toy Museum,
High Street, Godshill.
Tel: 0983 730055
(To)

Vectis Model Auctions,
Ward House, 12 York
Avenue, East Cowes.
Tel: 0983 292272
(To)

Kent
Amelia Dolls, Pantiles Spa
Antiques, The Pantiles,
Tunbridge Wells.
Tel: 0892 541377/0342
713223
(Do)

Amherst Antiques, 23
London Road, Riverhead,
Sevenoak.
Tel: 0732 455047
(Tr)

Antiques & Interiors,
22 Ashford Road,
Tenterden.
Tel: 05806 5422
(PM, T)

Beaubush House Antiques, 95 High Street, Sandgate, Folkestone.
Tel: 0303 49099
(SP)

Blackford, Rowena, at Penny Lampard's, Antique Centre, 31 High Street, Headcorn.
Tel: 0622 890682/861360
(AD, K)

Burman, Valerie, 69 High Street, Broadstairs.
Tel: 0843 862563
(ADC)

Candlestick & Bakelite, 30 Prescott Avenue, Petts Wood, Orpington.
Tel: 081-467 3743
(Te)

Collectables, PO Box 130, Rochester.
Tel: 0634 828767
(Col)

Dolls House Workshop, 54a London Road, Teynham.
Tel: 0795 533445
(DHF)

Falstaff Antiques Motor Museum, 63-67 High Street, Rolvenden, Nr. Cranbrook.
Tel: 0580 241234
(Au)

Hadlow Antiques, No. 1 The Pantiles, Tunbridge Wells.
Tel: 0892 29858
(Do)

Heggie, Stuart, 58 Northgate, Canterbury.
Tel: 0227 470422
(Ca, St, R)

Kirkham, Harry, Garden House Antiques, 118 High Street, Tenterden.
Tel: 05806 3664
(F)

Kollectomania, 4 Catherine Street, Rochester.
Tel: 0634 45099
(Ma)

Lace Basket, 1a East Cross, Tenterden.
Tel: 05806 3923
(L&L, H/HP)

Lampard, Penny, 28 High Street, Headcorn
Tel: 0622 890682
(K)

Magpie's Nest, 14 Palace Street, Canterbury.
Tel: 0227 764883
(Do, DHF)

Old Saddlers Antiques, Church Road, Goudhurst, Cranbrook.
Tel: 0580 211458
(J, M)

Page Angela Antiques, Tunbridge Wells.
Tel: 0892 22217
(P)

Reeves, Keith & Veronica, Burgate Antiques, 10c Burgate, Canterbury.
Tel: 0227 456500/0634 375098
(A&M)

Roses, 60 King Street, Sandwich.
Tel: 0304 615303
(Col)

Serendipity, 168 High Street, Deal.
Tel: 0304 369165/366536
(Ce)

Stevenson Brothers, The Workshop, Ashford Road, Bethersden, Ashford.
Tel: 0233 820363
(RH)

Strawsons Antiques, 33, 39 & 41 The Pantiles, Tunbridge Wells.
Tel: 0892 30607
(TW)

Sturge, Mike, 39 Union Street, Maidstone.
Tel: 0622 54702
(Po)

Up Country, Old Corn Stores, 68 St. John's Road, Tunbridge Wells.
Tel: 0892 23341
(K)

Variety Box, 16 Chapel Place, Tunbridge Wells.
Tel: 0892 31868/21589
(BH, G&CC, Fa, G, H/HP, Sew, S, TW)

Lancashire
A. S. Antiques, 26 Broad Street, Pendleton, Salford.
Tel: 061-737 5938
(AD)

British Heritage Telephones, 11 Rhodes Drive, Unsworth, Bury.
Tel: 061-767 9259
(Te)

Bunn Roy W. Antiques, 34-36 Church Street, Barnuldswick, Colne.
Tel: 0282 813703
(Ce, SP)

Lister Art Books, 22 Station Road, Banks, Southport.
Tel: 0704 232033
(Bk)

Old Bakery The, 36 Inglewhite Road, Longridge, Nr. Preston.
Tel: 0772 785411
(K)

Leicestershire
Charnwood Antiques, Coalville, Leicester.
Tel: 0530 38530
(BP)

Jessups of Leicester Ltd., 98 Scudamore Road, Leicester.
Tel: 0533 320033
(Ca)

Williamson Janice, 9 Coverdale Road, Meadows Wiston, Leicester.
Tel: 0533 812926
(Ce, D)

Lincolnshire
20th Century Frocks, Lincolnshire Art Centre, Bridge Street, Horncastle.
Tel: 06582 7794/06588 3638
(T)

Junktion, The Limes, Fen Road, Stickford, Boston.
Tel: 0205 480087/480431
(To, T&MS)

Legends Rocking Horses, Yew Tree Farmhouse, Holme Road, Kirton Holme, Boston.
Tel: 020 579 214
(To, RH)

Middlesex
Albert's Cigarette Card Specialists, 113 London Road, Twickenham.
Tel: 081-891 3067
(CC)

Ives, John, 5 Normanhurst Drive, Twickenham.
Tel: 081-892 6265
(Bk)

Norfolk
Bluebird Arts, 1 Mount Street, Cromer.
Tel: 0263 512384/78487
(Po)

Howkins, Peter, 39, 40 & 135 King Street, Great Yarmouth.
Tel: 0493 844639
(J)

Kensington Pottery, Winstanley Cats, 1 Grammar School Road, North Walsham.
Tel: 0692 402962
(Ce, P)

Pundole, Neville, 1 White House Lane, Attleborough.
Tel: 0953 454106
(ADC)

Trains & Olde Tyme Toys, Aylsham Road, Norwich.
Tel: 0603 413585
(To)

Yesteryear Antiques, 24d Magdalen Street, Norwich.
Tel: 0603 622908.
(Ce, D)

North Humberside
Marine Art Posters Services, 42 Ravenspur Road, Bilton, Hull.
Tel: 0482 874700/815115
(Sh)

Northamptonshire
Shelron, 9 Brackley Road, Towcester.
Tel: 0327 50242
(Po)

Nottinghamshire
Breck Antiques, 726 Mansfield Road, Nottingham.
Tel: 0602 605263
(Ce)

Keyhole The ,Dragonwyck, Far Back Lane, Farnsfield, Newark.
Tel: 0623 882590
(L&K)

Reflections of a Bygone Age, 15 Debdale Lane, Keyworth.
Tel: 06077 4079
(Po)

Vennett -Smith, T., 11 Nottingham Road, Gotham.
Tel: 0602 830541
(E,Po)

Vintage Wireless Shop, The Hewarths, Sandiacre, Nottingham.
Tel: 0602 393138
(R, TV)

Oxfordshire
Clockwork & Steam, The Old Marmalade Factory, 27 Parkend Street, Oxford.
Tel: 0865 200321
(To)

Comics & Showcase, 19-20 St. Clements Street, Oxford.
Tel: 0865 723680
(Co)

Key Antiques, 11 Horse Fair, Chipping Norton.
Tel: 0608 3777
(M)

Manfred Schotten, Crypt Antiques, 109 High Street, Burford.
Tel: 099 382 2302
(Go)

R.A.T.S., Unit 16, Telford Road, Bicester.
Tel: 0869 242161/40842
(T&MS)

Strange Peter, Restorer, The Willows, Sutton, Oxford.
Tel: 0865 882020
(Do)

Teddy Bears, 99 High Street, Witney.
Tel: 0993 702616
(TB)

Thames Gallery, Thameside, Henley-on-Thames.
Tel: 0491 572449
(S)

Shropshire
Antiques on the Square, 2 Sandford Court, Church Stretton.
Tel: 0694 724111
(ADC)

Manser, F. C., & Son Ltd., 53 Wyle Cop, Shrewsbury.
Tel: 0743 51120
(CaC, Fa, S)

Nock Deighton, Saleroom Centre, Tasley, Bridgnorth.
Tel: 0746 762666
(F)

Rocking Horse Workshop, Ashfield House, The Foxholes, Wem.
Tel: 0939 32335
(RH)

Scot Hay House Antiques, 7 Nantwich Road, Woore.
Tel: 063 081 7118
(K)

Stretton Models, 12 Beaumont Road, Church Stretton.
Tel: 0694 723737
(To)

Summers Roger, 17 Daddlebrook, Hollinswood, Telford.
(BM)

Tiffany Antiques, Unit 3, Shrewsbury Antique Centre, 15 Princess Howe, The Square, Shrewsbury.
Tel: 0270 257425
and
Unit 15, Shrewsbury Antique Market, Frankwell Quay Warehouse, Shrewsbury.
Tel: 0270 257425
(Col, K)

Vintage Fishing Tackle Shop & Angling Art Gallery, 103 Longden Coleham, Shrewsbury.
Tel: 0743 69373
(F)

Staffordshire
Gordon The 'Ole Bottleman, 25 Stapenhill Road, Burton-on-Trent.
Tel: 0283 67213
(Bot)

Midwinter Antiques, 13 Brunswick Street, Newcastle-under-Lyme.
Tel: 0782 712483
(T)

Somerset
House, Bernard G., Mitre Antiques, Market Place, Wells.
Tel: 0749 72607
(Ba)

London Cigarette Card Co. Ltd., Sutton Road, Somerton.
Tel: 0458 73452
(CC)

Spencer & Co., Margaret, Dept AD, Chard Road, Crewkerne.
Tel: 0460 72362
(RH)

Yesterday's Paper, 40 South View, Holcombe Rogus, Wellington.
Tel: 0823 672774
(Co)

Suffolk
Crafers Antiques, The Hill, Wickham Market.
Tel: 0728 747347
(Ce, SP, Sew)

Hoad, W. L., 9 St. Peter's Road, Kirkley, Lowestoft.
Tel: 0502 587758
(CC)

Surrey
Burns, David, 116 Chestnut Grove, New Malden.
Tel: 081-949 7356
(S&MI)

Church Street Antiques, 15 Church Street, Godalming.
Tel: 0483 860894
(ADC, Com)

Dorking Dolls House Gallery, 23 West Street, Dorking.
Tel: 0306 885785
(Do)

Nostalgia Amusements, 22 Greenwood Close, Thames Ditton.
Tel: 081-398 2141
(Ju)

Sheppard Press, Unit 2, Monk's Walk, Farnham.
Tel: 0252 734347
(Bk)

Victoriana Dolls, Reigate.
Tel: 0737 249525
(Do)

West Street Antiques, 63 West Street, Dorking.
Tel: 0306 883487
(A&M)

Wych House Antiques, Wych Hill, Woking.
Tel: 04862 64636
(K)

Sussex
Barclay Antiques, 7 Village Mews, Little Common, Bexhill-on-Sea.
Tel: 0797 222734
(TW)

Bartholomew, John & Mary, The Mint Arcade, 71 The Mint, Rye.
Tel: 0797 225952
(Po)

Beech, Ron, Brambledean Road, Portslade, Brighton.
Tel: 0273 423355
(Ce, PL)

Bygones, Collectors Shop, 123 South Street, Lancing.
Tel: 0903 750051/763470
(Col, Po)

Chateaubriand Antique Centre, High Street, Burwash.
Tel: 0435 882535
(Cor, O, L&L)

Dolls Hospital, 17 George Street, Hastings.
Tel: 0424 444117/422758
(Do)

Ginns, Ray & Diane, PO Box 129, East Grinstead.
Tel: 0342 326041
(SP)

Keiron James Designs, St Dominic's Gallery, 4 South Street, Ditchling.
Tel: 0273 846411
(TB)

Lingard, Ann, Rope Walk Antiques, Rye.
Tel: 0797 223486
(K, Ti)

Old Mint House, Pevensey.
Tel: 0323 762337
(P)

Pearson, Sue, 13½ Prince Albert Street, Brighton.
Tel: 0273 29247
(Do, TB)

Recollect Studios, Dept. M, The Old School, London Road, Sayers Common.
Tel: 0273 833314
(Do)

Rin Tin Tin, 34 North Road, Brighton.
Tel: 0273 672424/733689
(eves)
(Col, T&MS)

Russell, Leonard, 21 King's Avenue, Mount Pleasant, Newhaven.
Tel: 0273 515153
(Ce, Com)

Sussex Commemorative Centre, 88 Western Road, Hove.
Tel: 0273 773911
(Ce)

Trains, 67 London Road, Bognor Regis.
Tel: 0243 864727
(To)

V.A.G. & Co., Possingworth Craft Centre, Brownings Farm, Blackboys, Uckfield.
Tel: 0323 507488
(A&M)

Verrall Brian R. & Co., The Old Garage, High Street, Handcross, Haywards Heath.
Tel: 0444 400678
(Au)

Wallis & Wallis, West Street Auction Galleries, Lewes.
Tel: 0273 480208
(A&M, To)

Tyne & Wear
Ian Sharp Antiques (Maling Ware), 23 Front Street, Tynemouth.
Tel: 091-296 0656
(Ce)

Warwickshire
Arbour Antiques Ltd., Poet's Arbour, Sheep Street, Stratford-upon-Avon.
Tel: 0789 293453
(A&M)

Art Deco Ceramics, Stratford Antique Centre, Ely Street, Stratford-upon-Avon.
Tel: 0789 297496/297244
(ADC)

Bowler, Simon, Smith Street Antique Centre, Warwick.
Tel: 0926 400554
(O)

Central Antique Arms & Militaria, Smith Street Antique Centre, 7 Smith Street, Warwick.
Tel: 0926 497864
(A&M)

Fab, 130 Queens Road, Nuneaton.
Tel: 0203 382399
(Col)

Jazz, Civic Hall, Rother Street, Stratford-upon-Avon.
Tel: 0789 298362
(ADC)

Lions Den, 31 Henley Street, Stratford-upon-Avon.
Tel: 0789 415802
(ADC, P)

Midlands Goss & Commemoratives, Warwick Antique Centre, 22 High Street, Warwick.
Tel: 0926 495704
(Ce, Com, G&CC)

Paull, Janice, 125 Warwick Road, Kenilworth.
Tel: 0926 55253
(P, LB)

Rich Designs, 11 Union Street, Stratford-upon-Avon.
Tel: 0789 772111
(ADC)

Time Machine, Paul M. Kennelly, 198 Holbrook Lane, Coventry.
Tel: 0203 663557
(To)

West Midlands

Doghouse The, 309 Bloxwich Road, Walsall.
Tel: 0922 30829
(K)

Moseley Railwayana Museum, Birmingham.
Tel: 021-449 9707
(Ra, To)

Mr Morgan, F11 Swincross Road, Old Swinford, Stourbridge.
Tel: 0384 397033
(TB)

Nostalgia & Comics, 14-16 Smallbrook, Queensway City Centre, Birmingham.
Tel: 021-643 0143
(Co)

Railwayana Collectors Journal, 7 Ascot Road, Moseley, Birmingham.
(Ra)

Sawyer, George, 11 Frayne Avenue, Kingswinford.
Tel: 0384 273847
(Po)

Walton & Hipkiss, 111 Worcester Road, Hagley, Stourbridge.
Tel: 0562 885555/886688
(Au)

Wiltshire

Coppins of Corsham Repairs, 1 Church Street, Corsham.
Tel: 0249 715404
(J)

Expressions, 17 Princess Street, Shrewsbury.
Tel: 0743 51731
(ADC)

Oxley, P. A., The Old Rectory, Cherhill, Nr. Calne.
Tel: 0249 816227
(Ba)

Relic Antiques, Lea, Malmesbury.
Tel: 0666 822332
(T&MS)

Wells, David, Salisbury Antique & Collectors Market, 37 Catherine Street, Salisbury.
Tel: 0425 476899
(Po, To)

Yorkshire

Barnett, Tim, Carlton Gallery, 60a Middle Street, Driffield.
Tel: 0482 443954
(ADC)

British Bottle Review, 2 Strafford Avenue, Elsecar, Nr. Barnsley.
Tel: 0226 745156/0709 879303
(Bot)

Camera House, Oakworth Hall, Colne Road, Oakworth.
Tel: 0535 642333
(Ca)

Clarke, Andrew, 42 Pollard Lane, Bradford.
Tel: 0274 636042
(To)

Crested China Company, Station House, Driffield.
Tel: 0377 47042
(G&CC)

Danby Antiques, 65 Heworth Road, York.
Tel: 0904 415280
(B)

Echoes, 650a Halifax Road, Eastwood, Todmorden.
Tel: 0706 817505
(T)

Haley, John & Simon, 89 Northgate, Halifax.
Tel: 0422 822148
(To, MB)

Hewitt, Muir, Halifax Antiques Centre, Queens Road, Gibbet Street, Halifax.
Tel: 0442 366657
(ADC)

In Retrospect, 2 Pavement, Pocklington, York.
Tel: 0759 304894
(P)

Memory Lane, 69 Wakefield Road, Sowerby Bridge.
Tel: 0422 833223
(TB)

National Railway Museum, Leeman Road, York.
Tel: 0904 621261
(Ra)

Rouse, Sue, The Dolls House, Gladstone Buildings, Hope Street, Hebden Bridge.
Tel: 0422 845606
(Do)

Sheffield Railwayana Auctions, 43 Little Norton Lane, Sheffield.
Tel: 0742 745085
(Ra)

Spencer Bottomley, Andrew, The Coach House, Thongsbridge, Holmfirth.
Tel: 0484 685234
(A&M)

Windmill Antiques, 4 Montpelier Mews, Harrogate.
Tel: 0423 530502
(B, M, RH)

Scotland

AKA Comics & Books,, 33 Virginia Street, Glasgow,
Tel: 041-552 8731
(Co)

Black Laurance, 45 Cumberland Street, Edinburgh.
Tel: 031-557 4543
(Ta)

Bow Well Antiques, 103 West Bow, Edinburgh.
Tel: 031-225 3335
(Gr, SC)

Edinburgh Coin Shop, 2 Polwarth Crescent, Edinburgh.
Tel: 031-229 3007/2915
(A&M)

Koto Buki, The Milestone, Balmedie, Aberdeen.
Tel: 0358 42414
(O)

Maxtone Graham, Jamie, Lyne Haugh, Lyne Station, Peebles.
Tel: 07214 304
(F)

Millars, 9-11 Castle Street, Kirkcudbright.
Tel: 0557 30236
(ADC)

Miller, Jess, PO Box 1, Birnam, Dunkeld, Perthshire.
Tel: 03502 522
(F)

Now & Then Classic Telephones, 7/9 Cross-causeway, Edinburgh.
Tel: 031-668 2927/0592 890235
(Te)

Stockbridge Antiques, 8 Deanhaugh Street, Edinburgh.
Tel: 031 332 1366
(Do, T)

Toys & Treasures, Wendy B. Austin-Bishop, 65 High Street, Grantown on Spey, Morayshire,
Tel: 0479 2449
(Do)

Whittingham Crafts Ltd., 8 Pentland Court, Saltire Centre, Glenrothes, Fife.
Tel: 0592 630433
(RH)

Wales

Ayers, Brindley John, 45 St. Anne's Road, Hakin, Milford Haven, Pembrokeshire.
Tel: 06462 78359
(F)

Biffins, Ty Newydd, Gwalchmai Uchaf, Anglesey.
Tel: 0407 720550
(Po)

Corgi Toys Ltd., Kingsway, Swansea Industrial Estate, Swansea.
Tel: 0792 586223
(To)

Forbidden Planet, 5 Duke Street, Cardiff.
Tel: 0222 228885
(Co)

Gibbs, Paul, 25 Castle Street, Conwy.
Tel: 0492 593429
(BH, ADC, Ti)

Howards Antiques, 10 Alexandra Road, Aberystwyth, Dyfed.
Tel: 0970 624973
(P)

MacPherson, Stuart & Pam, A.P.E.S., Ty Isaf, Pont y Gwyddel, Llanfair T.H., Abergele, Clwyd.
Tel: 074 579 365
(RH)

Victorian Fireplaces, (Simon Priestley), Ground Floor, Cardiff Antique Centre, 69/71 St Mary Street, Cardiff.
Tel: 0222 30970/226049
(Ti)

Watkins, Islwyn, 1 High Street/29 Market Street, Knighton, Powys.
Tel: 0547 520145/528940
(P)

Williams, Paul, Forge Antiques, Synod Inn, Llandysul, Dyfed.
(T)

CALENDAR OF FAIRS

MAY

Sat 1
Exeter Livestock Centre,
Matford Park Road, Marsh
Barton, Exeter, Devon
Devon County Antiques Fairs
Tel: 0363 82571

Sat 1-3
The East Berkshire Antiques
Fair, Hall Place, Burchett's
Green, Maidenhead
Tel: 0548 531356

Sat 1-3
Mammoth Fair, Donington
Park, Leics
Four In One Promotions
Tel: 0455 233495

Sun 2
Picketts-Lock Leisure Centre,
Picketts-Lock Lane, Edmonton,
London N9
Jax Fairs
Tel: 0444 400570

Sun 2-3
Ceramics Fair, The Great
Danes Hotel, Hollingbourne,
Nr Maidstone, Kent
Wakefield Fairs
Tel: 0634 723461

Sun 2-3
The Sutton Coldfield Antiques
Fair, Penn's Hall Hotel, Sutton
Coldfield,
W. Midlands
Tel: 0952 595622

Wed 5-11
The BADA Fair, Pavilion, The
Duke of Yorks' H.Q., Chelsea,
London SW3

Fri 7-9
The Tatton Park Paintings
Fair, Knutsford, Cheshire
Robert Bailey
Tel: 0277 362662

Fri 7-9
The 9th West & Wales Antique
Ceramics Fair, The New Inn,
Langstone, Nr. Newport, Gwent
Antiques in Britain Fairs
Tel: 0273 423355

Fri 7-9
The Tyneside Antiques Fair,
Redworth Hall, Newton
Aycliffe, Co. Durham
Country House Events
Tel: 0937 541065

Sat 8-9
Antiques Fair, Hagley Hall,
Stourbridge
Wakefield Fairs
Tel: 0634 723461

Sat 8-9
The Leicester County Antiques
Fair, Prestwold Hall, Nr.
Loughborough
Cooper Antiques Fairs
Tel: 0672 515558

Sat 8-15
The 29th Buxton Antiques Fair,
Pavilion Gardens, Buxton,
Derbyshire
Cultural Exhibitions
Tel: 0483 422562

Wed 12-13
Mammoth Fair, The
Racecourse, Chepstow, Gwent
Four In One Promotions
Tel: 0455 233495

Fri 14-15
Truro Antiques, Collectors' and
Book Fair, City Hall, Truro
West Country Antiques &
Collectors' Fairs
Tel: 0225 424677

Fri 14-16
The Edinburgh Ceramics Fair,
The Roxburghe Hotel,
Charlotte Sq., Edinburgh
Wakefield Fairs
Tel: 0634 723461

Sat 15-16
Euro Antiques Fair, The
Showground, Oswestry,
Shropshire
Tel: 0565 634614

Sat 15-16
The Scottish Antiques Super
Fair, Scottish Exhibition
Centre, Glasgow
Tel: 091 537 2893

Wed 19-23
The 3rd Spring Grasmere
Antiques Fair, Grasmere Hall,
Grasmere, Cumbria
Tel: 0748 824095

Sat 22-23
Mammoth Fair, Springwood
Park Showground, Kelso,
Scotland
Four In One Promotions
Tel: 0455 233495

Mon 24-25
Mammoth Fair, Royal
Highland Centre, Ingliston,
Edinburgh
Four In One Promotions
Tel: 0455 233495

Thurs 27-29
Lewes Antiques Fair, The Corn
Exchange, Lewes, East Sussex
Antiques in Britain Fairs
Tel: 0273 423355

Fri 28-31
The Antique Dealers' Fair of
Wales, The Orangery, Margan
Park, Port Talbot
Tel: 0202 604306

Fri 28-31
The Harlaxton Antiques Fair,
Harlaxton Manor, Grantham,
Lincs
Robert Bailey
Tel: 0277 362662

Sat 29-30
Newton Abbot Antiques,
Collectors' & Book Fair, The
Racecourse, Newton Abbot
West Country Antiques &
Collectors' Fairs
Tel: 0225 424677

Sat 29-31
Antiques Fair, Carlton Towers,
Goole, N. Yorks
Tel: 0742 351502

Sat 29-31
The 1st Langley Park Antiques
Fair, Nr Loddon, Norfolk
Tel: 0603 737631

Sun 30-31
Fine Art & Antiques Fair,
Bellhouse Hotel, Beaconsfield,
Bucks
Midas Fairs
Tel: 0753 886993

Mon 31
Harrow Leisure Centre,
Christchurch Avenue, Harrow,
Middx
Jax Fairs
Tel: 0444 400570

JUNE

Thurs 3-4
North Devon Antique Dealers'
Fair, Queen's Hall, Barnstaple,
Devon
West Country Antiques &
Collectors' Fairs
Tel: 0225 424677

Thurs 3-13
The 1993 Fine Art & Antiques
Fair, Olympia, London W14
Tel: 071 370 8211

Sat 5
Exeter Livestock Centre,
Matford Park Road, Marsh
Barton, Exeter, Devon
Devon County Antiques Fairs
Tel: 0363 82571

Sat 5-6
Antiques Fair, Lamport Hall,
Nr Northampton
C.J. Antiques Fairs
Tel: 0952 595403

Sat 5-6
Antiques Fair, Pavilion
Gardens, Buxton
Unicorn Fairs
Tel: 098 987 312

Sat 5-6
The West Berkshire Antiques
Fair, Englefield House, Nr
Theale, Berks
Tel: 0548 531356

Sun 6
The London International
Antique Dolls, Toys, Miniatures
& Teddy Bear Fair, Kensington
Town Hall, W8
Tel: 081 693 5432

Sun 6
Picketts-Lock Leisure Centre,
Picketts-Lock Lane, Edmonton,
London N9
Jax Fairs
Tel: 0444 400570

Tues 8
Newark & Nottinghamshire
Showground, Newark
International Antique &
Collectors Fair Co., Ltd.
Tel: 0636 702326

Tues 8-10
The 16th Annual Aberdeen
Antiques Fair, New Marcliffe
Hall, Queens Road, Aberdeen
Antiques in Britain Fairs
Tel: 0273 423355

Wed 9-19
The Grosvenor House Antiques
Fair, Grosvenor House, Park
Lane, London W1
sTel: 0799 526699

Thurs 10-12
Petersfield Antiques Fair,
Petersfield, Hants
Gamlin Exhibition Services
Tel: 0452 862557

Fri 11-13
The South-East Counties
Antique Dealers' Fair,
Goodwood House, West Sussex
Country House Events
Tel: 0937 541065 .

Fri 11-13
Elegant Homes Show, Royal
Baths & Assembly Rooms,
Harrogate, N. Yorks Tel: 081
445 5040

Fri 11-13
The London Ceramics Fair,
Cumberland Hotel, Marble
Arch, London W1
Wakefield Fairs
Tel: 0634 723461

Fri 11-14
The International Ceramics
Fair & Seminar, Park Lane
Hotel, Piccadilly, London W1
Tel: 071 734 5491

Sat 12-13
Mammoth Fair, Donington
Park, Leics
Four In One Promotions
Tel: 0455 233495

Fri 18-20
The Thoresby Antiques Fair,
Thoresby Park Exhibition
Centre,
Nr Ollerton, Notts
Whittington Exhibitions
Tel: 081 644 9327

Fri 18-20
Giant Antique Fair, Bingley
Hall, County Showground,
Stafford
Bowman Fairs
Tel: 0532 843333

Fri 18-21
P.B.F.A. Book Fair, Hotel
Russell, London WC1
Tel: 0763 248400

Sat 19-20
Trent Park Antiques &
Collectors' Fair, Oakwood
London N14
Tel: 0923 852817

Tues 22-24
London Antiquarian Book Fair,
Park Lane Hotel, London W1
Tel: 071 379 3041

Thurs 24-27
The Westminster Antiques
Fair, Horticultural Old Hall,
London SW1
Penman Antiques Fairs
Tel: 0444 482514

Sat 26-27
Antiques Fair, Westpoint
Exhibition Centre, Exeter,
Devon
Devon County Antiques Fairs
Tel: 0363 82571

Tues 29-30
Euro Antiques Fair, Essex Co.
Showground, Gt. Leighs, Nr
Chelmsford
Tel: 0565 634614

JULY

Sun 4
Newmarket Racecourse
International Antique &
Collectors Fair Co., Ltd.
Tel: 0636 702326

Mon 5-8
Elegant Homes Pavilion, Royal
Show, Stoneleigh,
Warwickshire
Tel: 081 445 5040

Tues 6-8
Shropshire Summer Antiques
Fair, Lion Hotel, Shrewsbury
Antiques in Britain Fairs
Tel: 0273 423355

Thurs 8-11
The Sussex Oak & Country
Fair, Barkham Manor Barn,
Piltdown, Nr Newick, West
Sussex
Penman Antiques Fairs
Tel: 0444 482514

Fri 9-10
International Tyne & Wear
Antiques & Collectors' Fair,
Gosforth Park, Newcastle
Great Northern Antiques Fairs
Tel: 0642 550268

Sat 10-11
Antiques Fair, Showground,
Shepton Mallet, Somerset
Tel: 0278 691616

Mon 12-13
Mammoth Fair, The
Racecourse, Chepstow, Gwent
Four In One Promotions
Tel: 0455 233495

Wed 14-19
The Cambridge Art &
Sculpture Fair, Cambridge
Tel: 0223 242946

Fri 16-18
The Chester Racecourse
Antiques Fair, Chester
Robert Bailey
Tel: 0277 362662

Sat 17-18
Antiques Fair, Rhodes Centre,
Bishops Stortford
Britannia Antiques Fairs
Tel: 0984 31668

Sat 17-18
The North Cotswolds Antiques
Fair, Stanway House, Nr
Winchcombe, Glos
Cooper Antiques Fairs
Tel: 0672 515558

Wed 21
South of England Showground,
Ardingly, Sussex
International Antique &
Collectors Fair Co., Ltd.
Tel: 0636 702326

Thurs 22-24
Antiques Fair, The Game Fair,
Edinburgh
Robert Bailey
Tel: 0277 362662

Thurs 22-24
Elegant Homes Pavilion, The
Game Fair, Edinburgh
Tel: 081 455 5040

Thurs 22-25
The 27th Annual Snape
Antiques Fair, The Maltings,
Snape, Suffolk
Anglian Arts & Antiques
Tel: 0986 872368

Sat 24-25
Mammoth Fair, Kent County
Showground, Detling, Nr
Maidstone
Four In One Promotions
Tel: 0455 233495

Tues 27-28
Great Northern International
Antiques & Collectors' Fair,
Yorkshire Showground,
Harrogate
Great Northern Antiques Fairs
Tel: 0642 550268

Tues 27-29
The 22nd Annual Edinburgh
Antiques Fair, Roxburghe Hotel
Antiques in Britain Fairs
Tel: 0273 423355

Fri 30-1 Aug
Elegant Homes Show,
Kensington Town Hall, London
W8   Tel: 081 445 5040

AUGUST

Tues 3-5
The 1st West Highland
Antiques Fair, Argyllshire
Gathering Halls, Oban
Antiques in Britain Fairs
Tel: 0273 423355

Thurs 5-8
The NEC August Fair, National
Exhibition Centre, Birmingham
Tel: 021 780 4141

Sat 7
Exeter Livestock Centre,
Matford Park Road, Marsh
Barton, Exeter, Devon
Devon County Antiques Fairs
Tel: 0363 82571

Sat 7-8
Mammoth Fair, Donington
Park, Leics
Four In One Promotions
Tel: 0455 233495

Tues 10
Newark & Nottinghamshire
Showground, Newark
International Antique &
Collectors Fair Co., Ltd.
Tel: 0636 702326

Fri 13-15
Giant Antique Fair, Bingley
Hall, County Showground,
Stafford
Bowman Fairs
Tel: 0532 843333

Fri 13-15
The South Cotswolds Antiques
Fair, Westonbirt School,
Tetbury
Cooper Antiques Fairs
Tel: 0672 515558

Sat 14-15
Mammoth Fair, Springwood
Park Showground, Kelso,
Scotland
Four In One Promotions
Tel: 0455 233495

Tues 17-18
Mammoth Fair, Royal
Highland Centre, Ingliston,
Edinburgh
Four In One Promotions
Tel: 0455 233495

Thurs 19-22
West London Antiques Fair,
Kensington Town Hall, London
W8
Penman Antiques Fairs
Tel: 0444 482514

Fri 20-21
Truro Antiques, Collectors' &
Book Fair, City Hall, Truro
West Country Antiques &
Collectors' Fairs
Tel: 0225 424677

Fri 20-22
The Petworth Antiques Fair,
Seaford College, West Sussex
Robert Bailey
Tel: 0277 362662

Sat 21-22
Euro Antiques Fair, The
Showground, Oswestry,
Shropshire
Tel: 0565 634614

Fri 27-28
Antiques & Staffordshire
Figures Fair, King Edward
Hall, Lindfield, Sussex
Antiques in Britain Fairs
Tel: 0273 423355

Fri 27-30
The Ilkley Antiques Fair, Kings
Hall, Ilkley,
W. Yorks
Robert Bailey
Tel: 0277 362662

Sat 28-29
Antiques Fair, Pavilion
Gardens, Buxton
Unicorn Fairs
Tel: 098 987 312

Sun 29-30
Antiques Fair, Dorking Halls,
Dorking
Tel: 081 874 3622

Sun 29-30
Antiques Fair, Lamport Hall,
Nr Northampton
C.J. Antiques Fairs
Tel: 0952 595403

Sun 29-30
Fine Art & Antiques Fair,
Bellhouse Hotel, Beaconsfield
Midas Fairs
Tel: 0753 886993

Sun 29-30
Antiques Fair, Elvaston Castle,
Derby
Tel: 0602 459321

Mon 30
Harrow Leisure Centre,
Christchurch Avenue, Harrow,
Middx
Jax Fairs
Tel: 0444 400570

SEPTEMBER

Thurs 2-4
The 27th Annual East Anglia
Antiques Fair, Athenaeum,
Bury St. Edmunds, Suffolk
Antiques in Britain Fairs
Tel: 0273 423355

Fri 3-5
The Hatfield House Antiques
Fair, Hatfield House, Herts
Robert Bailey
Tel: 0277 362662

Fri 3-5
Great Northern International
Antiques & Collectors' Fair,
Yorkshire Showground,
Harrogate
Great Northern Antiques Fairs
Tel: 0642 550268

Sat 4-5
Ceramics Fair, Royal Crown
Derby Museum, Derby
Wakefield Fairs
Tel: 0634 723461

Sat 4-5
Mammoth Fair, Donington
Park, Leics
Four In One Promotions
Tel: 0455 233495

Sat 4-5
City of Plymouth Antiques
Fair, The Pavilions, Plymouth
Tel: 0934 624854

Sat 4-5
The Loseley Antiques Fair,
Loseley House,
Nr Guildford
Tel: 0548 531356

Sun 5
Picketts-Lock Leisure Centre,
Picketts-Lock Lane, Edmonton,
London N9
Jax Fairs
Tel: 0444 400570

Tues 7-12
The London Antique Dealers'
Fair, Café Royal, Regent Street,
London W1
Jane Sumner
Tel: 0672 870727

Thurs 9-11
Petersfield Antiques Fair,
Petersfield, Hants
Gamlin Exhibition Services Tel:
0452 862557

Thurs 9-11
24th Annual Welsh Antiques
Fair, Castle of Brecon Hotel,
Brecon, Powys
Antiques in Britain Fairs
Tel: 0273 423355

Fri 10-12
The Carlton Towers Antiques &
Fine Art Fair, Nr Goole, N.
Yorks
Whittington Exhibitions
Tel: 081 644 9327

Sat 11
Exeter Livestock Centre,
Matford Park Road, Marsh
Barton, Exeter, Devon
Devon County Antiques Fairs
Tel: 0363 82571

Sat 11-12
Ceramics Fair, Felbridge Hotel,
East Grinstead, Sussex
Wakefield Fairs
Tel: 0634 723461

Sat 11-12
Mammoth Fair, Kent County
Showground, Detling, Nr
Maidstone
Four In One Promotions
Tel: 0455 233495

Sun 12
The London International
Antique Dolls, Toys, Minatures
& Teddy Bear Fair, Kensington
Town Hall, W8
Tel: 081 693 5432

Tues 14-19
The Decorative Antiques &
Textiles Fair, Chelsea Harbour,
London SW10
Tel: 071 624 5173

Tues 14-25
The Chelsea Antiques Fair, Old
Town Hall, King's Road,
London SW3
Penman Antiques Fairs
Tel: 0444 482514

Wed 15-19
The Tatton Park Antiques Fair,
Knutsford, Cheshire
Robert Bailey
Tel: 0277 362662

Sat 18
Salisbury Leisure Centre, The
Butts, Hulse Road, Salisbury,
Wilts
Devon County Antiques Fairs
Tel: 0363 82571

Sat 18-19
Antiques Fair, Ragley Hall,
Warwickshire
Wakefield Fairs
Tel: 0634 723461

Wed 22
South of England Showground,
Ardingly, Sussex
International Antique &
Collectors Fair Co., Ltd.,
Tel: 0636 702326

Wed 22-26
20th Century British Art Fair,
The Royal College of Art,
Kensington Gore, London SW7
Tel: 071 603 0165

Thurs 23-25
Ceramics Fair, Pittville Pump
Room, Cheltenham
Wakefield Fairs
Tel: 0634 723461

Fri 24-25
The 51st London Arms Fair,
Earls Court Park Inn
International, Lillie Road,
London SW6
Tel: 071 405 7933

Fri 24-25
Great Northern International
Fair, Gosforth Park, Newcastle
Great Northern Antiques Fair
Tel: 0642 550268

Fri 24-26
The Harrogate Antiques Fair,
Crown Hotel, Harrogate
Robert Bailey
Tel: 0277 362662

Fri 24-26
The Thoresby Antiques Fair,
Nr Ollerton, Notts
Whittington Exhibitions
Tel: 081 644 9327

Sat 25-26
38th Warwickshire County
Antiques Fair, Cricket Ground,
Edgbaston, Birmingham
Tel: 021 743 2259

Sat 25-26
The Cotswolds Oak and
Country Antiques Fair,
Painswick House, Glos
Cooper Antiques Fairs
Tel: 0672 515558

Sat 25-26
Trent Park Antiques &
Collectors' Fair, Oakwood,
London N14
Tel: 0923 852817

UNICORN

ANTIQUE AND COLLECTORS' FAIRS

THE EXHIBITION HALLS
PARK HALL
CHARNOCK RICHARD
LANCASHIRE

EVERY SUNDAY
8.30 a.m. (TRADE) – 4.00 p.m.

300
STALLS

* The biggest weekly Fair in the North
* Established 16 years
* 300 stalls every Sunday offering a vast range of Antique and Collectable items
* Outside selling from 5.00 a.m.
* Easy access – directly behind M6 Charnock Richard Services
* Free and plentiful parking
* Level loading – no steps
* Refreshments
* Comfortable Halls, carpeted and heated
* Pegboarding (wall stalls) and power points at no extra charge
* Early Trade admission just £1

TO BOOK YOUR STALL PLEASE PHONE UNICORN FAIRS
061-773 7001
Venues and Dates 1993

The Pavilion Gardens, Buxton, Derbyshire
120 quality stalls. 8.30 a.m. (Trade) – 5.00 p.m. Adults £1.00
O.A.P.s 50p (accompanied children free). Stalls and enquiries
Tel: 061-773 7001

3rd and 4th April
5th and 6th June
10th and 11th July
28th and 29th August
2nd and 3rd October
13th and 14th November
Monday and Tuesday 27th and 28th December

The Exhibition Halls, Park Hall, Charnock Richard, Lancashire.
300 stalls every Sunday. The largest weekly fair in the North.
8.30 a.m. (Trade) – 4.00 p.m. Adults £1, O.A.P.s 50p
(accompanied children free).
Off the A49, immediately behind M6 Charnock Richard Services.
Stalls and enquiries 061-773 7001

Sat 25-26
Mammoth Fair, Showground,
Peterborough
Four In One Promotions
Tel: 0455 233495

Sat 25-27
The Aberdeen Antiques & Fine
Art Fair, Exhibition Centre,
Bridge of Don, Aberdeen
Tel: 0202 604306

Tues 28-29
Euro Antiques Fair, Essex
County Showground,
Gt. Leighs
Tel: 0565 634614

Thurs 30-6 Oct
Northern Antiques Fair 1993,
Royal Baths Assembly Rooms,
Harrogate, N. Yorks
Tel: 0223 832852

OCTOBER

Fri 1-3
Ceramics Fair, Margam Park,
Port Talbot, W. Glamorgan
Wakefield Fairs
Tel: 0634 723461

Fri 1-3
Antiques & Decorative Arts at
Rudding House, Nr Harrogate,
N. Yorks
Country House Events
Tel: 0937 541065

Fri 1-3
Giant Fair, Bingley Hall, Co.
Showground, Stafford
Bowman Fairs
Tel: 0532 843333

Fri 1-3
Harlaxton Antiques Fair,
Harlaxton Manor, Grantham
Robert Bailey
Tel: 0277 362662

Fri 1-5
25th Surrey Antiques Fair,
Civic Hall, Guildford
Cultural Exhibitions
Tel: 0483 422562

Sat 2-3
Antiques Fair, Pavilion
Gardens, Buxton
Unicorn Fairs
Tel: 098 987 312

Sun 3
Picketts-Lock Leisure Centre,
Picketts-Lock Lane, Edmonton,
London N9
Jax Fairs
Tel: 0444 400570

Mon 4-5
Little Chelsea Antiques Fair,
Old Town Hall, King's Road,
London SW3
Ravenscott Fairs
Tel: 071 727 5045

Wed 6-7
Mammoth Fair, The
Racecourse, Chepstow, Gwent
Four In One Promotions
Tel: 0455 233495

Wed 6-10
The Park Lane Antiques Fair,
The Park Lane Hotel,
Piccadilly, London W1
Tel: 071 603 0165

Sat 9-10
Antiques Fair, Westpoint
Exhibition Centre, Exeter
Devon County Antiques Fairs
Tel: 0363 82571

Tues 12-14
23rd Annual Hereford Antiques
Fair, Hereford Moathouse,
Hereford
Antiques in Britain Fairs
Tel: 0273 423355

Tues 12-17
The LAPADA Show 1993,
Royal College of Art,
Kensington Gore, London SW7
Tel: 071 823 3511

Fri 15-17
The Antique Dealers' Fair of
Scotland, Hopetoun House,
South Queensferry
Country House Events
Tel: 0937 541065

Fri 15-17
Cheshire County Antiques Fair,
Arley Hall, Knutsford
Cooper Antiques Fairs
Tel: 0672 515558

Sat 16-17
Antiques Fair, Potterspury
Lodge School, Towcester,
Northants
Tel: 0925 595622

Sat 16-17
Antiques Fair, Rhodes Centre,
Bishops Stortford
Britannia Antiques Fairs
Tel: 0984 31668

Sat 16-17
Ceramics Fair, Dyson Perrins
Museum, Worcester
Wakefield Fairs
Tel: 0634 723461

Sat 16-17
Mammoth Fair, Donington
Park, Leics
Four In One Promotions
Tel: 0455 233495

Tues 19
Newark & Nottinghamshire
Showground, Newark
International Antique &
Collectors Fair Co., Ltd.
Tel: 0636 702326

Tues 19-23
Kenilworth Antiques Fair,
Chesford Grange, Kenilworth,
Warwicks
Jane Sumner
Tel: 0672 870727

Wed 20-24
The 24th Grasmere Annual
Autumn Antiques Fair,
Grasmere, Cumbria
Tel: 0798 824095

Thurs 21-23
The Cheltenham Antiques &
Fine Art Fair, Pittville Pump
Room
Whittington Events
Tel: 081 644 9327

Thurs 21-23
22nd Annual St Edmunds
Antiques Fair, Athenaeum,
Bury St. Edmunds
Anglian Arts & Antiques
Tel: 0986 872368

Fri 22-23
Truro Antiques, Collectors' &
Book Fair, City Hall, Truro
West Country Antiques &
Collectors' Fairs
Tel: 0225 424677

Fri 22-24
The Brighton Antiques Fair,
Brighton
Robert Bailey
Tel: 0277 362662

Fri 22-24
The Lancashire Antique
Dealers' Fair, Up Holland, Nr
Wigan
Country House Events
Tel: 0937 541065

Fri 22-24
Antiques Fair, Royal Concert
Hall, Glasgow
Great Northern Antiques Fairs
Tel: 0642 550268

Sat 23-24
Ceramics Fair, Worksop
College, Worksop, Notts
Wakefield Fairs
Tel: 0634 723461

Sat 23-24
Rutland County Antiques Fair,
Uppingham College
Cooper Antiques Fairs
Tel: 0672 515558

Sat 23-24
Antiques Fair, Sherborne
School, Dorset
Devon County Antiques Fairs
Tel: 0363 82571

Tues 26
Harrow Leisure Centre,
Christchurch Avenue, Harrow,
Middx
Jax Fairs
Tel: 0444 400570

Wed 27-30
Bath Antiques & Fine Art Fair,
The Assembly Rooms, Bath
Tel: 0823 323363

Thurs 28-30
The 36th Bi-Annual High
Wycombe Antiques Fair, Royal
Grammar School
Tel: 0494 673674

Thurs 28-30
2nd East Anglian Antique
Dealers' Fair, Langley School,
Loddon, Norfolk
Tel: 0603 737631

Thurs 28-31
The East Berkshire Antiques
Fair, Hall Place, Burchett's
Green, Maidenhead
Tel: 0548 531356

Fri 29-31
2nd Annual Nuneaton Antiques
Fair, The Chase Hotel, Higham
Lane, Nuneaton
Antiques in Britain Fairs
Tel: 0273 423355

Fri 29-31
Chelsea Brocante Fair, Old
Town Hall, King's Road,
London SW3
Tel: 0428 685452

Fri 29-31
Antiques Fair, Stonyhurst, Nr
Whalley, Lancs
Robert Bailey
Tel: 0277 362662

Sat 30-31
36th Luton Antiques Fair,
Putteridge Bury, Luton, Beds
Tel: 0462 434525

Sat 30-31
The Bedford County Antiques
Fair, Woburn Abbey
Cooper Antiques Fairs
Tel: 0672 515558

NOVEMBER

Tues 2-7
42nd Kensington Antiques
Fair, Town Hall, Kensington,
London W8
Cultural Exhibitions
Tel: 0483 422562

Wed 3
South of England Showground,
Ardingly
International Antique &
Collectors Fair Co., Ltd.,
Tel: 0636 702326

Fri 5-6
Wells Antiques Fair, The
Bishop's Palace, Wells,
Somerset
West Country Antiques &
Collectors' Fairs
Tel: 0225 424677

Fri 5-6
The Dorset County Antiques
Fair, Bryanston School,
Blandford Forum
Cooper Antiques Fairs
Tel: 0672 515558

Fri 5-7
Antiques Fair, Puckrup Hall
Hotel, Nr Tewkesbury, Glos
Wakefield Fairs
Tel: 0634 723461

Fri 5-7
Great Northern International
Antiques Fair, Yorkshire
Showground, Harrogate
Great Northern Antiques Fairs
Tel: 0642 550268

Fri 5-7
The Antique Dealers' Fair of
North Wales, Portmeirion,
Porthmadog, Gwynedd
Country House Events
Tel: 0937 541065

Fri 5-7
The Hatfield House Antiques
Fair, Hatfield, Herts
Robert Bailey
Tel: 0277 362662

Sat 6
Exeter Livestock Centre,
Matford Park Road, Marsh
Barton, Exeter, Devon
Devon County Antiques Fairs
Tel: 0363 82571

Sun 7
Picketts-Lock Leisure Centre,
Picketts-Lock Lane, Edmonton,
London N9
Jax Fairs
Tel: 0444 400570

Thurs 11-14
The Solihull Antiques Show,
Conference Centre, Solihull
Tel: 0562 700791

Fri 12-14
The West of Scotland Antiques
Fair, Cameron House, Balloch,
Loch Lomond
Country House Events
Tel: 0937 541065

Fri 12-14
Ceramics Fair, Crown Hotel,
Harrogate, N. Yorks
Wakefield Fairs
Tel: 0634 723461

Fri 12-14
Holker Hall Antiques Fair,
Holker Hall, Cartmel, Cumbria
Robert Bailey
Tel: 0277 362662

Fri 12-17
The International Art &
Antiques Fair, Harrods (3rd
Floor), Knightsbridge, London
SW1
Tel: 071 734 5491

Sat 13-14
Antiques Fair, Showground,
Shepton Mallet, Somerset
Tel: 0278 691616

Sat 13-14
Antiques Fair, Pavilion
Gardens, Buxton
Unicorn Fairs
Tel: 098 987 312

Sun 14
The London International
Antique Dolls, Toys, Miniatures
& Teddy Bear Fair, Kensington
Town Hall, W8
Tel: 081 693 5432

Wed 17-23
Fine Art & Antiques Fair,
Olympia, London W14
Tel: 071 370 8211

Fri 19-21
The Christmas South-East
Counties Antiques Fair,
Goodwood House, Sussex
Country House Events
Tel: 0937 541065

Fri 19-21
16th Annual Edinburgh Winter
Antiques Fair, Roxburghe
Hotel, Edinburgh
Antiques in Britain Fairs
Tel: 0273 423355

Sat 20-21
Newton Abbot Antiques,
Collectors' & Book Fair, The
Racecourse, Newton Abbot,
Devon
West Country Antiques &
Collectors' Fairs
Tel: 0225 424677

Tues 23-24
The 14th English-Speaking
Union Antiques Fair,
Dartmouth House, Charles St.,
London W1
Tel: 071 493 3328

Tues 23-25
Elegant Homes Show, Royal
Horticultural Halls, London
SW1
Tel: 081 445 5040

Wed 24-28
The Castle Howard Antiques
Fair, Castle Howard, Malton,
Yorks
Robert Bailey
Tel: 0277 362662

Wed 24-29
City Antiques & Fine Art Fair
1993, Barbican Centre, London
EC2
Tel: 081 660 8008

Fri 26-28
Ceramics Fair, Michael Herbert
Hall, Wilton, Wilts
Wakefield Fairs
Tel: 0634 723461

Fri 26-28
The Welsh Decorative &
Antiques Fair, Dyffryn House,
St. Nicholas, Cardiff Tel: 0202
604306

Sat 27
Exeter Livestock Centre,
Matford Park Road, Marsh
Barton, Exeter, Devon
Devon County Antiques Fairs
Tel: 0363 82571

Sat 27-28
The Leicester County Antiques
Fair, Prestwold Hall, Nr
Loughborough
Cooper Antiques Fairs
Tel: 0672 515558

Sat 27-28
The City of Plymouth Antiques
Fair, The Pavilions
Tel: 0934 624854

Mon 29-30
Little Chelsea Antiques Fair,
Old Town Hall, King's Road,
London SW3
Ravenscott Fairs
Tel: 071 727 5045

DECEMBER

Thurs 2-5
The Winter Westminster
Antiques Fair, Royal
Horticultural Halls, London
SW1
Penman Antiques Fairs
Tel: 0444 482514

Fri 3-5
The Hoghton Tower Antiques
Fair, Nr Preston, Lancs
Robert Bailey
Tel: 0277 362662

Sat 4-5
Mammoth Fair, Donington
Park, Leics
Four In One Promotions
Tel: 0455 233495

Sun 5
Picketts-Lock Leisure Centre,
Picketts-Lock Lane, Edmonton,
London N9
Jax Fairs
Tel: 0444 400570

Tues 7
Newark & Nottinghamshire
Showground, Newark
International Antique &
Collectors Fair Co., Ltd.
Tel: 0636 702326

Fri 10-12
Giant Antique Fair, Bingley
Hall, County Showground,
Stafford
Bowman Fairs
Tel: 0532 843333

Fri 10-12
The Ilkley Antiques Fair, Kings
Hall, Ilkley,
W. Yorks
Robert Bailey
Tel: 0277 362662

Fri 17-18
Truro Antiques, Collectors' &
Book Fair, City Hall, Truro
West Country Antiques &
Collectors' Fairs
Tel: 0225 424677

Mon 27-28
Antiques Fair, Pavilion
Gardens, Buxton
Unicorn Fairs
Tel: 098 987 312

Tues 28
Harrow Leisure Centre,
Christchurch Avenue, Harrow,
Middx
Jax Fairs
Tel: 0444 400570

Tues 28-29
Mammoth Fair, Sheffield
Arena, Sheffield
Four In One Promotions
Tel: 0455 233495

Tues 28-29
2nd Gwent Antiques Fair, The
New Inn, Langstone, Newport
Antiques in Britain Fairs
Tel: 0273 423355

Fri 31-2 Jan
The Petworth Antiques Fair,
Seaford College, West Sussex
Robert Bailey
Tel: 0277 362662

DIRECTORY OF MARKETS & CENTRES

London

Alfie's Antique Market,
13-25 Church Street, NW8.
Tel: 071-723 6066
Tues-Sat 10-6pm

Angel Arcade, 116-118
Islington High Street,
Camden Passage, N1.
Wed & Sat

Antiquarius Antique
Market, 131/141 King's
Road, Chelsea, SW3.
Tel: 071-351 5353
Mon-Sat 10-6pm

Antiques & Collectors
Corner, North Piazza,
Covent Garden, WC2.
Tel: 071-240 7405
9-5pm every day

Bermondsey Antiques
Market, Corner of Long
Lane & Bermondsey
Street, SE1.
Tel: 071-351 5353
Friday 5am-2pm

Bermondsey Antiques
Warehouse, 173
Bermondsey Street, SE1.
Tel: 071-407 2040/4250
9.30-5.30pm, Thurs 9.30-
8pm, Fri 7-5.30pm, closed
Sat & Sun.

Bond Street Antiques
Centre, 124 New Bond
Street, W1.
Tel: 071-351 5353
Mon-Fri 10-5.45pm, Sat
10-4pm

Camden Antiques Market,
Corner of Camden High
Street & Buck Street,
Camden Town, NW1.
Thurs 7-4pm

Camden Passage Antique
Centre, 12 Camden
Passage, Islington, N1.
Tel: 071-359 0190
Stalls Wed 8-3pm (Thurs
books 9-4pm), Sat 9-5pm

Chelsea Antiques Market,
245-253 King's Road, SW3.
Tel: 071-352
5689/9695/1424
10-6pm

Chenil Galleries, 181-183
King's Road, SW3.
Tel: 071-351 5353
Mon-Sat 10-6pm

Corner Portobello Antiques
Supermarket, 282, 284,
288, 290 Westbourne
Grove, W11.
Tel: 071-727 2027
Fri 12-4pm, Sat 7-6pm

Cutler Street Antiques
Market, Goulston Street,
Nr Aldgate End, E1.
Tel: 071-351 5353
Sun 7-2pm

Crystal Palace Collectors
Market, Jasper Road,
Westow Hill, Crystal
Palace, SE19.
Tel: 081-761 3735
Wed 9-4pm, Fri 9-5pm, Sat
9-4pm, Sun 11-4pm

Dixons Antique Centre,
471 Upper Richmond Road
West, East Sheen, SW14.
Tel: 081-878 6788
10-5.30pm, Sun 1.30-
5.30pm, Closed Wed.

Franklin's Camberwell
Antiques Market, 161
Camberwell Road, SE5.
Tel: 071-703 8089
10-6pm, Sun 1-6pm

Georgian Village Antiques
Market, 100 Wood Street,
Walthamstow, E17.
Tel: 081-520 6638
10-5pm, Closed Thurs.

Georgian Village, Islington
Green, N1.
Tel: 071-226 1571
Wed 10-4pm, Sat 7-5pm

Good Fairy Open Market,
100 Portobello Road, W11.
Tel: 071-351 5950/221 8977
Sats only 5-5pm

Gray's Antique Market,
58 Davies Street, W1.
Tel: 071-629 7034
Mon-Fri 10-6pm

Gray's Mews,
1-7 Davies Street, W1.
Tel: 071-629 7034
Mon-Fri 10-6pm

Gray's Portobello, 138
Portobello Road, W11.
Tel: 071-221 3069
Sat 7-4pm

Greenwich Antiques
Market, Greenwich High
Road, SE10.
Sun 7.30-4.30 & Sat (June-
Sept)

Hampstead Antique
Emporium, 12 Heath
Street, Hampstead, NW3.
Tel: 071-794 3297
10-6pm, closed Mon & Sun.

Jubilee Market,
Covent Garden, WC2.
Tel: 071-836 2139
Open Mon

Kensington Church Street Antiques Centre, 58-60 Kensington Church Street, W8.
10-6

The London Silver Vaults, Chancery House, 53-65 Chancery Lane, WC2.
Tel: 071-242 3844
9-5.30pm, Sat 9-12.30pm

The Mall Antiques Arcade, 359 Upper Street, Islington, N1.
Tel: 071-354 2839
Tues, Thurs, Fri 10-5pm, Wed 7.30-5pm, Sat 9-6pm

Northcote Road Antiques Market, 155a Northcote Road, Battersea, SW11.
Tel: 071-228 6850
10-6pm, Sun 12-5pm

Peckham Indoor Market, Rye Lane Bargain Centre, 48 Rye Lane, Peckham, SE15.
Tel: 071-246 3639
Tues-Sat

Pierrepoint Arcade, Camden Passage, N1.
Tel: 071-359 0190
Wed & Sat

Portobello Road Market, W11.
Sat 5.30-5pm

Rochefort Antique Gallery, 32/34 The Green, Winchmore Hill, N21.
Tel: 081-886 4779/363 0910

Roger's Antiques Gallery, 65 Portobello Road, W11.
Tel: 071-351 5353
Sat 7-4pm

Steptoes Yard West Market, 52a Goldhawk Road, W12.
Tel: 071-602 2699
Fri, Sat & Sun

Streatham Traders & Shippers Market, United Reform Church Hall, Streatham High Street, SW16.
Tel: 071-764 3602
Tues 8-3pm

Wimbledon Market, Car Park, Wimbledon Greyhound Stadium, Plough Lane, SW19.
Tel: 07268 17809
Sun.

Willesden Market, Car Park, White Hart Public House, Willesden, NW10.
Tel: 081-569 3889

World Famous Portobello Market, 177 Portobello Road & 1-3 Elgin Crescent, W11.
Tel: 071-221 4964
Sat 5-6pm

York Arcade, 80 Islington High Street, N1.
Tel: 071-833 2640
Wed & Sat 8-5pm

Avon
Bartlett Street Antique Centre, 5-10 Bartlett Street, Bath.
Tel: 0225 466689
Mon-Sat 9.30-5pm, Wed Market 8-5pm

Bath Antiques Market, Guinea Lane, off Lansdown Road, Bath.
Wed 6.30-2.30pm

Bristol Antique Market, St Nicholas Markets, The Exchange, Corn Street, Bristol.
Tel: 0272 224014
Fri 9-3pm

Clifton Antiques Market, 26/28 The Mall, Clifton, Bristol.
Tel: 0272 741627
10-6pm, Closed Mon

Great Western Antique Centre, Bartlett Street, Bath.
Tel: 0225 424243
Mon-Sat 10-5pm, Wed 8.30-5pm

Bedfordshire
Dunstable Antique Centre, 38a West Street, Dunstable.
Tel: 0582 696953

Woburn Abbey Antiques Centre, Woburn.
Tel: 0525 290350
11-5pm Nov to Easter, 10-5.30pm Easter to Oct

Berkshire
Hungerford Arcade, High Street, Hungerford.
Tel: 0488 683701
9.30-5.30pm, Sun 10-6pm

Reading Emporium, 1a Merchant Place (off Friar Street), Reading.
Tel: 0734 590290
10-5pm

Twyford Antiques Centre, 1 High Street, Twyford.
Tel: 0734 342161
Mon-Sat 9.30-5.30pm, Sun 10.30-5pm, Closed Wed

Buckinghamshire
Amersham Antique Collectors Centre, 20-22 Whieldon Street, Old Amersham.
Tel: 0494 431282
Mon-Sat 10-6pm

Antiques at Wendover, The Old Post Office, 25 High Street, Wendover.
Tel: 0296 625335
Mon-Sat 10-5.30pm, Sun 11-5.30pm

Bell Street Antiques Centre, 20/22 Bell Street, Princes Risborough.
Tel: 08444 3034
9.30-5.30pm, Sun 12-5pm

Market Square Antiques, 20 Market Place, Olney.
Tel: 0234 712172
Mon-Sat 10-5.30pm, Sun 2-5.30pm

Olney Antiques Centre, Rose Court, Olney.
Tel: 0234 712172
10-5.30pm, Sun 12-5.30pm

Tingewick Antiques Centre, Main Street, Tingewick.
Tel: 0280 847922
10.30-5pm every day

Winslow Antique Centre, 15 Market Square, Winslow.
Tel: 0296 714540/714055
10-5

Cambridgeshire
Collectors Market, Dales Brewery, Gwydir Street (off Mill Road), Cambridge.
9.30-5pm

Fitzwilliam Antiques Centre, Fitzwilliam Street, Peterborough.
Tel: 0733 65415

Willingham Antiques & Collectors Market, 25-29 Green Street, Willingham.
Tel: 0954 60283
10-5pm, Closed Thurs

Cheshire
Davenham Antique Centre, 461 London Road, Davenham, Nr. Northwick.
Tel: 0606 44350
Mon-Sat 10-5pm, Closed Wed

Nantwich Antique Centre, The Old Police Station, Welsh Row, Nantwich.
Tel: 0270 624035
10-5.30pm, Closed Wed

Melody's Antique Galleries, 30-32 City Road, Chester.
Tel: 0244 328968
Mon-Sat 10-5.30pm

Stancie Cutler Antique & Collectors Fairs, Nantwich Civic Hall, Nantwich.
Tel: 0270 624288

Cornwall
New Generation Antique Market, 61/62 Chapel Street, Penzance.
Tel: 0736 63267
10-5pm

Waterfront Antique Complex, 1st Floor, 4 Quay Street, Falmouth.
Tel: 0326 311491
9-5pm

Cumbria
Carlisle Antique & Craft Centre, Cecil Hall, Cecil Street, Carlisle.
Tel: 0228 21970
Mon-Sat 9-5pm

Cockermouth Antiques Market, Courthouse, Main Street, Cockermouth.
Tel: 0900 824346
10-5pm

Derbyshire
Derby Antique Centre, 11 Friargate, Derby.
Tel: 0332 385002
Mon-Sat 10-5.30pm

Derby Antiques Market, 52-56 Curzon Street, Derby.
Tel: 0332 41861
Mon-Sat 9-5pm, closed Wed

Glossop Antique Centre, Brookfield, Glossop.
Tel: 0457 863904
Thurs-Sun 10-5pm

Devon
The Antique Centre on the Quay, Exeter.
Tel: 0392 214180
10-5pm

The Antique Centre, Abingdon House, 136 High Street, Honiton.
Tel: 0404 42108
Mon-Sat 10-5pm

Barbican Antiques Centre, 82-84 Vauxhall Street, Barbican, Plymouth.
Tel: 0752 266927
9.30-5pm

Dartmoor Antiques Centre, Off West Street, Ashburton.
Tel: 0364 52182
Tues 9-4pm

Dorset
The Antique Centre, 837-839 Christchurch Road, East Boscombe, Bournemouth.
Tel: 0202 421052
Mon-Sat 9.30-5.30pm

Barnes House Antiques Centre, West Row, Wimborne Minster.
Tel: 0202 886275
10-5pm

Bridport Antique Centre, 5 West Allington, Bridport.
Tel: 0308 25885
9-5pm

Gold Hill Antiques & Collectables,
3 Gold Hill Parade, Gold Hill, Shaftesbury.
Tel: 0747 54050

Sherborne Antique Centre, Mattar Arcade, 17 Newlands, Sherborne.
Tel: 0935 813464
9-5pm

R. A. Swift & Son, St Andrews Hall, 4c Wolverton Road (off Christchurch Road), Bournemouth.
Tel: 0202 394470
Mon-Fri 9-5.30pm

Wimborne Antique Centre, Newborough Road, Wimborne.
Tel: 0202 841251
Thurs 10-4pm, Fri 8.30-5pm, Sat 10-5pm, Sun 9.30-5pm

Essex
Abridge Antique Centre, Market Place, Abridge.
Tel: 0992 813113
10-5pm, Thurs 10-1pm

Battlesbridge Antiques Centre, The Green, Chelmsford Road, Battlesbridge, Nr Wickford.
Tel: 0268 764197

Essex Antiques Centre, Priory Street, Colchester.
Tel: 0206 871150
10-5.30pm

Grays Galleries Antiques & Collectors Centre, 23 Lodge Lane, Grays.
Tel: 0375 374883
10-5.30pm

Kelvedon Antiques Centre, 139 High Street, Kelvedon.
Tel: 0376 570896
Mon-Sat 10-5pm

Maldon Antiques & Collectors Market, United Reformed Church Hall, Market Hill, Maldon.
Tel: 07872 22826
1st Sat in month

Trinity Antiques Centre, 7 Trinity Street, Colchester.
Tel: 0206 577775
9.30-5pm

Townsford Mill Antiques Centre, The Causeway, Halstead.
Tel: 0787 474451
10-5pm, inc Sun

Gloucestershire
Antique Centre, London House, High Street, Moreton-in-Marsh.
Tel: 0608 51084
10-5pm

Charlton Kings Antique Centre, 199 London Road, Charlton Kings, Cheltenham.
Tel: 0242 510672
9.30-5.30pm

Cheltenham Antique Market, 54 Suffolk Road, Cheltenham.
Tel: 0242 529812
9.30-5.30pm

Cirencester Antique Market, Market Place, Cirencester.
Tel: 071-262 5003
Fri

Gloucester Antiques Centre, Severn Road, Gloucester.
Tel: 0452 529716
9.30-5pm, Sun 1-5pm

Cotswold Antiques Centre, The Square, Stow-on-the-Wold.
Tel: 0451 31585
10-5.30pm

Painswick Antique Centre, New Street, Painswick.
Tel: 0452 812431
10-5pm, Sat 9.30-5.30pm, Sun 11-5.30pm

Tewkesbury Antique Centre, Tolsey Hall, Tolsey Lane, Tewkesbury.
Tel: 0684 294091
9-5pm

Windsor House Antiques Centre, High Street, Moreton-in-Marsh.
Tel: 0608 50993
10-5.30pm, Sun 12-5.30pm

Hampshire
Creightons Antique Centre, 23-25 Bell Street, Romsey.
Tel: 0794 522758
9-6pm

Folly Antiques Centre, College Street, Petersfield.
Tel: 0730 64816
10-5pm, Thurs 10-1pm

Kingsley Barn Antique Centre, Church Lane, Eversley, Nr Wokingham.
Tel: 0734 328518
10.30-5pm, closed Mon

Lymington Antiques Centre, 76 High Street, Lymington.
Tel: 0590 670934
10-5pm, Sat 9-5pm

Squirrel Collectors Centre, 9 New Street, Basingstoke
Tel: 0256 464885
10-5.30pm

Hereford & Worcester
The Galleries Antiques Centre, Pickwicks, 503 Evesham Road, Crabbs Cross, Redditch.
Tel: 0527 550568
9.30-5pm, inc Sun

Hereford Antique Centre, 128 Widemarsh Street, Hereford.
Tel: 0432 266242
9-5pm, Sun 1-5pm

Leominster Antiques Market, 14 Broad Street, Leominster.
Tel: 0568 2189
10-5pm

Worcester Antiques Centre, Reindeer Court, Mealcheapen Street, Worcester.
Tel: 0905 610680/1
10-5pm

Hertfordshire
Antique & Collectors Market, Market Place, Hemel Hempstead.
Tel: 071-624 3214
Wed 9-2pm

Bushey Antiques Centre, 39 High Street, Bushey.
Tel: 081-95- 5040

By George! Antiques Centre, 23 George Street, St Albans
Tel: 0727 53032
10-5pm

The Herts & Essex Antique Centre, The Maltings, Station Road, Sawbridgeworth
Tel: 0279 722044
Tues-Fri 10-5pm, Sat & Sun 10-30-6pm, closed Mon

St Albans Antique Market, Town Hall, Chequer Street, St Albans
Tel: 0727 44957
Mon 9.30-4pm

Kent
The Antiques Centre, 120 London Road, Sevenoaks.
Tel: 0732 452104
9.30-5.30pm, Sat 10-5.30pm

Beckenham Antique Market, Old Council Hall, Bromley Road, Beckenham.
Tel: 081-777 6300
Wed 9.30-2pm

Bromley Antique Market, Widmore Road, Bromley.
Thurs 7.30-3pm

Burgate Antiques Centre, 10 Burgate, Canterbury.
Tel: 0227 456500
Mon-Sat 10-5pm

Castle Antiques Centre, 1 London Road, Westerham.
Tel: 0959 562492
Mon-Sat 10-5pm

Cranbrook Antiques Centre, 15 High Street, Cranbrook.
Tel: 0580 712173
10-5pm

Folkestone Market, Rotunda Amusement Park, Marine Parade, Folkestone.
Tel: 0850 311391
Sun

Hythe Antique Centre, 5 High Street, Hythe.
Tel: 0303 269043/269643
10-4pm, Sat 10-5pm
Closed Wed & Sun.

Malthouse Arcade, High Street, Hythe.
Tel: 0303 260103
Fri & Sat 10-6pm

Noah's Ark Antiques Centre, 5 King Street, Sandwich.
Tel: 0304 611144
10-5pm, closed Wed & Sun

Paraphernalia Antiques & Collectors Centre, 171 Widmore Road, Bromley.
Tel: 081-318 2997
10-5.30pm, Sun 10-2pm

Rochester Antiques & Flea Market, Corporation Street, Rochester.
Tel: 071 262 5003
Sat 8-1pm

Sandgate Antiques Centre, 61-63 High Street, Sandgate.
Tel: 0303 48987
10-6pm, Sun 11-6pm

Tenterden Antiques Centre, 66-66A High Street, Tenterden.
Tel: 05806 5885
10-5pm, inc Sun

Thanet Antiques Trade Centre, 45 Albert Street, Ramsgate.
Tel: 0843 597336
'9-5pm

Tudor Cottage Antiques Centre, 22-23 Shipbourne Road, Tonbridge.
Tel: 0732 351719
10-5.30pm

Tunbridge Wells Antique Centre, Union Square, The Pantiles, Tunbridge Wells.
Tel: 0892 533708
Mon-Sat 9.30-5pm

Lancashire
Blackpool Antiques Centre, 105-107 Hornby Road, Blackpool.
Tel: 0253 752514
9-5pm, closed Sat

Bolton Antiques Centre, Central Street, Bolton.
Tel: 0204 362694
9.30-5pm, inc Sun

Bygone Times, Times House, Grove Mill, The Green, Eccleston.
Tel: 0257 453780
8-6pm, inc Sun

Darwen Antique Centre, Provident Hall, The Green, Darwen.
Tel: 0254 760565
9.30-5pm, Sun 11-5pm, closed Tues

GB Antiques Centre, Lancaster Leisure Park, Wyresdale Road, Lancaster.
Tel: 0524 844734
10-5pm, inc Sun

Last Drop Antique & Collectors Fair, Last Drop Hotel, Bromley Cross, Bolton.
Sun 11-4pm

Levenshulme Antiques Hypermarket, Levenshulme Town Hall, 965 Stockport Road, Levenshulme, Manchester.
Tel: 061 224 2410
10-5pm

Memory Lane Antique Centre, Gilnow Lane, off Deane Road, Bolton.
Tel: 0204 380383
9-5pm, inc Sun

Preston Antique Centre, The Mill, New Hall Lane, Preston.
Tel: 0772 794498
Mon-Fri 8.30-5.30pm, Sat 10-4pm, Sun 9-4pm

Royal Exchange Shopping Centre, Antiques Gallery, St Anne's Square, Exchange Street, Manchester.
Tel: 061 834 3731/834 1427
Mon-Sat 9.30-5.30pm

Walter Aspinall Antiques, Pendle Antique Centre, Union Mill, Watt Street, Sabden, Nr Blackburn.
Tel: 0282 76311
9-5pm, weekends 11-4pm

Leicestershire
The Antiques Complex, St Nicholas Place, Leicester.
Tel: 0533 533343
9.30-5.30pm

Boulevard Antique & Shopping Centre, The Old Dairy, Western Boulevard, Leicester.
Tel: 0533 541201
10-6pm, Sun 2-5pm

Oxford Street Antiques Centre Ltd., 16-26 Oxford Street, Leicester.
Tel: 0533 553006
Mon-Fri 10-5.30pm, Sun 2-5pm

Lincolnshire
Boston Antiques Centre, 12 West Street, Boston.
Tel: 0205 361510
9-5pm, closed Thurs

Eastgate Antiques Centre, 6 Eastgate, Lincoln.
Tel: 0522 544404
9.30-5pm

Hemswell Antique Centre, Caenby Corner Estate, Hemswell Cliff, Nr Gainsborough.
Tel: 0427 668389
10-5pm, inc Sun

The Lincolnshire Antiques Centre, 26 Bridge Street, Horncastle.
Tel: 0507 527794
9-5pm

Portobellow Row Antiques Centre, 93-95 High Street, Boston.
Tel: 0205 369456
10-4pm

Talisman Antiques, 51 North Street, Horncastle.
Tel: 0507 526893
10-5pm, closed Mon.

Stamford Antiques Centre, The Exchange Hall, Broad Street, Stamford.
Tel: 0780 62605
10-5pm

Talisman Antiques, Regent House, 12 South Market, Alford.
Tel: 0507 463441
10.30-4.30pm, closed Thurs.

Merseyside
Hoylake Antique Centre, 128-130 Market Street, Hoylake.
Tel: 051-632 4231
9.15-5.30pm

Middlesex
Hampton Village Antiques Centre, 76 Station Road, Hampton.
Tel: 081-979 5871
10-5.30pm

The Jay's Antique Centre, 25/29 High Street, Harefield.
Tel: 0895 824738
10-6pm, Wed 10-1pm

Norfolk
Angel Antique Centre, Pansthorn Farmhouse, Redgrave Road, South Lopham, Nr Diss.
Tel: 037 988 317
9.30-6pm, inc Sun

Antique & Collectors Centre, St Michael at Plea, Bank Plain, Norwich.
Tel: 0603 619129
9.30-5.00pm

Cloisters Antiques Fair, St Andrew's & Blackfriars Hall, St Andrew's Plain, Norwich.
Tel: 0603 628477
Wed 9.30-3.30pm

Coltishall Antiques Centre, High Street, Coltishall.
Tel: 0603 738306
10-5pm

Fakenham Antique Centre, Old Congregational Chapel, 14 Norwich Road, Fakenham.
Tel: 0328 862941
10-5pm, Thurs 9.5pm

Gostling's Antique Centre, 13 Market Hill, Diss.
Tel: 0379 650360
10-5pm, Thurs 10-7pm

Norwich Antiques & Collectors Centre, Quayside, Fye Bridge, Norwich.
Tel: 0603 612582
10-5pm

The Old Granary Antique & Collectors Centre, King Staithe Lane, off Queens Street, King's Lynn.
Tel: 0553 775509
10-5pm

Wells Antique Centre, The Old Mill, Maryland.
Tel: 0328 711433
10-5pm, inc Sun

Wymondham Antique Centre, No 1 Town Green, Wymondham.
Tel: 0953 604817
10-5pm

Northamptonshire

Antiques & Bric-a-Brac Market, Market Square, Town Centre, Wellingborough.
Tel: 0905 611321
Tues 9-4pm

Finedon Antiques Centre, Church Street, Finedon, Nr Wellingborough.
Tel: 0933 681260
9.30-5.30pm, Sun 2-5

The Village Antique Market, 62 High Street, Weedon.
Tel: 0327 42015
9.30-5.30pm, Sun 10.30-5.30pm

Northumberland

Colmans of Hexham, 15 St Mary's Chare, Hexham.
Tel: 0434 603811/2
9-5pm

Nottinghamshire

Castle Gate Antiques Centre, 55 Castle Gate, Newark.
Tel: 0636 700076
9-5.30pm

Newark Antiques Centre, Regent House, Lombard Street, Newark.
Tel: 0636 605504
9.30-5pm, Sun 11-4

Newark Antique Warehouse, Kelham Road, Newark.
Tel: 0636 74869
8.30-5.30pm, Sat 10-4pm

Nottingham Antique Centre, British Rail Goods Yard, London Road, Nottingham.
Tel: 0602 504504/505548
9-5pm, closed Sat

Top Hat Antiques Centre, 66-72 Derby Road, Nottingham.
Tel: 0602 419143
9.30-5pm

Oxfordshire

Antique & Collectors Market, Town Hall, Thame.
Tel: 0844 28205
8.30-3.30pm, 2nd Tues of month

Cotswold Gateway Antique Centre, Cheltenham Road, Burford Roundabout, Burford.
Tel: 099 382 3678
10-5.30pm, Sun 2-5.30pm

Chipping Norton Antique Centre, Ivy House, Middle Row, Chipping Norton.
Tel: 0608 644212
10-5pm, inc Sun

Deddington Antique Centre, Laurel House, Bull Ring, Market Square, Deddington.
Tel: 0869 38968
Mon-Sat 10-5pm

Friday Street Antique Centre, 2 & 4 Friday Street, Henley-on-Thames.
Tel: 0491 574104
9.30-5.30, Sun 11-5

Goring Antique Centre, 16 High Street, Goring-on-Thames.
Tel: 0491 873300.
10-5pm, Sat 11-5pm, closed Wed pm

Henley Antique Centre, Rotherfield Arcade, 2-4 Reading Road, Henley-on-Thames.
Tel: 0491 411468

The Lamb Arcade, High Street, Wallingford.
Tel: 0491 35166/35048
10-5pm, Sat 10-5.30pm Wed 10-4pm

Oxford Antiques Centre, The Jam Factory, 27 Park End Street, Oxford
Tel: 0865 251075
Mon-Sat 10-5pm and 1st Sun every month

Oxford Antiques Market, Gloucester Green, Oxford.
Tel: 0865 242216
Every Thurs

Span Antiques, 6 Market Place, Woodstock.
Tel: 0993 811332
10-5pm, inc Sun, closed Wed

Shropshire

Cleobury Mortimer Antique Centre, Childe Road, Cleobury Mortimer, Nr Kidderminster.
Tel: 0299 270513
10-5pm, inc Sun, closed Thurs

Ironbridge Antique Centre, Dale End, Ironbridge.
Tel: 0952 433784
10-5pm, Sun 2-5pm

Pepper Lane Antique Centre, Pepper Lane, Ludlow.
Tel: 0584 876494
10-5pm

Shrewsbury Antique Market, Frankwell Quay Warehouse, Shrewsbury.
Tel: 0743 350916
9.30-5pm

Shrewsbury Antique Centre, 15 Princess House, The Square, Shrewsbury.
Tel: 0743 247704
9.30-5.30pm

St Leonards Antiques, Corve Street, Ludlow.
Tel: 0584 875573
9-5pm

Stretton Antiques Market, 36 Sandford Avenue, Church Stretton.
Tel: 0694 723718
9.30-5.30pm, Sun 10.30-4.30pm

Telford Antique Centre, High Street, Wellington, Telford.
Tel: 0952 256450
10-5pm, Sun 2-5pm

Somerset

Bridgwater Antiques Market, Marycourt Shopping Mall, Bridgwater.
Tel: 0823 451433
Friday 9-5pm, Sat 10-5pm

County Antiques Centre, 21/23 West Street, Ilminster.
Tel: 0460 54151
10-5pm

Dulverton Antique Centre, Lower Town Hall, Dulverton.
Tel: 0398 23522
10-5pm

Guildhall Antique Market, The Guildhall, Chard.
Thurs 9-3pm

Oscar's Antique Market, 13-15 Market Square, Crewkerne.
Tel: 0460 72718
10-5.30pm

Taunton Silver Street Antiques Centre, 27/29 Silver Street, Taunton.
Tel: 071-351 5353
Mon 9-4pm

Staffordshire

The Antique Centre, 128 High Street, Kinver.
Tel: 0384 877441
10-5.30pm

Antique Market, The Stones, Newcastle-under-Lyme.
Tel: 071-624 4848
Tues 9-4pm

Barclay House Antiques, 14-16 Howard Place, Shelton, Stoke-on-Trent.
Tel: 0782 274747
9.30-6pm

Rugeley Antique Centre, 161/3 Main Road,Brereton, Nr Rugeley.
Tel: 08895 77166
9-5pm

The Potteries Antique Centre, Waterloo Road, Cobridge, Stoke-on-Trent.
Tel: 0782 201455   9-6pm

Tudor of Lichfield Antique Centre, Lichfield House, Bore Street, Lichfield.
Tel: 0543 263951

Tutbury Mill Antiques, 6 Lower High Street, Tutbury, Nr Burton-on-Trent.
Tel: 0283 815999
9-5pm every day

Suffolk

The Barn, Risby, Bury St Edmunds.
Tel: 0284 811126
10-5pm, inc Sun

Clare Antique Warehouse, The Mill, Malting Lane, Clare, Nr. Sudbury.
Tel: 0787 278449
9.30-5.30pm

Debenham Antique Centre, The Forresters Hall, High Street, Debenham.
Tel: 0728 860777
10-5.30pm, Sun 2-5pm

Long Melford Antiques Centre, The Chapel Maltings, Long Melford.
Tel: 0787 79287
9.30-5.30pm

Old Town Hall Antiques Centre, High Street, Needham Market.
Tel: 0449 720773
10-5pm

Snape Antiques and Collectors' Centre, Snape Maltings, Snape.
Tel: 0728 888038
10-6pm, inc Sun

Waveney Antiques Centre, Peddars Lane, Beccles.
Tel: 0502 716147
10-5.30pm

Wrentham Antiques Centre, 7 High Street, Wrentham, Nr. Beccles.
Tel: 0502 75376
10-5.30pm, Sun 2-5.30pm

Surrey

Antiquarius Antique Centre, 56 West Street, Dorking.
Tel: 0306 743398
9.30-5.30pm

Antiques Arcade, 22 Richmond Hill, Richmond.
Tel: 081-940 2035
10.30-5.30pm, closed Wed

Antiques & Interiors, 64 Station Road East, Oxted.
Tel: 0883 712806
9.30-5.30pm

The Antiques Arcade,
77 Bridge Road,
East Molesey.
Tel: 081-979 7954
10-5pm

The Antiques Centre, 22
Haydon Place, corner of
Martyr Road, Guildford.
Tel: 0483 67817
10-4pm, closed Mon & Wed

Cambridge Parade
Antiques, 229-231
Carshalton Road,
Carshalton.
Tel: 081-643 0014
10-5.30pm

Dorking Antiques Centre,
17/18 West Street,
Dorking.
Tel: 0306 740915
10-5.30pm

Duke's Yard Antique
Market, 1a Duke Street,
Richmond.
Tel: 081-332 1051
10-6pm, closed Mon

Farnham Antique Centre,
27 South Street, Farnham.
Tel: 0252 724475
9.30-5pm

Fern Cottage Antique
Centre, 28/30 High Street,
Thames Ditton.
Tel: 081-398 2281
10-5.30pm

Maltings Monthly Market,
Bridge Square, Farnham.
Tel: 0252 726234
First Sat in month

The Old Smithy Antique
Centre, 7 High Street,
Merstham.
Tel: 073764 2306
10-5pm

Reigate Antiques Arcade,
57 High Street, Reigate.
Tel: 0737 222654
10-5.30pm

Surrey Antiques Centre,
10 Windsor Street,
Chertsey.
Tel: 0932 563313
10-5pm

Sutton Market, West
Street, Sutton.
Tel: 081-661 1245
Tues & Sat

Victoria & Edward
Antiques Centre,
61 West Street, Dorking.
Tel: 0306 889645
9.30-5.30pm

Wood's Wharf Antiques
Bazaar, 56 High Street,
Haslemere.
Tel: 0428 642125
Mon-Sat 9.30-5pm

Sussex East

Antique Market, Leaf Hall,
Seaside, Eastbourne.
Tel: 0323 27530
Tues & Sat, 9-5pm

Bexhill Antiques Centre,
Quakers Mill, Old Town,
Bexhill.
Tel: 0424 210182/221940
10-5.30pm

Brighton Antiques Gallery,
41 Meeting House Lane,
Brighton.
Tel: 0273 26693/21059
10-5.30pm

Brighton Market, Jubilee
Shopping Hall, 44-47
Gardner Street, Brighton.
Tel: 0273 600574
9-5pm

Chateaubriand Antiques
Centre, High Street,
Burwash.
Tel: 0435 882535
10-5pm, Sun 2-5pm

Cliffe Antiques Centre, 47
Cliffe High Street, Lewes.
Tel: 0273 473266
9.30-5pm

Cliffe Gallery Antique
Centre, 39 Cliffe High
Street, Lewes.
Tel: 0273 471877
9.30-5pm

The Collectors Market,
The Enterprise Centre,
Station Parade,
Eastbourne.
Tel: 0323 32690

The Courtyard Antiques
Market, 13, 15 & 17 High
Street, Seaford.
Tel: 0323 892091
8.30-5.30pm

Foundry Lane Antiques
Centre, 15 Cliffe High
Street, Lewes.
Tel: 0273 475361
10-5pm, closed Mon

George Street Antiques
Centre, 47 George Street,
Old Town, Hastings.
Tel: 0424 429339
9-5pm Sun 11-4pm

The Hastings Antique
Centre, 59-61 Norman
Road, Hastings.
Tel: 0424 428561
10-5.30pm

Horsebridge Antiques
Centre, 1 North Street,
Horsebridge, Nr Hailsham.
Tel: 0323 844414
10-5pm

Kollect-O-Mania, 25
Trafalgar Street, Brighton.
Tel: 0273 694229
10-5pm

Lewes Antique Centre,
20 Cliffe High Street,
Lewes.
Tel: 0273 476148
9.30-5pm

Mint Arcade,
71 The Mint, Rye.
Tel: 0797 225952
10-5pm

Newhaven Flea Market,
28 South Way, Newhaven.
Tel: 0273 517207/516065
Open every day

The Old Town Hall,
Antique Centre, 52
Ocklynge Road,
Eastbourne.
Tel: 0323 416016
9.30-5pm, Sun 10.30-5pm

Pharoahs Antiques Centre,
28 South Street,
Eastbourne.
Tel: 0323 38655
10-5pm

Prinnys Antique Gallery,
3 Meeting House Lane,
Brighton.
Tel: 0273 204554
9.30-5pm

Seaford's Barn Collectors
Market & Studio Book
Shop, The Barn, Church
Lane, Seaford.
Tel: 0323 890010
Tues, Thurs & Sat
10-4.30pm

Sussex West

Almshouses Arcade,
19 The Hornet, Chichester.
9.30-4.30pm

Antiques & Collectors
Market, Old Orchard
Building,
Old House, Adversane,
Nr Billingshurst.
Tel: 0403 783594
Every day

Copthorne Group
Antiques, Copthorne Bank,
Crawley.
Tel: 0342 712802
Mon-Sat 10-5.30pm

Eagle House Antiques
Market, Market Square,
Midhurst.
Tel: 0730 812718

Mamies Antiques Centre, 5
River Road, Arundel.
Tel: 0903 882012
Thurs-Sun, 9-5pm

Midhurst Antiques
Market, Knockhundred
Row, Midhurst.
Tel: 0730 814231
9.30-5pm

Shirley, Mostyns Antique
Centre, 64 Brighton Road,
Lancing.
Tel: 0903 752961
Mon-Fri 10-5pm

Petworth Antique Market,
East Street, Petworth.
Tel: 0798 42073
10-5pm

Tarrant Street Antique
Centre, Nineveh House,
Tarrant Street, Arundel.
Tel: 0903 884307
9.30-5pm, Sun 11-5pm

Treasure House Antiques
& Collectors Market, 31b
High Street, Arundel.
Tel: 0903 883101
9-5pm

Upstairs Downstairs
Antique Centre, 29
Tarrant Street, Arundel.
Tel: 0903 883749
10.30-5pm, inc Sun

Tyne & Wear

Antique Centre Newcastle,
8 St Mary Place East,
Newcastle-upon-Tyne.
Tel: 091-232 9832
Tues-Sat 10-5pm

Blaydon Antique Centre,
Bridge House, Bridge
Street, Blaydon,
Nr Newcastle-upon-Tyne.
Tel: 091-414 3535
10-5pm

Vine Lane Antique
Market, 17 Vine Lane,
Newcastle-upon-Tyne.
Tel: 091-261 2963/232 9832
10-5.30pm

Warwickshire

The Antiques Centre, High
Street, Bidford-on-Avon.
Tel: 0789 773680
10-5pm, Sun 2-5.30pm,
closed Mon

Antiques Etc., 22 Railway
Terrace, Rugby.
10-5pm, closed Tues &
Wed

The Antique Arcade, 4
Sheep Street, Stratford-
upon-Avon.
Tel: 0789 297249
10-5.30pm

Dunchurch Antique
Centre, 16/16a Daventry
Road, Dunchurch, Nr
Rugby.
Tel: 0788 817147
10-5pm, inc Sun

Leamington Pine &
Antiques Centre, 20
Regent Street, Leamington
Spa.
Tel: 0926 429679
9-6pm

Smith Street Antiques
Centre, 7 Smith Street,
Warwick.
Tel: 0926 497864
10-5.30pm

Spa Antiques Market, 4
Windsor Street,
Leamington Spa.
Tel: 0926 22927
9.30-5.30pm

Stratford Antiques Centre,
60 Ely Street, Stratford-
upon-Avon.
Tel: 0789 204180
10-5.30pm

Vintage Antique Market,
36 Market Place, Warwick.
Tel: 0926 491527
10-5pm

Warwick Antique Centre,
20-22 High Street,
Warwick.
Tel: 0926 495704
6 days a week

West Midlands
Birmingham Antique
Centre, 141 Bromsgrove
Street, Birmingham.
Tel: 021-692 1414/622 2145
Thurs from 9am

The City of Birmingham
Antique Market, St
Martins Market,
Edgbaston Street,
Birmingham.
Tel: 021-267 4636
Mon 6.30-2pm

Stancie Cutler Antique &
Collectors Fair, Town Hall,
Sutton Coldfield.
Tel: 0270 624288
Wed monthly, 11-8pm

Walsall Antiques Centre,
7a The Digbeth Arcade,
Walsall.
Tel: 0922 725163/5
10-5pm

Wiltshire
Antique & Collectors
Market, 37 Catherine
Street, Salisbury.
Tel: 0722 326033
9-5pm

The Avon Bridge Antiques
& Collectors Market,
United Reform Church
Hall, Fisherton Street,
Salisbury.
Tues 9-4pm

London House Antique
Centre, High Street,
Marlborough.
Tel: 0672 52331
Mon-Sat 9.30-5.30pm

The Marlborough Parade
Antiques Centre, The
Parade, Marlborough.
Tel: 0672 515331
10-5pm, inc Sun

Micawber's, 53 Fisherton
Street, Salisbury.
Tel: 0722 337822
9.30-5pm, closed Wed

Yorkshire
The Ginnel, Harrogate
Antique Centre, off
Parliament Street,
Harrogate.
Tel: 0423 508857
9.30-5.30pm

Grove Collectors Centre,
Grove Road, Harrogate.
Tel: 0423 561680
10-4.30pm

Halifax Antiques Centre,
Queen's Road/Gibbet
Street, Halifax.
Tel: 0422 366657
Tues-Sat, 10-5pm

Malton Antique Market, 2
Old Maltongate, Malton.
Tel: 0653 692732
9.30-5, closed Thurs

Micklegate Antiques
Market, 73 Micklegate,
York.
Tel: 0904 644438
Wed & Sat, 10-5.30pm

Montpelier Mews Antique
Market, Montpelier Street,
Harrogate.
Tel: 0423 530484
9.30-5.30pm

Treasure House Antiques
Centre, 4-10 Swan Street,
Bawtry, Nr Doncaster.
Tel: 0302 710621
10-5pm, inc Sun

West Park Antiques
Pavilion, 20 West Park,
Harrogate.
Tel: 0423 61758
10-5pm, closed Mon

York Antique Centre, 2
Lendal, York.
Tel: 0904 641445
Mon-Sat 9.30-5.30pm

Scotland
Bath Street Antique
Galleries, 203 Bath Street,
Glasgow.
Tel: 041-248 4220
10-5pm, Sat 10-1pm

Corner House Antiques,
217 St Vincent Street,
Glasgow.
Tel: 041-248 2560
10-5pm

King's Court Antiques
Centre & Market, King
Street, Glasgow.
Tel: 041-423 7216
Tues-Sun

The Victorian Village, 53 &
57 West Regent Street,
Glasgow.
Tel: 041-332 0808
10-5pm, Sat 10-1pm

Wales
Cardiff Antique Centre,
69-71 St Mary Street,
Cardiff.
Tel: 0222 30970

Carew Market, Carew
Airfield on A477, Port
Talbot.
Tel: 0639 886822
Sun

Jacobs Antique Centre,
West Canal Wharf, Cardiff.
Tel: 0222 390939
Thurs & Sat 9.30-5pm

Offa's Dyke Antiques
Centre, 4 High Street,
Knighton, Powys.
Tel: 0547 528634/528940
Mon-Sat 10-5pm

Pembroke Antique Centre,
The Hall, Hamilton
Terrace, Pembroke.
Tel: 0646 687017
10-5pm

Port Talbot Market,
Jubilee Shopping Hall, 64-
66 Station Road, Port
Talbot, Glamorgan.
Tel: 0639 883184
Mon-Sat

Swansea Antique Centre,
21 Oxford Street, Swansea.
Tel: 0792 466854
10-5pm

Channel Islands
Union Street Antique
Market, 8 Union Street,
St Helier, Jersey.
Tel: 0534 73805/22475
10-5pm

A Noddy
kaleidoscope,
1960s, 9in
(23cm) long.
£5-6 *FAB*

INDEX